Austen Layard

Nineveh and Babylon

A narrative of a second expedition to Assyria during the years 1849, 1850 and 1851

Austen Layard

Nineveh and Babylon
A narrative of a second expedition to Assyria during the years 1849, 1850 and 1851

ISBN/EAN: 9783337282608

Printed in Europe, USA, Canada, Australia, Japan

Cover: Foto ©ninafisch / pixelio.de

More available books at **www.hansebooks.com**

A NARRATIVE

OF

A SECOND EXPEDITION TO ASSYRIA

DURING THE YEARS 1849, 1850, & 1851

BY AUSTEN HENRY LAYARD M.P. D.C.L.

Abridged by the Author from his Larger Work

WITH NUMEROUS WOODCUTS

LONDON
JOHN MURRAY, ALBEMARLE STREET
1867

Palace of Sennacherib at Kouyunjik, restored

CONTENTS.

INTRODUCTION.

Excavations continued after my return to England in 1851—Success of Mr. H. Rassam's explorations—Description of the new sculptures—Their removal to England—Future researches must be of a different nature—Investigations of the arrow-headed characters—M. Grotefend's researches—M. Lassen, J. Martin, Burnouf, and others—Investigations of Sir H. Rawlinson—Dr. Hincks—his great learning—his death—ill-requital of his labours—Researches of M. Oppert, Mr. Fox Talbot, and Mr. Norris—The Royal Asiatic Society—Their plan for testing the accuracy of the various decipherments of the cuneiform inscriptions—Testimonies of Sir G. Wilkinson, Professor Wilson, and others, as to the correctness of these renderings—The French Academy—Reward of M. Oppert by the French Government—Assyrian chronology—Sir H. Rawlinson's theory respecting the ancient capital of Assyria—The inscriptions furnish but little information, yet sufficient to prove the great advancement of the Assyrians in the arts and sciences of a civilised nation xix

CHAPTER I.

Renewal of excavations in Assyria—Return to Mosul—Discoveries at Kouyunjik—Visit to Nimroud—Excavations in the Mound—Mr. H. Rassam.—Sculptures representing transport of winged bulls discovered at Kouyunjik—Fresh sculptures—Discovery of gateway—High Mound at Nimroud explored 1

CHAPTER II.

Discovery of the grand entrance to Sennacherib's palace—The inscriptions containing the annals of his reign—Account of his war with Hezekiah—Sculptures representing siege of Lachish—Jewish captives—Discovery of arched vault at Nimroud—of painted bricks—Attack of the Tai on village of Nimroud—Discovery of chamber containing bronze bowls, glass, and other relics . . . 40

CHAPTER III.

Visit to the winged lions by night—The bitumen springs—Removal of the winged lions to the river—Loss and recovery of lion—Visit to Bavian—Description of rock sculptures—Inscriptions—Sculptures at Kouyunjik 67

CHAPTER IV.

Preparations for a journey to the Khabour—Sheikh Suttum—His rediff—Departure from Mosul—First encampment—Abou Khameera—A storm—Tel Ermah—A stranger—Tel Jemal—A sunset in the desert—A Jebour encampment—The Bellad Sinjar—The Sinjar hill—The dress of the Yezidis—The Shomal—Return to the Bellad—A snake-charmer—Journey continued in the desert—Rishwan—Encampment of the Boraij—Dress of Arab women—Rathaiyah—Hawking—A deputation from the Yezidis—The Khabour—Arrival at Arban 80

CHAPTER V.

Encampment on the Khabour—Sheikh Suttum—Mohammed Emin—Discovery of winged bulls—of Assyrian relics—of lions—of human figure—of various objects of antiquity—The Chebar of the Captivity—Our tents—Bread of the Arabs—Their food—Their knowledge of medicine—The Deloul, or Dromedary—Adla—A storm—Animals on the Khabour—Visit to Moghamis . 116

CHAPTER VI.

Leave Arban—The banks of the Khabour—Artificial mounds—Mijwell—The cadi of the Bedouins—The 'thar,' or blood revenge—Caution of Arabs—A natural cavern—An extinct volcano—The confluents of the Khabour—Suleiman Agha—Encampment at Um-Jerjeh—Mohammed Emin leaves us—Visit to the Milli Kurds—Arab love-making—The Dakheel—Bedouin poets and poetry—Leave the Khabour—Arab sagacity—The Hol—Khatouniyah—Return of Suttum—Ferhan—Sinjar villages—Eski Mosul—Departure of Suttum 139

CHAPTER VII.

Discoveries at Kouyunjik—Procession of figures bearing fruit and game—Locusts—Led horses—An Assyrian campaign—Dagon, or the fish-god—The chambers of records—Inscribed clay tablets—Return to Nimroud—Effects of the flood—Discoveries—Small temple under high mound—The Evil Spirit—Fish-god—Fine bas-relief of the king—Great inscribed monolith—Cedar beams—Second temple 163

CHAPTER VIII.

The summer—Encampment at Kouyunjik—Mode of life—Departure for the mountains — Akra — Rock-tablets at Gunduk — District of Zibari—Namet Agha—District of Shirwan—of Baradost—of Gherdi—of Shemdina—Mousa Bey—Nestorian bishop—Convent of Mar Hananisho—District and plain of Ghaour-Dizza—An Albanian friend—Bash-Kalah—Izzet Pasha—A Jewish encampment—High mountain pass—Mahmoudiyah—First view of Wan. 184

CHAPTER IX.

Mehemet Pasha—Description of Wan—Its history—Improvement in its condition—The Armenian bishop—The cuneiform inscriptions—The caves of Khorkhor—The Meher Kapousi—A tradition—The Bairam—An Armenian school—Amikh—The convent of Yedi Klissia—Leave Wan—The Armenian patriarch—The island of Akhtamar—An Armenian church—History of the convent—Pass into Mukus—The district of Mukus—of Shattak—of Nourdooz—A Nestorian village—Encampments—Mount Ararat—Mar Shamoun—Jula-Merik—Valley of Diz—Pass into Jelu—Nestorian district of Jelu—An ancient church—The bishop—District of Baz—of Tkhoma—Return to Mosul. . . . 205

CHAPTER X.

Discoveries at Kouyunjik during the summer—Description of the sculptures—Capture of cities on a great river—Alabaster pavement—Conquest of tribes inhabiting a marsh—Their wealth—Chambers with sculptures belonging to a new king—Conquest of the people of Susiana—Portrait of the king—His guards and attendants—The city of Shushan—Captive prince—Musicians—Captives put to the torture—An inclined passage—Two small chambers—Colossal figures. 238

CHAPTER XI.

Departure for Babylon—The Awai—Descent of the river—Tekrit—The plain of Dura—The Naharwan—Samarrah—Kadesia—Palm groves—Kathimain—Approach to Baghdad—The City—Arrival—Modern Baghdad—Departure for Babylon—Abde Pasha's camp—Approach to Babylon—The ruins—Arrival at Hillah—The chiefs of Hillah—Present of lions—Description of the town—The ruins of Babylon—The walls—Visit to the Birs Nimroud—Description of the ruin—View from it—Excavations and discoveries in the Mound of Babel—in the Mujelibé or Kasr—The tree Athelé—Excavations in the ruin of Amran—Bowls, with inscriptions in Hebrew and Syriac characters—The Jews of Babylonia 260

CHAPTER XII.

State of the ruins of Babylon—Cause of the disappearance of buildings—Nature of original edifices—Babylonian bricks—The history of Babylon—Its commerce—Canals and rivers—The arts—Engraved gems—Fall of the city—The mounds of El Hymer—of Anana—Ruins in Southern Mesopotamia—Departure from Hillah—Sand-hills—Villages in the Jezirah—Sheikh Karboul—Ruins—First view of Niffer—The marshes—Arab boats—Arrive at Souk-El-Afaij—Sheikh Agab—Town of the Afaij—Description of the ruins of Niffer—Excavations in the mounds—Discovery of coffins—of various relics—Mr. Loftus' discoveries at Wurka—The Arab tribes—Wild beasts—Lions—Customs of the Afaij—Leave the marshes—Return to Baghdad—A mirage . . 294

CHAPTER XIII.

Departure from Baghdad—Journey through Mesopotamia—Early Arab remains—The Median wall—Tekrit—Horses stolen—Instance of Bedouin honesty—Excavations at Kalah Sherghat—Reach Mosul—Discoveries during absence—New chambers at Kouyunjik—Description of bas-reliefs—Extent of the ruins explored—Bases of pillars—Small objects—Absence of Assyrian tombs—Assyrian relics—Remains beneath the tomb of Jonah—Discoveries at Shereef-Khan—at Nimroud—Engraved cylinders . . . 329

CHAPTER XIV.

Results of the discoveries to chronology and history—Names of earliest Assyrian kings—Annals of Tiglath Pileser I.—The period of his reign—The dynasty of the Nimroud kings—Sardanapalus I.—His successor—Mention of Jehu, king of Israel—Annals of Tiglath Pileser II.—Mention of Menahem—Annals of Sargon—of Sennacherib—of Esar-haddon—of his son and grandson—Nature of Assyrian records—Political condition of Assyria—Religion—Extent of Nineveh—Assyrian architecture—Sennacherib's palace at Kouyunjik—The palaces at Nimroud—Fortifications of Nimroud, Khorsabad, and Kouyunjik—Conclusion . . . 351

LIST OF ILLUSTRATIONS.

	PAGE
Palace of Sennacherib at Kouyunjik, restored	*Frontispiece*
Hound held in Leash	xxiii
Lion let out of Trap	xxiv
Wounded Lioness	xxv
Lion seizing Chariot Wheel	xxv
King transfixing Lion with his Spear	xxvi
King in close Combat with a Lion	xxvi
Wild Ass captured by Hounds	xxvii
Wounded Wild Ass seized and pulled down by Hounds	xxvii
King hunting Lions	xxviii
Wild Ass captured with Lasso	xxix
Gazelle pursued by Huntsmen	xxix
Wounded Gazelle	xxix
King pouring Libation over Dead Lions	xxx
Sardanapalus and his Queen seated at a Banquet	xxxi
Statue of the God Nebo	xxxii
Palace of Sennacherib.—Plan I.	4
Underground Excavations at Kouyunjik	6
Head-dress of Captives employed by Assyrians in moving Bull. (Kouyunjik.)	19
Cart with Ropes and Workmen carrying Saws, Picks and Shovels, for moving colossal Bull. (Kouyunjik.)	21
Workmen carrying Ropes, Saws, and other Implements for moving Bull. (Kouyunjik.)	21
Stag. (Kouyunjik.)	23
Wild Sow and Young, amongst Reeds. (Kouyunjik.)	23
King superintending Removal of colossal Bull. (Kouyunjik.)	25
Village with conical Roofs, near Aleppo	26
Assyrians placing a human-headed Bull. (Kouyunjik.)	27
Plan of Northern Gateway to Inclosure of Kouyunjik	32
Square Tower and small Temples. Mound of Nimroud.—Plan II.	34
Tunnel along Eastern Basement Wall of Tower. (Nimroud.)	35

	PAGE
Western Face of Basement of Tower. (Nimroud.)	36
Northern Face of Basement of Tower. (Nimroud.)	36
Tower on a Mound. (From a Bas-relief, Kouyunjik.)	39
Remains of Façade and Grand Entrance of the Palace of Sennacherib. (Kouyunjik.)	41
Existing Remains at Khorsabad, showing original state of Grand Entrance at Kouyunjik	43
Bulls with historical Inscriptions of Sennacherib. (Kouyunjik.)	46
Sennacherib on his Throne before Lachish	49
Jewish Captives from Lachish. (Kouyunjik.)	51
Bronze Socket of the Palace Gate. (Nimroud.)	52
Vaulted Drain beneath South-east Palace. (Nimroud.)	53
Vaulted Drain beneath the North-west Palace at Nimroud.	54
Excavated Chamber in which the Bronzes were discovered. (Nimroud.)	57
Bronze Bells found in a Cauldron. (Nimroud.)	58
Handles of Bronze Dishes, from Nimroud	60
Bronze Vessels, taken from the Interior of a Cauldron	60, 61
Bronze Wine Strainer	61
Bronze Dish, from Nimroud	61
Bronze Cup, 6¼ in. diameter, and 1⅝ in. deep	61
Bronze Shields from Nimroud	63
Bronze Cube inlaid with Gold. (Original Size.)	64
Fallen Rock-Sculptures. (Bavian.)	72
Assyrian Fountain. (Bavian.)	73
A Captive. (Kouyunjik.)	76
Bas-relief from Kouyunjik, representing fortified City, a River with a Boat and Raft, and a Canal	77
Bas-relief representing a River, and Gardens watered by Canals, (Kouyunjik.)	78
Sheikh Suttum	85
Our First Encampment in the Desert	87
Interior of a Yezidi House at Bukra, in the Sinjar	96
A Group of Yezidis	99
Arab Nose Ring and Bracelet of Silver	107
Suttum, with his Wife, on his Dromedary	109
A trained Falcon	115
Artificial Mounds on the Khabour	117
Sheikh Mohammed Emin	119
Winged Bull discovered at Arban	121
Lion discovered at Arban	123
Bas-relief discovered at Arban	124
Arab Women grinding Corn with a Hand-mill, rolling out the Dough, and baking the Bread	128
Saddling a Deloul or Dromedary	133

LIST OF ILLUSTRATIONS.

	PAGE
Volcanic Cone of Koukab	143
The Tent of the Milli Chief	147
Women of the Milli Tribe	149
Town and Lake of Khatouniyah	157
Arab Camels	159
Attendants carrying Pomegranates and Locusts. (Kouyunjik.)	164
The King in his Chariot passing through a Stream in a Valley. (Kouyunjik.)	167
Assyrian Cylinder, with Dagon, or the Fish-god	168
Cylinder, with Assyrian Records	169
Clay Tablet with Cylinder impressed. (From Kouyunjik.)	170
Inscribed Tablet, with Inscription at one end in Cursive Characters	171
Piece of Clay with Impressions of Seals	172
Impression of a Seal on Clay	172
Back of the same Seal, showing the Marks of the String and the Fingers	172
Impressions of the Signets of the Kings of Assyria and Egypt. (Original Size.)	173
Part of Cartouche of Sabaco, enlarged from the Impression of his Signet	173
Royal Cylinder of Sennacherib	174
Entrance to Small Temple. (Nimroud.)	176
Fish-god at Entrance to small Temple. (Nimroud.)	177
Effigy of King	178
Entrance to a small Temple dedicated to Beltis. (Nimroud.)	181
Statue of King from Temple. (Nimroud.)	182
Landing Place with Ferryboats on the Tigris at Mosul	184
A Kurd	190
The Castle of Mahmoudiyah	202
The Town and Rock of Wan	207
Tombs in the Rock at Wan	209
Kurds of Wan	212
A Nestorian Family	224
Arabs and Nestorians moving a Slab at Kouyunjik	239
Assyrian Warriors in a Cart, captured from the Elamites. (Kouyunjik.)	246
Singers coming out to meet the Conquerors. (Kouyunjik.)	252
Musicians coming out to meet the Conquerors. (Kouyunjik.)	253
Assyrians flaying their Prisoners alive, and carrying away Heads of the Slain. (Kouyunjik.)	254
Assyrians torturing their Captives. (Kouyunjik.)	256
Colossal Figures at an Entrance. (Kouyunjik.)	257
Cases containing Sculptures ready for Embarkation	258
A Kellek, or Raft of Skins, on the Tigris	261

a

	PAGE
Plan of Part of the Ruins of Babylon on the Eastern Bank of the Euphrates	274
The Birs Nimroud, or Tower of Babel of early Travellers	278
Eastern Face of the Birs Nimroud with proposed Restoration	280
Mound of Babel: Ruins of Babylon	283
The Mujelibé, or Kasr: Ruins of Babylon. (From Rich.)	286
Babylonian Brick	287
Fragment from the Mujelibé. (Babylon.)	289
Inscribed Earthen Bowls, from Babylon	291
Terracotta Tablet from Babylon, representing a Dog	302
Babylonian Cylinder in Sienite. (Size of the Original.)	304
Engraved Gem from Babylon	304
Cylinder in the British Museum	305
Heads of Arab Delouls	312
Lid of Glazed Coffin	320
Glazed Coffins from Babylonia, in the British Museum	321
Terracotta Model of a Body in a Coffin	321
Throne-room, Teheran	327
Loading a Camel. (Kouyunjik.)	333
Captives in a Cart. (Kouyunjik.)	334
Captives resting	334
Battle in a Marsh in Southern Mesopotamia. (Kouyunjik.)	336
Assyrians cutting down the Palm Trees belonging to a captured City. (Kouyunjik.)	338
Assyrian Pedestal, from Kouyunjik	340
Cylinder in green Jasper	343
Ancient Assyrian Cylinder, in Serpentine	344
Assyrian Cylinders, in Serpentine	345
Babylonian Cylinders, in Agate, Porcelain, Iron Hæmatite, and Jasper	346, 347
Cylinders, with Semitic Characters	348
Persian Cylinders, in Red Cornelian, Chalcedony, Rock Crystal, and Onyx	349
Bas-relief, representing Pul, or Tiglath Pileser. (Nimroud.)	359
The Great Hall of Sardanapalus' Palace, restored *To face*	383
Court of Sargon's Palace at Khorsabad, restored after Fergusson	380
Exterior of a Building. (From a Bas-relief at Kouyunjik.)	384
Plan of the Mound of Nimroud	389
Mound of Nimroud	390
Plan of Mound and Inclosure of Nimroud	393
Plan of Mound and Inclosure of Kouyunjik	395
Ornament on Top of Walls. (Kouyunjik.)	396
Double Ditch and Walls of Inclosure of Kouyunjik	398
Last View of Mosul	402

INTRODUCTION.

AFTER THE TERMINATION of the expedition described in this volume and my return to England in the spring of 1851, the excavations at Kouyunjik were continued on a limited scale by Mr. Christian Rassam, the British Vice-consul at Mosul, their general direction having been confided by the Trustees of the British Museum to Sir Henry Rawlinson, then H.M. Consul General, and the Political Agent of the East India Company at Baghdad. Sir Henry visited the ruins in the early part of 1852. The excavations were chiefly carried on amongst the ruins of the palace of Sennacherib in the south-west corner of the mound of Kouyunjik, and at Shereef Khan, an ancient Assyrian site to the north of Nineveh.

The sculptures discovered at Kouyunjik formed for the most part a continuation of the bas-reliefs previously uncovered, representing various wars of the Assyrians. In that part of Sennacherib's palace, in which his grandson had caused to be executed the bas-reliefs representing the conquest of Elam or Susiana, discovered previously to my departure,[*] were found a number of clay tablets and fragments of cylinders of the same material, which form an important

---

[*] See Chap. x. Drawings of the sculptures discovered by Sir H. Rawlinson and Mr. C. Rassam were made by Mr. Hodder, and are now in the British Museum.

addition to the large collection of similar records sent by me to this country. At Shereef Khan, the ruins which I had discovered proved to be the remains of a palace built, according to Sir H. Rawlinson, by a younger brother of Esar-haddon, and of a temple dedicated to the Assyrian Neptune. No sculptures were found amongst them, but several inscriptions of interest were obtained from them, and a beautiful cylinder in chalcedony, bearing the name of a king of a dynasty tributary to Assyria, and ruling on the river Khabour.

The French Consul at Mosul, M. Place, also commenced excavations in the mound of Kouyunjik after my return to Europe. The only discovery of any interest which he made was that of an inscribed tablet bearing the name of Sardanapalus, the builder of the north-west palace at Nimroud, and apparently stating that that monarch erected a temple at Kouyunjik. If such be the case, other remains of the same period may still exist in some part of the mound hitherto unexplored, and it would be proved that, long anterior to Sennacherib, an Assyrian city stood on this site.

In the mound of Nebbi Yunus, a pair of winged, human-headed bulls were accidentally discovered by an inhabitant of the village, who was digging the foundations of his house. The Turkish authorities took possession of them, and carried on excavations for a short time, uncovering sculptured slabs and inscriptions. But these excavations were soon abandoned, as the mound is covered with the buildings surrounding the so-called tomb of Jonah and the burial-ground depending upon it, which could not, without giving offence to the people of Mosul, be disturbed. Sufficient, however, was discovered to lead to the belief that the mound covers the ruins of palaces of great interest and importance, richly adorned with sculpture, and built by three different kings—the grandson of the builder of the centre palace at Nimroud, Sennacherib, and Esar-haddon.

Mr. Vice-consul Rassam removed and packed for transport to England a collection of bas-reliefs which I had discovered in the palace of Sennacherib, but, unfortunately, the raft on which they were sent to Baghdad was plundered on the way by the Arabs, and the sculptures were destroyed.

Parliament having voted a grant of money for further researches in Assyria, Mr. Hormuzd Rassam, who had been my companion during my two expeditions, and to whose zeal, ability, and influence over the Arabs I had been so much indebted for their success, was requested by the Trustees of the British Museum to superintend the excavations. He had accompanied me to England, from whence he returned to Mosul, and was again amongst the ruins in the month of October, 1852. A general direction over the expedition was confided to Sir Henry Rawlinson.

Mr. Hormuzd Rassam's excavations proved highly successful, and to them we owe many discoveries of great interest and value. On his arrival at Mosul he placed workmen at Kouyunjik and Nimroud, and proceeded himself to the great mound of Kalah Sherghat, where, from the fragments dug up during previous explorations, ruins of great antiquity and importance might be presumed to exist. But the palaces, or temples, which may once have stood there, had been so completely destroyed, that, with the exception of the remains of a colossal human-headed bull and lion in black basalt (a material apparently very generally employed by the Assyrians at this place), and a few fragments of alabaster slabs, no traces of buildings were discovered. Mr. Hormuzd Rassam was, however, fortunate enough to find two cylinders, which, with the cylinder previously obtained by me from the same ruins, enable us to complete the annals of one of the earliest Assyrian kings of whom we have any detailed records. His name, if the cuneiform characters composing it be correctly interpreted, is Tiglath Pileser (corresponding with that of the later monarch mentioned in the

Bible), and he appears to have reigned between 1200 and 1100 years B.C.

At Kouyunjik Mr. H. Rassam discovered the entire obelisk in white limestone, and the upper part of a second, now in the British Museum. These highly important monuments are of the same shape as the black obelisk obtained from the centre palace at Nimroud,* and are covered with an inscription containing annals of the founder of the north west palace at Nimroud, and a series of small bas-reliefs representing his exploits in war, and captives, or tributaries with their offerings brought into his presence.

At the beginning of 1854 Mr. H. Rassam commenced excavations in the northern part of the mound of Kouyunjik. He was fortunate enough to discover, deep below the surface, the remains of a palace built by the grandson of Sennacherib, and son of Esar-haddon. His name, according to Sir Henry Rawlinson, is to be read Asshur-bani-pal; to Dr. Hincks, Asshur-idanna-bal; to M. Oppert, Assur-iddanna-palla. He was one of the last of the Assyrian kings, probably the last but one; and there are grounds for conjecturing that he can be identified with the Sardanapalus of the Greek and Roman legends. The inscriptions and sculptures belonging to his reign which have been preserved, prove that he was a great conqueror, and equally renowned for his feats in war and in the chase. They are for the most part in excellent condition, not having been exposed to fire like those in the palace of Sennacherib. Of the building itself the remains of some halls and chambers were uncovered, and probably a considerable part of it yet remains to be explored.

The most important bas-reliefs discovered by Mr. H. Rassam, and sent to this country, are those representing hunting scenes, in which the king takes the principal part, now placed in the Assyrian collection in the basement floor

* Nineveh and its Remains, p. 244.

of the British Museum. For extreme delicacy and minuteness of execution, and for remarkable truth to nature and vigour of treatment in the delineation of animals, they are equal if not superior to any other sculptures brought from Assyria. In that which constitutes the highest quality of art, in variety of detail and ornament, in attempts at composition, in severity of style, and purity of outline, they are inferior to the earliest Assyrian monuments with which we

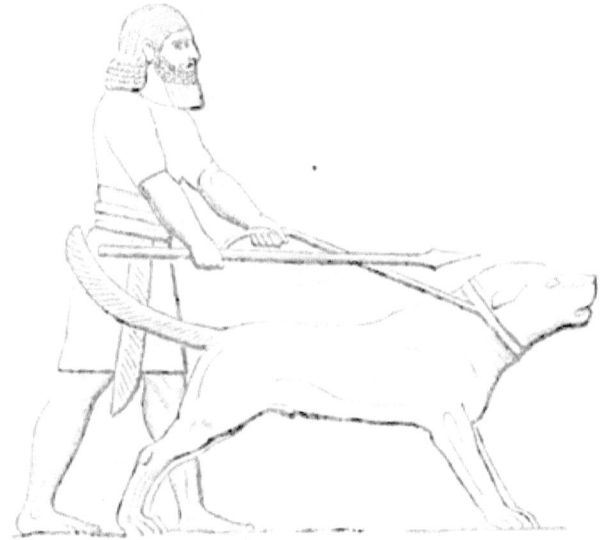

Hound held in Leash.

are acquainted—those from the north-west palace at Nimroud. They bear, indeed, the same relation to them as the later Egyptian monuments do to the earlier.

In these bas-reliefs Asshur-bani-pal is seen hunting the lion, sometimes engaged in close combat with the animal, and in pursuing the wild ass, the stag, and the gazelle. As usual in the sculptures adorning the walls of the Assyrian palaces of the later period, the sculptor has endeavoured to portray all the incidents of the events which he is recording. We have first the preparation for the chase. Huntsmen are seen leading the dogs or hounds in leashes, and men and mules are laden with the nets, ropes, and gins which were used in the capture of deer, gazelles, and wild asses.

The king appears to be represented as hunting in the parks or preserves attached to the royal palaces, which were stocked with wild animals, as well as in the open country. Lions, kept in cages, are turned loose for him to kill. The cage was drawn, probably by oxen, to the spot where the beast was to be set free. A box on the top of it protects a

Lion let out of Trap.

huntsman or attendant who, by raising a trap, opens the door from whence the lion issues. The wary motions of the animal on leaving the cage are admirably portrayed in the sculptures.

The king is seen hunting from his chariot, on horseback, and on foot. When in his chariot he is accompanied by the charioteer and two armed warriors. In some bas-reliefs he is seen transfixing a lion with arrows, and dead and dying lions lie scattered around him. The various attitudes of the beasts, whether wounded or in the last struggle, or stretched lifeless on the ground, are portrayed with singular vigour and truth to nature.

Wounded Lioness.

Sometimes the lion is represented as springing upon the chariot, when the king receives the animal upon his spear,

Lion seizing Chariot Wheel.

or transfixes it with a short sword, whilst his attendant warriors pierce it with their spears. In one bas-relief a wounded lion is seen seizing the wheel of the king's chariot, which, in its rage and agony, it is endeavouring to crush with its powerful jaws. The representation of the animal is full of life and artistic energy.

King transfixing Lion with his Spear.

King in close Combat with a Lion.

When the king is represented on horseback, he is attended by a horseman leading a second horse for his use. In some bas-reliefs the king is seen engaged on foot in close combat with the lion, and transfixing it with a spear or an arrow. Attendants standing behind are ready to supply him with fresh weapons, which they carry in their hands. He is sometimes attended and protected by a warrior who holds a shield before him.

An interesting series of bas-reliefs represents the chase of

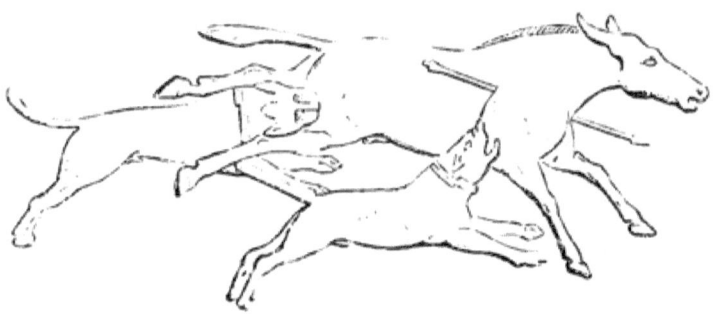

Wild Ass captured by Hounds.

the wild ass, an animal still found in the Mesopotamian desert. It is pursued by the king on horseback. He is

Wounded Wild Ass seized and pulled down by Hounds.

armed with bow and arrows, and followed by mounted attendants, who carry spare arrows and lead a second horse. The wild ass, when wounded, is represented as being pulled down by large and powerful hounds, apparently of the mastiff breed. The struggle between it and the dogs is portrayed with great spirit.

In one bas-relief the animal is represented as having been

King hunting Lions

Wild Ass captured with Lasso.

caught by a kind of lasso, with which the huntsmen lead it away.

Gazelle pursued by Huntsmen.

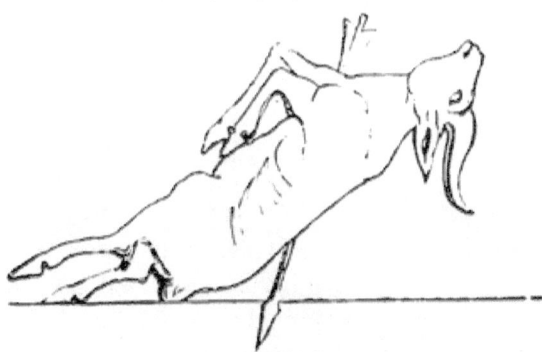

Wounded Gazelle.

The gazelles are also pursued by the king, armed with bow and arrows. They are portrayed (and always with the same spirit and truth to nature) in every variety of attitude—endeavouring to escape, falling transfixed by arrows, and lying wounded and dead upon the ground.

The deer are represented as driven into enclosures formed by nets, and then shot down with arrows.

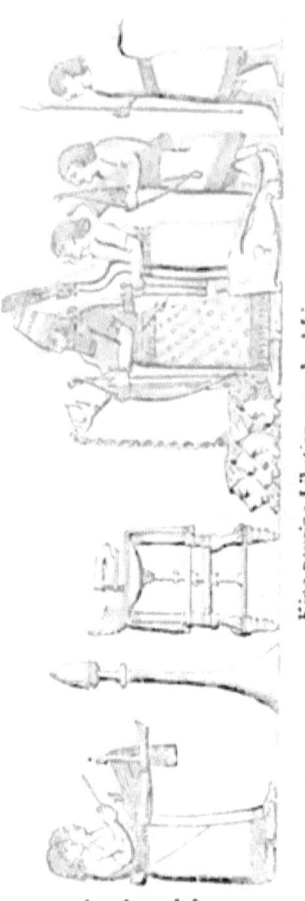

King pouring Libation over dead Lions

A series of bas reliefs represents the return of the huntsmen from the chase. They are seen bearing dead lions and birds, probably partridges. The slaughtered animals appear to have been placed before the king, who in one of the bas-reliefs is seen pouring a libation over them before an altar, attended by his fan and armour-bearers and by musicians who celebrate his exploits, accompanying their song on a kind of dulcimer.

Amongst the sculptures from the north-west palace of Kouyunjik which do not represent hunting scenes, the most remarkable is a highly finished and admirably preserved bas-relief, in which the king is seen lying on a couch or bed, beneath an arbour formed by vines, apparently at a banquet, as he is raising a cup in his right hand, and near him is a table on which are probably some viands. By his side, seated on a raised chair, richly attired and attended by two fan-bearers, is a woman, probably his queen. This is the only instance with which we are yet acquainted of an Assyrian lady of rank being represented in a bas-relief.

This sculpture, and one or two others from the same series now in the British Museum, especially a warrior on a horse at full speed, are carved with the sharpness, precision, and delicacy of a Greek gem. They are singularly fine examples of the perfection to which the Assyrians had attained in the technical part of the art of sculpture.

At Nimroud Mr. Hormuzd Rassam's researches were chiefly confined to the ruins of the south-east palace. He found that the building which I had partly explored had been erected over the remains of a more ancient edifice. Amongst the earlier ruins, which were at a considerable depth beneath the soil, were no chambers with sculptured walls, but bas-reliefs brought from the centre palace, and several detached objects of great interest were obtained from them. A large tablet, or stele, similar in form to the  one obtained from the temple in the north-west corner of the mound,* was found *in situ*. It contained the effigy of a king (believed to be the grandson of Sardanapalus), and an inscrip-

* See p. 178.

Statue of the God Nebo.

tion recording the annals of his reign. It is now in the British Museum. In another part of the building, supposed to be a temple dedicated to Nebo by a king, whose name, according to Sir Henry Rawlinson, is to be read Iva-lush, or Vama-Zala-Khus; or, according to M. Oppert, Hou-likhous, and who reigned about 800 B.C., were discovered two detached statues of the god, very rudely carved. On them is an inscription, which, according to Sir Henry Rawlinson, states that they were offered to Nebo by an officer who governed certain places in the Assyrian empire for the life of the king (Iva-lush), and of his wife Sammuramit, that the god might lengthen the king's life, prolong his days, increase his years, and give peace to his house and people, and victory to his armies.* This 'Sammuramit' has been identified, probably upon very slender grounds, with the Semiramis of classic story; and the group of cuneiform characters, supposed to represent her name upon these statues, has enabled Mr. Rawlinson to fix her place in history, to dispose of classic fables, and to show in a proper light her story, her character, her descent, and her true connection with the Assyrian monarchy.† The two statues are now in the national collection.

Whilst Mr. Hormuzd Rassam was carrying on the excavations near Mosul, the late Mr. Loftus, accompanied by Mr. Boutcher, an artist sent to the East by Messrs. Dickenson of Bond Street, had been engaged by the subscribers to the 'Assyrian Excavation Fund' to continue the examination of the mounds in Southern Mesopotamia and Babylonia, which he had commenced when attached to the mission of Sir Fenwick Williams of Kars, the British Commissioner for the determination of the boundaries between Turkey and Persia. To Mr. Loftus' skill and energy we owe many valuable discoveries in those ruins, the most important being the inscribed bricks and tablets containing the names of kings who are believed to have belonged to a dynasty that reigned at a very remote period—probably between 1900 and 1800 B.C.—in lower Chaldæa. Mr. H. Rassam having left Mosul for England early in the spring of 1854, the subscribers to the Assyrian Excavation Fund determined to continue the excavations at Kouyunjik and Nimroud, and Mr. Loftus was directed to proceed to Mosul. Mr. Vice-consul Rassam was at the same time requested by the Trustees of the British Museum to superintend the removal

---

* Rawlinson's Ancient Monarchies, vol. ii. p. 382, *note*.

† She was 'a Babylonian princess, the last descendant of a long line of kings, whom the Assyrian monarch wedded, to confirm through her his title to the southern provinces.' Instead of the heroine of the 'uncivilised ancients,' she was 'a very prosaic and commonplace princess,' like 'Atossa, or Elizabeth of York' ('Ancient Monarchies,' ii. 384, 385)!

and transport to England of the sculptures discovered by his brother, and to continue the excavations at Kouyunjik on a very reduced scale, chiefly for the purpose of retaining possession of the ground. Mr. Loftus discovered some new chambers in the palace of Asshur-bani-pal, on the northern side of the Kouyunjik mound, and found other bas-reliefs representing hunting scenes, which complete the series now in the British Museum. Very spirited and accurate drawings of these and other sculptures were made by Mr. Boutcher.

Excavations on a limited scale were carried on by Mr. Loftus at Nimroud—chiefly amongst the ruins of the centre palace, of the upper chambers connected with it, and of the earlier edifices beneath the south-east palace, but no discoveries of importance were made in them.

Mr. Loftus returned to Europe in 1854, and from that time no further excavations have been carried on by British agents amongst the Assyrian ruins. M. Place, the French Consul at Mosul, continued for a short period the exploration of the mounds of Khorsabad. No new sculptures were obtained from them; but a careful examination of the ruins, and the discovery of a variety of architectural details, have enabled him to restore many external features of the Assyrian palaces, and to settle several interesting questions of construction which had previously been undetermined. He also found a large inscribed clay cylinder and various tablets, several in gold, of the time of Sargon, the founder of the Khorsabad palace, whose annals by their assistance can now be almost entirely restored.

There yet remains much to be done before it can be said that the Assyrian ruins have been fully and satisfactorily explored, and that we possess all the materials which they are likely to afford for the investigation of Assyrian history. As yet owing to a variety of circumstances—to the limited means at the disposal of those who have been engaged in these researches, to the want of that knowledge which has since been partly furnished by a careful examination of the inscriptions, and by a comparison of the monuments now collected together, and to the condition of the country in which the ruins are situated—those extensive and systematic excavations which are absolutely necessary before we can determine the exact period and nature of the numerous ruins existing in Assyria, and before we can deal with confidence with the materials at our disposal, have yet to be carried on. For instance, there are now reasons for conjecturing that the mound of Kouyunjik covers the remains of edifices erected by some of the earliest Assyrian kings. As yet, with the exception of the obelisk in white stone, and of the solitary detached tablet of the time of Sardanapalus (about 900 B.C.) found by M. Place, no remains earlier than the palace of Sennacherib have been discovered there. It would appear from the inscriptions, that palaces or temples were built at Nimroud at least two or three hundred years before the foundation of the north-west palace, the most ancient edifice yet explored in that mound. According to Sir Henry Rawlinson, Kalah Sherghat represents the primitive Assyrian capital, founded many centuries before Nineveh. With the exception of the cylinders of Tiglath Pileser the First (about 1130 B.C.) and one or two bricks inscribed with doubtful royal names, no remains which can with confidence be ascribed to an earlier period than the son of Sardanapalus, the builder of the north-west palace at Nimroud (about 850 B.C.), have been discovered in that mound. That other extensive edifices with sculptured walls will be discovered in unexplored Assyrian mounds I do not anticipate; but the remains of bas-reliefs of an earlier date than anything we yet possess, and, what is even more important, inscriptions belonging to the times of the earlier kings—to those who, there is reason to believe, reigned in Assyria more than twenty centuries before the Christian era—may still be buried below the soil, and are probably far beneath the foundations of the edifices hitherto explored. It is evident that the arts and manufactures did not spring at once into existence at the time of the erection of the north-west palace at Nimroud, where we find them already at the highest perfection they appear to have at any time attained in Assyria. They were probably brought to that perfection by many successive ages of slow, perhaps almost imperceptible, development, unless, indeed, the Assyrians borrowed them wholesale from elsewhere, of which we have no evidence whatever. So far from this being the case, Assyrian art appears to have been original, and peculiar to the people who inhabited the northern part of Mesopotamia. Nothing has hitherto been discovered in Babylonia which would warrant us in asserting that the Assyrians derived their sculpture or their architecture from that country. The contrary, indeed, would appear to be the case. It is more probable that Babylonia owed these arts to Assyria. As regards the alphabet and literature of the Assyrians, however, this may not have been the case; but as yet we have no proof that they derived them from Babylonia, or any other country.

The researches to be hereafter made amongst the Assyrian ruins must be of a very different nature to those hitherto carried on. The explorer can no longer hope for that rich harvest of sculptures and inscribed monuments which has rewarded those who first discovered the Assyrian palaces, although there is probably still much left to be gleaned. All that we can expect is, that by patient toil and a most careful and systematic examination of all the principal mounds, we may be able to determine their relative antiquity, to add to the large collection of inscriptions already brought together for the elucidation of Assyrian history and philology, and to obtain materials for the restoration of the architecture of the Assyrians. To accomplish this will be a matter of immense labour and expense, as the vast mounds of earth which cover the Assyrian ruins will have to be explored to their very foundations, and tunnels or trenches carried through them in every direction; for it is impossible to conjecture what may yet remain beneath the edifices hitherto explored at Nimroud, Kouyunjik, and elsewhere. In addition, these edifices themselves should be still further examined, not with the view alone of collecting sculptures and other objects of art, however great their interest, but of obtaining a complete plan of them, and of ascertaining all the architectural features and details that may still remain. This has been hitherto only partially attempted in one Assyrian ruin—that of Khorsabad, at the expense of the French Government. It is very probable that many years may elapse before such a systematic examination of the Assyrian ruins will be made. But until these mounds are explored in the manner I have indicated, it cannot be said that we have obtained the materials which are necessary to enable us to restore the history and to illustrate the arts and manners of the ancient Assyrians.

That a vast deal—far more than the most sanguine explorer could have anticipated—has been done during the last few years is indisputable. Although our knowledge is far from complete, yet the sculptures and inscriptions have enabled us to put together a part of the skeleton of Assyrian history, and to illustrate to a certain extent the manners, arts, sciences, and literature of the Assyrian people. So much unreasonable incredulity still exists as to the extent to which this has been effected through the interpretation of the cuneiform inscriptions, and the evidence upon which that interpretation rests has been so summarily rejected by English writers of great and deserved authority,* that a short account of the

---

* Sir George Lewis, who was one of the most incredulous of these writers, and who was wont to quiz, with his ready and kindly wit, the cuneiform decipherer, as well as the Egyptologer, admitted to me shortly before his death, that he had never seriously investigated the principles

history of cuneiform decipherment may be interesting to some of my readers, and may tend to remove those erroneous impressions which exist on the subject.

The investigation of the arrow-headed character is by no means a new study. It was first seriously attempted in the year 1802, by Grotefend, a learned German scholar. At that time the only materials accessible for this purpose, with the exception of the well-known inscribed bricks from the ruins of Babylon, were the inscriptions carved on rocks and on the remains of edifices at Persepolis and Hamadan (Ecbatana), and near other ancient sites in Persia. Copies of these inscriptions, more or less accurate, had been brought to Europe by various travellers from the time of Tavernier and Chardin. Fortunately, although short, they afforded the most important materials for breaking ground and taking the first step in the interpretation of the cuneiform character. They are trilingual—that is to say, that the same inscription is repeated three times in a different language and in a different character; but, unfortunately, unlike the trilingual inscription on the celebrated Rosetta stone, which furnishes a key for the decipherment of the Egyptian hieroglyphics, neither the languages nor the

and the evidence upon which the interpretation of the arrow-headed inscriptions rested. Lord Macaulay rejected the interpretations with undisguised contempt, and other classical scholars of scarcely less authority have contributed to form the unfavourable opinion upon the subject which prevails in England. I attribute this, in a great measure, to the fact that those who have been hitherto engaged in the work of deciphering the cuneiform inscriptions have not placed before the public, in a popular and elementary form, a history of their discoveries, and of the process which has led to them; showing how, step by step, the results have been arrived at, and explaining the contradictions and discrepancies which exist in the interpretation of names, &c., as well as those which are inevitable in the first attempts to interpret an unknown character and language. Supposed discoveries have also been announced with too much confidence, and afterwards abandoned or ignored without sufficient explanation, whilst theories, more ingenious than sound, have been put forward to reconcile apparent discrepancies between the contents of the inscriptions and accepted biblical and profane history.

Trilingual Tablet (Persepolis).

FIRST COLUMN.

SECOND COLUMN.

THIRD COLUMN.

characters were previously known to us. The trilingual inscriptions of Persia are generally divided into three parallel columns, or arranged in three distinct tablets, each containing the same inscription expressed in a different language, and in a different modification of the cuneiform character—the letters and signs in each column being formed by the same elementary wedges arranged in different combinations or groups. That the inscriptions are the same is evident from the fact of the recurrence of the same groups of letters, or words, in each column or tablet, at the same regular intervals. I give a copy, in the preceding page, of one of these trilingual tablets from Persepolis, in order that my readers may understand their nature, and the process by which they were deciphered.

It will be perceived that the combination of wedges forming a letter or sign differs in each column. The most simple combination, and that which usually takes the place of honour in the first column of these tablets, is only found on monuments of the Persian period, and the language of the inscriptions is allied to the ancient Sanscrit. This is called the Persian cuneiform character. The characters in the second or centre column are commonly called the Median, or, more correctly, the Touranian or Scythic, because they are believed to express a Touranian or Tatar language, one of the three great families of languages spoken by the subjects of the ancient Persian kings. The inscriptions of the third column are in a character and language nearly identical with those of the monuments of Nineveh and Babylon. They have been consequently termed the Assyrian and the Babylonian, or sometimes the Assyro-Babylonian.*

It will be further observed that in the first, or Persian column, a single oblique arrow-head or wedge constantly

* It is to be observed that there is a slight difference between the Babylonian and Assyrian characters; but the difference is only graphical, like that between roman and italic type.

recurs. It first occurred to the German scholars, Tychsen and Münter, that this sign might mark the division of words. This conjecture was confirmed by the recurrence of the same group of letters forming a word, sometimes with terminal variations which might indicate case endings, marked off, as it were, by these single oblique wedges. Instances of this will be perceived in the first and second lines of the inscription which I have given. A comparison of a number of inscriptions led to the further discovery, that whilst the greater number of words or groups of signs in each were generally the same, certain groups had disappeared, and other groups which had before appeared in another part of the inscription, had taken their place. These again were succeeded by a new group. This circumstance led Grotefend to conjecture that these signs so changing position represented proper names of persons in the relation of father and son, and that when a new king had ascended the throne his name appeared in the place of his predecessor. The name of the grandfather would then disappear altogether, and be replaced by that of the father. For instance, if in one inscription Darius was called the son of Hystaspes, in a second carved after his death Xerxes would be called son of Darius, the name of Darius taking the place of that of Hystaspes, which would no longer be found in the inscription.

This ingenious conjecture led to the discovery of the clue to the decipherment of the inscriptions. Grotefend assumed that these groups of letters or signs were the names of these very Persian kings. Supposing such to be the case, and admitting that the ancient Persian forms of these names varied considerably from those handed down to us by the Greeks, yet he felt convinced that the value of certain letters in them must be the same. By various tentative processes he satisfied himself that he had hit upon the right names, and that he had determined the proper value of some, if not of all, the letters composing them. This enabled him to verify the conjecture, based upon historical evidence, that the language of the inscription was an Indo-Germanic dialect, spoken in Persia at the time of the Macedonian conquest, and allied to the Zend or Sanscrit, and consequently in a certain degree to the modern Persian.*

Proceeding always in the same tentative way, Grotefend next attempted a translation of some of the inscriptions, and the results of his investigations, and an analysis of his method of interpretation, were given in an appendix to Heeren's work on the principal nations of antiquity, which was published in 1815.†

Lassen, Rask, Burnouf, and other eminent Sanscrit and Oriental scholars, applied themselves to the examination of Grotefend's system and of his interpretations, bringing to bear upon the inquiry a profounder knowledge of the ancient Indo-Germanic tongues than he claimed to possess, though scarcely more skill and ingenuity as decipherers. Through their labours, what had been at first the result of happy conjecture was reduced to a certainty. It was proved that Grotefend had been mistaken in the value he had assigned to several letters, but that he had been right in his method of interpretation, and in his conjectures as to the names of the kings contained in the inscriptions which he had examined.

The short trilingual inscription which I have given contains the name of Xerxes, and may be translated thus:

KHSHIYÁRSHÁ KHSHÁYATHIYA WAZAR-
    Xerxes   the king   great,

-KA KHSHÁYATHIYA KHSHAYATHIYÁ-
    The king   of kings;

---

* The Persian names preserved by the Greek and Roman writers leave no doubt whatever that the language spoken by the ancient Persians was of this character.

† Historical Researches into the Politics, &c., of the Principal Nations of Antiquity, vol. ii. English edition of 1833. Oxford.

·NÁM DÁRYAVAHUSH KHSHÁYATH·
Of Darius   the king.
·IYAHYÁ PUTRA HAKHÁMANISHIYA.
The son,   the Achæmenid.

Hitherto the materials for the investigation of the cuneiform character had been comparatively limited. The inscriptions copied by travellers in Persia were short, rarely consisting of more than ten or twelve lines, and they were for the most part of nearly the same import. A trilingual inscription of great length was known to exist on the rock of Behistun, near Kermanshah, on the western frontiers of Persia; but it was in a position inaccessible to the ordinary traveller, and too high to admit of its being copied from below. Sir Henry Rawlinson was the first to obtain an imperfect transcript of it by the aid of a powerful telescope in the year 1835; but it was not until 1844 that, assisted by Captain Jones, and other gentlemen attached to the mission at Baghdad, he was able to reach the tablets, and to make copies and paper casts of the inscriptions. Like those of Persepolis and Hamadan, they consist of the same record, repeated three times in the three languages spoken by the three great races under the dominion of the Persian kings, and written in different modifications of the cuneiform character. The Persian column contains no less than 406 lines. The application to this great inscription of the key furnished by the short records previously deciphered by Grotefend and other investigators, completely corroborated the soundness of their system of interpretation. The Behistun tablets were found to contain a narrative of the principal events of the reign of Darius, the son of Hystaspes, which, in many respects, coincide with those recorded by the Greek historians. The effigy of the king himself is sculptured on the rock. Behind him stand his attendants, and in front are nine captive kings or chiefs, one of whom lies prostrate at his feet. Above each figure are short

trilingual inscriptions, recording the name of the person re
presented.

By the aid of the Behistun inscription, which has furnished
the most ample and reliable materials we yet possess for the
investigation of the cuneiform character, Sir Henry Rawlinson
has been able to add largely to the results obtained by Grotefend, Lassen, Burnouf, and others, from the scanty records
in their possession. He published the text of the Persian
column, with a complete translation of it, in the 'Journal' of
the Royal Asiatic Society for 1846. This translation has
been subjected to the most rigorous examination and criticism by Sanscrit scholars; and those who have taken the
trouble to acquaint themselves with the subject, and are
competent to form an opinion upon it, do not hesitate to
admit that the interpretation of the Persian cuneiform is
placed beyond a doubt.

The Persian column of the trilingual inscription having
thus been deciphered, a key was afforded to the interpretation of the two other inscriptions, supposing always that
their contents were the same, and that the language was one
which either still existed, or was allied to one still spoken
or written. That the contents of the three inscriptions
were the same was evident from the corresponding recurrence of certain groups in each column. But the Assyro-
Babylonian inscriptions offered far greater difficulties than
the Persian. The letters or signs used in the Persian were
limited in number, not exceeding thirty-six; and, as we
have seen, each word was separated, and marked by an
oblique wedge. In the Assyrian inscription there was no
division between the words, the letters and signs seemed not
only to be unlimited in number, but to be used in the most
arbitrary manner. As, however, the inscriptions contained
names of persons, countries, cities, &c.,* many of which could

---

* A list, in the three cuneiform characters, of the various satrapies included within the dominions of the King of Persia, had previously been

be identified with those preserved in classical or biblical literature, the value of many letters could be determined with sufficient confidence; and thus a clue was afforded to a few words of constant recurrence, and proof afforded that the language of the Assyro-Babylonian inscriptions, as might have been expected, was a Semitic dialect, allied to the Chaldee, Hebrew, Arab, and other cognate languages, either still existing, or of which written remains have been preserved.

Whilst European scholars were thus occupied in deciphering the trilingual tablets, the discoveries at Nimroud, Khorsabad and Kouyunjik, and amongst other Assyrian ruins, furnished a vast number of inscriptions which will afford materials for years to come for the study of the cuneiform character. During the excavations in Assyria I was too much occupied to be able to devote much time to the decipherment of the inscriptions; but whilst copying them, I was able to compare them and to classify to a certain extent the various signs and letters which they contain. One fact soon became evident to me, that the Assyrians, unlike the Persians, rarely, if ever, divided a word at the end of a line, preferring to finish it by cutting letters on the sculpture itself, or on the side or even back of a slab. As the 'Standard inscription' of the north-west palace of Nimroud, containing the names, titles, and part of the annals of the founder of the edifice, was repeated upon almost every slab discovered in the ruins, and in every variety of space, sometimes only one or two letters forming a line, I was able, by a careful comparison of the endings, to determine and mark off almost every word in the inscription. I soon also found, by the relative position of certain groups, the signs or letters marking the names of the kings, their titles, and the names of their fathers, and, in many instances, of their grandfathers.

discovered at Persepolis, and had enabled Burnouf and Lassen to determine the value of several letters of the Persian cuneiform alphabet.

On my return to England from my first expedition I edited, for the Trustees of the British Museum, a volume containing transcripts of inscriptions from Nimroud, Kouyunjik, Kalah Sherghat, and other Assyrian ruins. Their publication, and that of the cuneiform inscriptions discovered by M. Botta at Khorsabad, afforded fresh materials for investigation, and several eminent scholars took up the subject: amongst whom were the late Dr. Hincks,[*] Mr. Norris, Mr. Fox Talbot, and M. Oppert. Sir Henry Rawlinson, in 1850, announced that he had succeeded in reading the inscription on the black obelisk discovered in the centre palace at Nimroud, and shortly after communicated his version of its contents at a meeting of the members of the Royal Institution. On my return to England in 1851, after my second expedition, I spent some time with Dr. Hincks

---

[*] By the death of Dr. Hincks we have lost one of the ablest and most successful investigators of the cuneiform inscriptions. To profound scholarship in the Semitic tongues, and to the most extensive literary and scientific acquirements, he added a wonderful ingenuity, acuteness, and sagacity, and a singularly retentive memory, which peculiarly fitted him for a decipherer. His power of dealing with the most complicated and difficult cipher was exhibited at a very early age. After making many discoveries in Egyptology, he applied his great talents to the investigation of the cuneiform inscriptions, and with marvellous success, when it is remembered that he was the incumbent of a small living in Ireland, far from any public library, without the books and materials necessary for the prosecution of his studies, and so circumscribed in means that at one time he was, I believe, obliged to dispose of a part of his library. In any other country but England, a man of such attainments, and so eminently calculated to confer honour upon the nation to which he belonged, would have received some reward, or would have been placed in a position of independence, to enable him to pursue his studies. But, in spite of numerous representations to government by one or two of his friends in his behalf, and of the European reputation which he had established for himself by his discoveries, he was allowed to remain at Killyleagh with a decreasing income, and without any public recognition whatever of his literary and scientific acquirements. He died there at the commencement of this year. It is not detracting from the deserved reputation of Sir H. Rawlinson to say, that we owe to Dr. Hincks some of the most important discoveries in cuneiform literature, the present advanced state of our knowledge of the subject, and more especially the progress that has been made in placing upon firm ground the grammatical construction of the Assyrian language.

in Ireland in examining the cuneiform inscriptions which I had brought from Assyria and Armenia, and I am indebted to him for the translation of those inscriptions which I published in the work of which this book is an abridgment. Dr. Hincks had already deciphered the names of Sargon, Sennacherib, and Esar-haddon, and had thus proved that which I had been led to conjecture from a comparison of the monuments and from other evidence, that the palaces at Kouyunjik and Khorsabad, and in the south-west corner of the mound of Nimroud, owed their foundation to those kings. He also determined the Assyrian numerals from the Wan inscriptions. He had previously (in June, 1846) discovered the names of Nebuchadnezzar and Babylon on the well-known Babylonian bricks from the ruins near Hillah. On August 23, 1851, Sir Henry Rawlinson announced in the 'Athenæum' that he had found in the inscriptions from Kouyunjik notices of the reign of Sennacherib, 'which placed beyond the reach of dispute his historic identity;' and he gave a recapitulation of the principal events recorded on the monuments, including the war with Hezekiah and the siege and capture of Lachish.

Constant additions were made to our knowledge of the contents of the cuneiform inscriptions in communications from Dr. Hincks, Sir H. Rawlinson, Mr. Fox Talbot, and Mr. Norris, to the 'Journals' of the Royal Asiatic Society, to the 'Transactions' of the Royal Irish Academy, to the 'Athenæum,' and to other literary and scientific periodicals. But scholars in this country, whose learning was limited to the classics, were little inclined to accept these interpretations, and were rather disposed to reject them altogether as ingenious fictions. In the year 1857 Sir H. Rawlinson had superintended for the Trustees of the British Museum the publication of a transcript of the inscription upon the clay cylinders discovered at Kalah Sherghat. A copy of this inscription had been sent to Mr. Fox Talbot before its publication, and before Sir H. Rawlinson had placed before the public any account of its contents. In March, Mr. Fox Talbot forwarded a sealed packet to the late Professor Wilson, then President of the Royal Asiatic Society, enclosing his translation of the inscription, with a request that it might not be opened until Sir Henry Rawlinson, with whom he had had no communication on the subject, had published the translation of the same inscription which he had announced—adding his opinion, that 'all candid inquirers must acknowledge, that if any special agreement should appear between such independent versions, it must indicate that they have truth for their basis.'

The Council of the Royal Asiatic Society considered that this was a favourable occasion for testing the general accuracy of the interpretation of the cuneiform writing, and they requested not only Sir Henry Rawlinson, but Dr. Hincks and M. Oppert also, to furnish them with translations of the same inscription, under sealed covers, and without any previous communication with each other. A committee of gentlemen of the highest literary attainments, and of entirely independent opinions upon such matters, including Dr. Milman (the Dean of St. Paul's), Dr. Whewell, Sir Gardner Wilkinson, Mr. Grote, the Rev. Mr. Cureton, and Professor Wilson, were named to open the packets, and to examine and report upon the translations. Mr. Cureton, Dr. Whewell, and Professor Wilson were absent when the packets were opened; but the other three members of the committee, after having carefully examined and compared their contents, reported their opinions to the Council of the Asiatic Society. Dr. Milman and Mr. Grote certified that 'the coincidences between the translations, both as to the general sense and verbal rendering, were very remarkable. In most parts there was a strong correspondence in the meaning assigned, and occasionally a curious identity of expression as to particular words. When the versions differed very materially, each translator had, in many cases, marked the passage as one of doubtful or unascertained signification. In the interpretation of numbers there was throughout a singular correspondence.' Sir Gardner Wilkinson, in a separate report, expressed himself somewhat more strongly in favour of the decipherers, and declared that 'the resemblance (very often exactly the same, word for word) was so great, as to render it unreasonable to suppose that the interpretation could be arbitrary, or based on uncertain grounds.' Professor Wilson declares in his report to the Society that, 'upon the whole, the result of this experiment—than which a fairer test could scarcely be desired—may be considered as establishing almost definitively the correctness of the valuation of the characters of these inscriptions.'*

Since the period of the publication of the translations of this inscription, much has been added to our knowledge of the cuneiform character. Other scholars have entered into the field of investigation, and many remarkable instances of independent evidence confirming the general accuracy of the interpretation of the inscription could be cited. I may mention the short trilingual inscriptions containing the name of Artaxerxes, in the three forms of cuneiform writing, the Persian, Touranian, and Babylonian, accompanied by an Egyptian cartouche with the same royal name, upon an alabaster vase in the treasury of St. Mark's at Venice, of which, singularly enough, a duplicate was discovered by Mr. Newton amongst the ruins of the mausoleum at Halicarnassus. These inscriptions furnish a test of the accuracy of the decipherment of both the cuneiform character and the hieroglyphics.

The first literary and scientific body in the world, the French Academy, has publicly recognised the progress made,

---

* Inscription of Tiglath Pileser I., king of Assyria, B.C. 1150, as translated by Sir H. Rawlinson, Fox Talbot, Esq., Dr. Hincks, and Dr. Oppert. Published by the Royal Asiatic Society, 1857.

the accuracy of the principles upon which the decipherment of the cuneiform inscriptions is based, and the importance of the results already obtained, by recommending Dr. Oppert to the French government for the great prize of 20,000 francs, conferred periodically upon the author who has rendered the greatest service to literature or science. In England, however, the same doubts and misgivings still prevail with regard to the interpretation of the arrow headed character, and the writer of a recent article in a leading periodical criticises with the utmost severity the labours of the decipherer, and seems to reject altogether the additions to our knowledge of the history and language of the Assyrians, which the inscriptions are believed to afford.* But the critic in this case had no special knowledge of the subject, and he somewhat unfairly keeps out of view the evidence that can be adduced in support of the system of interpretation which has now been accepted by so many distinguished scholars, and the explanations which can be afforded of contradictions and inconsistencies that undoubtedly occur in the versions given at different times by the same decipherer of the same inscription. For instance, the fact that the same proper name has been rendered in various ways, and that no certainty exists with regard to the value of the signs and letters composing it, although put forward as a conclusive argument against the progress alleged to have been made in the interpretation of the cuneiform character, admits of a satisfactory explanation. The names of places and persons, and especially those of Assyrian and Babylonian kings, are frequently composed of the name of a god,† usually represented by one sign, of which we do not know the phonetic reading, and the sound or value of which, consequently, must be more or less a matter of conjecture.

---

* See 'Edinburgh Review' for January, 1867 (No. 255), article on 'Rawlinson's Ancient Monarchies.'
† The names of foreign kings, which are not Assyrian, are written phonetically, and are consequently deciphered with more certainty.

In some instances the equivalent of this sign in letters has been ascertained, and then the name of which it forms a part can be determined with confidence, as for example that of Sennacherib. But it must be admitted that, owing to the fact I have mentioned, the reading of many of the royal names which occur in the Assyrian inscriptions is more or less doubtful, and must be received with caution. This, however, does not prove that they are not royal names, or that their places in the Assyrian dynastic lists cannot be fixed with accuracy.*

A more weighty argument is furnished to the adverse critic by the attempts which, it appears to me, have been somewhat injudiciously made to reconcile the contents of the inscriptions with the very vague and doubtful notices of ancient Assyria contained in the fragments of ancient writers, most of which are of little or no authority, and to the tendency which some interpreters of the inscriptions have shown to build up theories altogether opposed to authentic history, upon the slightest possible foundation. An instance of this is furnished by the author of a learned work in which all the available information with regard to Babylonia and Assyria has been collected together with much industry— 'The History of the Five Great Monarchies of the Ancient Eastern World.' A primitive empire of Chaldæa is called into existence, and the history, arts, manners, and religion of an imaginary people described, upon no better foundation than a few bricks dug out of Babylonian mounds and believed

---

* I have not thought it necessary to point out in the text the various reasons why the interpretation of the cuneiform character is liable to so much uncertainty, as far as the literal reading, though not always of the meaning, of words is concerned. As for instance, the fact that the number of the characters seems to be almost unlimited, and that some only of them are phonetic, the remainder being syllabic and ideographic. The exact value of many of these signs has however been satisfactorily determined by the aid of the very curious and important lists of signs with their equivalents in letters, discovered amongst the clay tablets in the British Museum.

to bear royal names which cannot be said to have been yet satisfactorily deciphered, and some pottery and other remains of doubtful antiquity. Although very great progress has undoubtedly been made in the interpretation of the cuneiform inscriptions, the time is not yet come for the historian to accept their presumed contents as authentic and well-established materials for the reconstruction of a history of the ancient Assyrian empire, mixing with them the scattered and semi-fabulous notices of ancient authors of no authority. Any such attempt must inevitably expose its author to severe criticism, and must rather tend to throw a doubt upon, than to establish, the soundness of the principles upon which the decipherment of the cuneiform inscriptions has been carried on.

The study of the writing and language of the ancient Assyrians and Babylonians is still too much in its infancy to warrant the acceptance, without questioning, of the literal interpretation of any one considerable inscription. As yet the number of scholars who have seriously and independently turned their attention to the decipherment of the cuneiform character is very limited. An immense mass of materials for the investigation has been accumulated in the British Museum, in the collection of clay tablets and of the monuments brought from Assyria and Babylonia. These materials will gradually be made accessible to foreign scholars through their publication by the Trustees, under the able editorship of Sir Henry Rawlinson. A most important aid to the student will be furnished by a dictionary, or vocabulary of all known Assyrian words, now in the course of compilation by that eminent and most industrious scholar, Mr. Edwin Norris. What is now principally required is the independent examination of the inscriptions by learned Orientalists of different countries. As yet little has been done in Germany, and yet the accurate and penetrating intellect and patient analysis of the German scholar are peculiarly fitted for investigations of this nature. I have little doubt that, in a few years, such progress will have been made in our knowledge of the contents of the inscriptions, and in our acquaintance with the comparative dates of the monuments, that we shall be able to restore much of the history of the ancient Assyrian empire, and to obtain a considerable insight into the religion, arts, sciences, literature, and political institutions of its people.

Some doubts exist as to the dates which are assigned to the various Assyrian monuments and inscriptions that have been discovered; and it has been asked, upon what evidence we are able to restore Assyrian chronology. Although we may not be able to assign a place with confidence to any event, such as the accession of a king to the throne, in our system of chronology, yet the inscriptions have furnished the means for ascertaining with certainty the year of his reign in which any event of importance occurred. It would appear that each Assyrian year was known by the name of a highpriest or some great dignitary, as the Athenian year was connected with the name of an Archon; the first year of a king's reign being frequently identified with the royal name itself. Fragments of clay tablets containing lists of these 'eponyms,' as they are termed, have been discovered amongst the collections in the British Museum. Although as yet a complete list has not been restored, a sufficient number of names has already been found to enable us to fix the relative dates of most of the events mentioned in the annals of the later Assyrian kings, as those annals are usually marked, year by year, by the name of the eponym.* These kings filled the Assyrian throne at a time when we approach authentic history, and the epoch of their reigns can be determined with some degree of certainty from sources independent of the Assyrian monuments and inscriptions.

* This important discovery was announced by Sir H. Rawlinson, in the 'Athenæum' for May 31 and July 19, 1862.

Although, therefore, it may be impossible as yet to ascertain the very year before Christ of any particular event, we can get near enough to it for all useful purposes.* The dates of the accession of the very early kings, and of the principal events of their reigns, have been doubtfully determined by references to them in the inscriptions themselves. But when we endeavour to deal with them we tread upon very uncertain ground. As yet it cannot be asserted that they can be fixed otherwise than approximately. It would seem, however, that the Assyrians kept a very accurate computation of time, and future discoveries may enable us to restore a great part of Assyrian chronology.

Sir Henry Rawlinson has put forward a theory, that the ancient capital of Assyria was a city called Asshur, of which the great mound of Kalah Sherghat marks the site, and that Nineveh was a comparatively recent capital to which the seat of government was only transferred about seven centuries B.C., and whose foundation does not date beyond the 10th or 12th century. But it appears to me that this view cannot be supported by sufficient evidence. It is undoubtedly opposed to sacred and profane history, and to the testimony afforded by Egyptian monuments, on which the name of Nineveh is found as far back as the 15th century B.C., whilst no mention of such a city as Asshur occurs.†

It has been remarked that, after all, the contents of the Assyrian inscriptions, admitting them to have been deciphered, have afforded us no useful information, and have added but little to our knowledge of the ancient world, as they only contain a dry record of the wars and conquests of

---

* If the discovery of the notice of an eclipse of the sun upon an Assyrian tablet be confirmed, we should then be able to determine with complete certainty the date of the principal events mentioned in the Assyrian annals.

† The Rev. G. Rawlinson ('Ancient Monarchies,' vol. ii. p. 303) gets over the difficulty of the mention of Nineveh in Genesis by suggesting that the 11th and 12th verses of the 10th chapter 'were possibly an addition made by Ezra on the return from the captivity.'

eastern tyrants, and of a barbarous people. What, it might be asked, should we know of the Greeks if only their monumental records had been preserved to us? Fortunately, however, the Assyrian inscriptions contain more than mere royal annals; and although we cannot ascertain the intellectual advancement which the Assyrian people may have made, as we have no written literature belonging to them, such as happily has been preserved to us from ancient Greece, yet we have in the vast collection of inscriptions on marble and baked clay, dug up from the ruins of Nineveh and Babylon, and in the monuments themselves, ample materials to prove that the Assyrians had made great progress in those arts and sciences which distinguish a civilised people. The discoveries in Assyria and Babylonia have enabled us to reach one of the remotest sources of that mighty stream of human progress which has developed, through Greece and Rome, into our present civilisation. It is in this that their great interest and importance consist.

Erratum.

Page 292, note ‡, line 3 from foot, *for* Appian *read* Apion.

NINEVEH AND BABYLON.

CHAPTER I.

Renewal of excavations in Assyria—Return to Mosul—Discoveries at Kouyunjik—Visit to Nimroud—Excavations in the Mound—Mr. H. Rassam—Sculptures representing transport of winged bulls discovered at Kouyunjik—Fresh sculptures—Discovery of gateway—High Mound at Nimroud explored.

IN the summer of 1849 I had returned to my post at Constantinople as an attaché to her Majesty's Embassy. The general interest expressed in England at the result of the discoveries on the site of Nineveh, during my first expedition to Assyria, induced the Trustees of the British Museum to continue the excavations, and, having obtained a grant of money for that purpose from the Government, they requested me to undertake their direction. I cheerfully consented to return to Mosul, and to carry on further researches amongst the Assyrian ruins. My preparations having been soon completed, I left the Turkish capital at the end of August. I was accompanied by Mr. F. Cooper, an artist sent out by the Trustees to make drawings of such objects as might be discovered; by Dr. Sandwith, an English physician on a visit to the East; and by my faithful friend and former companion, Mr. Hormuzd Rassam. Cawal Yusuf, a priest and chief of the sect of the Yezidis, availed himself of my escort to return to his native mountains. He was the bearer of a Firman, which he had obtained through the mediation of Lord Stratford de Redcliffe, releasing his people from various unjust and oppressive burdens and laws to which they had previously been subject.

I chose for our route to Mosul the little known districts of Eastern Armenia, and the Kurdish mountains between the Lake of Wan and Jezirah. I was thus able to follow and determine the track of the ten thousand Greeks in their memorable retreat under Xenophon, to trace the head waters of the Tigris, and to visit the two important Turkish towns of Erzeroom and Bitlis. We travelled through a highly interesting and picturesque country without accident, although not without risk from Kurdish and Arab marauders, and at the end of September I again found myself in the Assyrian plains.*

The first stage of my journey homewards, on leaving Mosul two years before, had been at the Chaldæan village of Tel Kef. It was the last on my return. As we rode wearily towards the village, on a hot and sultry afternoon at the end of September, I left the high road with Hormuzd to quench my thirst at some Arab tents. As we drew near, we were greeted with exclamations of joy, and were soon in the midst of a crowd of men and women, kissing our knees, and giving us other marks of welcome. They were Arabs of the Jebour tribe, who had been formerly employed in the excavations. They eagerly enquired whether we were again going to dig for old stones, and hearing that such was the object of my journey, they at once set about striking their tents, to be ready to join us at Mosul or Nimroud.

As we neared Tel Kef we found groups of my old superintendents and workmen by the road side. There were fat Toma, Mansour, Behnan, and Hannah, joyful at meeting me once more, and at the prospect of fresh service. In the village were Mr. Rassam (the English vice-consul) and Khodja Toma, his dragoman, who had made ready the feast for us at the house of the Chaldæan bishop. Next morning, as we rode the last three hours of our journey, we met fresh groups of old friends :—Merjan, with my groom holding the stirrup

---

* A full narrative of my journey will be found in the first three chapters of my larger edition of 'Nineveh and Babylon.'

ready for me to mount, the noble animal looking as beautiful, as fresh, and as sleek as when I last saw him, although two long years had passed; former servants, Awad and the Sheikhs of the Jebours, even the very greyhounds who had been brought up under my roof. Then as we ascend an eminence midway, walls, towers, minarets, and domes rise boldly from the margin of the broad river, cheating us into the belief, too soon to be dispelled, that Mosul is still a not unworthy representative of the great Nineveh. As we draw near, the long line of lofty mounds, the only remains of mighty bulwarks and spacious gates, detach themselves from the low undulating hills: now the vast mound of Kouyunjik overtops the surrounding heaps; then above it peers the white cone of the tomb of the prophet Jonah; many other well-remembered spots follow in rapid succession; but we cannot linger. Hastening over the creaking bridge of boats, we force our way through the crowded bazars, and alight at the house I had left two years ago. Old servants take their places as a matter of course, and, uninvited, pursue their regular occupations as if they had never been interrupted. Indeed it seemed as if we had but returned from a summer's ride; two years had passed away like a dream.

On the morning after our arrival in Mosul, I rode at sunrise to Kouyunjik. On my return to Europe in 1847, Mr. Ross had continued the excavations in the palace of Sennacherib, where I had left off, and had uncovered several interesting bas-reliefs. That gentleman had, to my great regret, left Mosul. Since his departure the excavations had been placed under the charge of Mr. Rassam, who was directed by the Trustees of the British Museum to employ a small number of men, rather to retain possession of the spot, and to prevent interference on the part of others, than to carry on extensive operations. Toma Shishman, or 'the Fat,' was still the overseer of the workmen, and accompanied me on my first visit to the ruins.

But little change had taken place in the great mound since I had last seen it. It was yellow and bare, as it always is at this time of the year. Heaps of earth marked the site of former excavations, the chambers first discovered having been again completely buried with rubbish. Of the sculptured walls laid bare two years before no traces now remained.

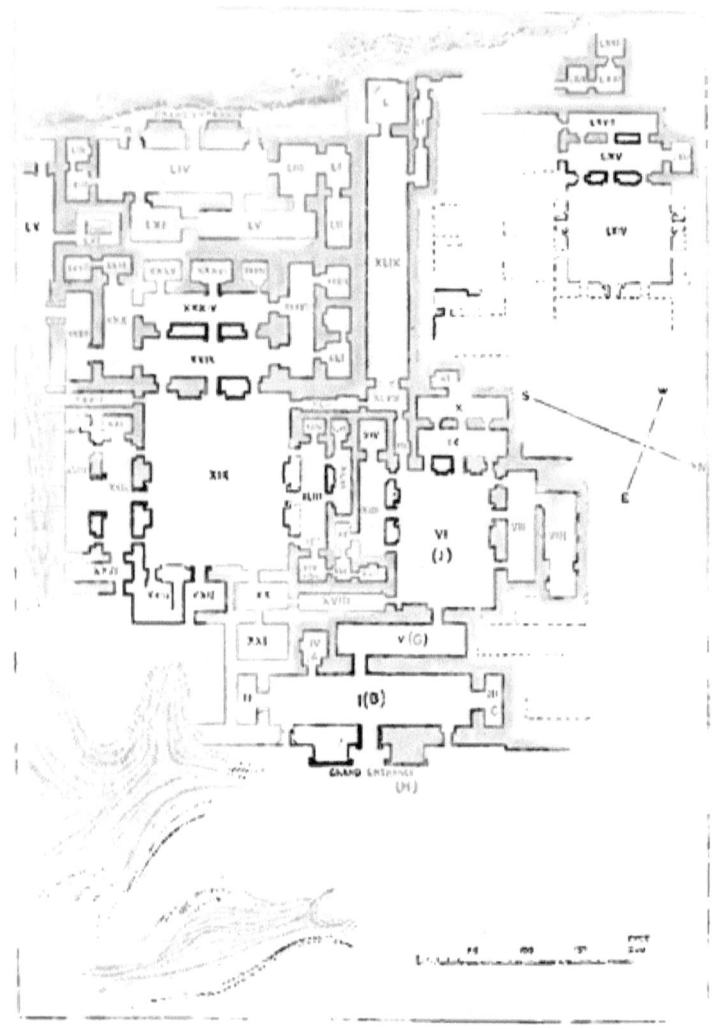

PLAN I.—Palace of Sennacherib.

The trenches dug under Mr. Ross's directions, in the southern corner, opposite the town of Mosul, were still open. The two chambers he had explored formed part of the great palace standing on this angle of the mound, already partly explored.* The bas-reliefs, however, were much defaced.

They recorded the conquest by Sennacherib of a nation inhabiting the banks of a river. The captive women were distinguished by long embroidered robes fringed with tassels. The walls of the castles had a peculiar wedge-shaped ornament, and stood on the bank of a river or marsh, indicated by canes or reeds, and in a district producing the palm tree. The Assyrians having captured the strong places by escalade, were carrying the inhabitants into captivity, and driving away cattle, camels, and carts drawn by oxen. Some of the men bore large baskets of osier work, and the women vases or cauldrons. The king, standing in his chariot, attended by his warriors, and preceded by an eunuch registering the number of prisoners and the amount of the spoil, received the captive chiefs. We may conjecture, from the marsh or river and the palm trees, that the conquered people inhabited some district in southern Mesopotamia. They were, probably, one of the numerous tribes who lived in the marshes formed by the Euphrates and Tigris, and whose subjection is recorded in the inscriptions of Sennacherib. In the southern wall of this chamber was a doorway formed by plain, upright slabs of close-grained magnesian limestone, almost as hard as flint ; between them were two small, crouching lions, in the usual alabaster. This entrance led into a further room, of which only a small part had been explored.† The walls were panelled with unsculptured slabs of the same compact limestone.

The sculptured remains hitherto discovered in the mound of Kouyunjik had been reached by digging down to them from the surface. The accumulation of rubbish was, however, so considerable in this part of the ruins, frequently exceeding thirty feet, that the workmen, to avoid the labour of clearing it away, began to tunnel along the buried walls, sinking shafts at intervals to admit light and air. The underground passages were narrow, and were propped up when necessary either by leaving columns of soil, as in mines, or by wooden

* No. LI. Plan I.   † No. LIII. Plan I.

beams. These long galleries, dimly lighted, and lined with the remains of ancient art—the wild Arabs and Nestorians wandering through their intricacies, or working in their dark recesses—were singularly picturesque.

Toma Shishman had removed the workmen from the

Underground Excavations at Kouyunjik.

southern corner of the mound, where the sculptures were much injured, and had opened tunnels in a part of the building previously explored, commencing where I had left off in 1847.* I descended into the underground passages by an inclined way, through which the workmen issued with the rubbish

* No. VI. Plan I. p. 4.

dug out from the ruins. At the bottom I found myself before a wall forming the southern side of the great hall, discovered, though only partly explored, during my former researches.* The sculptured slabs faintly seen through the gloom, although almost reduced to lime by the fire which had destroyed the palace, were still fairly preserved. They had been entirely covered with figures, varying from three inches to one foot in height, carefully finished, and designed with great spirit.

In this series of bas-reliefs the history of an Assyrian conquest was more fully portrayed than in any other yet discovered, from the going out of the monarch to battle to his triumphal return after victory. Sennacherib, accompanied by his chariots and horsemen, was seen passing through a mountainous and wooded district and entering the high country. The mountains, valleys, and streams, the vines and dwarf oaks, indicated a region north of Assyria, either Armenia, Media, or Kurdistan, countries we know to have been invaded by this monarch. His troops, cavalry and infantry, were represented in close combat with the enemy, pursuing them over hills and through valleys, beside streams, and in the midst of vineyards. The vanquished turned to ask for quarter; or, wounded, fell under the feet of the advancing horses, raising their hands imploringly to ward off the impending death-blow. The triumph followed. The king standing in his chariot, beneath the royal parasol, attended by long lines of dismounted warriors leading richly caparisoned horses, and by foot soldiers variously armed and accoutred, was receiving the captives and spoil taken from the conquered people. First approached the spearmen throwing the heads of the slain into heaps before the officers appointed to number them. Then came other soldiers, leading, and urging onwards with staves, the prisoners—men chained together, or bound singly in fetters, and women, some on foot, carrying their children on their shoulders, or leading them by the hand, others riding on mules. Asses, mules, and flocks of sheep, formed the spoil. The dress of the men consisted of a short tunic; that of the women, of a shirt falling to the ankles, and cut low in front of the neck.†

* No. VI. Plan I. p. 4.
† Two plates from these spirited sculptures are given in the 2nd series

In the side of the hall or court sculptured with these bas-reliefs was a wide portal, formed by a pair of colossal human-headed bulls. They had suffered, like all those previously discovered, from the fire, and the upper part—the wings and human head—had been completely destroyed. The lower half had, however, escaped, and the inscriptions were consequently nearly entire. By the side of each bull were two small figures, one above the other. They had long hair, falling in large and massive curls on their shoulders, wore short tunics descending to the knee, and held in one hand a pole topped by a kind of cone, and raised the other in act of adoration.* At right angles with the slabs bearing these sculptures were colossal figures carrying the oft-repeated cone and basket.

In this entrance a well, cut through the large pavement slab between the bulls, was afterwards discovered. It contained fragments of pottery, human bones, and some pieces of calcined sculptured alabaster, evidently detached from the bas-reliefs on the walls. Like many other wells discovered during the excavations, it had probably been sunk by those who had built on the mound above the Assyrian ruins.

A small doorway to the right of the portal formed by the winged bulls, led into a further chamber,† in which an entrance had been found into another room,‡ whose walls had been completely uncovered. The dimensions of this third room were 26 feet by 23, and it had but one door, flanked on either side by two colossal figures, whose lower extremities alone remained, the upper part of the slabs having been destroyed: one appeared to have been eagle-headed, with the body of a man, and the other a monster, with human head and the feet of a lion. The bas-reliefs represented the siege of a castle standing on an artificial mound, and surrounded by houses. The besieged defended themselves on the walls and turrets with bows, spears, and stones. As

of the 'Monuments of Nineveh,' Plates 37, 38. They represent the battle, and part of the triumph.

* One such figure has been placed in the British Museum, and see 2nd series of the 'Monuments of Nineveh,' Plate 6.

† No. XIII. Plan I. p. 4. ‡ No. XIV. same Plan.

syrian spearmen, slingers, and bowmen had already gained the housetops. Male and female captives had been taken and heads cut off—the victorious warriors, according to custom and probably to claim a reward,* bringing them to the registrars. The led horses and body-guard of the king were still preserved, but the figure of the monarch himself had been destroyed. The country was indicated by wooded mountains, vines, and various trees, and a river. The dress of the male prisoners consisted either of a long robe falling to the ankles, or of a tunic reaching to the knees, over which was an outer garment, apparently made of the skins of animals, and they wore greaves laced up in front. The women were clothed in a robe descending to the feet, with an outer fringed garment thrown over the shoulders; a kind of hood or veil covered the back of the head, and fell over the neck. Above the castle was the fragment of an inscription in two lines, containing the name of the city, of which unfortunately the first character is wanting, and which cannot, therefore, be satisfactorily determined. We may infer, however, from the nature of the country represented, that it stood in a mountainous district to the north of Assyria.† In this chamber, as in others afterwards explored, some of the slabs (those adjoining the entrance) had been purposely defaced, every vestige of sculpture having been carefully removed by a sharp instrument.

Returning to the great hall, I found that a third entrance had been discovered, opening to the west. It had been guarded by six colossal figures, three on each side. The upper part of all of them had been destroyed. They had been eagle-headed and lion-headed monsters.

This doorway led into a narrow passage, only one side of which had been excavated; ‡ on it was represented the siege of a walled city, divided into two parts by a river. One-half of the place had been captured by the Assyrians, who had

---

* It is still the custom in Persia, and was so until lately in Turkey, for soldiers to bring the heads of the slain to their officers after a battle, for the purpose of claiming a reward.

† Such parts of the bas-reliefs as could be moved are now in the British Museum; see also 2nd series of the 'Monuments of Nineveh,' Plate 39.

‡ No. xii. Plan I. p. 4.

gained possession of the towers and battlements; the other, on the opposite bank of the stream, was still defended by slingers and bowmen. Against its walls had been thrown banks or mounds, built of stones, bricks, and branches of trees. The battering-rams, covered with skins or hides, had been rolled up these inclined ways, and had already made a breach in the fortifications. Archers and spearmen were hurrying to the assault, whilst others were driving off the captives, and carrying away their gods or idols. The dress of the male prisoners consisted of a plain under-shirt, an upper garment falling below the knees, divided in the front and buttoned at the neck, and laced greaves. Their hair and beards were shorter and less elaborately curled than those of the Assyrians. The women were distinguished by high rounded turbans, ornamented with plaits or folds. A veil fell from the back of this headdress over their shoulders.* No inscription remained to record the name of the vanquished nation.

The opposite side of this narrow chamber, or passage, was shortly afterwards uncovered. The bas-reliefs on its walls represented Sennacherib in his chariot, preceded and followed by his warriors. The only remarkable feature in the sculptures was the highly decorated trappings of the horses, whose bits were in the form of a horse at full speed.

Such were the discoveries that had been made during my absence. There could be no doubt whatever that all the chambers hitherto excavated belonged to one great edifice, built by one and the same king. I have already shown how the bas-reliefs of Kouyunjik differed from those of the older palaces of Nimroud, but closely resembled those of Khorsabad in the general treatment, in the costumes of the Assyrian warriors, as well as of the nations with whom they warred, and in the character of the ornaments, inscriptions, and details.† Those newly uncovered were, in all these respects, like the bas-reliefs found before my departure, and upon which I

---

* Such is the costume of the women in ships in a bas-relief discovered during my former researches (see 'Monuments of Nineveh,' Plate 71), which, there is reason to believe, represents the capture of Tyre or Sidon.
† See 'Nineveh and its Remains,' chap. xiii.

had ventured to form an opinion as to the respective antiquity and origin of the various ruins hitherto explored in Assyria. The bas-reliefs of Nimroud, the reader may remember, were divided into two bands or friezes by inscriptions; the subject being frequently confined to one tablet, or slab, and arranged with some attempt at composition, so as to form a separate picture. At Kouyunjik the four walls of a chamber were generally occupied by one series of sculptures, representing a consecutive history, uninterrupted by inscriptions, or by the divisions in the alabaster panelling. Figures, smaller in size than those of Nimroud, covered from top to bottom the face of slabs eight or nine feet high, and sometimes of equal breadth.

The sculptor could thus introduce more action, and far more detail, into his subject. He aimed even at conveying, by rude representations of trees, valleys, mountains, and rivers, a general idea of the natural features of the country in which the events recorded took place. Thus a chamber generally contained the whole story of one campaign, from the going out of the king to his triumphal return. We are thus able to identify, in many instances, the sculptured records with the descriptive accounts contained in the great inscriptions carved upon the bulls, at the various entrances to the palace, which relate the principal events of the reign of the king. At Kouyunjik there were probably few bas-reliefs, particularly those containing representations of castles and cities, that were not accompanied by a short epigraph, or label, giving the name of the conquered king and country, and even the names of the principal prisoners, especially if royal personages. Unfortunately these inscriptions having been usually placed on the upper part of the slabs, which has very rarely escaped destruction, but few of them remain.

I lost no time in making arrangements for continuing the excavations. Toma Shishman was placed over Kouyunjik; Mansour, Behnan (the marble cutter), and Hannah (the carpenter), again entered my service. Ali Rahal, a sheikh of the Jebours, who, hearing of my return, had hastened to Mosul, was sent to the desert to collect such of my old workmen from his tribe as were inclined to re-enter my service.

He was appointed 'sheikh of the mound,' and duly invested with the customary robe of honour on the occasion.

The accumulation of soil above the ruins was so great, that I determined to continue the tunnelling, removing only as much earth as was necessary to show the sculptured walls. The rubbish was carried away through shafts sunk at intervals for this purpose, and to admit light and air, and was raised in baskets by rude wooden pulleys.

Many of the Nestorians formerly in my service as diggers, having heard of my expected return, had left their mountains and had joined me a day or two after my arrival. There were Jebours enough in the immediate neighbourhood of the town to make up four or five gangs of workmen, and I placed parties at once in the galleries already opened, and also in different parts of Kouyunjik not previously explored, and at a high mound in the north-west walls, forming one side of the great inclosure opposite Mosul—a ruin which I had only partially examined during my previous visit.

After a short visit to the Yezidi shrine at Sheikh Adi, I was again at Mosul on the 12th October. By this time all my preparations were completed. The Jebours had pitched their tents over the excavations at Kouyunjik. About one hundred workmen, divided into twelve or fourteen parties, were employed at the mound. The Arabs, as before, removed the earth and rubbish, whilst the more difficult labour with the pick was left entirely to the hardy Nestorian mountaineers. My old friend, Yakoub, the Rais of Asheetha, made his appearance one morning, declaring that things were going on ill in the mountains; and that, although the head of a village, he hoped to spend the winter more profitably and more pleasantly in my service than at home. He was accordingly named superintendent of the Nestorian workmen, for whom I built mud huts near the foot of the mound.

The work having been thus began at Kouyunjik, I rode with Hormuzd to Nimroud for the first time on the 18th of October. It seemed but yesterday that we had followed the same track. We stopped at each village, and found in each old acquaintances ready to welcome us. From the crest of the hill half way, the first view of Nimroud opened upon us; the great mound, on which I had gazed so often from this spot, and with which so many happy recollections were bound up, rising boldly above the Jaif, the river winding through the plain, the distant wreaths of smoke marking the villages of Naifa and Nimroud. At Selamiyah we sought the house of the Kiayah, where I had passed the first winter whilst excavating at Nimroud; but it was now a house of mourning. The good old man had died two days before, and the wails of the women, telling of a death within, met our ears as we approached the hovel. Turning from the scene of woe, we galloped over the plain, and reached Nimroud as the sun went down. Saleh Shahir, with the elders of the village, was there to receive us. I dismounted at my old house, which was still standing, though somewhat in ruins, for it had been the habitation of the Kiayah during my absence. To avoid the vermin swarming in the rooms, my tent was pitched in the courtyard, and I dwelt entirely in it.

The village had still, comparatively speaking, a flourishing appearance, and had not diminished in size since my last visit. The *tanzimat*, or reformed system of local administration, had been introduced into the pashalic of Mosul, and although many of its regulations were evaded, and arbitrary acts were still occasionally committed, yet on the whole a marked improvement had taken place in the dealings of the authorities with the subjects of the Sultan. The great cause of complaint was the want of security. The troops under the command of the Pasha were not sufficient in number to keep the Bedouins in check, and there was scarcely a village in the low country which had not suffered more or less from their depredations. Nimroud was particularly exposed to their incursions, and the inhabitants lived in continual agitation and alarm.

The evening was spent with the principal people of the village, talking with them of their prospects, taxes, harvests, and the military conscription, now the great theme of discontent in Southern Turkey, where it had been newly introduced.

By sunrise next morning I was amongst the ruins. The

mound had undergone no change. There it rose from the plain, the same sun-burnt yellow heap that it had stood for twenty centuries. The earth and rubbish, which had been heaped over the excavated chambers and sculptured slabs, had settled, and had left uncovered, in sinking, the upper part of several bas-reliefs. A few colossal heads of winged figures rose calmly above the level of the soil, and with two pairs of winged bulls, which had not been reburied on account of their mutilated condition, was all that remained above ground of the north-west palace, that great storehouse of Assyrian history and art. Since my departure the surface of the mound had again been furrowed by the plough, and ample crops had this year rewarded the labours of the husbandman. The ruins of the south-west palace were still uncovered. The Arabs had respected the few bas-reliefs which stood against the crumbling walls, and Saleh Shahir pointed to them as a proof of the watchfulness of his people during my long absence.

Collecting together my old excavators from the Shemutti and Jehesh (the Arab tribes which inhabit Nimroud and Naifa), and from the tents of a few Jebours, I placed workmen in different parts of the mound. The north-west palace had not been fully explored. I consequently directed a party of workmen to resume the excavations where they had been formerly abandoned.* New trenches were also opened in the ruins of the centre palace, where, as yet, no sculptures had been discovered in their original position against the walls. The high conical mound at the north-west corner of Nimroud had not been examined. With the exception of a shaft, about forty feet deep, sunk nearly in its centre, and passing through a solid mass of sundried bricks, no opening had been made into this singular ruin. I now ordered a tunnel to be carried into its base on the western face, and on a level with the conglomerate rock upon which it rests.

Whilst riding among the ruins giving directions to the workmen, we had not escaped the watchful eyes of the Abou-Salman Arabs, whose tents were scattered over the Jaif. Not

* To the south of Chamber X. Plan II. p. 42, 'Nineveh and its Remains.'

having heard of my visit, and perceiving horsemen wandering over the mound, they took us for Bedouin marauders, and mounting their mares, sallied forth to reconnoitre. Seeing Arabs galloping over the plain I rode down to meet them, and soon found myself in the embrace of Schloss, the nephew of Sheikh Abd-ur-Rahman. We turned together to the tents of the chief, still pitched on the old encamping ground. The men, instead of fighting with Bedouins, now gathered round us in the *muzaf**, and a sheep was slain to celebrate my return. The Sheikh himself was absent, having been thrown into prison by the Pasha for refusing to pay some newly-imposed taxes. I was able to announce his release, at my intercession, to his wife, who received me as his guest.

As I ascended the mound next morning I perceived a group of travellers on its summit, their horses picketed in the stubble. Ere I could learn what strangers had thus wandered to this remote region, my hand was seized by the faithful Bairakdar. Beneath, in an excavated chamber, wrapped in his travelling cloak, was Rawlinson deep in sleep, wearied by a long and harassing night's ride. For the first time we met in the Assyrian ruins, and besides the greetings of old friendship there was much to be seen together, and much to be talked over. The fatigues of the journey had, however, brought on fever, and we were soon compelled, after visiting the principal excavations, to take refuge from the heat of the sun in the mud huts of the village. The attack increasing in the evening, it was deemed prudent to ride into Mosul at once, and we mounted our horses in the middle of the night. Three days afterwards he continued his journey to Constantinople.

I had now nearly all my old adherents and workmen about me. The Bairakdar, who had hastened to join me as soon as he had heard of my return, was named principal cawass, and had the general management of my household. One Latiff Agha, like the Bairakdar, a native of Scio, carried off as a slave after the massacre, and brought up as a Mussulman, was appointed an overseer over the workmen. He had been

---

* The *muzaf* is that part of an Arab tent in which guests are received.

strongly recommended to me by the British consul at Kaiseriyah, and fully justified in my service by his honesty and fidelity the good report I had received of him.

During the months of October and November my time was spent between Kouyunjik and Nimroud, and the excavations were carried on at both places without interruption. Mr. Cooper was occupied in drawing the bas-reliefs discovered at Kouyunjik—living in Mosul, and riding over daily to the ruins. To Mr. Hormuzd Rassam, who usually accompanied me in my journeys, were confided, as before, the general superintendence of the operations, the payment of the workmen, the settlement of disputes, and various other offices, which only one, as well acquainted as himself with the Arabs and men of various tribes and sects employed in the works, and exercising so much personal influence over them, could undertake. To his unwearied exertions, and his faithful and punctual discharge of all the duties imposed upon him, to his inexhaustible good humour, combined with necessary firmness, to his complete knowledge of the Arab character, and the attachment with which even the wildest of those with whom we were brought in contact regarded him, the Trustees of the British Museum owe not only much of the success of these researches, but the economy with which I was enabled to carry them through. Without him it would have been impossible to accomplish half what has been done with the means placed at my disposal.

The Kouyunjik workmen received their weekly pay in the subterranean galleries, some convenient space where several passages met being chosen for the purpose; those of Nimroud generally in the village. A scene of wild confusion ensued on pay-days, from which an inexperienced observer might have argued a sad want of order and method. This was, however, but the way of doing business usual in the country. When there was a difference of opinion, he who cried the loudest gained the day, and after a desperate struggle of voices matters relapsed into their usual state, every one being perfectly satisfied. Screaming and gesticulation with Easterns by no means signify ill-will, or even serious disagreement. Without them, except of course amongst the

Turks, who are staid and dignified to a proverb, the most
ordinary transactions cannot be carried on. Sometimes the
Arabs employed at Kouyunjik would cross the river to Mosul
to receive their pay. They would then walk through the
town in martial array, brandishing their weapons and chanting their war cries in chorus, to the alarm of the authorities
and the inhabitants, who generally concluded that the place
had been invaded by the Bedouins. It was Mr. Hormuzd
Rassam's task to keep in check these wild spirits.

By the end of November several entire chambers had been
excavated at Kouyunjik, and many bas-reliefs of great interest had been discovered. The four sides of the court,*
part of which has already been described, had now been
explored.† In the centre of each side was a grand entrance,
guarded by colossal human-headed bulls.‡ This court was
124 feet in length by 90 feet in breadth, the longest sides
being those to the north and south. It appears to have
formed a centre, around which the principal chambers in this
part of the palace were grouped. Its walls had been completely covered with the most elaborate and highly finished
sculptures. Unfortunately all the bas-reliefs, as well as the
colossal figures at the entrances, had suffered more or less
from the fire which had destroyed the edifice.

The narrow passage leading from the great hall at the
south-west corner had been completely explored. Its sculptures have already been described.§ It opened into a chamber 24 feet by 19, from which branched two other passages.‖
The one to the west was entered by a wide doorway, in which
stood two plain spherical stones about three feet high, having

---

* I have called this part of the palace, in the larger edition of this
work, 'a hall;' it was more probably a court entirely open to the sky,
like the courts of modern Mosul houses.

† No. VI. Plan I. p. 4. It will be borne in mind that it was necessary
to carry tunnels round the chambers, and along the walls, leaving the
centre buried in earth and rubbish, a very laborious and tedious operation
with no other means at command than those afforded by the country.

‡ All these entrances were formed in the same way as that in the
south-eastern side, described p. 8, namely, by a pair of human-headed
bulls, flanked on each side by a winged giant, and two smaller figures
one above the other.

§ P. 9. ‖ Nos. XLVIII. and XLII. Plan I. p. 4.

the appearance of the bases of columns, although no traces of the columns themselves could be found. This was the entrance into a broad and spacious gallery, about 218 feet long and 25 wide.* A tunnel at its western end, cut through the solid wall, as there was no doorway on this side of the gallery, led into the chambers excavated by Mr. Ross,† thus connecting them with the rest of the building.

I have already described the bas-reliefs on the southern side of the great hall, representing the conquest of a mountainous country.‡ The same subject was continued on the western wall, without much variety in the details. But on the northern, the sculptures differed from any others yet discovered, and were of great interest. They represented the moving of the great human-headed bulls to their places in the palaces.

The whole gallery, to the west of the great hall, had been occupied by one continuous series, representing the different processes adopted by the Assyrians in moving and placing various objects used in their buildings, and especially the human-headed bulls, from the first transport of the huge stone in the rough from the quarry, to the raising of these gigantic sculptures in the gateways of the palace. In the great hall the same subjects were repeated, and other details introduced.

A huge block of stone (probably of the alabaster used in the Assyrian edifices), somewhat elongated in form so as to resemble an obelisk in the rough,§ was lying on a low flat-bottomed boat floating on a river. It had probably been towed down the Tigris from some distant quarry, and was to be landed near the site of the intended palace, to be carved by the sculptor into the form of a colossal bull. It exceeded the boat considerably in length, projecting beyond both the head and stern, and was held by upright beams fastened to the sides of the vessel, and kept firm in their places by

---

* No. XLIX. Plan I. p. 4.   † Nos. LI. and LII. same Plan.

‡ P. 7. I assume the building to be due north and south, although it is not so. It faces nearly north-east and south-west.

§ It is just possible that this object really represents an obelisk; but I think it more probable, for several reasons, that it is a block in the rough from the quarry, to be sculptured into the form of a winged bull.

wooden wedges. Two cables were passed through holes cut in the stone itself, and a third was tied to a strong pin projecting from the head of the boat. Each cable was held by a large body of men, who pulled by means of small ropes fastened to it and passed round their shoulders. Some of these trackers walked in the water, others on dry land. The number altogether represented must have been nearly 300, about 100 to each cable, and they appeared to be divided into distinct bands, each distinguished by a peculiar costume. Some wore a kind of embroidered turban, through which their long hair was gathered behind; the heads of others were encircled by a fringed shawl, whose ends hung over the ears and neck, leaving the hair to fall in long curls upon the shoulders.

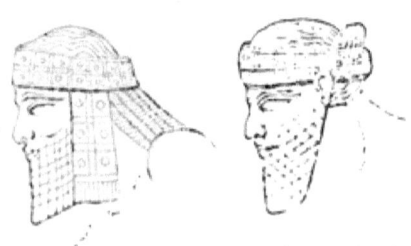

Head-dress of Captives employed by Assyrians in moving Bull. (Kouyunjik.)

Many were represented naked, but the greater number were dressed in short chequered tunics, with a long fringe attached to the girdle. They were urged on by taskmasters armed with swords and staves. The boat was also pushed by men wading in the stream. An overseer, who regulated the whole proceedings, was seated astride on the fore-part of the stone. His hands were stretched out in the act of giving commands. As the upper part of all the bas-reliefs had unfortunately been destroyed, it cannot be ascertained what figures were represented above the trackers; probably Assyrian warriors drawn up in martial array, or may be the king himself in his chariot, accompanied by his body-guard, and presiding over the operations.*

The huge stone having been landed, and carved by the Assyrian sculptor into the form of a colossal human-headed bull, was to be moved from the bank of the river to the site it was meant to occupy in the palace. This process was re-

---

* For the details of these interesting bas-reliefs, I must refer my readers to Plates 10 and 11, in the second series of the 'Monuments of Nineveh.'

presented on the walls of the great hall. From these bas-reliefs, as well as from discoveries to be hereafter mentioned, it is evident that the Assyrians sculptured these gigantic figures before moving them to their places, leaving only the details and the finishing touches to be put in; the smaller sculptures appear to have been executed after the slabs had been placed.

In one bas-relief the colossal bull was seen resting horizontally on a sledge similar in form to the boat containing the rough block from the quarry. It faced the spectator, and the human head rested on the fore part of the sledge, which was curved upwards and strengthened by a thick beam, apparently running completely through from side to side. The upper part, or deck, was otherwise nearly flat; the keel, being slightly curved throughout. Props, probably of wood, were placed under different parts of the sculpture to secure an equal pressure. The sledge was dragged by cables, and helped onwards by levers. The cables were four in number; two fastened to strong projecting pins in front, and two to similar pins behind. They were pulled by small ropes passing over the shoulders of the men. The workmen were distinguished by various costumes, to show that they were captives from different conquered nations, and were urged on by task-masters. The sledge moved over rollers, which, as soon as left behind, were brought again to the front by parties of men, who were under the control of overseers armed with staves. Although these rollers materially facilitated the motion, it would be almost impossible, when passing over rough ground, or if the rollers were jammed, to give the first impetus to so heavy a body by mere force applied to the cables. The Assyrians, therefore, lifted, and consequently eased, the hinder part of the sledge with huge levers of wood, and in order to obtain the necessary fulcrum they carried with them during the operations wedges of different sizes. Kneeling workmen were represented using these levers and wedges. The levers were worked by ropes, and on a detached fragment, discovered in the long gallery, men were seen seated astride upon them to add by their weight to the force applied.

MOVING THE BULLS.

On the bull were four persons, probably the superintending officers. The first was kneeling, and appeared to be clapping his hands, probably beating time, to regulate the

Cart with Ropes and Workmen carrying Saws, Picks and Shovels, for moving colossal Bull. (Kouyunjik.)

motions of the workmen, who unless they applied their strength at one and the same moment would be unable to move so large a weight. Behind him stood a second officer

Workmen carrying Ropes, Saws, and other Implements for moving Bull. (Kouyunjik.)

with outstretched arm, evidently giving the word of command. The next held to his mouth an object resembling the modern speaking-trumpet. In no bas-relief hitherto discovered does a similar object occur as an instrument of music. The fourth officer, also standing, carried a mace, and was probably stationed behind to give directions to those who worked the levers. The sledge bearing the sculpture was followed by men with coils of ropes and various implements, and drawing carts laden with cables and beams. Even the landscape was not neglected; and the country in which these operations took place was indicated by trees, and a river. In the river were seen men swimming on skins; and boats and rafts, resembling those still in use in Assyria, impelled by oars with wedge-shaped blades.

The same subject was represented in other bas-reliefs, with even fuller details. The bull was placed in the same manner on a sledge, which was also moved by cables and levers. It was accompanied by workmen with saws, hatchets, pickaxes, shovels, ropes, and props, and by carts carrying cables and beams. Upon the bull itself were three officers directing the operations, one holding the speaking trumpet in his hands; and in front walked four other overseers. Above the sledge and the workmen were rows of trees, and a river on which were circular boats resembling in shape the 'kufas,' now used on the lower part of the Tigris, and probably, like them, built of reeds and ozier twigs, covered with square pieces of hide.* They were heavily laden with the beams and implements required for moving and placing the bulls. They appeared to have been near the sledge when dragged along the bank of the river, and were impelled by four oars. Near the boats, astride on inflated skins in the water, were fishermen angling with hook and line.†

On a fallen slab, forming part of the same series, was represented the king standing in a richly-decorated chariot, the pole of which, curved upwards at the end, and ornamented with the head of a horse, was raised by two eunuchs. From the peculiar form of this chariot and the absence of a

---

* Such appear to have been the boats described by Herodotus (lib. i. c. 194). The modern 'kufa' is covered with bitumen.

† This bas-relief is now in the British Museum, and see Plate 12, 2nd series of 'Monuments of Nineveh.'

yoke, it would seem to have been a kind of movable throne drawn by men and not by horses.* Behind the monarch, who holds in one hand a kind of flower, or ornament in the shape of a pine cone, stood two other eunuchs, one raising a parasol to shade him from the sun, the other fanning him. He appeared to have been superintending the transport of one of the colossal sculptures, and his chariot was preceded and followed by his body-guard armed with maces. In the upper part of the slab was a jungle of high reeds, or canes, in which were seen a wild sow with its young, and a stag and two hinds †

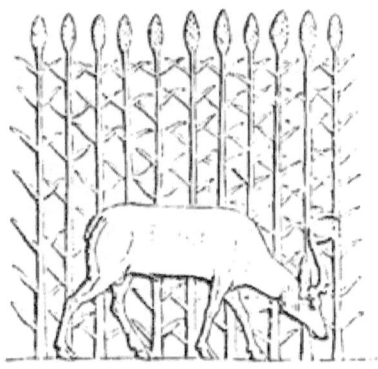

Stag   (Kouyunjik.)

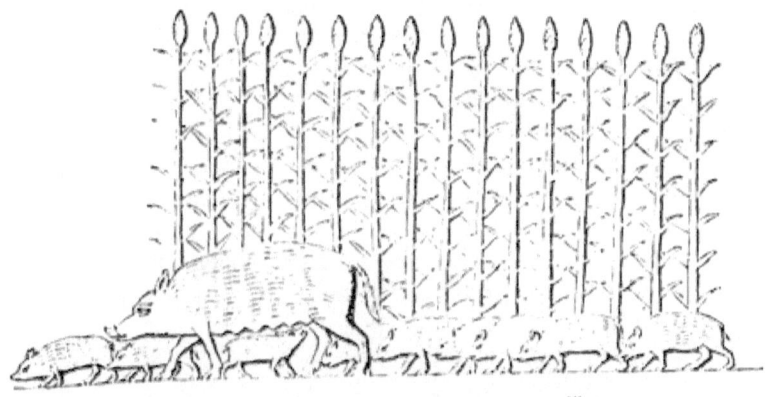

Wild Sow and Young, amongst Reeds.   (Kouyunjik.)

The next series of bas-reliefs represented workmen building the artificial platforms on which the palaces were erected.

* A throne on wheels, with a yoke, carried by two eunuchs, is represented in a bas-relief at Khorsabad. Botta. Plate 17.
† See Plate 12, 2nd series of 'Monuments of Nineveh.'

and moving to their summit the colossal bulls.* The king, attended by his guards, and seated in his chariot drawn by eunuchs, with an attendant raising the parasol above his head, superintended the operations. Above him were low hills covered with various trees, amongst which could be distinguished by their fruit the vine, the fig, and the pomegranate. At the bottom of the slab was represented either a river divided into two branches and forming an island, as the Tigris does to this day opposite Kouyunjik, or the confluence of that stream and the Khauser, which once probably took place at the very foot of the mound. On the banks were seen men raising water by a simple machine, still generally used for irrigation in the East, as well as in Southern Europe—a pole, balanced on a shaft of masonry, with a stone at one end and a bucket at the other.

The building of the artificial mound was then represented.† Men, apparently engaged in making bricks, were crouching round the clay pit. These brickmakers were between two mounds, on which were gangs of workmen, carrying up large stones and baskets filled with bricks, earth, and rubbish, and returning for fresh materials.

They appeared to be captives and malefactors, for many of them were in chains, some singly, others bound together by an iron rod attached to rings in their girdles. The fetters either confined the legs, and were supported by a bar fastened to the waist, or consisted of simple shackles round the ankles. The workmen wore a short tunic, and a conical cap somewhat resembling the Phrygian bonnet, with the top turned backwards. Each gang was attended by task-masters armed with staves.

The mound, having been thus built, partly with regular layers of sundried bricks and partly with mere heaped-up earth and rubbish,‡ the next step was to drag to its summit

---

* See Plates 14 and 15, 2nd series of 'Monuments of Nineveh.'
† Part of this bas-relief is in the British Museum. The whole series occupied about twenty-five slabs in the N.E. walls of the great hall. Unfortunately some of the slabs had been entirely destroyed.
‡ Subsequent excavations at Kouyunjik and Nimroud fully verified this fact.

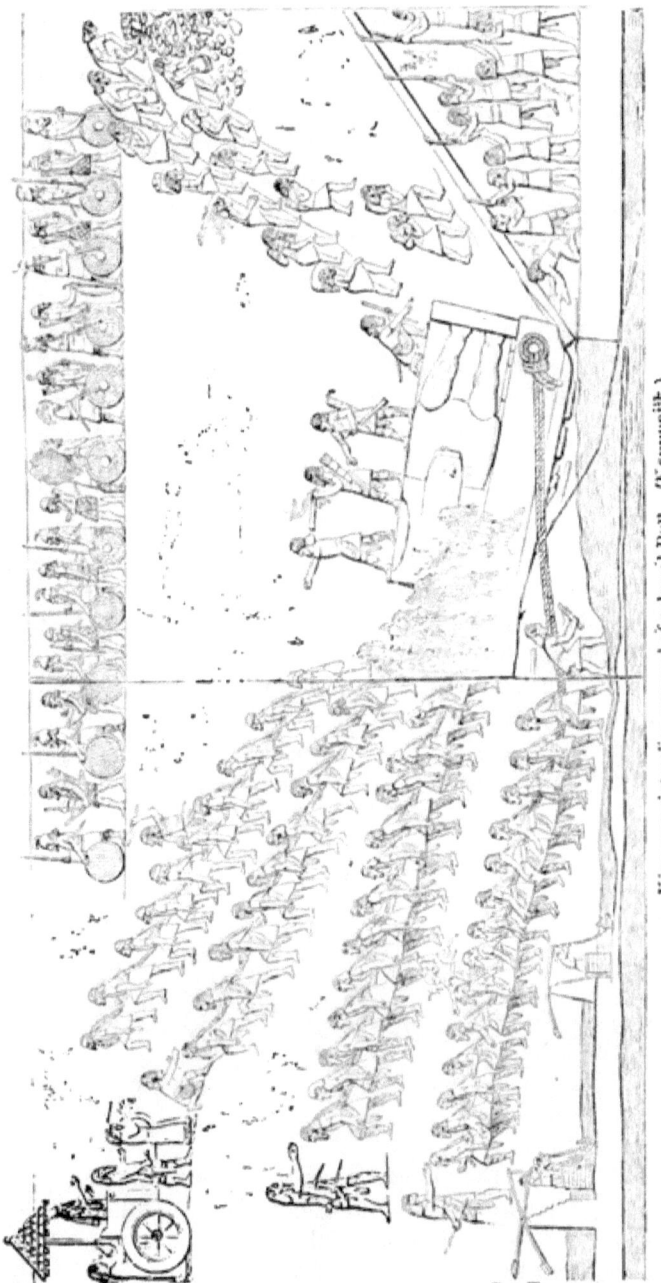

King superintending; removal of colossal Bull. (Kouyunjik.)

the colossal figures prepared for the palace. As some of the largest of these sculptures were full twenty feet square, and must have weighed between forty and fifty tons, this was no easy task when the only mechanical powers possessed by the Assyrians appear to have been the roller and the lever. A sledge was used similar to that already described, and drawn in the same way. In the bas-relief representing the operation, four officers were seen on the bull, the first apparently clapping his hands to make the drawers keep time, the second using the speaking trumpet, the third directing the men who had the care of the rollers, and the fourth kneeling down behind to give orders to those who worked the lever. Two of the groups were preceded by overseers, who turned back to encourage the workmen in their exertions; and in front of the royal chariot, on the edge of the mound, knelt an officer, probably the chief superintendent, looking towards the king to receive orders direct from him.

Behind the monarch were carts bearing the cables, wedges, and implements required in moving the sculpture. A long beam or lever was slung by ropes from the shoulders of three men, and one of the great wedges was carried in the same way. In the upper compartment of this slab was a stream issuing from the foot of hills wooded with vines, fig-trees,

Village with conical Roofs, near Aleppo.

and pomegranates. Beneath stood a town or village, the houses of which had domes and high conical roofs, probably built of mud, as in parts of Northern Syria.

This interesting series was completed by a bas-relief, showing, it would seem, the final placing of the colossal bull.

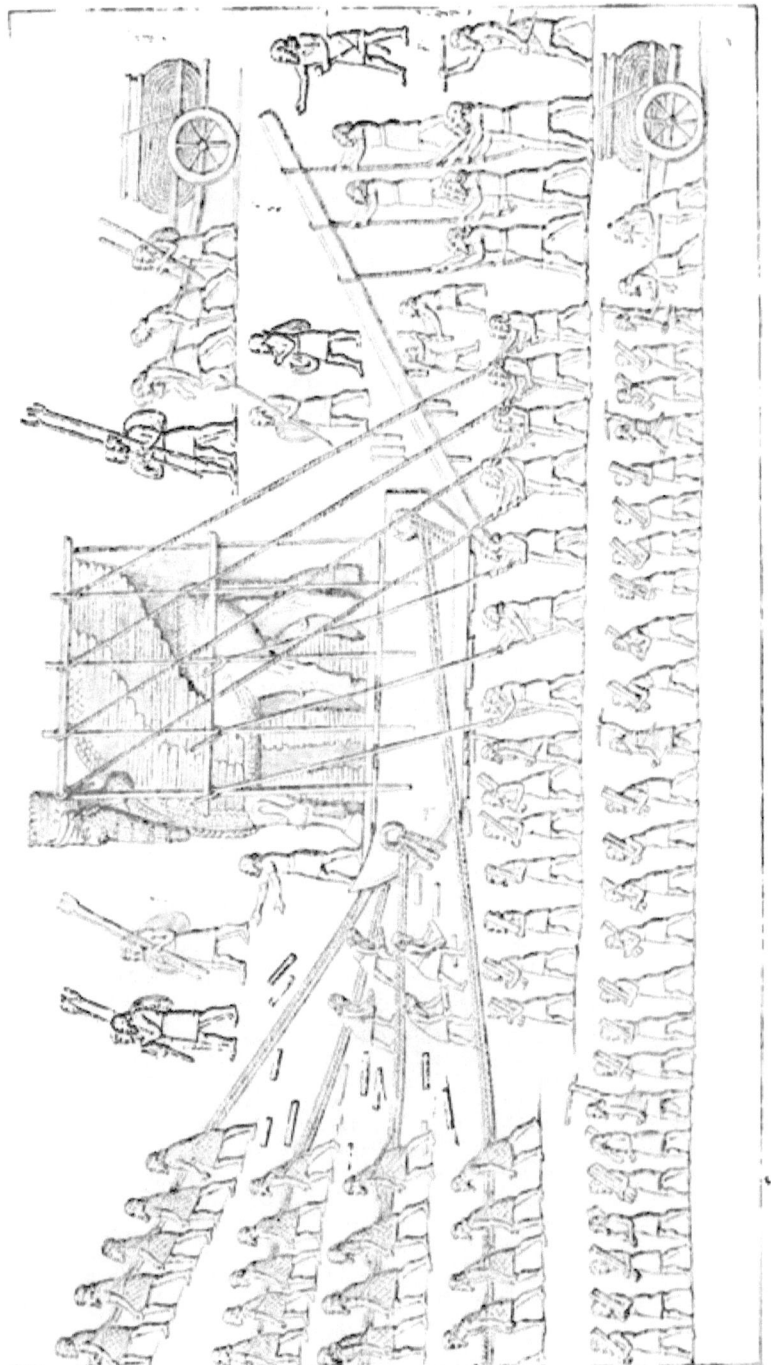

Assyrians placing a human-headed bull. (Kouyunjik.)

The figure no longer lay on its side on the sledge, but was held upright by men with ropes and forked wooden props. It was kept in its erect position by beams, held together by cross bars and wedges*, and was further supported by blocks of stone or wood. On the sledge, in front of the bull, stood an officer giving directions with outstretched hands to the workmen. Cables, ropes, rollers, and levers were used by the workmen. Unfortunately the upper part of all the slabs had been destroyed, and much of the subject was consequently wanting.

Thus was represented with remarkable fidelity and spirit, the several processes employed to place these colossi where they still stand—from the transport down the river of the rough block to the final removal of the sculptured figure to the palace. When moving the winged bulls and lions now in the British Museum from the ruins to the banks of the Tigris, I used almost the same means as the ancient Assyrians, employing, however, a cart instead of a sledge.

No traces whatever, notwithstanding the most careful search, have yet been found of the quarries from whence the builders of the Assyrian palaces obtained their large slabs of alabaster. They were probably not far from Nineveh, as strata of this material abound in Assyria.

We learn from short inscriptions cut upon the slabs that the king represented as superintending the construction of the mounds, and the placing of the colossal bulls, is Sennacherib, and that the sculptures record the building at Nineveh by that monarch of his great palace and its adjacent temples. The inscriptions on the winged bulls at Kouyunjik describe the manner in which the edifice itself was erected, its general plan, and the various materials employed in decorating the halls, chambers, and roofs.†

* It may be remarked, that precisely the same framework was used in the British Museum for moving and placing the great sculptures.

† In a fragment of an epigraph upon one of the slabs mention appears to be made of wood 'brought from Mount Lebanon and taken up (to the top of the mound) from the Tigris.' This may refer to cedarwood, of which beams have been found in the ruins of Nineveh. We thus find that the Assyrians brought this precious wood from Lebanon,

That captives from foreign countries were employed in the great public works undertaken by the Assyrian kings, may be inferred from the variety of costume represented in the bas-reliefs, and from the fetters on the legs of some of the workmen. The Jews themselves, after their captivity, may have been thus condemned to labour, as their forefathers had been in Egypt, in erecting the monuments of their conquerors; and we may, perhaps, recognise them amongst the workmen portrayed in the sculptures.

I have mentioned that the long gallery containing the bas-reliefs representing the moving of the great stone, led out of a chamber whose walls had been completely uncovered.* The sculptures upon them were partly preserved, and recorded the conquest of a city standing on a broad river, in the midst of mountains and forests. The Assyrians appear to have entered the enemy's country by a valley, to have forded the stream frequently, and to have continued during their march along its banks. Warriors on foot led their horses, and dragged chariots over precipitous rocks. On each side of the river were wooded hills, with small streams flowing amongst vineyards. As they drew near to the city, the Assyrians cut down the woods to clear the approaches. Amongst the branches of a tree exceeding the others in size, and standing immediately beneath the walls, were birds and two nests containing their young. The sculptor probably introduced these accessories to denote the season of the year. The river appeared to flow through or behind the city. Long low walls and equidistant towers, surmounted by cornices and angular battlements, stood on one side of the stream. Within the walls were large square buildings, curiously ornamented, and whose windows, immediately beneath the roof, were flanked by small pillars with capitals having the Ionic volute. The doors, except the entrance to the castle which was arched, were square, and, in some instances, surmounted by a plain cornice. Part of the city seemed to consist of a

as did Solomon for the choicest wood-work of the Temple and of his own palaces.

* No. XLVIII. Plan I. p. 4. See 'Monuments of Nineveh,' 2nd series, Plate 40.

number of detached forts and houses, some of which had open balustrades to admit the light. Flames issued from the dwellings, and on the towers were men apparently cutting down trees growing within the walls. Assyrian warriors, marching in a long line, carried away the spoil from the burning city. Some were laden with arms; others with furniture, such as chairs, stools, couches, and tables of various forms.

The last bas-relief of the series represented the king seated within a fortified camp, on a throne of elaborate workmanship. He was receiving the captives, who wore long robes falling to their ankles. Unfortunately no inscription remained by which we might identify the conquered people. It is probable, from the nature of the country represented, that they inhabited some district in the western part of Asia Minor, or in Armenia, in which direction Sennacherib more than once carried his victorious arms.

Excavations had been resumed in a lofty mound in the north-west line of walls forming the square inclosure in which stands Kouyunjik. It was apparently the remains of a gate leading into this quarter of the city, and part of a building, with fragments of two colossal winged figures, had already been discovered in it. By the end of November the whole had been explored, and the results were of considerable interest. As the mound rises nearly fifty feet above the plain, I was obliged to tunnel along the walls of the building within it, through a compact mass of rubbish, consisting almost entirely of loose bricks. Following the rows of low limestone slabs, from the south side of the mound, and passing through two halls or chambers, we came at length to the opposite side of the gateway. It faced the open country, and was formed by a pair of majestic human-headed winged bulls, fourteen feet in length, still entire, though cracked and injured by fire. They were similar in form to those of Khorsabad and Kouyunjik, wearing the lofty head-dress, richly ornamented with rosettes, and surmounted by a crest of feathers. Behind them were colossal winged figures of the same height, bearing the pine cone and basket. Their faces were in full, and the relief was high and bold. More knowledge of art was shown in the outline of the limbs and in the delineation of the muscles, than in any sculpture I have seen of this period. The naked leg and foot were designed with a spirit and truthfulness not unworthy of a Greek artist.* It is, however, remarkable that the four figures were unfinished, none of the details having been put in. They stood as if the sculptors had been interrupted by some public calamity, and had left their work incomplete. Perhaps the murder of Sennacherib by his sons, as he worshipped in the house of Nisroch his god, put a sudden stop to the great undertakings he had commenced in the beginning of his reign.

The sculptures to the left, on entering from the open country, were in a far more unfinished state than those on the opposite side. The hair and beard were but roughly marked out, square bosses being left for carving the elaborate curls. The horned cap of the human-headed bull was, as yet, unornamented, and the wings merely outlined. The limbs and features were hard and angular, still requiring to be rounded off, and to have expression given to them by the finishing touches of the artist. The other two figures were more perfect. The curls of the beard and hair (except on one side of the head of the giant) and the ornaments of the head-dress had been completed. The limbs of the winged deity and the body and legs of the bull had been sufficiently finished to give a bold and majestic character to the figures, which might have been rather lessened than improved by the addition of details. The wings of the giant were merely in outline. The sculptor had begun to mark out the feathers in those of the bull, but had been interrupted after finishing one row and commencing a second.† No inscription had yet been carved on either sculpture.

The entrance formed by these colossal bulls was fourteen

* The bulls and winged figures resembled in form those from Khorsabad, now in the great hall at the British Museum, but exceeded them in the beauty of the sculpture and in grandeur, as well as in preservation. As nearly similar figures had thus already been sent to England, I did not think it advisable to remove them.

† See Plate 3, of the 2nd series of the 'Monuments of Nineveh.' The giant is correctly represented in its unfinished state in this plate, but the artist by mistake has filled up the details in the wings of the bulls.

feet and a quarter wide. It was paved with large slabs of limestone, on which could be seen the grooves worn by the wheels of the chariots, which in the days of the Assyrians had passed through the city gates. The sculptures were buried in a mass of brick and earth, mingled with charcoal and charred wood. They were lighted from above by a deep shaft sunk from the top of the mound. It would be difficult to describe the effect produced by these solemn and

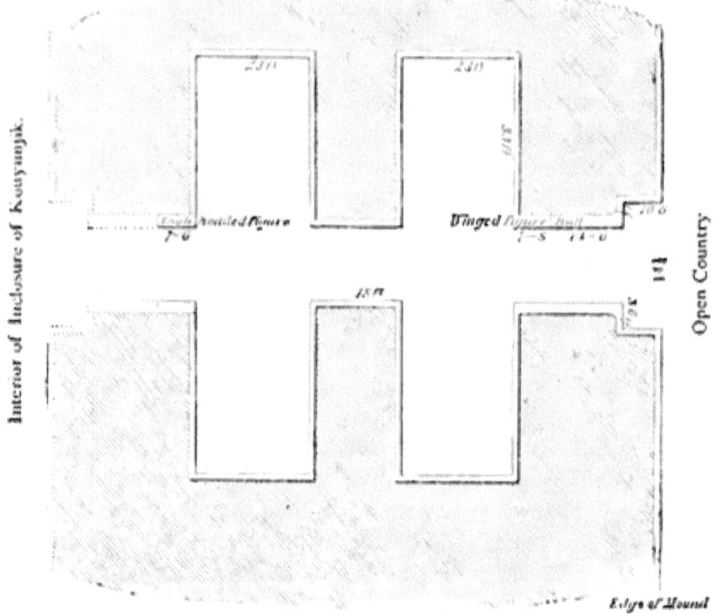

Plan of Northern Gateway to Inclosure of Kouyunjik.

majestic figures, dimly visible amidst the gloom, when, after winding through the dark, underground passages, you suddenly came into their presence. Between them Sennacherib with his hosts had gone forth in all his might and glory to the conquest of distant lands, and had returned rich with spoils and captives, amongst whom may have been the handmaidens and youths of Israel. Through them, too, the Assyrian monarch had entered his capital in shame, after his fatal defeat. Then the lofty walls, now but long lines of low, wave-like mounds, had stretched far to the right and to the left—a basement of stone supporting a curtain of solid brick masonry, crowned with battlements and studded with frowning towers.

This entrance may have been arched like the castle gates represented in the bas-reliefs, and the mass of burnt bricks around the sculptures may be the remains of the vault. A high tower evidently rose above this gate, which formed the principal northern access to this quarter of Nineveh.

Behind the colossal figures, and between the outer and inner face of the gateway, were two chambers, nearly 70 feet in length by 23 in breadth. Of that part of the entrance which was within the city walls, only the fragments of winged figures, discovered during my previous researches, now remained.* It is probable, however, that a second pair of human-headed bulls once stood there. They may have been 'the figures of animals,' described to Mr. Rich as having been casually uncovered in this mound, and which were broken up nearly fifty years ago to furnish materials for the repair of a bridge.†

The city gate thus consisted of two distinct chambers and three doors, two flanked by human-headed bulls, and a third between them simply panelled with low limestone slabs like the chambers. Its original height, including the tower, must have been full one hundred feet. Most of the baked bricks found amongst the rubbish bore the name of Sennacherib. A similar gateway, but without any remains of sculptured figures, and panelled with plain alabaster slabs, was subsequently discovered in the inner line of walls forming the eastern side of the quadrangle, where the road to Baashiekhah and Baazani leaves the ruins.

At Nimroud discoveries of considerable importance were made in the high conical mound at the north-west corner. Desirous of fully exploring that remarkable ruin, I had employed nearly all the workmen in opening a tunnel into its western base. After penetrating for no less than eighty-four feet through a compact mass of rubbish, composed of loose

* See 'Nineveh and its Remains,' p. 104.
† See Rich's 'Residence in Kurdistan and Nineveh,' vol. ii. p. 39.

gravel, earth, burnt bricks, and fragments of stone, the excavators came to a wall of solid stone masonry. The man-

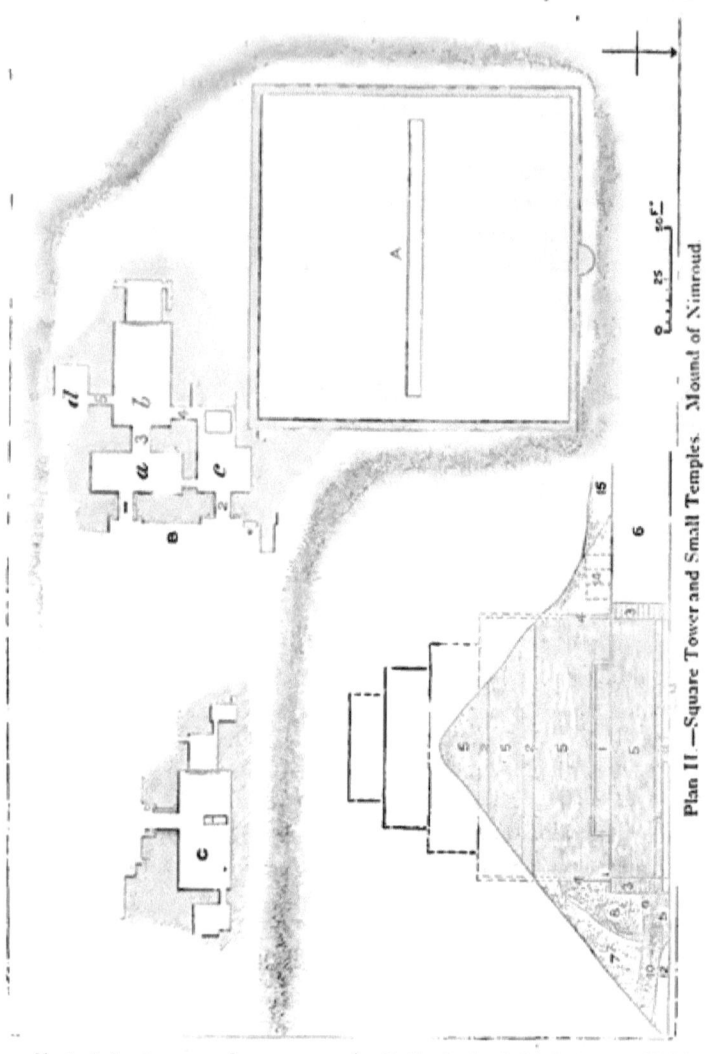

Plan II.—Square Tower and Small Temples. Mound of Nimroud

1. Vaulted chamber or tomb.
2. Excavated tunnel.
3. Basement stone wall.
4. Brick outside wall.
5. Mass of sun-dried bricks.
6. Artificial platform or mound.
7. Earth mixed with a few fragments of bricks.
8. Earth mixed with fragments of brick, stone, and bones.
9. Line of deposit of broken brick.
10. The line of pebble deposit.
11. Cutting.
12. Loose gravel.
13. Natural conglomerate.
14. Temple B. of Plan.
15. Level of Nimrod mound.

ner in which this structure had been buried is so curious, that I have given a section of the different strata through which the tunnel passed.* I have already observed that the edifice covered by this high mound was originally built upon the natural rock—a mass of hard conglomerate rising about

Tunnel along Eastern Basement Wall of Tower. (Nimroud.)

fifteen feet above the plain, and washed in days of yore by the waters of the Tigris. The tunnel was carried for thirty-four feet on a level with this rock, which appears to have been covered by a kind of flooring of sun-dried bricks, probably forming a platform in front of the building. It

* See section of conical mound, Plan II. p. 34.

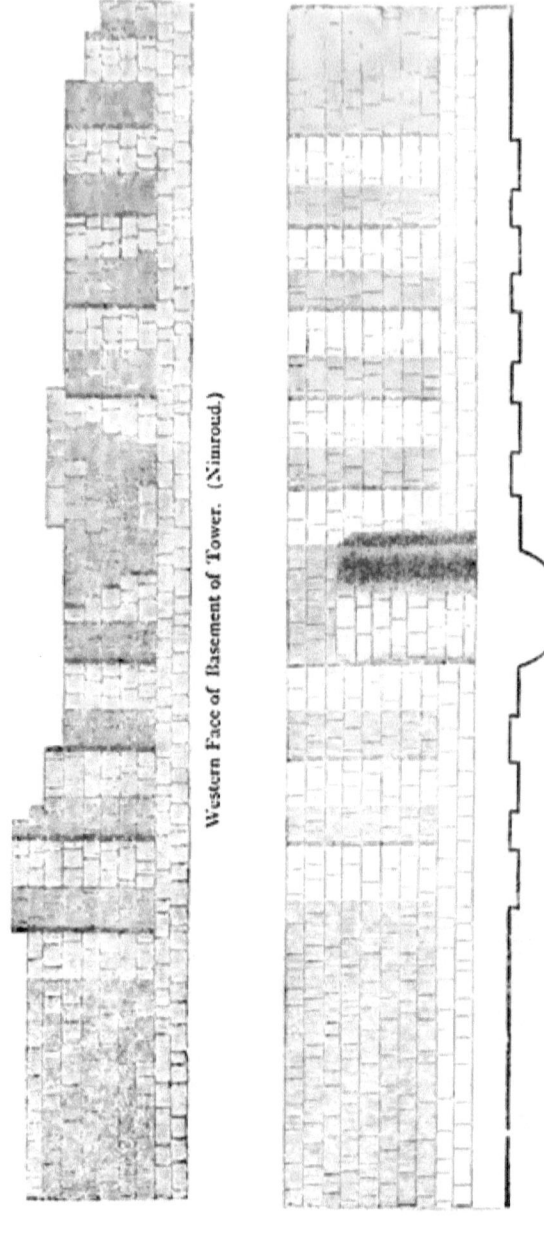

Western Face of Basement of Tower. (Nimroud.)

Northern Face of Basement of Tower. (Nimroud.)

was buried to the distance of thirty feet from the wall, by baked bricks broken and entire, and by fragments of stone, remains of the superstructure once resting upon the basement of still existing stone masonry. This mass of rubbish was about thirty feet high, and in it were found bones apparently human, and a yellow earthen jar rudely coloured with simple black designs.* The rest of this part of the mound consisted of earth, through which ran two thin lines of extraneous deposit, one *of pebbles*, the other of fragments of brick and pottery.

I carried tunnels along the basement wall, hoping to reach an entrance, but it was found to consist of solid masonry, extending nearly the whole length of the mound. Its height was twenty feet, which exactly coincides with that assigned by Xenophon to the stone basement of the wall of Larissa, as he calls the city of which Nimroud marks the site.† It was finished at the top by an ornamental battlement in gradines, similar to those represented on castles in the sculptures. These gradines had fallen, and some were discovered in the rubbish. The stones in this structure were levelled and carefully fitted together, though not united with mortar. In the face of the wall were eight recesses.

The northern side of the basement was of the same height as, and resembled in its masonry, the western. It had a semicircular projection in the centre, sixteen feet in diameter, on the east side of which were two recesses, and on the west four. That part of the basement against which the great artificial mound or platform abutted, and which was consequently concealed by it, that is, the eastern and southern sides, was of simple stone masonry without recesses or ornament. The upper part of the edifice, resting on the stone substructure, consisted of compact masonry of burnt bricks, which were mostly inscribed with the name of the founder of the centre palace (the son of Sardanapalus), the inscription being in many instances turned outwards.

It was thus evident that the high conical mound is the ruin of a square tower, and not of a pyramid, as had previously

---

* These relics may have belonged to tombs made in the mound after the edifice had fallen into ruins.   † Anab. lib. iii. c. 4.

been conjectured; and it may be the tomb of Sardanapalus, which, according to the Greek geographers, stood at the entrance of the city of Nineveh. Subsequent discoveries proved that a king supposed to bear this name raised the stone substructure, although his son may have completed the building. It was, of course, natural to conjecture that some traces of the chamber in which the royal remains were deposited, were to be found in the ruin, and I determined to examine it as fully as I was able.

After searching in vain for a sepulchral chamber at the base of the mound, I opened a tunnel on a level with the top of the stone basement wall, which was also the level of the platform of the north-west palace. The workmen soon came to a narrow gallery, about 100 feet long, 12 feet high, and 6 feet broad, blocked up at the two ends. It was vaulted with sun-dried bricks, a further proof of the use of the arch at a very early period, and the vault had in one or two places fallen in.* No remains whatever were found in it—neither fragments of sculpture nor inscription. There were evident signs that this chamber had been broken into at some remote period, and the remains which it may have contained, perhaps the embalmed body of the king, with vessels of precious metals and other objects of value buried with it, had been, no doubt, then carried away. I explored, with feelings of great disappointment, the empty chamber, and then opened other tunnels, without further results, in the upper parts of the mound. They only exposed a compact and solid mass of sun-dried brick masonry. I much doubt, for many reasons, whether any sepulchral chamber exists in the rock beneath the foundations of the tower, though, of course, it is not impossible that such may be the case.

As the ruin is 140 feet high, the building could scarcely have been much less than 200, whilst the immense mass of rubbish surrounding and covering the base shows that it

---

* The walls, as well as the vault, were of sun-dried bricks. It is curious that between one row of bricks was a layer of reeds, as in the Babylonian ruins; the only instance of this mode of construction yet met with in Assyria.

might have been considerably higher. It is probable that its original shape was that of a square tower, formed by a series of stages or platforms, on the top of which may have been placed an altar with the sacred fire. A bas-relief with the representation of a tower of this precise shape, with recesses in the basement, and built upon an artificial mound, was subsequently discovered at Kouyunjik. It is not a little curious that a door, with a kind of portcullis, is seen in this

Tower on a Mound. (From a Bas-relief, Kouyunjik.)

sculpture, on the level of the top of the basement wall, exactly where the entrance to the vaulted gallery, which I have conjectured to be the sepulchral chamber, may be supposed to have been placed. A river washes the foot of the mound, as the Tigris formerly washed that of Nimroud. Can this bas-relief represent the very tower the remains of which I have been describing, and with which it appears to correspond so nearly in form?

CHAPTER II.

Discovery of the grand entrance to Sennacherib's palace — The inscriptions containing the annals of his reign — Account of his war with Hezekiah — Sculptures representing siege of Lachish — Jewish captives — Discovery of arched vault at Nimroud — Of painted bricks — Attack of the Tai on village of Nimroud — Discovery of chamber containing bronze bowls, glass, and other relics.

DURING the month of December, several discoveries of the greatest interest and importance were made, both at Kouyunjik and Nimroud. I will first describe the results of the excavations in the ruins opposite Mosul.

Shortly before my departure for Europe in 1848, the forepart of a human-headed bull of colossal dimensions had been uncovered on the east side of the Kouyunjik Palace.* This sculpture then appeared to form one side of an entrance or doorway. The excavations had, however, been abandoned before any attempt could be made to ascertain the fact. On my return, a tunnel, nearly 100 feet in length, was opened at right angles to the winged bull, but without coming upon any other remains but a pavement of square limestone slabs, which continued as far as the excavation was carried.

On uncovering the bull which was still partly buried in the rubbish, it was found that adjoining it were other sculptures, and that it formed part of an exterior façade. The upper half of the next slab had been destroyed, upon the lower was part of the figure of the Assyrian Hercules strangling the lion, similar to that discovered between the bulls in the propylæa of Khorsabad, and now in the Louvre. The hinder part of the lion was still preserved. The legs, feet, and drapery of the god were in the boldest relief, and designed with great truth and vigour. Beyond this figure, in the same line, was a second bull. Then came a wide portal, guarded

* Plan I. Chamber II, p. 4.

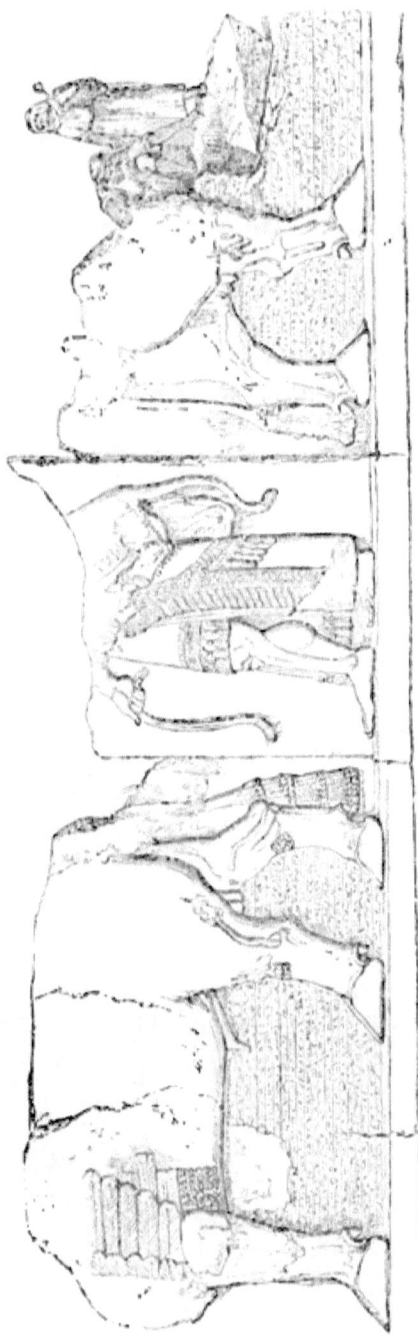

Remains of Façade and Grand Entrance of the Palace of Sennacherib. (Kouyunjik.)

by a pair of winged bulls, twenty feet long, and probably, when entire, more than twenty feet high, and two gigantic winged figures in low relief.* Flanking them were two smaller figures, one above the other. Beyond this entrance the façade was continued by a group similar to that on the opposite side, by a smaller entrance into the palace, and by a wall of sculptured slabs; then all traces of building and sculpture ceased near the edge of a water-worn ravine.

Thus, part of the façade of the south-east side of the palace, forming apparently the grand entrance to the edifice, had been discovered. Ten colossal bulls, with six human figures of gigantic proportions, altogether 180 feet in length, were here grouped together.† Although the bas-reliefs to the right of the entrance had apparently been purposely destroyed with a sharp instrument, enough remained to allow me to trace their subject. They had represented the conquest of a district, probably part of Babylonia, watered by a broad river and wooded with palms, spearmen on foot in combat with Assyrian horsemen, castles besieged, long lines of prisoners, and beasts of burden carrying away the spoil. Amongst various animals brought as tribute to the conquerors, could be distinguished a lion led by a chain. There were no remains whatever of the superstructure which once rose above the colossi, guarding this magnificent entrance.

Although the upper part of the winged bulls was destroyed, fortunately the lower part, and, consequently, the inscriptions, had been more or less preserved. To this fact we owe the recovery of some of the most precious records of the ancient world.

On the two great bulls forming the centre entrance, was one continuous inscription, injured in parts, but still so far preserved as to be legible almost throughout. It contained 152 lines. On the four bulls of the façade were two inscrip-

---

* Grand entrance, S.E. side, Plan I. p. 4. These figures were those of winged priests, or deities, carrying the fir-cone and basket.

† The frontispiece to this volume will convey to the reader some idea of this magnificent façade when entire. This restoration, for which I am mainly indebted to Mr. Ferguson, has been made with a careful regard to the exact proportions.

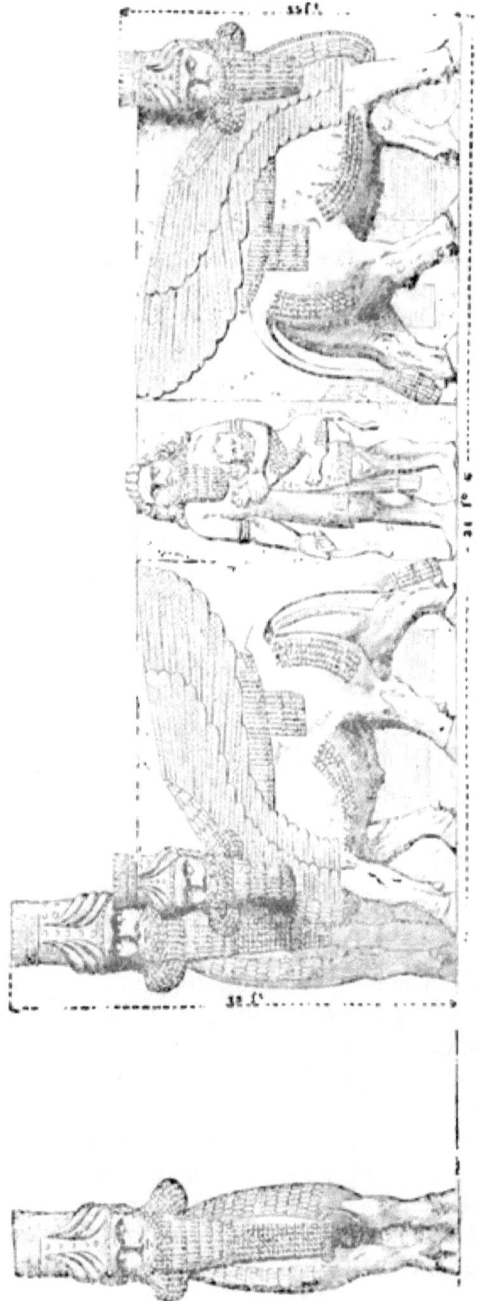

Existing Remains at Khorsabad, showing original State of Grand Entrance at Kouyunjik.

tions, one inscription being carried over each pair, and the two being precisely of the same import. These two different inscriptions complete the annals of six years of the reign of Sennacherib, and contain numerous particulars connected with the religion of the Assyrians, their gods, their temples, and the erection of their palaces. We gather from them that, in the third year of his reign, Sennacherib turned his arms against Merodach-Baladan, king of Babylon, whom he entirely defeated, capturing his cities and a large amount of spoil. The fourth year appears to have been chiefly taken up with expeditions against the inhabitants of the mountainous regions to the north and east of Assyria. In the fifth he crossed the Euphrates into Syria, the inhabitants of which country are called by their familiar Biblical name of Hittites. He first took possession of Phœnicia, which was abandoned by its King Luliya (the Eululæus of the Greeks). He then restored to his throne Padiya, or Padi, king of Ekron, and a tributary of Assyria, who had been deposed by his subjects and given over to Hezekiah, king of Jerusalem. The king of Ethiopia and Egypt sent a powerful army to the assistance of the people of Ekron, but it was entirely defeated by Sennacherib, who afterwards marched against Hezekiah, probably to punish him for having imprisoned Padiyah. The inscriptions record this expedition, according to the translation of the late Dr. Hincks, in the following terms:—'Hezekiah, king of Judah, who had not submitted to my authority, forty-six of his principal cities, and fortresses and villages depending upon them, of which I took no account, I captured and carried away their spoil. I *shut up* (?) himself within Jerusalem, his capital city. The fortified towns, and the rest of his towns, which I spoiled, I severed from his country, and gave to the kings of Ascalon, Ekron, and Gaza, so as to make his country small. In addition to the former tribute imposed upon their countries, I added a tribute, the nature of which I fixed.' The next passage is somewhat illegible, but the substance of it appears to be, that he took from Hezekiah the treasure he had collected in Jerusalem, 30 talents of gold and 800 talents of silver, the treasures of his palace, besides his sons and his daughters, and his male and female servants or slaves, and brought them all to Nineveh.* The city itself, however, he does not pretend to have taken.

There can be no doubt that the campaign against the cities of Palestine, recorded in the inscriptions of Sennacherib in his palace, is that described in the Old Testament; and it is of great interest, therefore, to compare the two accounts, which will be found to agree in the principal incidents mentioned to a very remarkable extent. In the Second Book of Kings† it is said—'Now, in the fourteenth year of king Hezekiah‡ did Sennacherib, king of Assyria, come up against all the fenced cities of Judah, and took them. And Hezekiah, king of Judah, sent to the king of Asssyria, to Lachish, saying, I have offended: return from me: that which thou puttest on me will I bear. And the king of Assyria appointed unto Hezekiah 300 talents of silver and 30 talents of gold. And Hezekiah gave him all the silver that was found in the house of the Lord and in the treasures of the king's house. At that time did Hezekiah cut off [*the gold from*] the doors of the temple of the Lord, and [*from*] the pillars which Hezekiah, king of Judah, had overlaid, and gave it to the king of Assyria.'

The coincidence of the amount paid in gold by Hezekiah

---

* The translation of this passage by Sir H. Rawlinson varies in some particulars from that given in the text: it is as follows:—'Because Hezekiah, king of Judah, would not submit to my yoke, I came up against him, and by force of arms, and by the might of my power, I took forty-six of his fenced cities; and of the smaller towns which were scattered about I took and plundered a countless number. And from these places I captured and carried off as spoil 200,150 people, old and young, male and female, together with horses and mares, asses and camels, oxen and sheep, a countless multitude. And Hezekiah himself I shut up in Jerusalem, his capital city, like a bird in a cage, building towers round the city to hem him in, and raising banks of earth against the gates, so as to prevent escape. . . . Then upon this Hezekiah there fell the fear of the power of my arms, and he sent out to me the chiefs and the elders of Jerusalem with 30 talents of gold and 800 talents of silver, and divers treasures, a rich and immense booty. . . . . All these things were brought to me at Nineveh, the seat of my government, Hezekiah having sent them by way of tribute, and as a token of his submission to my power. (Rawlinson's 'Ancient Monarchies,' vol. ii. p. 435.)

† Chap. xviii.

‡ There is a chronological discrepancy in this date which I shall not attempt to explain. Dr. Hincks proposed to read 'twenty-fifth' year for the 'fourteenth.'

to Sennacherib in the Assyrian and Jewish records, is certainly very curious. The discrepancy between the amount of silver may perhaps be attributed to the fact, that the Assyrian account included the silver ornaments stripped from the temple, as well as the metal in bars or rings which formed the currency of the Jews.

Having thus compelled Hezekiah to consent to the payment of what was probably a yearly tribute, Sennacherib returned to Nineveh*, and in the following year made another successful expedition into Babylonia and Chaldæa. In the

Bulls with historical Inscriptions of Sennacherib. (Kouyunjik.)

sixth year of the records on the bulls, he conquered a country to the north of Assyria, probably Armenia, or some part of Asia Minor; and, in the last year mentioned in these annals, he invaded Elam or Susiana, and some tribes probably living on the Persian Gulf, as, according to the inscriptions, he was compelled, in order to reach them, to construct a fleet

---

* Sennacherib appears to have undertaken a second expedition against Hezekiah, when he was defeated by the Egyptians; but this campaign is not alluded to in the inscriptions on the bulls.

of ships, and to man them with mariners from Tyre, Sidon, and *Yavan* (conjectured to be some island in the Mediterranean).

Such are the principal historical facts recorded in the inscriptions carved by Sennacherib on the great commemorative bulls which he placed in his palace at Nineveh.*

As, unfortunately, the upper parts of nearly all the slabs at Kouyunjik have been destroyed, the short inscriptions or epigraphs which were usually placed above the bas-reliefs, and which indicated the events, persons, or places portrayed by the sculptor, were wanting. We are thus unable to identify the greater part of the sculptures with the events recorded in the inscriptions on the bulls. However, one chamber was discovered, in which some of the slabs were almost entire, though cracked and otherwise injured by fire, and the epigraph explaining the sculptures was complete.† These bas-reliefs represent the siege and capture by the Assyrians of a city evidently of great extent and importance. It appears to have been defended by double walls, with battlements and towers, and by fortified outworks. The country around it was hilly and wooded, producing the fig and the vine. The whole power of the great king seems to have been called forth to take this stronghold. In no other sculptures are so many armed warriors seen drawn up in array before a besieged city. In the first rank are the kneeling archers, those in the second are bending forward, whilst those in the third discharge their arrows standing upright, and are mingled with spearmen and slingers, the whole forming a compact and organised phalanx. The reserve consists of large bodies of horsemen and charioteers. Against the fortifications have been thrown up as many as ten banks or mounts, built of stones, bricks, earth, and branches of trees, and seven battering-rams have already been rolled up to the walls. The besieged defend themselves with great determination. Spear-

---

* Many other of the principal events of this reign, extending over sixteen years, are found recorded on clay cylinders and tablets preserved in the British Museum. They have been translated by those who have deciphered the cuneiform character, and the substance of them will be found in Rawlinson's 'Ancient Monarchies,' vol. ii. chap. ix.

† No. XXXVI. Plan 1. p. 4.

men, archers, and slingers throng the battlements and towers, showering arrows, javelins, stones, and blazing torches upon their assailants. On the battering-rams are bowmen, discharging their arrows, and men with large ladles, pouring water upon the flaming brands, which, hurled from above, threatened to destroy the engines. Ladders, probably used for escalade, are falling from the walls upon the soldiers who mount the inclined ways to the assault. Part of the city has, however, been taken. Beneath its walls are seen Assyrian warriors impaling their prisoners, and from the gateway of an advanced tower, or fort, issues a procession of captives, reaching to the presence of Sennacherib himself, who, gorgeously arrayed, receives them seated on his throne. Amongst the spoil are furniture, arms, shields, chariots, vases of metal of various forms, camels, carts drawn by oxen, and laden with women and children, and many objects the nature of which cannot be determined. The vanquished people are distinguished from the conquerors by their dress. Those who defend the battlements wear a pointed helmet, differing from that of the Assyrian warriors in having a fringed lappet falling over the ears. Some of the captives have a kind of turban with one end hanging down to the shoulder, not unlike that worn by the modern Arabs of the Hedjaz. Others have no head-dress, and short hair and beards. Their garments consist either of a robe reaching to the ankles, or of a tunic scarcely falling lower than the thigh, and confined at the waist by a girdle. The latter appears to be the dress of the fighting-men. The women wear long shirts, with an outer garment thrown, like the veil of modern Eastern ladies, over the back of the head and falling to the feet.

Several prisoners are already in the hands of the torturers. Two are stretched naked on the ground to be flayed alive, others are being slain by the sword before the throne of the king. The haughty monarch is receiving the chiefs of the conquered nation, who crouch and kneel humbly before him. They are brought into the royal presence by the Tartan or general of the Assyrian forces, probably the Rabshakeh, or chief cup-bearer, himself,* followed by his principal officers.

* Isaiah, ch. xxxvi.

SIEGE OF LACHISH.

He is clothed in embroidered robes, and wears on his head a fillet adorned with rosettes and long tasseled bands.

The throne of the king stands upon an elevated platform. Its arms and sides are supported by three rows of figures one above the other. The wood is richly carved, or encased in embossed metal, and the legs end in pine-shaped ornaments, probably of bronze. Over the high back is thrown an embroidered cloth, doubtless of some rare and beautiful material.

The royal feet rest upon a high footstool of elegant form, fashioned like the throne, and cased with embossed metal, the legs ending in lion's paws. Behind the king are two attendant eunuchs raising fans above his head, and holding embroidered napkins.

The monarch himself is attired in long loose robes richly ornamented, and edged with tassels and fringes. In his right hand he raises two arrows, and his left rests upon a bow; an attitude, probably, denoting triumph over his enemies, and in which he is usually portrayed when receiving prisoners after a victory.

Sennacherib on his Throne before Lachish.

Behind the king is the royal tent;* and beneath him are his led horses, and an attendant on foot carrying the parasol, the emblem of royalty. His two chariots, with their charioteers, are waiting for him. One has a peculiar semi-

---

* Above it is an inscription, to the effect, that it is 'the *tent* (?) of Sennacherib, king of Assyria.'

circular ornament of considerable size, rising from the pole between the horses, and spreading over their heads. It may originally have contained the figure of a deity, or some mythic symbol. Two quivers, holding a bow, a hatchet, and arrows, are fixed to the side of the chariot. The trappings of the horses are richly decorated.

On the last bas-relief * is the ground-plan of a castle, or of a fortified camp containing tents and houses. Within the walls is seen a fire-altar with two beardless priests, wearing high conical caps, standing before it. In front of the altar, on which burned the sacred flame, is a table bearing various sacrificial objects, and beyond it two sacred chariots, probably such as accompanied the Persian kings in their wars.† The horses have been taken out, and the yokes rest upon stands. Each chariot carries a lofty pole surmounted by a globe, and long tassels or streamers.

Above the head of the king is an inscription, which may be translated, 'Sennacherib, the mighty king, king of the country of Assyria, sitting on the throne of judgment, before (or at the entrance of) the city of Lachish (Lakhisha). I give permission for its slaughter.'

This highly interesting series of bas-reliefs, which has now been placed in a lower chamber in the British Museum, consequently represents the siege and capture of Lachish, as described in the Second Book of Kings, and in the inscriptions on the human-headed bulls. Sennacherib himself is seen seated on his throne and receiving the submission of the inhabitants of the city, whilst he had sent his generals to demand the payment of tribute from Hezekiah.‡ The defenders of the castle walls and the prisoners tortured and crouching at the conqueror's feet are Jews, and the sculptor has evidently endeavoured to indicate the peculiar physiognomy of the race, and the dress of the people.

The value of this discovery can scarcely be overrated. Whilst we have thus the representation of an event recorded

---

* For detailed drawings of these bas-reliefs, see 2nd series of the 'Monuments of Nineveh,' Plates 20 to 24.

† Xenophon, Cyrop. lvii. c. 3. Quintus Curtius, liii. c. 3.

‡ 2 Kings xviii. 14; Isaiah xxxvi. 2. From 2 Kings xix. 8 and Isaiah xxxvii. 8, we may infer that the city of Lachish soon yielded to the arms of Sennacherib.

in the Old Testament, of which consequently these bas-reliefs furnish a most interesting and important illustration. they serve to a certain extent to test the accuracy of the interpretation of the cuneiform inscriptions, and to remove any doubt that might still exist as to the identification of the King, who built the palace on the mound of Kouyunjik, with the Sennacherib of Scripture. Had these bas-reliefs been the only remains dug up from the ruins of Nineveh, the labour of the explorer would have been amply rewarded, and the sum expended by the nation on the excavations more than justified. They furnish, together with

Jewish Captives from Lachish. (Kouyunjik.)

the inscriptions which they illustrate, and which are also now deposited in the national collection, the most valuable cotemporary historical record possessed by any museum in the world. They may be said to be the actual manuscript, caused to be written or carved by the principal actor in the events which it relates. Who would have believed it probable or possible, before these discoveries were made, that beneath the heap of earth and rubbish which marked the site of Nineveh, there would be found the history of the wars between Hezekiah and Sennacherib, written at the very time when they took place by Sennacherib himself, and con firming even in minute details the Biblical record? He who would have ventured to predict such a discovery would have been treated as a dreamer or an impostor. Had it been known that such a monument really existed, what sum would have been considered too great for the precious record?

The gigantic human-headed lions, first discovered in the north-west palace at Nimroud*, were still standing in their original position. Having been carefully covered up with earth previous to my departure in 1848, they had been preserved from exposure to the effects of the weather, and to wanton injury from the Arabs. The Trustees of the British Museum wishing to add these fine sculptures to the national collection, I was directed to remove them entire. A road through the ruins, for their transport to the edge of the mound, was in the first place necessary, and it was commenced early in December. They would thus be ready for embarkation as soon as the waters of the river were sufficiently high to bear a raft so heavily laden, over the rapids and shallows between Nimroud and Baghdad. Whilst cutting the road I found some carved fragments of ivory similar to those already placed in the British Museum; and two massive sockets in bronze, in which turned the hinges of a gate of the palace. No remains of the doorposts, or other parts of the gate, were discovered, and it is uncertain whether these rings were fixed in stone or wood.

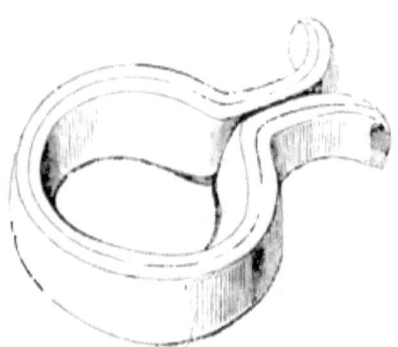

Bronze Socket of the Palace Gate. (Nimroud.)

In the south-eastern corner of the mound tunnels carried beneath the ruined edifice, which is of the seventh century B. C., showed the remains of an earlier building.† A

---

* Nineveh and its Remains, p. 52.

† This building was afterwards explored by Mr. Loftus, and would appear to have been founded, according to some inscriptions discovered amongst the ruins, by Tiglath Pileser.

vaulted drain, about five feet in width, was also discovered. The arch was turned with large kiln-burnt bricks, and rested upon side walls of the same material. The bricks being square, and not expressly made for vaulting, a space was left above the centre of the arch, which was filled up by bricks laid longitudinally.

Other examples were not wanting in the ruins to prove

Vaulted Drain beneath South-east Palace. (Nimroud.)

that the Assyrians were well acquainted at an early period with the true principle of the arch. The earth falling away from the sides of the deep trench opened in the north-west palace for the removal of the bull and lion during the former excavations, left uncovered the entrance to a vaulted drain or passage built of sun-dried bricks. Beneath was a small water-course, inclosed by square slabs of alabaster.* A third arch was found beneath the ruins of the south-east edifice almost at the very foot of the mound.

In the south-east corner of the quadrangle, formed by the low mounds marking the walls once surrounding this quarter

Vaulted Drain beneath the North-west Palace at Nimroud.

of the city of Nineveh, or the park attached to the royal residence, the level of the soil is considerably higher than in any other part of the inclosed space. This sudden inequality evidently indicates the site of some ancient edifice. Con-

* This drain was beneath chambers S and T of the north-west palace. (See Plan II. 'Nineveh and its Remains,' p. 42.)

nected with it, rising abruptly, and almost perpendicularly, from the plain, and forming one of the corners of the walls, is a lofty, irregular mound, known to the Arabs by the name of the Tel (mound) of Athur, the Lieutenant of Nimrod.* Several tunnels and trenches opened in it showed nothing but earth, unmingled with bricks or fragments of stone. Remains of walls and a pavement of baked bricks were, however, discovered at the foot of the high mound. The bricks had evidently been taken from some other building, for upon them were traces of coloured figures and patterns, of the same character and style as those on the sculptured walls of the palaces. Their painted faces were placed downwards, as if purposely to conceal them, and the designs upon them were in most instances injured or destroyed. A few fragments were collected, and are now in the British Museum. The colours have faded, but were probably once as bright as the enamels of Khorsabad. The outlines are white, on a pale blue or olive green ground. The only other colour used is a dull yellow.†

All these fragments probably belong to the same subject, the conquest of some distant nation by the Assyrians. They may have been taken from the same building as the detached bas-reliefs in the south-west palace, and may consequently be attributed to the same king.‡

During the greater part of the month of December I resided at Nimroud. One morning, I was disturbed by the reports of firearms, mingled with the shouts of men and the shrieks of women. Issuing immediately from the house, I found the open space behind it a scene of wild excitement and confusion. Horsemen, galloping in all directions and singing their war song, were driving before t. em with their long spears the cattle and sheep of the inhabitants of the village. The men were firing at the invaders; the women, armed with tent poles and pitchforks, and filling the air with their

---

* 'Out of that land went forth Asshur, and builded Nineveh.' (Gen. x. 11.)

† For facsimiles of these coloured fragments, see 2nd series of 'Monuments of Nineveh.' Plates 53, 54, 55.

‡ That is, as will be hereafter shown, to Tiglath Pileser.

shrill screams, were trying to rescue the animals. The horsemen of the Arab tribe of Tai had taken advantage of a thick mist hanging over the Jaif, to cross the Zab early in the morning, and to fall upon us before we were aware of their approach. No time was to be lost to prevent bloodshed, and all its disagreeable consequences. My horse was soon ready, and I rode towards the one who appeared to be the chief of the attacking party. Although his features were concealed by the *keffieh* closely drawn over the lower part of his face, after the Bedouin fashion in war, he had been recognised as Saleh, the brother of the Howar, the Sheikh of the Tai. He saluted me as I drew near, and we rode along side by side, whilst his followers were driving before them the cattle of the villagers. Directing Hormuzd to keep back the Shemutti, I asked the chief to restore the plundered property. Fortunately, hitherto, only one man of the attacking Arabs had been seriously wounded. The expedition was chiefly directed against the Jebours, who some days before had carried off a large number of the camels of the Tai. I promised to do my best to recover them. At length Saleh, for my sake, as he said, consented to restore all that had been taken, and the inhabitants of Nimroud were called upon to claim each his own property. As we approached the ruins, for the discussion had been carried on as we rode from the village, my Jebour workmen, who had by this time heard of the affray, were preparing to meet the enemy. Some had ascended to the top of the high conical mound, where they had collected stones and bricks ready to hurl against the Tai should they attempt to follow them. Others advanced towards us, stripped to their waists, brandishing their swords and short spears in defiance, and shouting their war-cry. It was with difficulty that, with the assistance of Hormuzd, I was able to check this display of valour, and prevent them from renewing the engagement. The men and women of the village were still following the retreating horsemen, clamouring for various articles, such as cloaks and handkerchiefs, not yet restored. In the midst of the crowd of wranglers, a hare suddenly sprang from her form and darted over the plain. My greyhounds, who had followed me from the house, immediately pursued her. This was too much for the Arabs; their love of the chase overcame even their propensity for appropriating other people's property; cattle, cloaks, swords, and *keffiehs* were abandoned to their respective claimants, and the whole band of marauders joined wildly in the pursuit. Before we had reached the game we were far distant from Nimroud. I seized the opportunity to conclude the truce, and Saleh with his followers rode slowly back towards the ford of the Zab

Excavated Chamber in which the Bronzes were discovered. (Nimroud.)

to seek his brother's tents. I promised to visit the Howar in two or three days, and we parted with mutual assurances of friendship.

Two days after the attack upon Nimroud, I paid my promised visit to the Howar. During my absence a new chamber had been discovered in the north-west palace.* Its walls were

* It was parallel to, and to the south of, the chamber marked AA, in the plan of the north-west palace. (Nineveh and its Remains, p. 42.)

of sun-dried brick, panelled round the bottom with large burnt bricks, about three feet high. They were coated with bitumen, and, like those forming the pavement, were inscribed with the name and usual titles of the royal founder of the building. In one corner was a well, the circular mouth of which was formed by brickwork. Its sides were also bricked down to the conglomerate rock, and holes had been left at regular intervals for descent. When first discovered it was filled with earth. The workmen emptied it until they came, at the depth of nearly sixty feet, to brackish water.*

The first objects found in this chamber were two plain copper cauldrons, about 2½ feet in diameter and 3 feet deep, resting upon a stand of brickwork, with their mouths closed

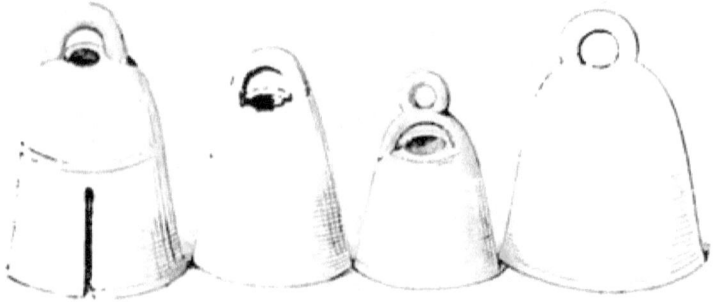

Bronze Bells found in a Cauldron. Nimroud.)

by large tiles. Near them was a copper jar, which fell to pieces almost as soon as uncovered. In the cauldrons were a number of small bronze bells† with iron tongues, and various small copper ornaments, some suspended to wires. With them were a quantity of tapering bronze rods, bent into a hook, and ending in a kind of lip. Beneath were several bronze cups and dishes, which I succeeded in removing entire. Scattered in the earth, amongst these objects, were several hundred studs and buttons in mother of pearl and ivory, with many small rosettes in metal.

* Few wells in the plains bordering on the Tigris yield sweet water.
† The cauldrons contained about eighty bells. They are now in the British Museum with the other objects found in this chamber.

All the objects contained in these cauldrons, with the exception of the cups and dishes, were probably ornaments of horse and chariot furniture. The horses of the Assyrian cavalry, as well as those harnessed to chariots, are continually represented in the sculptures with bells round their necks, and in the Bible we find allusion to such ornaments.*

Beneath the cauldrons were heaped lions' and bulls' feet of bronze; and the remains of iron rings and bars, probably parts of tripods, or stands, for supporting vessels and bowls;† which, as the iron had rusted away, had fallen to pieces, leaving such parts entire as were in the more durable metal.

Two other cauldrons, found further within the chamber, contained, besides several plates and dishes, four crown shaped bronze ornaments, perhaps belonging to a throne or couch; two long ornamented bands of copper, rounded at both ends, apparently belts, such as were worn by warriors in armour;‡ a grotesque head in bronze, probably the top of a mace; a metal wine strainer of elegant shape; various metal vessels of peculiar form, and a bronze ornament, probably the handle of a dish or vase.

Eight more cauldrons and jars were found in other parts of the chamber. One contained ashes and bones, the rest were empty. Some of the larger vessels were crushed almost flat, probably by the falling in of the roof. With the cauldrons were discovered two circular metal vessels, nearly six feet in diameter, and about two feet deep, which I can only compare with the brazen sea that stood in the temple of Solomon.§

Behind the cauldrons was a heap of curious and interesting objects. In one place were piled, one above the other, bronze cups, bowls, and dishes of various sizes and shapes.

---

* Zech. xiv. 20.
† Tripod-stands, consisting of a circular ring raised upon feet, to hold jars and vases, are frequently represented in the bas-reliefs. (See particularly Botta's large work, Plate 141.) The rings were of iron, bound in some places with copper, and the feet of iron cased in bronze.
‡ Resembling those of the eunuch warriors in Plate 28 of the 1st series of the 'Monuments of Nineveh.'
§ 2 Chron. iv. 2. The dimensions, however, of this vessel were far greater. It is singular that, in some of the bas-reliefs, large metal cauldrons supported on brazen oxen, like those in Solomon's temple, are represented.

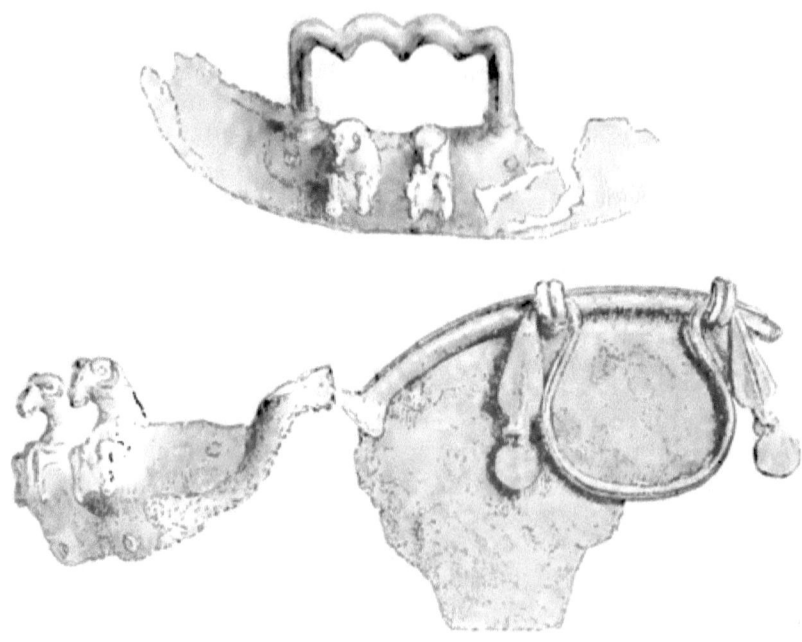

Handles of Bronze Dishes, from Nimroud.

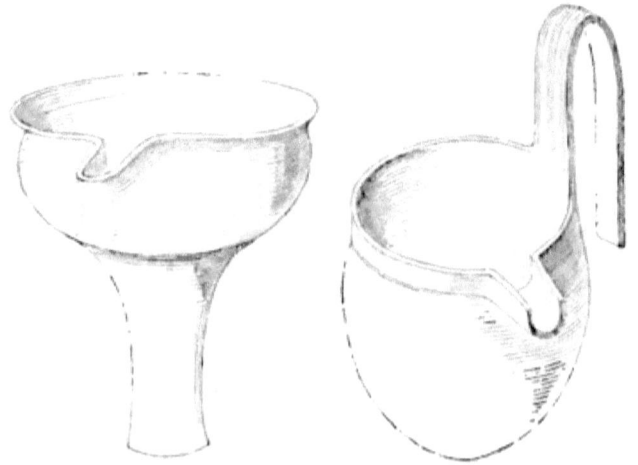

Bronze Vessels taken from the Interior of a Cauldron.

The upper vessels having been most exposed to damp, the metal had been eaten away by rust, and was crumbling into fragments, or into a green powder. As they were cleared away, more perfect specimens were taken out, until, near the pavement of the chamber, some were found almost entire.

Bronze Vessel, taken from the Interior of a Cauldron.   Bronze Wine Strainer.

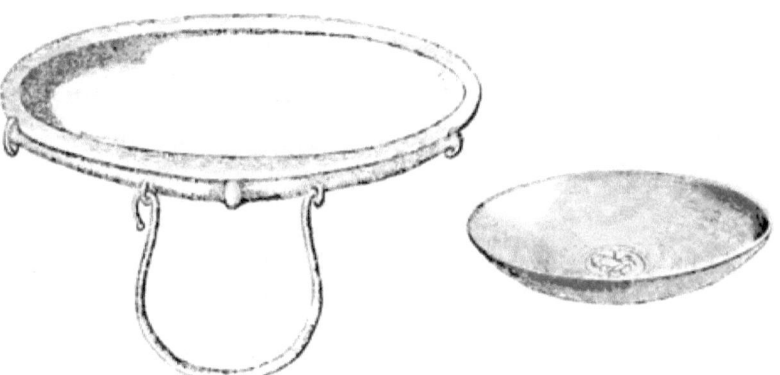

Bronze Dish, from Nimroud.   Bronze Cup, 6¼ in. diameter, and 1⅝ in. deep.

Although a green crystalline deposit, arising from the decomposition of the metal, encrusted all the vessels, I could distinguish upon many of them traces of embossed and engraved ornaments. They have since been carefully and skilfully cleaned by the late Mr. Doubleday, of the British Museum, and the very beautiful and elaborate designs upon them brought to light.*

* Engravings of the most interesting of these vessels will be found in the 2nd series of my 'Monuments of Nineveh.'

The bronze objects thus discovered may be classed under four heads — dishes with handles, plates, deep bowls, and cups. Some are plain, others have a simple rosette, scarab, or star in the centre, and many are most elaborately ornamented with the figures of men and animals, and with elegant designs, either embossed or incised. The inside, and not the outside, of these vessels is ornamented. The embossed figures have been raised in the metal by a blunt instrument.* Even those ornaments which are not embossed but incised, appear to have been formed by a similar process, except that the punch was applied on the inside. The tool of the graver has been sparingly used.†

About 150 bronze vessels discovered in this chamber are now in the British Museum. The metal of the dishes, bowls, and rings contain one part of tin to ten of copper, being exactly the relative proportions of the best ancient and modern bronze. The bells, however, have fourteen per cent. of tin, showing that the Assyrians were well aware of the effect produced by changing the proportions of the metals. These two facts show the advance made by them in the metallurgic art.

The tin was probably obtained from Phœnicia, whose vessels, it has been conjectured, brought this metal from the coasts of Cornwall; and consequently that used in the bronzes in the British Museum may actually have been exported, nearly three thousand years ago, from the British Isles!

The embossed and engraved vessels from Nimroud afford many interesting illustrations of the progress made by the ancients in metallurgy. From the Egyptian character of the designs, and especially of the drapery of the figures, in several of the specimens, it may be inferred that some of them were not Assyrian, but had been brought from a foreign people. As in the ivories, however, the workmanship, subjects, and

---

* The embossing appears to have been produced by a process still practised by silversmiths. The metal was laid upon a bed of mixed clay and bitumen, and then punched from the outside.

† For a full description of the bronzes and other objects found in this chamber, see the unabridged edition of my 'Nineveh and Babylon,' chap. viii.

mode of treatment are more Assyrian than Egyptian, and seem to show that the artist either copied from Egyptian models, or was a native of a country, perhaps Phœnicia, under the influence of Egypt.

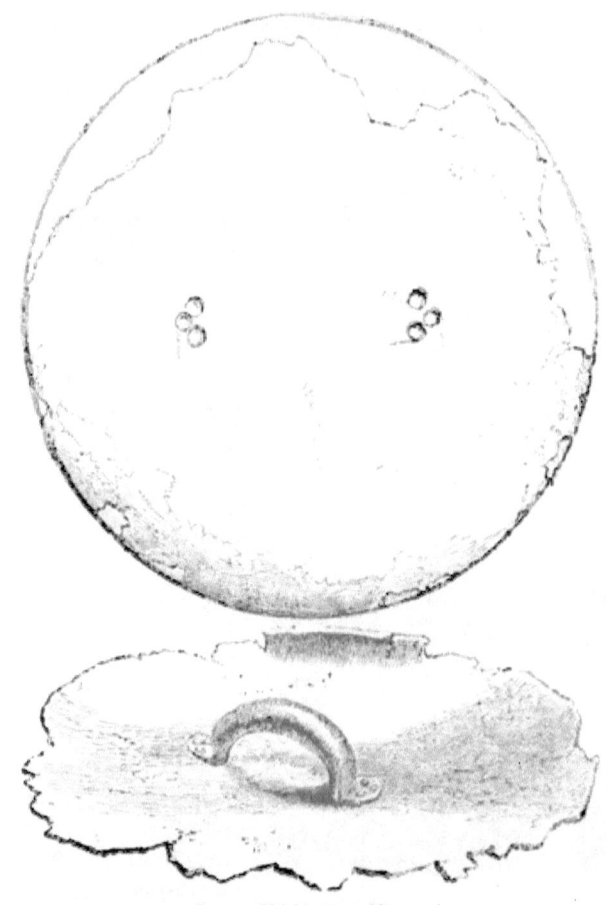

Bronze Shields from Nimroud.

Around the vessels I have described were heaped arms, remains of armour, iron instruments, glass bowls, and various objects in ivory and bronze. The arms consisted of swords, daggers, shields, and the heads of spears and arrows, which being chiefly of iron fell to pieces almost as soon as exposed to the air. A few specimens have alone been preserved. The shields stood upright, one against the other, supported by a square piece of brick work, and were so much decayed that only two could be sent to England. They are of bronze, and circular, the rim bending inwards, and forming a groove round the edge. The handles are of iron, and fastened by six bosses or nails, the heads of which form an ornament on the outer face of the shield.* The diameter of the largest and most perfect is 2 feet 6 inches.

The armour consisted of parts of breast-plates (?) and of other fragments, embossed with figures and ornaments.

Amongst the iron instruments were the head of a pick, a double-handled saw (about 3 feet 6 inches in length), several objects resembling the heads of sledge-hammers, and a large blunt spear-head, such as we find from the sculptures were used during sieges to force stones from the walls of besieged cities.†

The most interesting of the ivory relics were, a carved staff, perhaps a ︎al sceptre, part of which has been preserved; and severa︎ ︎ire elephants' tusks, the largest being about 2 feet 5 inche︎ ︎ng. Amongst the smaller objects were several figures and ︎ettes, and four oval bosses, with the nails of copper still remaining, by which they were fastened to wood or some other material.

Bronze Cube inlaid with Gold. (Original Size.)

Amongst various small objects in bronze were two cubes, each having on one face the figure of a scarab with outstretched wings, inlaid in gold; very interesting specimens of *niello*, and probably amongst the earliest known of an art carried in modern times to great perfection in the East.

---

* Such may have been the 'bosses of the bucklers' mentioned in Job, xv. 26.

† Monuments of Nineveh, 1st series, Plate 66.

Two entire glass bowls, with fragments of others, were also found in this chamber;* the glass is covered with pearly scales, which, on being removed, leave prismatic opal-like colours of the greatest brilliancy, showing, under different lights, the most varied and beautiful tints. This is a well known effect of age, arising from the decomposition of certain component parts of the glass. These bowls are probably of the same period as the small bottle found in the ruins of the north-west palace during the previous excavations, and now in the British Museum.†

With the glass bowls was discovered a rock-crystal lens, with opposite convex and plane faces. Its properties could scarcely have been unknown to the Assyrians, and we have consequently the earliest specimen of a magnifying and burning glass. The extreme minuteness of some of the inscriptions on the clay tablets, and of the engravings on the gems discovered in the Assyrian ruins, must lead to the conviction that the Assyrians possessed a magnifying power.‡ It was found under fragments of blue opaque glass, apparently the enamel of some object in ivory or wood, which had perished.

In the further corner of the chamber stood the royal throne. Although it was impossible, from its complete state of decay, to move it entire, I was able to ascertain that it resembled in shape the chair of state of the king, as seen in the sculptures of Kouyunjik and Khorsabad, and particularly that represented in the bas-relief of Sennacherib before the city of Lachish.§ With the exception of the legs, which appear to have been partly of ivory, it was of wood, cased or overlaid with bronze.‖ The metal was elaborately engraved and embossed with symbolical figures and ornaments, like those em-

---

* The larger, 5 inches in diameter, and 2¾ inches deep; the other, 4 inches in diameter, and 2¼ deep.
† See 'Nineveh and its Remains' (abridged), p. 242.
‡ For a description of this lens, by Sir David Brewster, see unabridged edition of 'Nineveh and Babylon,' note, p. 197.
§ See p. 49.
‖ This is a highly interesting illustration of the work in Solomon's palaces. The earliest use of metal amongst the Greeks appears also to have been as a casing to wooden objects. The throne of Solomon was of ivory overlaid with gold. (1 Kings, x. 18.)

broidered on the robes of the early Nimroud king, such as winged deities struggling with griffins, mythic animals, the sacred tree, and the winged lion and bull. In front of the throne was the footstool, also of wood overlaid with embossed metal, and adorned with the heads of bulls. The feet ended in lion's paws and pine cones, like those of the throne. The metal fragments sent to England have been skilfully put together, so that the Assyrian king's throne upon which Sennacherib himself sat, and the footstool which he used, may now be seen in the British Museum. A rod with loose rings, to which was once hung an embroidered curtain, appears to have belonged to the back of the chair, or to a framework raised above or behind it.

Near the throne, and leaning against the mouth of the well, was a circular band of bronze, 2 feet, 4 inches in diameter, studded with nails. It appears to have been the metal casing of a wheel, or of some object of wood.

Such, with an alabaster jar, and a few other objects in metal, were the relics found in the newly-opened room. This accidental discovery, after the examination I had made of the building during my former excavations, proves that other treasures may still exist in the mound of Nimroud, and increases my regret that means were not at my command to remove the rubbish from the centre of the other chambers in the palace.

CHAPTER III.

Visit to the winged lions by night—The bitumen springs—Removal of the winged lions to the river—Loss and recovery of lion—Visit to Bavian—Description of rock sculptures—Inscriptions—Sculptures at Kouyunjik.

By the 28th of January, the colossal lions forming the portal to the great hall in the north-west palace of Nimroud were ready to be dragged to the river-bank. The walls and their sculptured panelling had been removed from around them, and they stood isolated in the midst of the ruins. I rode one calm cloudless night to the mound, to look on them for the last time before they were taken from their old restingplaces. The moon was at her full, and as I drew nigh to the edge of the deep trench in which they stood, her soft light was creeping over the stern features of the human heads, and driving before it the dark shadows which still clothed the lion forms. One by one the limbs of the gigantic sphinxes emerged from the gloom, until the monsters were unveiled before me. I shall never forget that night, or the emotions which those venerable figures caused within me. A few hours more and they were to stand no longer where they had stood for ages, unscathed amidst the wreck of man and his works. It seemed almost sacrilege to tear them from their old haunts to make them a mere wonder-stock to the busy crowd of a new world. They were better suited to the desolation around them; for they had guarded the palace in its glory, and it was for them to watch over it in its ruin. Sheikh Abd-ur-Rahman, who had ridden with me to the mound, was troubled with no such reflections. He gazed listlessly at the grim images, wondered at the folly of the Franks, thought the night cold, and turned his mare towards his tents. I scarcely heeded his going, but stood speechless in the deserted portal, until the shadows again began to creep over its hoary guardians.

Beyond the ruined palaces a scene scarcely less solemn awaited me. I had sent a party of Jebours to the bitumen springs, outside the walls to the east of the inclosure. The Arabs having lighted a small fire with brushwood awaited my coming to throw the burning sticks upon the pitchy pools. A thick heavy smoke rolled upwards in curling volumes, hiding the light of the moon, and spreading wide over the sky. Tongues of flame and jets of gas, driven from the burning pit, shot through the murky canopy. As the fire brightened, a thousand fantastic forms of light played amidst the smoke. To break the cindered crust, and to bring fresh slime to the surface, the Arabs threw large stones into the springs; a new volume of fire then burst forth, throwing a deep red glare upon the figures and upon the landscape. The Jebours danced round the burning pools, like demons in some midnight orgie, shouting their war-cry, and brandishing their glittering arms. In an hour the bitumen was exhausted for the time,* the dense smoke gradually died away, and the pale light of the moon again shone over the black slime pits.

The colossal lions were moved by still simpler and ruder means than those adopted on my first expedition. They were tilted over upon loose earth heaped behind them. They were then lowered upon the cart by gradually removing the soil. A road paved with flat stones had been made to the edge of the mound, and the sculptures were, without difficulty, dragged from the trenches.

Beneath the lions, embedded in earth and bitumen, were a few bones, which, on exposure to the air, fell to dust before I could ascertain whether they were human or not. The sculptures rested simply upon the platform of sun-dried bricks without any other substructure, a mere layer of bitumen, about an inch thick, having been placed under the plinth.

Owing to recent heavy rains, which had left in many places deep swamps, we experienced much difficulty in dragging the

---

* In a few hours the pits are sufficiently filled to take fire again.

cart over the plain to the river side. Three days were spent in transporting each lion. The men of Naifa and Nimroud again came to our help, and the Abou-Salman horsemen, with Sheikh Abd-ur-Rahman at their head, encouraged us by their presence. The unwieldy mass was propelled from behind by enormous levers of poplar wood; and in the costumes of those who worked, as well as in the means adopted to move the colossal sculptures, except that we used a wheeled cart instead of a sledge, the procession closely resembled that which in days of yore moved the same great figures to the palace, and which had been so graphically represented on the walls of Kouyunjik.* As they had been brought so were they taken away.

It was necessary to humour and excite the Arabs to induce them to persevere in the arduous work of dragging the cart through the deep soft soil into which it continually sank. At one time, after many vain efforts to move the buried wheels, it was unanimously declared that Mr. Cooper, the artist, brought ill luck, and no one would work until he retired. The cumbrous machine crept onwards for a few more yards, but again all exertions were fruitless. Then the Frank lady would bring good fortune if she sat on the sculpture. The wheels rolled heavily along, but were soon clogged once more in the yielding soil. An evil eye surely lurked among the workmen or the bystanders. Search was quickly made, and a man having been detected upon whom this curse had alighted, he was ignominiously driven away with shouts and execrations. This impediment having been removed, the cart drew nearer to the village, but soon again came to a standstill. All the Sheikhs were now summarily degraded from their rank and honours, and a weakly ragged boy having been dressed up in tawdry kerchiefs, and invested with a cloak, was pronounced by Hormuzd to be the only fit chief for such puny men. The cart moved forwards, until the ropes gave way, under the new excitement caused by this reflection upon the character of the Arabs. When that had subsided, and the presence of the youthful Sheikh no longer encouraged

* See woodcut, p. 25.

his subjects, he was as summarily deposed as he had been elected, and a greybeard of ninety was raised to the dignity in his stead. He had his turn; then the most unpopular of the Sheikhs were compelled to lie down on the ground, as if the groaning wheels were to pass over them, like the car of Juggernaut over its votaries. With yells, shrieks, and wild antics the cart was drawn within a few inches of the prostrate men. As a last resource I seized a rope myself, and with shouts of defiance between the different tribes, who were divided into separate parties and pulled against each other, and amidst the deafening *tahlel* of the women, the lion was at length fairly brought to the water's edge.

It was not until the month of April, after I had left Mosul on my journey to the Khabour, that the floods caused by the melting of the snows in the mountains of Kurdistan enabled me to send these sculptures by rafts to Baghdad. After receiving the necessary repairs they floated onwards to Busrah. The waters of the Tigris throughout its course had risen far above their usual level. The embankments, long neglected by the Turkish government, had given way, and the river, bursting from its bed, spread itself over the surrounding country in vast lakes and marshes. One of the rafts, notwithstanding the exertions of the raftmen, aided by the crew of a boat that accompanied them, was left in the middle of a swamp, about a mile from the stream. The other raft fortunately escaped, and reached Busrah without accident.

For some time the stranded raft was given up for lost. But Captain Jones, the commander of the British flotilla on the Mesopotamian rivers, with his usual skill and intrepidity, took a steamer over the ruined embankment, and into the unexplored morass. After great exertion, under a burning sun in the middle of summer, he succeeded in conveying the sculpture to its destination.

During a hasty visit in the autumn to the remarkable rock-sculptures of Bavian, I had been unable to make drawings, or to copy the inscriptions. The winged lions having been removed from the Nimroud mound, I found time to revisit these important monuments. Our road thither from Mosul ran across the rocky range of the Gebel Makloub. The ascent was difficult and precipitous, scarcely practicable for heavily laden beasts. On the eastern side, the hills sink gradually into a broad plain. The small Kurdish hamlet of Bavian is situated at the foot of the next and higher limestone range. The sculptures are carved on the face of the rock, near the entrance to a narrow ravine, from whence issues a brawling mountain torrent, called the Gomel, one of the confluents of the Ghazir, the Bumadus of the Greeks, upon the banks of which was fought the great battle of Arbela. They consist of a number of tablets cut on the smoothed face of the cliff. The principal one is twenty-eight feet high, and contains two Assyrian deities standing on mythic animals, with two kings, one on each side, apparently in the act of adoration. It would seem that these two royal figures represent one and the same monarch, and the inscriptions identify him with Sennacherib. This colossal bas-relief has not only suffered from the effect of time, but has been further defaced by the entrances to tombs excavated in the rock. I succeeded in entering these tombs, having been lowered from above by ropes, but found them empty. They had, no doubt, been rifled at a remote period.

In a second tablet is represented an Assyrian horseman, of colossal proportions, riding at full speed with couched lance. In front of him stands Sennacherib, behind him an Assyrian deity, and above a row of gods standing on animals. On other parts of the cliff are eleven smaller tablets in arched recesses, each containing a figure of Sennacherib. Across three of them are inscriptions in the cuneiform character, and of precisely the same import. They appear to record certain extensive works for irrigation undertaken by that monarch, and his expedition against Merodach Baladan, and the capture and plunder of Babylon, mentioned in the records on the bulls at Nineveh. A very remarkable passage, if rightly interpreted, states that Sennacherib brought back to Assyria certain images of the gods which had been carried away 418 years before by a king of Mesopotamia. If this be the true interpretation, it shows that at that remote period the Assyrians kept an exact computation of time. Sennacherib declares that, on his return from Babylon, he had caused these tablets to be carved in the rock.

Beneath the sculptured tablets, and in the bed of the Gomel, are two enormous fragments of rock, which have fallen from the overhanging cliff into the torrent below. The pent-up waters eddy round them in deep and dangerous whirlpools, and when swollen by the winter rains sweep com-

Fallen Rock-Sculptures (Bavian.)

pletely over them.* They still bear the remains of sculpture. One has been broken by the fall into two pieces. On it is the Assyrian Hercules strangling the lion between two winged human-headed bulls, back to back, as at the grand entrances of the palaces of Kouyunjik and Khorsabad.

* It was at this spot that Mr. Bell, the youthful artist sent out by the Trustees of the British Museum, was unfortunately drowned when bathing, in the month of July, 1851, shortly after my departure from Mosul.

Above this group is the king, worshipping between two deities, who stand on mythic animals with the heads of eagles, the bodies and fore feet of lions, and hind legs armed with the talons of a bird of prey.

Near the entrance to the ravine the face of the cliff has been scarped for some yards to the level of the bed of the

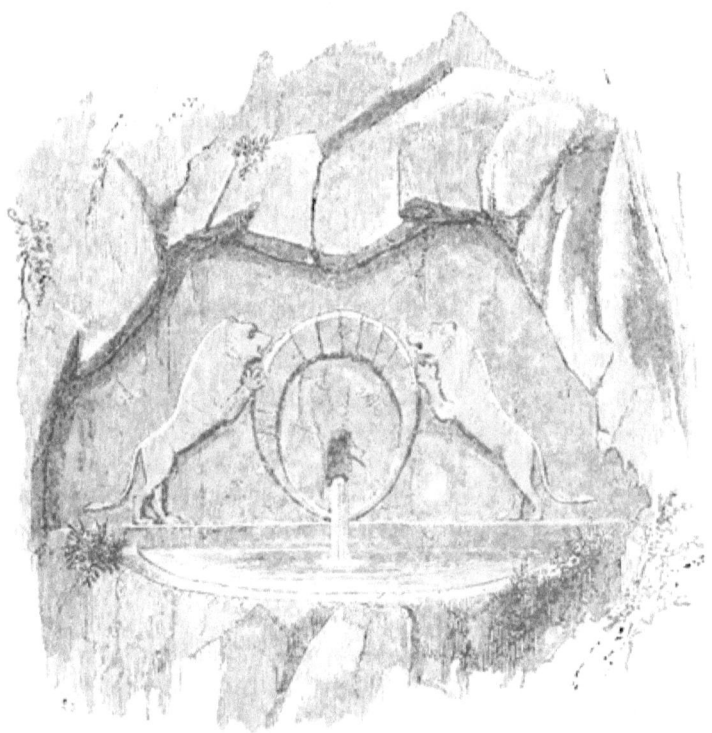

Assyrian Fountain. (Bavian.)

torrent. A party of Kurds were hired to excavate at this spot, as well as in other parts of the narrow valley. Remains and foundations of buildings in hewn stone were discovered. Higher up the gorge, on removing the earth, I found a series of basins cut in the rock, and descending in steps to the stream. The water had originally been led from one to the other through small conduits, the lowest of which was ornamented at its mouth with two rampant lions in relief. These outlets were choked up, but we cleared them, and by pouring water into the upper basin restored the fountain as it had been in the time of the Assyrians.

From the nature and number of the monuments at Bavian, it would seem that this ravine was a sacred spot, devoted to religious ceremonies and to national sacrifices. When the buildings, whose remains still exist, were used for these purposes, the waters must have been pent up between quays or embankments. They now occasionally spread over the bottom of the valley, leaving no pathway at the foot of the lofty cliffs. The remains of a well-built raised causeway of stone, leading to Bavian from Nineveh, may still be traced across the plain to the east of the Gebel Makloub.

The place, from its picturesque beauty and its cool refreshing shade even in the hottest days of summer, is a grateful retreat, well suited to devotion and to holy rites. The brawling stream almost fills the bed of the narrow ravine with its clear and limpid waters. The beetling cliffs rise abruptly on each side, and above them tower the wooded declivities of the Kurdish hills. As the valley opens into the plain, the sides of the limestone mountains are broken into a series of distinct strata, and resemble a vast flight of steps leading up to the high lands of central Asia. The banks of the torrent are clothed with shrubs and dwarf trees, amongst which are the green myrtle and the gay oleander, bending under the weight of its rosy blossoms.

I remained two days at Bavian to copy the inscriptions, and to explore the Assyrian remains.

During my absence, several new chambers had been opened at Kouyunjik. The western portal of the great hall, whose four sides were now completely uncovered,[*] led into a long narrow chamber (eighty-two feet by twenty-six), the walls of which had unfortunately been almost entirely destroyed.[†] On such fragments, however, as remained were traces of the usual subjects,—battles and victories. There was nothing remarkable in the dresses of the captives, or in the details,

---

[*] No. VI. Plan I. p. 4.   [†] No. IX. same Plan.

to give any clue to the conquered people, whose country was represented by wooded mountains and a broad river.

In the chamber beyond* a few slabs were still standing in their original places. In length this room was the same as that parallel to it, but in breadth it was only eighteen feet. The bas-reliefs represented the siege and sack of one of the many cities taken by Sennacherib, and the transfer of the captives to some distant province of Assyria. The prisoners were dressed in garments falling to the calves of their legs, and the women wore a kind of turban. Although the country was mountainous, its inhabitants used the camel as a beast of burden, and in the sculptures it was represented laden with the spoil. The Assyrians, as was their custom, carried away in triumph the images of the gods of the conquered nation, which were placed on poles and borne in procession on men's shoulders. 'Hath any god of the nations delivered his land out of the hand of the king of Assyria?' exclaimed the Assyrian general to the Jews. 'Where are the gods of Hamath and Arphad? where are the gods of Sepharvaim?'† They had been carried away with the captives, and the very idols that were represented in this bas-relief may have been amongst those to which Rabshakeh made this boasting allusion. The captured gods were three, a human figure with outstretched arms, a lion-headed man carrying a long staff in one hand, and an image enclosed by a square frame. Within a fortified camp, defended by towers and battlements, the priests were offering up the sacrifices usual upon a victory; the pontiff was distinguished by a high conical cap, and, as is always the case in the Assyrian sculptures, was beardless. By his side stood an assistant. Before the altar, on which were some sacrificial utensils, was the sacred chariot, with its elaborate yoke. On a raised band, across the centre of the castle, were inscribed the name and titles of Sennacherib.‡

On the northern side of the great hall the portal formed by the winged bulls, and the two smaller doorways guarded by colossal winged figures, led into a chamber one hundred

---

* No. x. Plan. I. p. 4.   † Isaiah, xxxvi. 18, 19.
‡ Plate 50, 2d series of 'Monuments of Nineveh.'

feet by twenty-four, which opened into a further room of somewhat smaller dimensions.* In the first were a few slabs, representing some warlike expedition of the Assyrian king, and, as usual, the triumphant issue of the campaign. The monarch, in his chariot, and surrounded by his body-guard, was seen receiving the captives and the spoil in a hilly country, whilst his warriors were dragging their horses up a steep mountain near a fortified town, driving their chariots along the banks of a river, and slaying with the spear the flying enemy.†

The bas-reliefs of the second chamber had recorded the wars of the Assyrians with a maritime people, represented in other sculptures, and who may probably be identified with some nation on the Phœnician coast. Their galleys, rowed by double banks of oarsmen, and the high conical head-dress of their women, have already been described.‡ On the best preserved slab was the interior of a fortified camp, amidst mountains. Within the walls were tents whose owners were engaged in various domestic occupations, cooking in pots placed on stones over the fire, receiving the blood of a slaughtered sheep in a jar, and making ready the couches. Warriors were seated before a table, with their shields hung to the tent-pole above them.

A Captive. Kouyunjik.

---

* Nos. VII. and VIII. Plan I. p. 4.
† Plate 29, of 2nd series of 'Monuments of Nineveh.'
‡ Nineveh and its Remains, chap. xiii.

In the southern part of the palace a chamber had been opened, in which several bas reliefs of considerable interest had been discovered.* Its principal entrance, facing the west, was formed by a pair of colossal human-headed lions, carved in coarse limestone, so much injured that even the inscriptions on the lower part of them were nearly illegible. Unfortunately the bas reliefs were equally mutilated, four

Bas-relief from Kouyunjik, representing fortified City, a River with a Boat and Raft, and a Canal.

slabs only retaining any traces of sculpture. One of them represented Assyrian warriors leading captives, wearing a head-dress of high feathers, forming a kind of tiara like that of an Indian chief, and a robe confined at the waist by an ornamented girdle. Some of them carried an object resembling a torch.

* No. XXII. Plan I. p. 4.

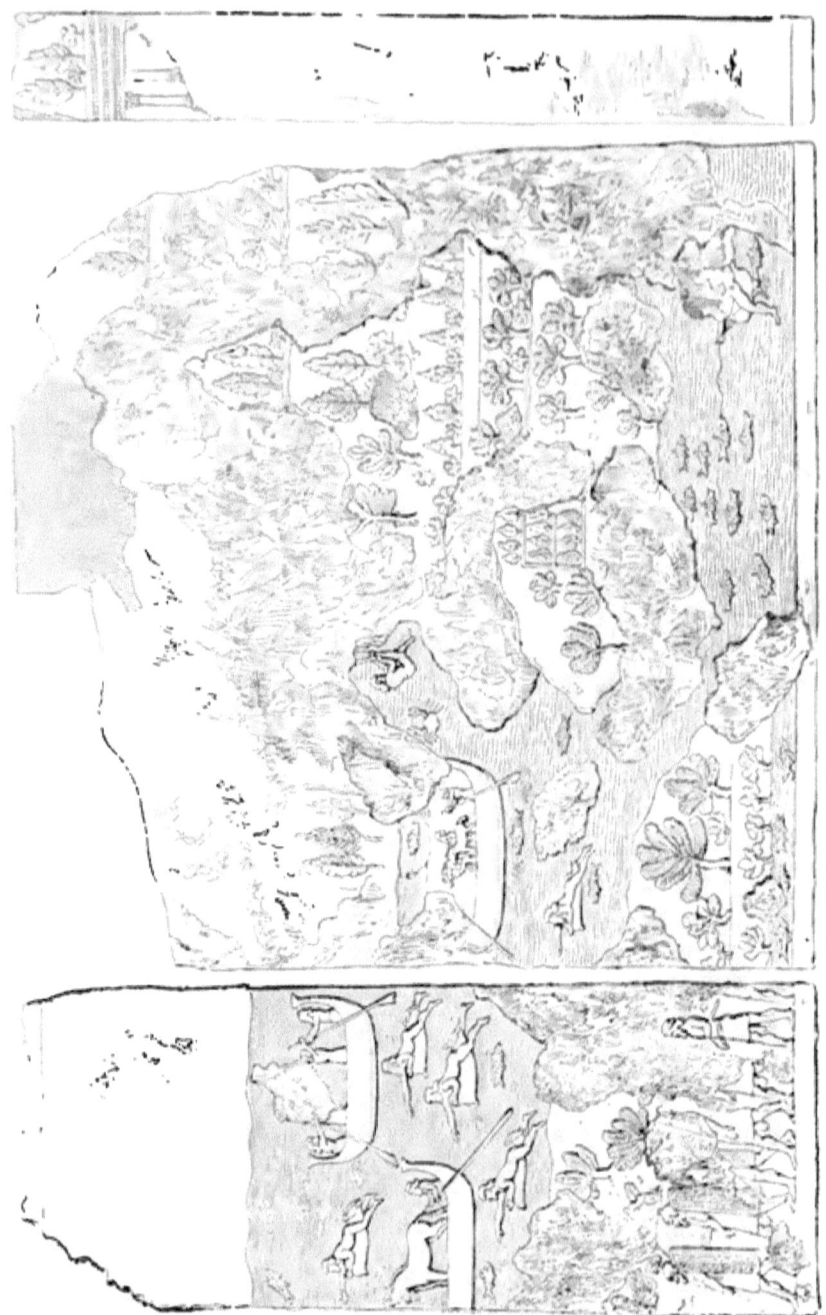

Bas-relief representing a River, and Gardens watered by Canals. (Kouyunjik).

On a second slab, preserved in this chamber, was represented a double-walled city with arched gateways, and inclined approaches leading to them from the outer walls. Within were warriors with horses; outside the fortifications was a narrow stream or canal, planted on both sides with trees, and flowing into a broad river, on which were large boats, holding several persons, and a raft of skins, bearing a man fishing, and two others seated before a pot or cauldron. Along the banks, and apparently washed by the stream, was a wall with equidistant towers and battlements. On another part of the same river were men ferrying horses across the river in boats, whilst others were swimming over on inflated skins. The water swarmed with fish and crabs. Gardens and orchards, with various kinds of trees, appeared to be watered by canals similar to those which once spread fertility over the plains of Babylonia, and of which the choked-up beds still remain. A man, suspended by a rope, was being lowered into the water. Upon the corner of a slab, almost destroyed, was a hanging-garden, supported upon columns, whose capitals were not unlike those of the Corinthian order. This representation of ornamental gardens was highly curious. It is much to be regretted that only fragments of these interesting bas-reliefs have been preserved.

CHAPTER IV.

Preparations for a journey to the Khabour—Sheikh Suttum—His rakiff—Departure from Mosul—First encampment—Abou Khameera—A storm—Tel Ermah—A stranger—Tel Jemal—A sunset in the desert—A Jebour encampment—The Belled Sinjar—The Sinjar hill—The dress of the Yezidis—The Shomal—Return to the Belled—A snake-charmer—Journey continued in the desert—Rishwan—Encampment of the Boraij—Dress of Arab women—Rathaiyah—Hawking—A deputation from the Yezidis—The Khabour—Arrival at Arban.

I HAD long wished to visit the banks of the Khabour. This river, the Chaboras of the Greek geographers, and the Habor, or Chebar, of the Samaritan captivity[*], rises in the north of Mesopotamia, and flowing to the west of the Sinjar hill, falls into the Euphrates near the site of the ancient city of Carchemish[†] or Circesium, still known to the Bedouins by the name of Carkeseea. As it winds through the midst of the desert, and its rich pastures are the resort of wandering tribes of Arabs, it is always difficult of access to the traveller. It was examined, for a short distance from its mouth, by the expedition under Colonel Chesney; but the general course of the river was imperfectly known, and several geographical questions of interest connected with it were undetermined previous to my visit.

With the Bedouins, who were occasionally my guests at Mosul or Nimroud, as well as with the Jebours, whose encamping grounds were originally on its banks, the Khabour was a constant theme of exaggerated praise. The richness of its pastures, the beauty of its flowers, its jungles teeming with game of all kinds, and the leafy thickness of its trees yielding an agreeable shade during the hottest days of sum-

[*] 2 Kings, xviii. 11; Ezek. i. 1.   [†] 2 Chron. xxxv. 20.

mer, formed a terrestrial paradise to which the wandering Arab eagerly turned his steps when he could lead his flocks thither in safety. Ruins, too, as an additional attraction, were declared to abound on its banks, and formed the principal inducement for me to undertake a long and somewhat hazardous journey. During the winter my old friend Mohammed Emin, Sheikh of one of the principal branches of the Jebour tribe, had pitched his tents on the river. Arabs from his encampment would occasionally wander to Mosul. They generally bore an invitation from their chief, urging me to visit him when the spring rendered a march through the desert both easy and pleasant. But when a note arrived from the Sheikh, announcing that two colossal idols, similar to those of Nimroud, had suddenly appeared in a mound by the river side, I hesitated no longer, and determined to start at once for the Khabour.

As the Shammar Bedouins were scattered over the desert between Mosul and the Khabour, and their horsemen continually scoured the plains in search of plunder, it was necessary that we should be protected and accompanied by an influential chief of the tribe. I accordingly sent to Suttum, a Sheikh of the Boraij, one of the principal branches of the Shammar, whose tents were at that time pitched between the river and the ruins of El Hather. Suttum was well known to me, and had already given proofs of his trustworthiness and intelligence on more than one similar occasion. He lost no time in obeying the summons. Arrangements were soon made with him. He agreed to furnish camels for our baggage, and to remain with me himself until he had seen my caravan in safety again within the gates of Mosul. He returned to the desert to fetch the camels, and to make other preparations for our journey, promising to be with me in a few days.

Punctual to his appointment, Sheikh Suttum brought his camels to Mosul on the 19th of March. He was accompanied by Khoraif, his *radif*, as the person who sits on the dromedary* behind the owner is called by the Bedouins.

---

* I use the word 'dromedary' for a swift riding camel, the *Deloul* of the Arabs, and *Hejin* of the Turks: it is so applied generally, although incorrectly, by Europeans in the East.

G

In the two great nomade tribes of the Shammar and Aneyza, the word 'rediff' frequently infers a more intimate connection than mere companionship on a camel. It is customary with them for a warrior to swear a kind of brotherhood with a person not only not related to him by blood, but frequently even of a different tribe. Two men connected by this tie are inseparable. They go together to war, they live in the same tent, and are allowed to see each other's wives. They become, indeed, more than brothers. Khoraif was of the tribe of the Aneyza, who have a deadly feud with the Shammar. Having left his own kith and kin on account of some petty quarrel, he had joined their enemies, and had become the rediff of Suttum, dwelling under his canvass, accompanying him in his expeditions, and riding with him on his deloul. Although he had deserted his tribe, Khoraif had not renounced all connection with his kindred, nor had he been cut off by them. Being thus allied to two powerful clans, he was able to render equal services to any of his old or new friends, who might fall into each other's hands. It is on this account that a warrior generally chobses his rediff from a tribe with which he is at enmity, for if taken in war he would then be *dakheel*, that is, protected, by the family, or rather particular sept, of his companion. On the other hand, should one of the rediff's friends become the prisoner of the sept into which his kinsman has been adopted, he would be under its protection, and could not be molested. Thus Khoraif would have been an important addition to our party had we fallen in, during our journey, with Aneyza Arabs, against whom, of course, Suttum could not protect us. On warlike expeditions the rediff generally leads the mare which is to be ridden by his companion in the fight. When in face of the enemy he is left in charge of the dromedary, and takes part in the battle from its back. He rides, when travelling, on the naked back of the animal, clinging to the hinder part of the saddle, his legs crouched up almost to his chin—a very uncomfortable position for one not accustomed from childhood to a hard seat and a rough motion.

As our desert trip would probably last for more than two months, during which time we should meet with no villages, or permanent settlements, we were obliged to take with us supplies of all kinds, both for ourselves and the workmen; consequently flour, rice, burghoul (prepared wheat, to be used as a substitute for rice), and biscuits, formed a large portion of our baggage. Two enormous boxes held various luxuries, such as sugar, coffee, tea, and spices, with robes of silk and cotton, and red and yellow boots, presents for the various chiefs whom we might meet in the desert. Baskets, tools for excavating, tents, and working utensils, formed the rest of our baggage.

I knew that I should have no difficulty in finding workmen when once in Mohammed Emin's encampment. As, however, it was my intention to explore any ruins of importance that we might see on our way, I chose about fifty of my best Arab excavators, and twelve Tiyari, or Nestorians, to accompany us. They were to follow on foot, but one or two extra camels were provided in case any were unable from fatigue to keep up with the caravan. The camels were driven into the small Mussulman burial-ground, adjoining my house in Mosul. The whole morning was spent in dividing and arranging the loads, always the most difficult part of the preparations for a journey in the East. The pack-saddles of the Bedouins, mere bags of rough canvass stuffed with straw, were ill-adapted to carry anything but sacks of wheat and flour. As soon as a load was adjusted, it was sure to slip over the tail, or to turn over on one side. When this difficulty was overcome, the animals would suddenly kneel and shake off their burdens. Their owners were equally hard to please: this camel was galled, another vicious, a third weak. Suttum and Khoraif exerted themselves to the utmost, and the inhabitants of the quarter, together with stray passers-by, joined in the proceedings, adding to the din and confusion, and of course considerably to our difficulties. At length, as the muezzin called to midday prayer, the last camel issued from the Sinjar gate. A place of general rendezvous had been appointed outside the walls, that our party might be collected together for a proper start, and that those who were good Mussulmans might go through their prayers before commencing a perilous journey.

When we had all assembled, our party had swollen into a little army. The Doctor, Mr. Cooper, and Mr. Hormuzd Rassam, of course, accompanied me. Mr. and Mrs. Rolland with their servants had joined our expedition. My Yezidi fellow-traveller from Constantinople, Cawal Yusuf, with three companions, was to escort me to the Sinjar, and to accompany us in our tour through that district. Several Jebour families, whose tribe was encamped at Abou-Psera, near the mouth of the Khabour, seized this opportunity to join their friends, taking with them their tents and cattle. Thirteen or fourteen Bedouins had charge of the camels, so that, with the workmen and servants, our caravan consisted of nearly one hundred well-armed men; a force sufficient to defy almost any hostile party with which we were likely to fall in during our journey. We had about five and twenty camels, and as many horses, some of which were led. As it was spring time and the pastures were good, it was not necessary to carry much provender for our animals.

Suttum, with his rediff, rode on a light fleet dromedary, which had been taken in a plundering expedition from the Aneyza. Its name was Dhwaila. Its high and picturesque saddle was profusely ornamented with brass bosses and nails; over the seat was thrown the Baghdad double bags adorned with long tassels and fringes of many-coloured wools, so much coveted by the Bedouin. The Sheikh had the general direction and superintendence of our march. The Mesopotamian desert had been his home from his birth, and he knew every spring and pasture. He was of the Saadi, one of the most illustrious families of the Shammar*, and he possessed great personal influence in the tribe. His intelligence was of a very high order, and he was as well known for his skill in Bedouin intrigue, as for his courage and daring in war. In person he was of middle height, of spare habit, but well made, and of noble and dignified carriage; although a musket wound in the thigh, from which the ball had not been extracted, gave

---

* An Arab tribe is divided into septs, and each sept is composed of certain families. Thus Suttum was a Shammar, of the branch called the Boraij, and of the family of Saadi, besides being a member of a peculiar division of the great tribe called the Khorusseh.

him a slight lameness in his gait. His features were regular and well-proportioned, and of that delicate character so frequently found amongst the nomades of the desert. A restless and sparkling eye of the deepest black seemed to scan and

Sheikh Suttum.

penetrate everything within its ken. His dark hair was platted into many long tails; his beard, like that of the Arabs in general, was scanty. He wore the usual Arab shirt, and over it a cloak of blue cloth trimmed with red silk and lined with fur, a present from some pasha as he pretended, but more probably a part of some great man's wardrobe that had been appropriated without its owner's consent. A coloured kerchief, or keffieh, was thrown loosely over his head, and confined above the temples by a rope of twisted camel's hair. At his side hung a scimitar, an antique horse-pistol was held by a rope, tied as a girdle round his waist, and a long spear, tufted with black ostrich feathers, and ornamented with scarlet streamers, rested on his shoulder. He was the very picture of a true Bedouin Sheikh, and his liveliness, his wit, and his singular powers of conversation, which made him the most agreeable of companions, did not belie his race.

As we wound slowly over the low rocky hills to the west of the town of Mosul, in a long straggling line, our caravan had a strange and motley appearance; Europeans, Turks, Bedouins, town-Arabs, Tiyari, and Yezidis, adding, by difference of costume and a profusion of bright colours, to the general picturesqueness and gaiety of the scene.

The Tigris, from its entrance into the low country at the foot of the Kurdish mountains near Jezirah, to the ruined town of Tekrit, is separated from the Mesopotamian plains by a range of low limestone hills. We rode over this undulating ground for about an hour and a half, and then descended into the plain of Zerga, encamping for the night near the ruins of a small village, with a falling castle, called Sahaghi, about twelve miles from Mosul. The place had been left by its inhabitants, like all others on the desert side of the town, on account of the depredations of the Bedouins. There is now scarcely one permanent settlement on the banks of the Tigris from Jezirah to the immediate vicinity of Baghdad, with the exception of Mosul and Tekrit. One of the most fertile countries in the world, watered by a river navigable for nearly six hundred miles, has been turned into a desert and a wilderness, by continued misgovernment, oppression, and neglect.

Our tents were pitched near a pool of rain water, which, although muddy and scant, sufficed for our wants. There are no springs in this part of the plain, and the Bedouins are entirely dependent upon such temporary supplies. The remains of ancient villages show, however, that water is not concealed far beneath the surface, and that wells once yielded all that was required for irrigation and human consumption.

The loads had not yet been fairly divided amongst the camels, and the sun had risen above the horizon, before the Bedouins had arranged them to their satisfaction, and were ready to depart. The plain of Zerga was carpeted with tender grass, scarcely yet forward enough to afford pasture for our animals. Scattered here and there were tulips of a bright scarlet hue, the earliest flower of the spring.

Our first Encampment in the Desert.

A ride of three hours and a quarter brought us to a second line of limestone hills, the continuation of the Tel Afer and Sinjar range, dividing the small plain of Zerga from the true Mesopotamian desert. From a peak which I ascended to take bearings, the vast level country, stretching to the Euphrates, lay like a map beneath me, dotted with mounds, but otherwise unbroken by a single eminence. The nearest and most remarkable group of ruins was called Abou Khameera, and consisted of a lofty, conical mound surrounded by a square inclosure, or ridge of earth, marking, as at Kouyunjik and Nimroud, the remains of ancient walls. From the foot of the hill on which I stood there issued a small rivulet, winding amongst rushes, and losing itself in the plain. This running water had drawn together the black tents of the Jehesh, a half sedentary tribe of Arabs, who cultivate the lands around the ruined village of Abou Maria. Their flocks grazing on the plain, and the shepherds who watched them, were the only living objects in that boundless expanse.

As the caravan issued from the defile leading from the hills into the plain, the Arabs brought out bowls of sour milk and fresh water, inviting us to spend the night in their encampment. Eight or ten of my workmen, under a Christian superintendent, had been for some days excavating in the Assyrian ruins of Abou Khameera. I therefore ordered the tents to be pitched near the reedy stream, and galloped to the mounds, which were rather more than a mile distant.

A broad and lofty mound shows the traces of several distinct platforms or terraces rising one above the other. It is almost perpendicular on its four sides, except where, on the south-eastern, there appears to have been an inclined ascent, or a flight of steps, leading to the summit, and it stands nearly in the centre of an inclosure of earthen walls forming a regular quadrangle about 660 paces square. The workmen had opened deep trenches and tunnels in several parts of the principal ruin, and had found walls of sun-dried brick, unsculptured alabaster slabs, and some circular stone sockets for the hinges of gates, similar to those discovered at Nimroud. The baked bricks and the pieces of gypsum and pottery scattered amongst the rubbish bore no inscriptions; nor could I, after the most careful search, find the smallest fragment of sculpture.

One of those furious and sudden storms, which frequently sweep over the plains of Mesopotamia during the spring season, burst over us in the night. Whilst incessant lightnings broke the gloom, a raging wind almost drowned the deep roll of the thunder. The united strength of the Arabs could scarcely hold the flapping canvass of the tents. Rain descended in torrents, sparing us no place of shelter. Towards dawn the hurricane had passed away, leaving a still and cloudless sky. When the sun rose from the broad expanse of the desert, as out of the sea, a most delightful calm and freshness pervaded the air.

During the day's journey we trod on a carpet of the brightest verdure, mingled with gaudy flowers. Men and animals rejoiced equally in these luxuriant pastures, and leaving the line of march strayed over the meadows. On all sides of us rose Assyrian mounds, now covered with soft herbage. I rode with Suttum from ruin to ruin, examining each, but finding no other remains than fragments of pottery and baked bricks. The Bedouin chief had names for them all, but they were mere Arab names, derived generally from some local peculiarity; the more ancient had been long lost. From his childhood his father's tents had been pitched amongst them nearly every year; when in the spring the tribe journeyed towards the banks of the Khabour, and again when in autumn they re-sought their winter camping-grounds around Babylon. These lofty mounds, seen from a great distance, are the best of landmarks in a vast plain, and guide the Bedouin in his wanderings.

Tel Ermah, 'the mound of the spears,' had been visible from our tents, rising far above the surrounding ruins. As it was a little out of the direct line of march, Suttum mounted one of our led horses, and leaving Khoraif to protect the caravan, rode with me to the spot. The mound is precisely similar in character to Abou Khameera and Mokhamour, and, like them, stands within a quadrangle of earthen walls. On its south-eastern side a ravine marks the remains of the ascent to the several terraces of the building. The principal ruin has assumed a conical form, like the high mound at Nimroud, and from the same cause. It was, I presume, originally square. Within the inclosure are traces of ancient dwellings, but I was unable to find any inscribed fragments of stone or brick.

Whilst I was examining the ruins, Suttum, from the highest mound, had been scanning the plain with his eagle eye. At length it rested upon a distant moving object. Although with a telescope I could scarcely distinguish that to which he pointed, the Sheikh saw that it was a rider on a dromedary. He now, therefore, began to watch the stranger with that eager curiosity and suspicion always shown by a Bedouin when the solitude of the desert is broken by a human being of whose condition and business he is ignorant. Suttum soon satisfied himself as to the character of the solitary wanderer. He declared him to be a messenger from his own tribe, who had been sent to lead us to his father's tents. Mounting his horse, he galloped towards him. The Arab soon perceived the approaching horseman, and then commenced on both sides a series of manœuvres practised by those who meet in the desert, and are as yet distrustful of each other. I marked them from the ruin as they cautiously approached, now halting, now drawing nigh, and then pretending to ride away in an opposite direction. At length, recognising one another, they met, and, having first dismounted to embrace, came together towards me. As Suttum had conjectured, a messenger had been sent to him from his father's tribe. The Boraij were now moving towards the north in search of the spring pastures, and their tents would be pitched in three or four days beneath the Sinjar hill. Suttum at once understood the order of their march, and made arrangements to meet them accordingly.

Leaving the ruins of Tel Ermah, we found the caravan halting near some wells of sweet water, called Marzib. From this spot the old castle of Tel Afer, standing boldly on an eminence about ten miles distant, was plainly visible. Continuing our march we reached, towards evening, a group of mounds known as Tel Jemal, and pitched our tents in the midst of them on a green lawn, enamelled with flowers, that furnished a carpet unequalled in softness of texture, or in richness of colour, by the looms of Cashmere. A sluggish stream, called by the Arabs El Abra, and by the Turcomans of Tel Afer, Kharala, crept through the ruins.

The tents had scarcely been raised when a party of horsemen were seen coming towards us. As they approached our encampment they played the Jerid with their long spears, galloping to and fro on their well-trained mares. They were the principal inhabitants of Tel Afer with Ozair Agha, their chief, who brought us a present of lambs, flour, and fresh vegetables. The Agha rode on a light chestnut mare of beautiful proportions and rare breed. His dress, as well as that of his followers, was singularly picturesque. His people are Turcomans, a solitary colony in the midst of the desert; and although their connection with the Bedouins has taught them the tongue and the habits of the wandering tribes, yet they still wear the turban of many folds, and the gay flowing robes of their ancestors. They allow their hair to grow long, and to fall in curls on their shoulders.

As the evening crept on, I watched from the highest mound the sun as it gradually sank in unclouded splendour below the sea-like expanse before me. On all sides, as far as the eye could reach, rose the grass-covered heaps marking the sites of ancient habitations. The great tide of civilisation had long since ebbed, leaving these scattered wrecks on the solitary shore. Are those waters to flow again, bearing back the seeds of knowledge and of wealth that they have wafted to the West? We wanderers were seeking what they had left behind, as children gather up the coloured shells on the deserted sands. At my feet there was a busy scene, making more lonely the unbroken solitude which reigned in the vast plain around, where the only moving thing were the shadows of the lofty mounds as they lengthened before the declining sun. Above three years before, when, watching the approach of night from the old castle of Tel Afer, I had counted nearly one hundred ruins, now, when in the midst of them, no less than double that number were seen from Tel Jemal. Our tents crowning the lip of a natural amphitheatre bright with flowers, Ozair Agha and his Turcomans seated on the greensward in earnest talk with the Arab chief, the horses picketed in the long grass, the Bedouins driving home their camels for their night's rest, the servants and grooms busied with their various labours; such was the foreground of a picture of perfect calm and stillness. In the distance was the long range of the Sinjar hills, furrowed with countless ravines, each marked by a dark purple shadow, gradually melting into the evening haze.

We had a long day's march before us to the village of Sinjar. The wilderness appeared still more beautiful than it had done the day before. The recent storm had given new life to a vegetation which, concealed beneath a crust of apparently unfruitful earth, only waits for a spring shower to burst, as if by enchantment, through the thirsty soil. Here and there grew patches of a shrub-like plant with an edible root, having a sharp pungent taste like mustard, eaten raw and much relished by the Bedouins. Among them lurked game of various kind. Troops of gazelles sprang from the low cover, and bounded over the plain. The greyhounds coursed hares; the horsemen followed a wild boar of enormous size, and nearly white from age; and the Doctor, who was the sportsman of the party, shot a bustard, with a beautiful speckled plumage, and a ruff of long feathers round its neck. This bird was larger than the common small bustard, but apparently of the same species. Other bustards, the great and the middle-sized (the Houbron and Houbara of the Arabs*), and the lesser, besides many birds of the plover kind†, rose from these tufts, which seemed to afford food and shelter to a variety of living creatures. We scanned the horizon in vain for the wild ass, which is but thinly scattered over the plains. The Arabs found many eggs of the Houbara. They were laid in the grass without any regular nest, the bird simply making a form somewhat like that of a hare, and sitting very close, frequently not rising until it was nearly trodden under foot. One or two eggs of the great bustard were also brought to me during the day.

We still wandered amongst innumerable mounds. The largest I examined were called Hathail and Usgah. They resembled those of Abou Khameera and Tel Ermah, with

---

* The Houbron is the *Otis tarda*, or great bustard; the Houbara, the *Otis Houbara*. I believe that more than one species of the lesser bustard (*Otis tetrax*) is found in the Mesopotamian plains.

† The most abundant was a large grey plover, called by the Bedouins 'Smoug.'

the remains of terraces, the ascent to them being on the south-eastern side, and the inclosure of earthen walls.

We rode in a direct line to the Belled Sinjar, the residence of the governor of the district. There was no beaten track, and the camels wandered along as they listed, cropping as they went the young grass. The horsemen and footmen, too, scattered themselves over the plain in search of game. Suttum rode from group to group on his swift deloul, urging them to keep together, as the Aneyza *gazous** occasionally swept this part of the desert. But to little purpose; the feeling of liberty and independence which these boundless meadows produced was too complete and too pleasing to be controlled by any fear of danger, or by the Sheikh's prudent counsel. All shared in the exhilarating effects of the air and scene. Hormuzd would occasionally place himself at the head of the Jebours, and chant their war songs, improvising words suited to the occasion. The men answered in chorus, dancing as they went, brandishing their weapons, and raising their bright-coloured kerchiefs, as flags, on the end of their spears. The more sedate Bedouins smiled in contempt at these noisy effusions of joy, only worthy of tribes who have touched the plough; but they indulged in no less keen, though more suppressed, emotions of delight. Even the Nestorians caught the general enthusiasm, and sung their mountain songs as they walked along.

As we drew near to the foot of the hills we found a large encampment, formed partly by Jebours belonging to Sheikh Abd-ul-Azeez, and partly by a Sinjar tribe called Mendka, under a chief known as the 'Effendi,' who enjoys considerable influence in this district. I dismounted at a short distance, to avoid a breach of good manners, as to refuse to eat bread, or to spend the night, after alighting near a tent, would be thought a grave slight upon its owner.

It was with difficulty that I resisted the entreaties of the Effendi to partake of his hospitality. We did not reach the Belled Sinjar until after the sun had gone down, the caravan having been ten hours in unceasing march. The tents were

---

* A plundering party, the *chappou* of the Persian tribes.

pitched on a small plot of ground, watered by numerous rills, and in the centre of the ruins. Although almost a swamp, it was the only spot free from stones and rubbish. In front of the tent door rose a leaning minaret, part of a mosque, and other ruins of Arab edifices. To the right was an old wall with a falling archway, from beneath which gushed a most abundant stream of clear sweet water, still filling the ancient fountains and reservoirs of the city.

My tent was soon filled with the people of the Belled, and they remained in animated discussion until the night was far spent.

The ruins amongst which we had encamped are those of the town of Sinjar, the capital of an Arab principality in the time of the Caliphs. Its princes frequently asserted their independence, coined money, and ruled from the Khabour and Euphrates to the neighbourhood of Mosul. The province was included within the dominions of the celebrated Saleh-ed-din (the Saladin of the Crusades), and was more than once visited by him.

Wishing to visit the villages of the *Shomal*, or northern side of the mountain, and at the same time to put an end, if possible, to the bloodshed between their inhabitants, and to induce them to submit to the governor, I quitted the Belled in the afternoon of the following day, accompanied by Cawal Yusuf, leaving the tents, baggage, and workmen under the charge of the Bairakdar. We followed a precipitous pathway along the hill-side to Mirkan, the village destroyed by Tahyar Pasha on my first visit to the Sinjar.* This part of the mountain is coated with thin strata of a white fossiliferous limestone, which detach themselves in enormous flakes, and fall into the ravines, leaving an endless variety of singular forms in the rocks above. In some places the declivities are broken into stupendous flights of steps, in others they have the columnar appearance of basalt. This limestone produces scarcely a blade of vegetation, and its milk-white colour, throwing back the intense glare of the sun's rays, is both painful and hurtful to the eyes.

* Nineveh and its Remains, p. 214, 215.

Mirkan was in open rebellion, and had refused to pay taxes and to receive the officer of the Pasha of Mosul. I was, at first, somewhat doubtful of our reception. Esau, the chief, came out, however, to meet me, and led us to his house. We were soon surrounded by the principal men of the village. They were also at war with the tribes of the 'Shomal.' A few days before they had fought with the loss of several men on both sides. Seconded by Cawal Yusuf, I endeavoured to make them feel that peace and union amongst themselves was not only essential to their own welfare, but to that of the Yezidis of Kurdistan and Armenia, who had, at length, received a promise of protection from the Turkish government. After a lengthened discussion the chief consented to accompany me to the neighbouring village of Bukra, with whose inhabitants his people had been for some time at war.

There are two pathways from Mirkan to the Shomal, one winding through narrow valleys, the other crossing the shoulder of the mountain. I chose the latter, as it enabled me to obtain an extensive view of the surrounding country, and to take bearings of many points of interest. The slopes around the villages are most industriously and carefully cultivated. Earth, collected with great labour, is spread over terraces, supported by walls of loose stones, as on the declivities of Mount Lebanon. These stages, rising one above the other, are planted with fig-trees, between which is occasionally raised a scanty crop of wheat or barley. The neatness of these terraced plots conveys a very favourable impression of the industry of the Yezidis.

Near the crest of the hill we passed a white conical building, shaded by a grove of trees. It was the tomb of the father of Murad, one of Yusuf's companions, a Cawal of note, who had died of the plague near the spot some years before. The walls were hung with the horns of sheep, slain in sacrifice, by occasional pilgrims.

I had little anticipated the beauty and extent of the view which opened round us on the top of the pass. The Sinjar hill is a solitary ridge rising abruptly in the midst of the desert; from its summit, therefore, the eye ranges on one side over the vast level wilderness stretching to the Euphrates,

and on the other over the plain bounded by the Tigris and
the lofty mountains of Kurdistan. Nisibin and Mardin were
both visible in the distance. I could distinguish the hills

Interior of a Yezidi House at Bukra, in the Sinjar

of Baadri and Sheikh Adi, and many well-known peaks of
the Kurdish Alps. Behind the lower ranges, each distinctly
marked by its sharp, serrated outline, were the snow-covered

heights of Tiyari and Bohtan. Whilst to the south of the Sinjar artificial mounds appeared to abound, to the north I could distinguish but few such remains. We dismounted to gaze upon this truly magnificent scene lighted up by the setting sun. I have rarely seen any prospect more impressive than these boundless plains viewed from a considerable elevation. Besides the idea of vastness they convey, the light and shade of passing clouds flitting over the face of the land, and the shadows as they lengthen towards the close of day, produce constantly changing effects of singular variety and beauty.*

It was night before we reached Bukra, where we were welcomed with great hospitality. The best house in the village had been made ready for us, and was scrupulously neat and clean, as the houses of the Yezidis usually are. It was curiously built, being divided into three principal rooms, opening one into the other. They were separated by a wall about six feet high, upon which were placed wooden pillars supporting the ceiling. The roof rested on trunks of trees, raised on rude stone pedestals at regular intervals in the centre chamber, which was open on one side to the air, like a Persian Iwan. The sides of the rooms were honeycombed with small recesses like pigeon-holes, tastefully arranged. The whole was plastered with the whitest plaster, fancy designs in bright red being introduced here and there, and giving the interior of the house a very quaint and original appearance.

The elders of Bukra came to me after we had dined, and seated themselves respectfully and decorously round the room. They were not averse to the reconciliation I proposed, received the hostile chiefs without hesitation, and promised to accompany me on the morrow to the adjoining village of Ossofa, with which they were also at war.

In the morning we visited several houses in the village. They were all built on the same plan, and were equally neat and clean. The women received us without concealing their

---

* The traveller who has looked down from Mardin, for the first time, upon the plains of Mesopotamia, can never forget the impression which that singular scene must have made upon him. The view from the Sinjar hill is far more beautiful and varied.

faces, which are, however, far from pleasing, their features being irregular, and their complexion sallow. Those who are married dress entirely in white, with a white kerchief under their chins, and another over their heads held by the *agal*, or woollen cord, of the Bedouins. The girls wear white shirts and drawers, but over them coloured *zabouns*, or long silk dresses, open in front, and confined at the waist by a girdle ornamented with pieces of silver. They twist gay kerchiefs round their heads, and adorn themselves with coins, and glass and amber beads, when their parents are able to procure them. But the Yezidis of the Sinjar are now very poor, and nearly all the trinkets of the women have long since fallen into the hands of the Turkish soldiery, or have been sold to pay taxes and arbitrary fines. The men have a dark complexion, black and piercing eyes, and frequently a fierce and forbidding countenance. They are of small stature, but have well-proportioned limbs strongly knit together, and are muscular, active, and capable of bearing great fatigue. Their dress consists of a shirt, loose trowsers and cloak, all white, and a black turban, from beneath which their hair falls in ringlets. Their long rifles are rarely out of their hands, and they carry pistols in their girdle, a sword at their side, and a row of cartouche cases, generally made of cut reeds, on their breast. These additions to their costume, and their swarthy features, give them a peculiar look of ferocity, which, according to some, is not belied by their characters.

The Yezidis are, by one of their religious laws, forbidden to wear the common Eastern shirt open in front, and this article of their dress is always closed up to the neck. This is a distinctive mark of the sect by which its members may be recognised at a glance. The language of the people of Sinjar is Kurdish, and few speak Arabic. According to their traditions they are the descendants of a colony from the north of Syria, which settled in Mesopotamia at a comparatively recent period, but I could obtain no positive information on the subject. It is probable, however, that they did not migrate to their present seats before the fall of the Arab principality, and the invasion of Timourleng, towards the end of the fourteenth century.

The north side of the mountain is thickly inhabited, and well cultivated as far as the scanty soil will permit. Scarcely three-quarters of a mile to the west of Bukra is the village of Naksi, the interval between the two being occupied by terraces planted with fig-trees. We did not stop there, although the inhabitants came out to meet us, but rode on to Ossofa, or Usifa, only separated from Naksi by a rocky valley. The people of this village were at war with their neighbours, and as this was one of the principal seats of rebellion and discontent, I was anxious to have an interview with its chief.

A Group of Yezidis.

The position of Ossofa is very picturesque. It stands on the edge of a deep ravine; behind it are lofty crags and narrow gorges, whose sides are filled with natural caverns. On overhanging rocks, towering above the village, are two *ziarehs*, or holy places, of the Yezidis, distinguished from afar by their white fluted spires.

Pulo, the chief, met us at the head of the principal inhabitants, and led me to his house, where a large assembly was soon collected to discuss the principal object of my visit.

The chiefs of Mirkan and Bukra were induced to make offers of peace, which were accepted, and, after much discussion, the terms of an amicable arrangement were agreed to and ratified by general consent. Sheep were slain to celebrate the event. The meat, after the Yezidi fashion, was boiled with onions and a kind of parched pea, and afterwards served up, like porridge, in large wooden bowls. The mess is not unsavoury, and is the principal dish of the Sinjar. Dried figs, strung in rows and made up into grotesque figures, were brought to us as presents. After the political questions had been settled, the young men adjourned to an open spot outside the village to practise with their rifles. They proved excellent shots, seldom missing the very centre of the mark.

The villages of Bouran (now deserted), Gundi-Gayli, Kushna, and Aldina, follow to the west of Ossofa, scarcely half a mile intervening between each. They are grouped together on the mountain side, which, above and below them, is divided into terraces and planted with fig-trees. The loose stones are most carefully removed from every plot of earth, however small, and built up into walls; on the higher slopes are a few vineyards. We passed the night at Aldina. Below the village is a remarkable *ziareh*, inclosed by a wall of cyclopean dimensions. In the plain beneath, in the midst of a grove of trees, is the tomb of Cawal Hussein, the father of Cawal Yusuf, who died in the Sinjar during one of his periodical visitations. He was a priest of sanctity and influence, and his grave is still visited as a place of pilgrimage. Sacrifices of sheep are made there, but they are merely in remembrance of the deceased, and have no particular religious meaning attached to them. The flesh is distributed amongst the poor, and a sum of money is frequently added. Approving the ceremony as one tending to promote charity and kindly feeling, I gave a sheep to be sacrificed at the tomb of the Cawal, and one of my fellow travellers added a second, the carcases being afterwards divided among the needy.

All the villages we had passed during our short day's journey stand high on the mountain side, where they have been built for security against the Bedouins, and command extensive views of the plain, the snowy range of Kurdistan forming a magnificent back-ground. The springs, rising in the hill, are either entirely absorbed in irrigation, or are soon lost in the thirsty plain beneath. Parallel to the Sinjar range is a long narrow valley, scarcely half a mile in width, formed by a bold ridge of white limestone rocks, so friable that the plain for some distance is covered with their fragments.

I returned to the Belled by a direct and precipitous pass, and we were nearly two hours in reaching the summit. We then found ourselves on a broad green platform thickly wooded with dwarf oak. I was surprised to see snow still lying in the sheltered nooks. On both sides of us stretched the great Mesopotamian plains. To the south, glittering in the sun, was a small salt lake about fifteen miles distant from the Sinjar, called by the Arabs, Munaif. From it the Bedouins, when in their northern pastures, obtain their supplies of salt.

We descended to the Belled through a narrow valley thick with oak and various shrubs. Game appeared to abound. A Yezidi, who had accompanied us from Aldina, shot three wild boars, and we put up several coveys of the large red partridge. The ibex is also found amongst the rocks. We were nearly five hours in crossing the mountain.

Suttum and his Bedouin companions, whom he had fetched from his father's tents during my absence, were waiting for us, but were not anxious to start before the following morning. A Yezidi snake-charmer, with his son, a boy of seven or eight years old, came to my tents in the afternoon, and exhibited his tricks in the midst of a circle of astonished beholders. He first pulled from a bag a number of snakes knotted together, which the bystanders declared to be of the most venomous kind. The child took the reptiles fearlessly from his father, and placing them in his bosom allowed them to twine themselves round his neck and arms. The Bedouins gazed in mute wonder at these proceedings, but when the Sheikh, feigning rage against one of the snakes which had drawn blood from his son, seized it, and biting off its head with his teeth threw the writhing body amongst them, they could no longer restrain their horror and indignation. They uttered loud curses on the infidel snake charmer and his kindred to the remotest generations. Suttum did not regain his composure during the whole evening, frequently relapsing into profound thought, then suddenly breaking out in a fresh curse upon the Sheikh, who, he declared, had a very close and unholy connection with the evil one. Many days passed before he had completely got over the horror the poor Yezidi's feats had caused him.

Suttum had changed his deloul for a white mare of great beauty, named Athaiba. She was of the race of Kohaila, of exquisite symmetry, in temper docile as a lamb, yet with an eye of fire, and of a proud and noble carriage when excited in war or in the chase. His saddle was the simple stuffed pad generally used by the Bedouins, without stirrups. A halter alone served to guide the gentle animal. Suttum had brought with him several of the principal members of his family, all of whom were mounted on high-bred mares. One youth rode a bay filly, for which, I was assured, one hundred camels had been offered.

We followed a pathway over the broken ground at the foot of the Sinjar, crossing deep watercourses worn by the small streams, which lose themselves in the desert. The villages, as on the opposite slope, or 'Shomal,' are high up on the hill-side. The first we passed was Gabara, inhabited by Yezidis and Mussulmans. Its chief, Ruffo, with a party of horsemen, came to us, and intreated me to show him how to open a spring called *Soulak*, which, he said, had suddenly been choked up, leaving the village almost without water. Unfortunately, being ignorant of the arts for which he gave me credit, I was unable to afford him any help. We encamped, after a short ride, upon a pleasant stream beneath the village of Jedaila.

We remained here a whole day in order to visit Suttum's tribe, which was now migrating towards the Sinjar. Early in the morning a vast crowd of moving objects could be faintly perceived on the horizon. These were the camels and sheep of the Boraij, followed by the usual crowd of men, women, children, and beasts of burden. We watched them as they scattered themselves over the plain, and gradually settled in different pastures. By midday the encampment had been formed and all the stragglers collected. We could scarcely distinguish the black tents, and their site was only marked by curling wreaths of white smoke.

In the afternoon Suttum's father, Rishwan, came to us, accompanied by several Sheikhs of the Boraij. He rode on a white deloul, celebrated for her beauty and swiftness. His saddle and the neck of the animal were profusely adorned with woollen tassels of many colours, glass beads, and small shells, after the manner of the Arabs of Nejd. The well-trained dromedary having knelt at the door of my tent, the old man alighted, and throwing his arms around my neck kissed me on both shoulders. He was tall, and of noble carriage. His beard was white with age, but his form was still erect and his footsteps firm. Rishwan was one of the bravest warriors of the Shammar. He had come, when a child, with his father from the original seat of the tribe in northern Arabia. As the leader of a large branch of the Boraij he had taken a prominent part in the wars of the tribe, and the young men still sought him to head their distant forays. But he had long renounced the toils of the *gazou*, and left his three sons, of whom Suttum was the second, to maintain the honour of the Saadi. He was a noble specimen of the true Bedouin, both in character and appearance. With the skill and daring of the Arab warrior he united the hospitality, generosity, and good faith of a hero of Arab romance. He spoke in the rich dialect of the desert tongue, with the eloquence peculiar to his race. He sat with me during the greater part of the afternoon, and having eaten bread returned to his tent.

The Yezidi chiefs of Kerraniyah or Sekkiniyah (the village is known by both names) came to our encampment soon after Rishwan's arrival. As they had a feud with the Bedouins, I took advantage of their visit to effect a reconciliation, both parties swearing on my hospitality to abstain from plundering one another hereafter.

Being anxious to reach the end of our journey I declined Suttum's invitation to sleep in his tent, but sending the caravan to the place appointed for our night's encampment. I made a detour to visit his father, accompanied by Mr. and Mrs. R., the Doctor, Mr. C., and Hormuzd. Although the Boraij were above six miles from the small rivulet of Jedaila, they were obliged to send to it for water.* As we rode towards their tents we passed their camels and sheep slowly wandering towards the stream. The camels, spreading far and wide over the plain, were divided according to their colours; some herds being entirely white, some yellow, and others brown or black. Each animal bore the well-known mark of the tribe branded on his side. The Arabs, who drove them, were mounted on dromedaries carrying the capacious *rouweis*, or buckets made of bullock skins, in which water is brought to the encampment for domestic purposes.

A Bedouin warrior, armed with his long tufted spear, and urging his fleet deloul, occasionally passed rapidly by us leading his high-bred mare to water, followed by her colt gambolling unrestrained over the greensward. In the throng we met Sahiman, the elder brother of Suttum. He was riding on a bay horse, whose fame had spread far and wide amongst the tribes, and whose exploits were a constant theme of praise and wonder with the Shammar. It was of the race of Obeyan Sherakh, a breed now almost extinct, and perhaps more highly prized than any other of the desert.

Near the encampment of the Boraij was a group of mounds resembling in every respect those I have already described. The Bedouins call them Abou-Khaima. Their similarity of form,—a centre mound divided into a series of terraces, ascended by an inclined way or steps, and surrounded by equilateral walls,—would lead to the conjecture that these mounds are the remains of fire temples, or vast altars, destined for the worship of the heavenly bodies. It will be seen hereafter that the well-known ruin of the Birs Nimroud, on or near the site of ancient Babylon, is very nearly the same in shape.

* In the spring months, when the pastures are good, the sheep and camels of the Bedouins require but little water, and the tents are seldom pitched near a well or stream; frequently as much as half a day's journey distant.

The Bedouins who accompanied us galloped to and fro, engaging in mimic war with their long quivering spears, until we reached the encampment of the Boraij. The tents were scattered far and wide over the plain; for so they are pitched during this season of the year when the pastures are abundant, and no immediate danger is apprehended from hostile tribes. At other times they are ranged in parallel lines close together, the Sheikh always occupying the foremost place, facing the side from which the guest, as well as the enemy, is expected, that he may be the first to exercise hospitality, and the first to meet the foe. This position, however, varies in winter, when the tent must be closed completely on one side, according to the direction of the wind, so that when the wind changes, the whole camp suddenly, as it were, turns round, the last tent becoming the foremost. It is thought unmannerly to approach by the back, to step over tent-ropes, or to ride towards the women's compartment, which is almost always on the right. During warm weather the whole canvass is raised on poles to allow the air to circulate freely, a curtain being used in the morning and evening to ward off the rays of the sun. The Bedouin can tell at once, when drawing near to an encampment, the tent of the Sheikh. It is generally distinguished by its size, and frequently by the spears stuck in the ground in front of it. If the stranger be not advancing directly towards it, and wishes to be the guest of the chief, he goes out of his way, that on approaching he may ride at once to it without passing any other, as it is considered uncourteous and almost an insult to go by a man's tent without stopping and eating his bread. The owner of a tent has even the right to claim any one as his guest who passes in front of it on entering an encampment.

Rishwan, Suttum, Mijwell his younger brother, and the elders of the tribe, were standing before the tent ready to receive us. All the old carpets and coverlets of the family, and ragged enough they were, had been spread out for their guests. As we seated ourselves two sheep were slain before us for the feast; a ceremony it would not have been considered sufficiently hospitable to perform previous to our arrival, as it might have been doubtful whether the animals had been slain wholly for us. The chief men of the encampment collected round us, crouching in a wide circle on the grass. We talked of Arab politics and Arab war, *ghazous*, and Aneyza mares stolen or carried off in battle by the Shammar. Huge wooden platters, heavy with the steaming messes of rice and boiled meat, were soon brought in and placed on the ground before us. Immense lumps of fresh butter were then heaped upon them, and allowed to melt, the chief occasionally mixing and kneading the whole up together with his hands. When the dishes had cooled * the venerable Rishwan stood up in the centre of the tent, and called in a loud voice upon each person by name and in his turn to come to the feast. We fared first with a few of the principal Sheikhs. The most influential men were next summoned, each however resisting the honour, and allowing himself to be dragged by Suttum and Mijwell to his place. The children, as is usual, were admitted last, and wound up the entertainment by a general scramble for the fragments and the bones. Neither Rishwan nor his sons would eat of the repast they had prepared, the laws of hospitality requiring that it should be left entirely to their guests.

After we had eaten, I accompanied Mrs. R. to the harem, where we found assembled the wives and daughters of Rishwan, of his sons, and of the elders of the tribe, who had met together to see the Frank lady. Amongst them were several of considerable beauty. The wife of Sahiman, the eldest of the three brothers, was most distinguished for her good looks. They were all dressed in the usual long blue shirt, and striped or black abba, with a black headkerchief, or keffieh, confined round the temple by a band

---

* It is considered exceedingly inhospitable amongst the Shammar to place a hot dish before guests, as they are obliged to eat quickly out of consideration for others, who are awaiting their turn, which they cannot do, unless the mess be cool, without burning their mouths, or wasting half their time picking out the colder bits. On one occasion, Ferhan, the great chief of the Shammar, and a large number of horsemen having alighted at my tent, I prepared a dinner for them. The Sheikh was afterwards heard to say that the Bey's feast was sumptuous, but that he had not treated his guests with proper hospitality, as the dishes were so hot nobody could eat his fill.

of spun camel's wool. Massive rings of silver, adorned with gems and coral, hung from their noses,* and bracelets in the same metal, and also set with precious stones, encircled their wrists and ankles. Some wore necklaces of coins, coarse amber, agate, cornelian beads and cylinders, mostly Assyrian relics picked up amongst ruins after rain. These ornaments were confined to the unmarried girls, and to the youngest and prettiest wives, who on waxing old are obliged to transfer them to a more favoured successor.

Arab Nose Ring and Bracelet of Silver.

When Bedouin ladies leave their tents, or are on a march, they sometimes wear a black kerchief over the lower part of the face, showing only their sparkling eyes. Like the men they also use the keffieh, or head-kerchief, to cover their features. Their complexion is of a dark rich olive. Their eyes are large, almond-shaped, expressive, and of extraordinary brilliancy and fire. They suffer their black and luxuriant hair to fall in clusters of curls. Their carriage in youth is erect and graceful. They are able to bear much fatigue, and show great courage and spirit in moments of difficulty and danger. But their beauty is only the companion of extreme youth. With few exceptions, soon after twenty, and the birth of one or two children, they rapidly change into the most hideous of old hags, the lightning-like brightness of the eye alone surviving the general wreck. When young, the daughters and wives of the chiefs are well cared for; they

---

* These are 'the rings and nose jewels,' which Isaiah (iii. 21.) describes as worn by the Jewish women. It is curious that no representation of them has hitherto been found in the Assyrian sculptures.

move with the tribe in the covered camel-saddle, shaded by carpets from the rays of the sun. Daughters are looked upon in the desert* as a source of strength and advantage, from the alliances they enable the father to make with powerful and influential chiefs, being frequently the means of healing feuds which have existed for many years. The children of Rishwan's family were naked, and, of course, dirty.

Before we left the encampment Suttum led before me as a present a handsome grey colt, which was as usual returned with a request to take care of it until it was required, the polite way of declining a gift of this nature.

Suttum having saddled his deloul was ready to accompany us on my journey. As he was to be for some time absent from his tents, he asked my leave to take his wife with him, and I willingly consented. Rathaiyah was the sister of Suttâm el Meekh, chief of the powerful tribe of the Abde, one of the principal divisions of the Shammar. Although no longer young she still retained much of her early beauty. There was more than the usual Bedouin fire in her large black eyes, and her hair fell in many ringlets on her shoulders. Her temper was haughty and imperious, and she evidently held more sway over Suttum than he liked to acknowledge, or was quite consistent with his character as a warrior. He had married her from motives of policy, as cementing an useful alliance with a powerful tribe. She soon carried matters with a high hand, for poor Suttum had been compelled, almost immediately after his marriage, to send back a young and beautiful wife to her father's tent. This prior claimant upon his affections was now on the Khabour with her tribe, and it was probably on this account that Rathaiyah, knowing the direction he was about to take, was so anxious to accompany her husband. She rode on the dromedary behind her lord, a comfortable seat having been made for her with a rug and a coverlet. The Sheikh carried his hawk, Hattab, on his wrist, guiding the deloul by a short hooked stick held in the right hand. Khoraif, his rediff, rode

---

* Amongst the inhabitants of towns, a daughter is considered a kind of flaw in the family, and the death of a girl, too frequently purposely brought about, is rarely a cause of grief.

on this occasion a second dromedary named Sheiala, with a Shammar Bedouin.

The true Sinjar mountain ends about nine miles from Jedaila, the high ridge suddenly subsiding into low broken hills. From all parts of the plain it is a very beautiful object. Its limestone rocks, wooded here and there with dwarf oak, are of a rich golden colour; and the numberless ravines which

Suttum, with his Wife, on his Dromedary.

furrow its sides, form ribs of deep purple shadow. The western part of the Sinjar is inhabited by the Yezidi tribe of Kherraniyah. We rode over the plain in a line parallel to the mountain, and about seven or eight miles from it. Towards nightfall we skirted a ridge of very low hills rising to our left. They are called Alouvi and Yusuf Beg.

The desert abounded in the houbara, or middle-sized bustard, the bird usually hawked by the Arabs, and esteemed by them a great delicacy. Hattab, the falcon, had been principally trained to this game, and sat on the raised wrist of Suttum, scanning the plain with his piercing eye. He saw the crouching quarry long before we could distinguish it, and spreading his wings struggled to release himself from the tresses. Once free he made one straight, steady swoop towards the bustard, which rose to meet the coming foe, but was soon borne down in his sharp talons. A combat ensued, which was ended by a horseman riding up, substituting the lure for the game, and hooding the hawk, which was again placed on his master's wrist.

Thus we rode joyously over the plain, night setting in before we could see the tents. No sound except the mournful note of the small desert-owl, which has often misled the weary wanderer,* broke the deep silence, nor could we distinguish the distant fires usually marking the site of an encampment. Suttum, however, well knew where the Bedouins would halt, and about an hour after dark we heard the well-known voice of Dervish, and others of my workmen, who, anxious at our delay, had come out to seek us. The tents stood near a muddy pool of salt water, thick with loathsome living things and camels' dung. The Arabs call the place Om-el-Dhiban, 'the mother of flies,' from the insects which swarm around it, and madden by their sting the camels and horses that drink at the stagnant water.

Our encampment was full of Yezidis of the Kherraniyah tribe, who had ridden from the tents to see me, bringing presents of sheep, flour, and figs. They were at war, both with the Bedouins and the inhabitants of the northern side of the mountain. My large tent was soon crowded with guests. They squatted down on the ground in double ranks. For the last time I spoke on the advantage of peace and union amongst themselves, and I exacted from them a solemn promise that they would meet the assembled tribes at the next great festival in the valley of Sheikh Adi, referring their dif-

* Its note resembles the cry of the camel-driver, when leading the herds home at night.

ferences in future to the decision of Hussein Bey, Sheikh Nasr, and the Cawals, instead of appealing to arms. I also reconciled them with the Bedouins, Suttum entering into an engagement for his tribe, and both parties agreeing to abstain from lifting each other's flocks when they should again meet in the pastures at the foot of the hills. The inhabitants of the Sinjar are too powerful and independent to pay *kowee**, or black mail, to the Shammar, who, indeed, stand in much awe of their Yezidi enemies. They frequently raise their annual revenues, and enrich themselves almost entirely at the expense of the Arabs. They watch their opportunity, when the tribes are migrating in the spring and autumn, and falling by night on their encampments, plunder their tents and drive off their cattle. Returning to the hills, they can defy in their fastnesses the revenge of the Bedouins.

The Yezidis returned to their encampment late at night, but about a hundred of their horsemen were again with me before the tents were struck in the morning. They promised to fulfil the engagements entered into on the previous evening, and accompanied me for some miles on our day's journey. Cawal Yusuf returned with them on his way back to Mosul.

After leaving Om-el-Dhiban we entered an undulating country crossed by deep ravines, worn by the winter torrents. Veins of Mosul marble, the alabaster used by the Assyrian sculptors, occasionally appeared above the soil, interrupting the carpet of flowers spread over the face of the country. We drew near to the low hills into which the Sinjar subsides to the west. They are called Jeraiba, are well wooded with the ilex and dwarf oak, and abound in springs, near which the Shammar Bedouins encamp during the summer. Skirting them we found a beaten path, the first we had seen since entering the desert, leading to the

---

* Literally, 'strength-money;' the small tribes, who wander in the desert, and who inhabit the villages upon its edge, are obliged to place themselves under the protection of some powerful tribe to avoid being utterly destroyed. Each great division of the Shammar receives a present of money, sheep, camels, corn, or barley, from some tribe or another for this protection, which is always respected by the other branches of the tribe. Should another branch of the Shammar plunder, or injure, tribes thus paying kowee, their protectors are bound to make good, or revenge, their losses.

Jebour encampments on the Khabour, and we followed it for the rest of the day. It seemed irksome after wandering, as we had listed, over the boundless untrodden plain, to be again confined to the narrow track of the footsteps of man. However, the Bedouins declared that this pathway led to the best water, and we had committed ourselves to their guidance. Four hours' ride brought us to a scanty spring; half an hour beyond we passed a second; and in five and a half hours pitched the tents, for the rest of the day, near a small stream. All these springs are called Maalaga, and, rising in the gypsum or Mosul marble, have a brackish and disagreeable taste. The Bedouins declare that, although unpalatable, they are exceedingly wholesome, and that even their mares fatten on the waters of Jeraiba.

Near our tents were the ruins of an ancient village surrounded by a wall. The spring once issued from the midst of them, but its source had been choked by rubbish, which, as some hours of daylight still remained, Hormuzd employed the Jebours and Nestorians in removing. Before sunset the supply and quality of the water had much improved. Suttum, who could not remain idle, wandered over the plain on his deloul with his hawk in search of game, and returned in the evening with a bag of bustards. He came to me before nightfall, somewhat downcast in look, as if a heavy weight were on his mind. At length, after various circumlocutions, he said that his wife would not sleep under the white tent which I had lent her, such luxuries being, she declared, only worthy of city ladies, and altogether unbecoming the wife and daughter of a Bedouin. 'So determined is she,' said Suttum, 'in the matter, that, Billah! she deserted my bed last night and slept on the grass in the open air; and now she swears she will leave me and return on foot to her kindred, unless I save her from the indignity of sleeping under a white tent.' It was inconvenient to humour the fancies of the Arab lady, but as she was inexorable, I gave her a black Arab tent, used by the servants for a kitchen. Under this sheet of goat-hair canvass, open on all sides to the air, she said she could breathe freely, and feel again that she was a Bedouin.

As the sun went down we could distinguish, in the extreme distance, a black line marking the wooded banks of the Khabour, beyond which rose the dark hills of Abd-ul-Azeez. Columns of thin curling smoke showed that there were encampments of Bedouins between us and the river, but we could neither see their tents nor their cattle. The plains to the south of our encampment were bounded by a range of low hills, called Rhoua and Haweeza.

We crossed, during the following day, a beautiful plain covered with sweet smelling flowers and aromatic herbs, and abounding in gazelles, hares, and bustards. We reached in about two hours the encampments, whose smoke we had seen during the preceding evening. They belonged to Bedouins of the Hamoud branch of the Shammar. The tents were pitched closely together in groups, as if the owners feared danger. We alighted at some distance from them to avoid entering them as guests. The chiefs soon came out to us, bringing camels' milk and bread. From them we learnt that they had lately plundered, on the high road between Mosul and Mardin, a caravan conveying, amongst other valuable loads, a large amount of government treasure. The Turkish authorities had called upon Ferhan, as responsible chief of the Shammar, to restore the money, threatening, in case of refusal, an expedition against the whole tribe. The Hamoud, unwilling to part with their booty, and fearing lest the rest of the Shammar might compel them to do so in order to avoid a war, were now retreating towards the north, and, being strong in horsemen, had openly defied Ferhan. They had been joined by many families from the Assaiyah, who had crossed the Euphrates, and united with the Aneyza on account of a blood feud with the Nejm. The Hamoud are notorious for treachery and cruelty, and certainly the looks of those who gathered round us, many of them grotesquely attired in the plundered garments of the slaughtered Turkish soldiery, did not belie their reputation. They fingered every article of dress we had on, to learn its texture and value.

Leaving their encampments, we rode through vast herds of camels and flocks of sheep belonging to the tribe, and at length came in sight of the river. The Khabour flows through the richest pastures and meadows. Its banks were now covered with flowers of every hue, and its windings through the green plain were like the coils of a mighty serpent. I never beheld a more lovely scene. An uncontrollable emotion of joy seized all our party when they saw the end of their journey before them. The horsemen urged their horses to full speed; the Jebours dancing in a circle, raised their coloured kerchiefs on their spears, and shouted their war cry, Hormuzd leading the chorus; the Nestorians sang their mountain songs and fired their muskets in the air. Trees in full leaf lined the water's edge. From amongst them issued a body of mounted Arabs. As they drew nigh we recognised at their head Mohammed Emin, the Jebour Sheikh, and his sons, who had come out from their tents to welcome us. We dismounted to embrace, and to exchange the usual salutations, and then rode onwards, through a mass of flowers, reaching high above the horses' knees, and such as I had never before seen, even in the most fertile parts of the Mesopotamian wilderness.

The tents of the chief were pitched under the ruins of Arban, and on the right or northern bank of the river, which was not at this time fordable. As we drew near to them, after a ride of nearly two hours, Mohammed Emin pointed in triumph to the sculptures, which were the principal object of my visit. They stood a little above the water's edge, at the base of a mound of considerable size. We had passed several *tels* and the banks of ancient canals, showing that we were still amidst the remains of former civilisation. Flocks of sheep and herds of camels were spread over the meadows on both sides of the river. They belonged to the Jebours, and to a part of the Boraij tribe under Moghamis, a distinguished Arab warrior, and the uncle of Suttum. Buffaloes and cattle tended by the Sherabbeen and Buggara, small clans pasturing under the protection of Mohammed Emin, stood lazily in the long grass, or sought refuge in the stream from the flies and noonday heat.

At length we stopped opposite to the encampment of the Jebour Sheikh, but it was too late to cross the river, some time being required to make ready the rafts. We raised our tents, therefore, for the night on the southern bank. They were soon filled by a motley group of Boraij, Hamoud, Assaiyah, and Jebour Arabs. Moghamis himself came shortly after our arrival, bringing me as a present a well-trained hawk and some bustards, the fruits of his morning's sport. The falcon was duly placed on his stand in the centre of the spacious tent, and remained during the rest of my sojourn in the East a member of my establishment. A Sheikh of the Hamoud also brought me a wild-ass colt, scarcely two months old, which had been caught whilst following its dam, and had been since fed upon camel's milk.* Indeed, nearly all those who came to my tent had some offering, either sheep, milk, curds, or butter; even the Arab boys had caught for us the graceful jerboa, which burrows in vast numbers on the banks of the river. Suitable presents were made in return. Dinner was cooked for all our guests, and we celebrated our first night on the Khabour by general festivities.

A trained Falcon.

* The Arabs of Mesopotamia frequently capture this beautiful animal when young, and generally kill it at once for food. It is almost impossible to take it when full grown. The colt mentioned in the text died before we returned to Mosul. A second, after living eight or nine months, also died; and a third met with the same fate. I was desirous of sending a live specimen to England, but failed in all my attempts to rear one. They became very playful and docile. That which I had at Mosul followed like a dog.

CHAPTER V.

Encampment on the Khabour—Sheikh Suttum—Mohammed Emin—Discovery of winged bulls—of Assyrian relics—of lions—of human figures—of various objects of antiquity—The Chabor of the Captivity—Our tents—Bread of the Arabs—Their food—Their knowledge of medicine—The Deloul, or Dromedary—Adla—A storm—Animals on the Khabour—Visit to Meghamis.

On the morning after our arrival in front of the encampment of Sheikh Mohammed Emin we crossed the Khabour on a small raft, and pitched our tents on its right, or northern bank. I found the ruins to consist of a large artificial mound of irregular shape, washed, and indeed partly carried away by the river, which was gradually undermining the perpendicular cliff left by the falling earth. The Jebours were encamped to the west of it. I chose for our tents a recess, like an amphitheatre, facing the stream. We were thus surrounded and protected on all sides. Behind us and to the east rose the mound, and to the west were the family and dependents of Mohammed Emin. In the desert, beyond the ruins, were scattered far and wide the tents of the Jebours, and of several Arab tribes who had placed themselves under their protection. From the top of the mound the eye ranged over a level country bright with flowers, and spotted with black tents, and innumerable flocks of sheep and camels. During our stay at Arban the colour of these great plains was undergoing a continual change. After being for some days of a golden yellow, a new family of flowers would spring up, and it would turn almost in a night to a bright scarlet, which would again as suddenly give way to the deepest blue. Then the meadows would be mottled with various hues, or would put on the emerald green of the most luxuriant of pastures. The glowing descriptions I had so frequently received from the Bedouins of the beauty and fertility of the banks of the Khabour were more than realised. The Arabs boast that its meadows bear three crops of grass during the year, and the wandering tribes look upon its wooded banks and constant greensward as a paradise during the summer months, where man can enjoy a cool shade, and beast can find fresh and tender herbs, whilst all around is yellow, parched, and sapless.

In the extreme distance, to the east of us, rose a solitary

Artificial Mounds on the Khabour.

conical elevation, called by the Arabs, Koukab. In front, to the south, was the beautiful hill of the Sinjar, ever varying in colour and in outline as the declining sun left fresh shadows on its furrowed sides. Behind us, and not far distant, was the low, wooded range of Abd-ul-Azeez. Artificial mounds, smaller in size than Arban, rose here and there above the thin belt of trees and shrubs skirting the river bank.

I had brought with me a tent large enough to hold full

two hundred persons, and intended as a 'museef,' or place of reception, always open to the wayfarer and the Arab visitor; for the first duty of a traveller wishing to mix with true Bedouins, and to gain an influence over them, is the exercise of hospitality. This great pavilion was pitched in the centre of my encampment, with its entrance facing the river. To the right were the tents of the Cawass and servants; one fitted up expressly for the Doctor to receive patients, of whom there was no lack at all times, and the black Arab tent of Rathaiyah, who would not mix with the Jebours. To the left were those of my fellow travellers, and about 200 yards beyond, near the excavations, my own private tent, to which I retired during the day, when wishing to be undisturbed, and to which the Arabs were not admitted. In it, also, we usually breakfasted and dined, except when there were any Arab guests of distinction with whom it was necessary to eat bread. In front of our encampment, and between it and the river, was a small lawn, on which were picketed our horses. Suttum and Mohammed Emin usually eat with us, and soon became perfectly reconciled to knives and forks, and the other restraints of civilised life. Suttum's tact and intelligence were indeed remarkable. Nothing escaped his hawk-like eye. A few hours had enabled him to form a correct estimate of the character of each one of the party, and he had detected peculiarities which might have escaped the notice of the most observant European. The most polished Turk would have been scarcely less at home in the society of ladies, and during the whole of our journey he never committed a breach of good manners. As a companion he was delightful,—full of anecdote, of unclouded spirits, acquainted with the history of every Bedouin tribe, their politics and their wars, and intimate with every part of the desert, its productions and its inhabitants. Many happy hours I spent with him, seated, after the sun went down, on a mound overlooking the great plain and the winding river, listening to the rich flow of his graceful Bedouin dialect, to his eloquent stories of Arab life, and to his animated descriptions of forays, wars, and single combats.

Mohammed Emin, the Sheikh of the Jebours, was a good

natured portly Arab, in intelligence greatly inferior to Suttum, and wanting many of the qualities of the pure Bedouin. During our intercourse I had every reason to be satisfied with his hospitality and the cordial aid he afforded me. His chief fault was a habit of begging for everything. Always

willing to give he was equally ready to receive. In this respect, however, all Arabs are alike; and, when the habit is understood, it is no longer a source of inconvenience, as on a refusal no offence is taken. The Jebour chief was a complete patriarch in his tribe, having no less than sixteen children, of whom six sons were horsemen and the owners of mares. The youngest, a boy of four years old, named Sultan, was his favourite. His usual costume consisted simply of a red Turkish skull cap, or fez. He scarcely ever left his father, who always brought the child with him when he came to our tent. He was as handsome and dirty as the best of Arab children. His mother, who had recently died, was the beautiful sister of Abd'rubbou. I chanced to be her brother's guest when the news of her death was brought to him. An Arab of the tribe, weary and wayworn, entered the tent and seated himself without giving the usual salutation; all present knew that he had come from the Khabour and from distant friends. His silence argued evil tidings. By an indirect remark, immediately understood, he told his errand to one who sat next him, and who in turn whispered it to Sheikh Ibrahim, the chief's uncle. The old man said aloud, with a sigh, 'It is the will and mercy of God; she is not dead but released!' Abd'rubbou at once understood of whom he spake. He arose and went forth, and the wailing of the mother and of the women soon issued from the inner recesses of the tent.

We were for a day or two objects of curiosity to the Arabs who assembled in crowds around our tents. Having never before seen an European, it was natural that they should hasten to examine the strangers. They soon, however, became used to us, and things went on as usual. It is a circumstance well worthy of mention, and most strongly in favour of the natural integrity of the Arab when his guests are concerned, that during the whole of our journey and our residence on the Khabour, although we lived in open tents, and property of all kinds was scattered about, we had not to complain of a single loss from theft.

My first care, after crossing to Arban, was to examine the sculptures described by the Arabs. The river having gradually worn away the mound had, during the recent floods, left uncovered a pair of winged human-headed bulls, some six feet above the water's edge, and full fifty beneath the level of the ruin. Only the forepart of these figures had been exposed to view, and Mohammed Emin would not allow any of the soil to be removed before my arrival. The earth was soon cleared away, and I found them to be of a coarse limestone, not exceeding 5½ feet in height by 4½ in length. Between them was a pavement slab of the same material. They resembled in general form the well-known

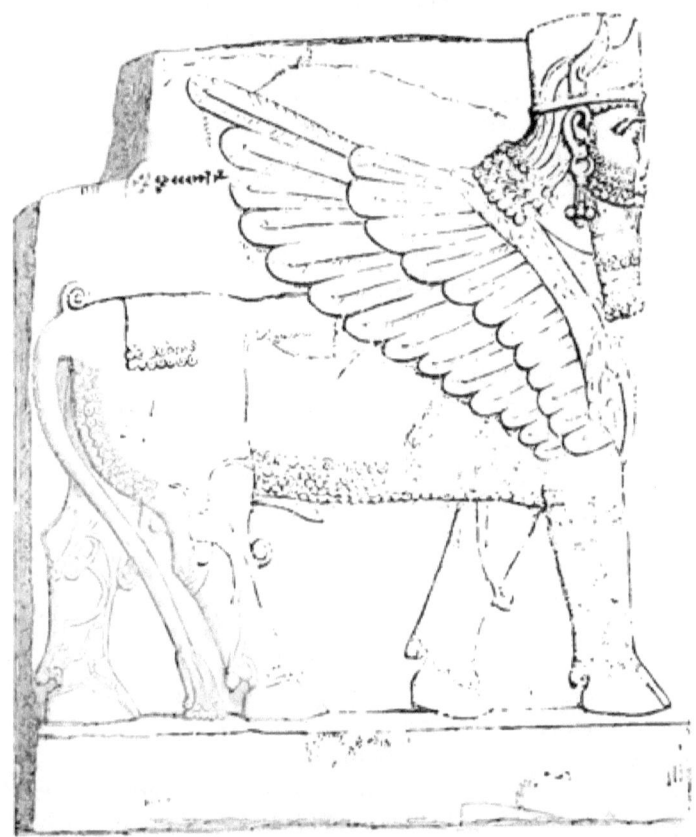

Winged Bull discovered at Arban.

winged bulls of Nineveh, but in the style of art they differed considerably from them. The outline and treatment was bold and angular, with an archaic feeling conveying the impression of great antiquity. The human features were unfortunately much injured, but such parts as remained were sufficient to show that the countenance had a peculiar character, differing from the usual Assyrian type. The sockets of the eyes were deeply sunk, probably to receive the white and the ball of the eye in ivory or glass. The nose was flat and large, and the lips thick like those of a negro. Human ears were attached to the head, and bull's ears to the horned cap, which was low and square at the top. The wings were small, and had not the majestic spread of those of the bulls that adorned the palaces of Nineveh. Upon the slab was a short inscription in Assyrian cuneiform characters.*

The great accumulation of earth above these sculptures proves that, since the destruction of the edifice in which they stood, other habitations had been raised upon its ruins. Arban, indeed, is mentioned by the Arab geographers as a flourishing city, in a singularly fertile district of the Khabour. Part of a minaret, whose walls were cased with coloured tiles, and ornamented with cufic inscriptions in relief, like that of the Sinjar, and the foundations of buildings, are still seen on the mound; and at its foot, on the western side, are the remains of a bridge which once spanned the stream. But the river has changed its course. The piers, adorned with elegantly shaped arabesque characters, are now on the dry land.

Tunnels were opened behind the bulls, and in various parts of the ruins on the same level. Trenches were also dug into the surface of the mound. Behind the bulls were found various Assyrian relics; amongst them a copper bell, like those from Nimroud, and fragments of bricks with arrow-headed characters painted yellow with white outlines. upon a pale green ground. In other parts of the mound were discovered glass and pottery, some Assyrian. others of a more doubtful character. Several fragments of earthenware, ornamented with flowers and scroll-work, and highly

* This inscription contains a name which Sir Henry Rawlinson reads, 'Mushis-Bar,' and believes to be that of a sacerdotal tributary of Assyria, belonging to a family which founded the city of Sidikan, of which Arban marks the site. The name of this personage, with those of his father and grandfather, has been found on a cylinder from Sheriff Khan, now in the British Museum. The grandfather paid tribute to Sardanapalus, the Nimroud king. The date of the monuments at Arban would be about 820 B.C. according to Sir H. Rawlinson.

glazed, had assumed the brilliant and varied iridescence of ancient glass.*

It was natural to conclude, from the usual architectural arrangement of Assyrian edifices, that the two bulls described stood at an entrance to a hall or chamber. We searched in

Lion discovered at Arban.

vain for the remains of walls, although digging for three days to the right and left of the sculptures, a work of considerable difficulty in consequence of the immense heap of superincumbent earth. I then directed a tunnel to be carried towards the centre of the mound, hoping to find a corresponding doorway opposite. I was not disappointed. On

* These relics are now in the British Museum.

the fifth day a similar pair of winged bulls were discovered. They were of the same size, and inscribed with the same characters. A part of one having been originally broken off, either in carving the sculpture or in moving it, a fresh piece of stone had been carefully fitted into its place. I also dug to the right and left of these sculptures for remains of walls, but without success, and then resumed the tunnelling towards the centre of the mound. In a few days a lion, with extended jaws, sculptured in the same coarse limestone, and in the same bold archaic style as the bulls, was discovered. It had five legs, and the tail had the claw at the end, as in the Nineveh bas-reliefs. In height it was nearly the same as the bulls. I searched in vain for the one which must have formed the opposite side of the doorway.

Bas-relief discovered at Arban.

With the exception of these sculptures, no remains of building were found in this part of the mound. In another tunnel, opened at some distance from the bulls, half of a human figure in relief was discovered.* The face was in full. One hand grasped a sword or dagger; the other held some object to the breast. The hair and beard were long and flowing, and ornamented with a profusion of curls as in the Assyrian bas-reliefs. The head-dress appeared to consist of a kind of circular helmet, ending in a sharp point. The treatment and style marked the sculpture to be of the same period as the bull and lion.

Such were the sculptures discovered in the mound of Arban.

* The height of this fragment was 5 ft. 8 in.

Amongst smaller objects of different periods were some of considerable interest, jars, vases, funeral urns, highly-glazed pottery, fragments of glass, a large copper ring, apparently Assyrian; an ornament in earthenware, resembling the pine-cone of the Assyrian sculptures; a bull's head in terracotta; fragments of painted bricks, probably of the same period; a small bottle with Chinese characters, of doubtful date; and several Egyptian scarabæi. It is singular that engraved stones and scarabs bearing Egyptian devices, and in some instances even royal cartouches, should have been found on the banks of the Khabour. Similar objects were subsequently dug up at Nimroud, and were brought to me by the Arabs from various ruins in Assyria.* They are mostly of the time of the 18th Egyptian dynasty, or of the 15th century before Christ; a period when, as we learn from Egyptian monuments, there was a close connection between Assyria and Egypt.

Several tombs were also found in the ruins, consisting principally of sarcophagi of earthenware, like those existing above the Assyrian palaces near Mosul. Some, however, were formed by two large earthen jars, like the common Eastern vessel for holding oil, laid horizontally, and joined mouth to mouth. These terracotta coffins appear to be of the same period as those found in all the great ruins on the banks of the rivers of Mesopotamia, and are not Assyrian. They contained human remains turned to dust, with the exception of the skull and a few of the larger bones, and generally three or four urns of highly glazed blue pottery.†

Fewer remains and objects of antiquity were discovered in the mounds on the Khabour than I had anticipated. They were sufficient, however, to prove that the ruins are of the same character as those on the banks of the Tigris. A deep interest, at the same time, attaches to the site they occupy. To the Chebar, or Khabour, were transported by the Assyrian king, after the destruction of Samaria, the captive children of Israel, and on its banks 'the heavens were

---

* A description of the most important of the Egyptian scarabs discovered at Arban will be found in the larger edition of this work, p. 281.

† Most of the small objects described in the text are now in the British Museum.

opened' to Ezekiel, and 'he saw visions of God,' and spake his prophecies to his brother exiles.* Around Arban may have been pitched the tents of the sorrowing Jews, as those of the Arabs were during my visit. To the same pastures they led their sheep, and they drank of the same waters. Then the banks of the river were covered with towns and villages, and a palace-temple still stood on the mound, reflected in the transparent stream. We have, however, but one name connected with the Khabour recorded in Scripture, that of Tel-Abib, 'the mound of Abib, or, of the heaps of ears of corn.'† but whether it applies to a town, or to one of those artificial mounds, such as still abound, and are still called 'tels,' is a matter of doubt. I sought in vain for some trace of the word amongst the names now given by the wandering Arab to the various ruins on the Khabour and its confluents.

We know that Jews still lingered in the cities of the Khabour until long after the Arab invasion; and we may perhaps recognise in the Jewish communities of Ras-al-Ain, at the sources of the river, and of Carkeseea, or Carchemish, at its confluence with the Euphrates, visited and described by Benjamin of Tudela in the latter end of the twelfth century of the Christian æra, the descendants of the captive Israelites.

But the hand of time has long since swept even this remnant away, with the busy crowds which once thronged the banks of the river. From its mouth to its source, from Carchemish to Ras-al-Ain, there is now no single permanent human habitation on the Khabour.‡ Its rich meadows and

---

* 2 Kings, xvii. 6, Ezek. i. 1. In the Hebrew text the name of this river is spelt in two different ways. In Kings we have Khabour, answering exactly to the Chaboras of the Greeks and Romans, and the Khabour of the Arabs. In Ezekiel it is written Kebar. There is no reason, however, to doubt that the same river is meant.

† Ezekiel, iii. 15. 'Then I came to them of the captivity at *Tel-Abib*, that dwelt by the river of Chebar.' To the west of Arban and on the Khabour there are many artificial mounds. The principal which I visited were Tel Hamer, Shedadi, Ledjmiyat, Fedghami, and Shemshani. Remains of the early Arab occupation, such as ruined castles, bridges, &c., are also frequent.

‡ Since my visit to the Khabour, the Turkish Government has placed a colony of Circassians at Ras-al-Ain, and has built a small town there.

its deserted ruins are alike become the encamping places of the wandering Arab.

During the time we dwelt at Arban, we were the guests and under the protection of Mohammed Emin, the Sheikh of the Jebours. On the day we crossed the river, he celebrated our arrival by a feast after the Arab fashion, to which the notables of the tribe were invited. Sheep, as usual, were boiled and served up piecemeal in large wooden bowls, with a mass of butter and bread soaked in the gravy. The chief's tent was spacious, though poorly furnished. It was the general resort of those who chanced to wander, either on business or for pleasure to the Khabour, and was, consequently, never without a goodly array of guests; from a company of Shammar horsemen out on a foray to the solitary Bedouin who was seeking to become a warrior in his tribe, by first stealing a mare from some hostile encampment.

My own large tent was no less a place of resort than that of Mohammed Emin, and as we were objects of curiosity, Bedouins from all parts flocked to see us. With some of them I was already acquainted, having either received them as my guests at Mosul, or met them during excursions in the desert. They generally passed one night with us, and then returned to their own tents. A sheep was always slain for them, and boiled with rice, or prepared wheat, in the Arab way: if there were not strangers enough to consume the whole, the rest was given to the workmen or to the needy, as it is considered derogatory to the character of a truly hospitable man to keep meat until the following day, or to serve it up a second time when cold. Even the poorest Bedouin who kills a sheep, invites all his friends and neighbours to the repast, and if there be still any remnants, distributes them amongst the poor and the hungry, although he should himself want on the morrow.

We had brought a supply of flour with us, and the Jebours had a little wheat raised on the banks of the river. The wandering Arabs have no other means of grinding their corn than by handmills, which they carry with them wherever they go. They are always worked by the women, for it is considered unworthy of a man to engage in any domestic occupation.

These handmills are simply two circular flat stones, generally about eighteen inches in diameter, the upper turning loosely upon a wooden pivot, and moved quickly round by a wooden handle. The grain is passed through the hole of the pivot, and the flour is collected in a cloth spread under the mill. It is then mixed with water, kneaded in a wooden bowl, and pressed by the hand into round balls ready for baking. During these processes, the women are usually seated on the bare ground: hence, in Isaiah,* is the daughter

Arab Women grinding Corn with a Hand-mill, rolling out the Dough, and baking the Bread

of Babylon told to sit in the dust and on the ground, and 'to take the millstones to grind meal.'

The tribes, who are always moving from place to place, bake their bread on a slightly convex iron plate, called a *sadj*, moderately heated over a low fire of brushwood or camels' dung. The lumps of dough are rolled, on a wooden platter, into thin cakes, a foot or more in diameter, and laid by means of the roller upon the iron. They are baked in a

* Chap. xlvii. 1, 2.

very short time, and should be eaten hot.* The Kurds, whose flour is far whiter and more carefully prepared than that of the Arabs, roll the dough into larger cakes, scarcely thicker than a sheet of paper. When carefully baked by the same process, it becomes crisp, and is exceedingly agreeable to the taste. The Arab tribes that remain for many days in one place, make rude ovens by digging a hole in the ground about three feet deep, shaping it like a reversed funnel, and plastering it with mud. They heat it by burning brushwood within, and then stick the lumps of dough, pressed into small cakes about half an inch thick, to the sides with the hand. The bread is ready in two or three minutes. When horsemen go on an expedition, they either carry with them the thin bread first described, or a bag of flour, which, when they come to water, they moisten and knead on their cloaks, and then bake by covering the balls of dough with hot ashes. All Arab bread is unleavened.

If a Bedouin tribe be moving in great haste before an enemy, the women sometimes prepare bread whilst riding on camels. The fire is then lighted in an earthen vessel. One woman kneads the flour, a second rolls out the dough, and a third bakes, boys or women on foot passing the materials, as required, from one to the other.

The fuel used by the Arabs consists chiefly of dwarf shrubs, growing in the desert, of dry grass, and of camels' dung. They frequently carry bags of the latter with them when in summer they march over very arid tracts. On the banks of the great rivers of Mesopotamia, the tamarisk and other trees furnish them with abundant firewood. They are entirely dependent for their supplies of wheat upon the villages on the borders of the desert, or on the sedentary Arabs, who, whilst living in tents, cultivate the soil. Sometimes a tribe is fortunate enough to plunder a caravan laden with corn, or to

---

* Such was probably the process of making bread mentioned in 2 Sam. xiii. 8, 9. 'So Tamar went to her brother Amnon's house; and he was laid down. And she took flour and kneaded it, and made cakes *in his sight*, and did bake the cakes. And she took a pan and poured them out before him.' It will be observed that the bread was made at once, without leaven; such also was probably the bread that Abraham commanded Sarah to make for the three angels. (Gen. xviii. **6**.)

K

sack the granaries of a village: they have then enough to satisfy their wants for some months. But the Bedouins usually draw near to the towns and cultivated districts soon after the harvest, to lay in their stock of grain. A party of men and women, chosen by their companions, then take with them money, or objects for sale or exchange, and drive the camels to the villages, where they load them and then return to their tents. Latterly a new and extensive trade has been opened with the Bedouins for sheep's wool, much prized for its superior quality in European markets. As the time for shearing is soon after the harvest, the Arabs have ready means of obtaining their supplies, as well as of making a little money, and buying finery and arms.

Nearly the whole revenue of an Arab Sheikh, whatever it may be, is laid out in corn, rice, and other provisions. The quantity of food consumed in the tents of some of the great chiefs of the Bedouins is very considerable. Almost every traveller who passes the encampment eats bread with the Sheikh, and there are generally many guests dwelling under his canvass. In times of difficulty or scarcity, moreover, the whole tribe frequently expects to be fed by him; and he considers himself bound, even under such circumstances, by the duties of hospitality, to give all that he has to the needy. The extraordinary generosity displayed on such occasions by their chiefs forms some of the most favourite stories of the Arabs.

The common Bedouin can rarely get meat. His food consists almost exclusively of wheaten bread with truffles, which are found in great abundance during the spring, a few wild herbs, such as asparagus, onions, and garlic, fresh butter, curds, and sour milk. But, at certain seasons, even these luxuries cannot be obtained; for months together he often eats bread alone. The Sheikhs usually slay a sheep every day, of which their guests, a few of their relatives, and their immediate adherents partake. The women prepare the food, and always eat after the men, who rarely leave them much wherewithal to satisfy their hunger.

The dish usually placed before a guest in the tent of a Bedouin chief is a mess of boiled meat, sometimes mixed with onions, upon which a lump of fresh butter is placed and allowed to melt. The broad tail of the Mesopotamian sheep is used for grease when there is no butter. Sometimes cakes of bread are laid under the meat, and the entertainer tearing up the thin loaves into small pieces, soaks them in the gravy with his hands. The Aneyza make very savoury dishes of chopped meat and bread mixed with sour curds, over which, when the huge platter is placed before the guest, is poured a flood of melted butter. Roasted meat is very rarely seen in a Bedouin tent. Rice is only eaten by the Sheikhs, except amongst the tribes who encamp in the marshes of Southern Mesopotamia, where rice of an inferior quality is very largely cultivated. There it is boiled with meat and made into pillaus.

The Bedouins do not make cheese. The milk of their sheep and goats is shaken into butter or turned into curds: it is rarely drank fresh, new milk being thought very unwholesome, as by experience I soon found it to be, in the desert. I have frequently had occasion to describe the process of making butter by shaking the milk in skins. This is also an employment confined to the women, and one of a very laborious nature. The curds, or 'leben,' are formed by boiling the milk, and then putting some of the curds made on the previous day into it, and allowing it to stand. When the sheep no longer give milk, some curds are dried, to be kept for leaven. Leben is thick and acid, but very agreeable and grateful to the taste in a hot climate. The sour milk, or sheneena, an universal beverage amongst the Arabs, is either butter-milk pure and diluted, or curds mixed with water. Camel's milk is drank fresh. It is pleasant to the taste, rich, and exceedingly nourishing. It is given in large quantities to the horses. The Shammar and Aneyza Bedouins have no cows nor oxen, those animals being looked upon as the peculiar property of tribes who have forgotten their independence, and degraded themselves by the cultivation of land. The sheep are milked at dawn, or even before daybreak, and again in the evening on their return from the pastures. The milk is immediately turned into leben, or boiled to be shaken into butter. Amongst the

Bedouins and Jebours it is considered derogatory to the character of a man to milk a cow or a sheep, but not to milk a camel. The Sheikhs occasionally obtain dates from the cities. They are either eaten dry with bread and leben, or fried in butter, a very favourite dish of the Bedouin.

To this spare and simple diet the Bedouins owe their freedom from sickness, and their extraordinary power of bearing fatigue. Diseases are rare amongst them; and the epidemics, which rage in the cities, seldom reach their tents. The cholera, which visited Mosul and Baghdad with fearful severity, has not yet struck the Bedouins, and they have frequently escaped the plague, when the settlements on the borders of the desert have been nearly depopulated by it. The small pox, however, occasionally makes great havoc amongst them, vaccination being still unknown to the Shammar, and intermittent fever prevails in the autumn, particularly when the tribes encamp near the marshes in Southern Mesopotamia. Rheumatism is not uncommon, and is treated, like most local complaints, with the actual cautery, a red hot iron being applied very freely to the part affected. Another cure for rheumatism consists in killing a sheep and placing the patient in the hot reeking skin, Ophthalmia is common in the desert as well as in all other parts of the East, and may be attributed as much to dirt and neglect as to any other cause.

The Bedouins are acquainted with few medicines. The desert yields some valuable simples, which are, however, rarely used. Dr. Sandwith hearing from Suttum that the Arabs had no opiates, asked what they did with one who could not sleep. "Do!" answered the Sheikh, "why, we make use of him, and set him to watch the camels." If a Bedouin be ill, or have received a wound, he sometimes comes to the nearest town to consult the barbers, who are frequently not unskilful surgeons. Hadjir, one of the great chiefs of the Shammar, having been struck by a musket ball which lodged beneath the shoulder-blade, visited the Pasha of Mosul to obtain the aid of the European surgeons attached to the Turkish troops. They declared an operation to be impossible, and refused to undertake it. The Sheikh applied to a barber, who in his shop, in the open bazaar, quietly cut down to the ball, and taking it out brought it to the Pasha in a plate, to claim a reward for his skill. It is true that the European surgeons in the service of the Porte are not very eminent in their profession. The Bedouins set broken limbs by means of rude splints.

The women suffer little in labour, which often takes place during a march, or when they are far from the encampment watering the flocks or collecting fuel. They allow their children to remain at the breast until they are nearly two and even three years old, and, consequently, have rarely many offspring.

Soon after our arrival at the Khabour I bought a deloul, or dromedary, as more convenient than a horse for making excursions in the desert. Her name was Sahaima, and she belonged to Moghamis, the uncle of Suttum, having been

Saddling a Deloul, or Dromedary.

taken by him from the Aneyza; she was well trained, and swift and easy in her paces. The best delouls come from Nedjd and the Gebel Shammar. They are small and lightly made, the difference between them and a common camel being as great as that between a high bred Arab mare and an English cart-horse. Their powers of endurance are very great.* The deloul is much prized, and the race is carefully preserved. The Arabs breed from them once in two years, and are very particular in the choice of the male. An ordinary animal can work for twenty years. Suttum assured me that they could travel in the spring as many as six days without water. Their colour is generally light brown and white, darker colours and black are more uncommon. Their pace is a light trot kept up for many hours together without fatigue; they can increase it to an unwieldy gallop, a speed they cannot long maintain. A good deloul is worth at the most 10*l*., the common price is about 5*l*.

The grass around Arban having been eaten by the flocks, the Jebours struck their tents at dawn on the 4th of April, and wandered down the Khabour in search of fresh pastures. The Boraij, too, moved further inland from the river. During the whole morning the desert around the ruins was a busy scene; sheep, camels, cattle, beasts of burden, men, women, and children being scattered far and wide over the plain. By midday the crowd had disappeared, and the meadows, which a few hours before had been teeming with living things, were now again left lonely and bare. I know no feeling more melancholy than that caused by the sudden breaking up of a large tribe, and by the sight of the spent fires and rubbish-heaps of a recent encampment; the silence and solitude which have suddenly succeeded to the busy scene of an Arab community. Mohammed Emin alone, with a few Sherabeen Arabs, remained to protect us.

Soon after our arrival at the Khabour, Adla, Suttum's first wife, came to us with her child. After the Sheikh's marriage

---

* Burckhardt ('Notes on the Bedouins,' &c. p. 262.) mentions as the best authenticated instance of the wonderful speed and endurance of a deloul which had come to his knowledge, a journey for a wager, of 115 miles in eleven hours, including twenty minutes in crossing the Nile twice in a ferry-boat. As that traveller, however, justly remarks, it is by the ease with which they can carry their rider during an uninterrupted journey of several days and nights at a kind of easy amble of five, or five and a half miles, an hour, that they are unequalled by any other animal.

with Rathaiyah, she had been driven from her husband's tent by the imperious temper of his new bride, and had returned to Moghamis her father. Her eldest sister was the wife of Suttum's eldest brother, Sahiman, and her youngest, Maizi, was betrothed to Suttum's youngest brother, Mijwell. The three were remarkable for their beauty; their dark eyes had the true Bedouin fire, and their long black hair fell in clusters on their shoulders. Their cousins, the three brothers, had claimed them as their brides according to Bedouin law.* Adla now sought to be reconciled through me to her husband. Rathaiyah, the new wife, whose beauty was already on the wane, dreaded her young rival's share in the affections of her lord, over whom she had established more influence than a lady might be supposed to exercise over her spouse amongst independent Arabs. The Sheikh was afraid to meet Adla, until, after much negotiation, Hormuzd acting as ambassador, the proud Rathaiyah consented to receive her in her tent. Then the injured lady refused to accept these terms, and the matter was only finished by Hormuzd taking her by the arm and dragging her by force over the grass to her rival. There all the outward forms of perfect reconciliation were satisfactorily gone through, although Suttum evidently saw that there was a different reception in store for himself when there were no European eye-witnesses. Such are the trials of married life in the desert!

I may here mention that polygamy is very common amongt the Bedouins. It is considered disgraceful for a man to accept money for his daughter, according to the custom in towns and amongst the cultivating tribes; and a girl cannot be forced against her will to marry a man unless he be her cousin, and legally entitled to demand her hand.

On the 6th of April we witnessed a remarkable electrical phenomenon. During the day heavy clouds had been hanging on the horizon, foreboding one of those furious storms which at this time of the year occasionally visit the desert. Late in the afternoon these clouds had gathered into one vast circle, which moved slowly round like an enormous

---

* Amongst the Bedouins a man has a right to demand his cousin in marriage, and she cannot refuse him.

wheel, presenting one of the most extraordinary and awful appearances I ever saw. From its sides leaped, without ceasing, forked flames of lightning. Clouds springing up from all sides of the heavens, were dragged hurriedly into the vortex, which advanced gradually towards us, and threatened soon to break over our encampment. Fortunately, however, we only felt the very edge of the storm,—a deluge of rain and hail of the size of pigeon's eggs. The great rolling cloud, attracted by the Sinjar hill, soon passed away, leaving in undiminished splendour the setting sun.

On the 8th of April, the Mogdessi, one of my servants, caught a turtle in the river measuring three feet in length. The Arabs have many stories of the voracity of these animals, which attain, I am assured, to even a larger size, and Suttum declared that a man had been pulled under water and devoured by one, probably an Arab exaggeration.

A Bedouin, who had been attacked by a lion whilst resting, about five hours lower down on the banks of the river, came to our encampment. He had escaped with the loss of his mare. Lions are not uncommon in the jungles of the Khabour, and the Bedouins and Jebours frequently find their cubs in the spring season.

The waters of the river had been rising rapidly since the recent storm, and had now spread over the meadows. We moved our tents on the 11th April, and the Arabs took refuge on the mound, which stood like an island in the midst of the flood. The Jebours killed four beavers, and brought three of their young to us alive. They had been driven from their holes by the swollen stream. Mohammed Emin eagerly accepted the musk bags, which are much valued as *majouns* by the Turks, and, consequently, fetch a large price in the towns. The Arabs eat the flesh, and it was cooked for us, but proved coarse and tough. The young we kept for some days on milk, but they eventually died. Their cry resembled that of a newborn infant. The Khabour beavers appeared to me to differ in several respects from the American. The tail, instead of being large and broad, was short and pointed. They do not build huts, but burrow in the banks, taking care to make the entrance to their holes below the surface of the stream to avoid detection, and the chambers above, out of reach of ordinary floods.

Beavers were formerly found in large numbers on the Khabour, but in consequence of the value attached to the musk bag, they have been hunted almost to extermination by the Arabs.

On April 18th we visited the tents of Moghamis and his tribe; they were pitched about five miles from the river. The face of the desert was as burnished gold. Its last change was to flowers of the brightest yellow hue,[*] and the whole plain was dressed with them. Suttum rioted in the luxuriant herbage and scented air. I never saw him so exhilarated. 'What kef (delight) has God given us equal to this?' he continually exclaimed, as his mare waded through the flowers. 'It is the only thing worth living for. Ya Bej! what do the dwellers in cities know of true happiness, they have never seen grass nor flowers? May God have pity on them!'

The tents were scattered far and wide over the plain. The mares wandered loose in the midst of them, cropping the rich grass. We were most hospitably received by Moghamis, who wore a shirt of chain armour. Such luxuries, in the way of a ragged carpet and an old coverlet, as his tent could afford, had been spread for Mrs. R., whose reputation had extended far and wide amongst the Arabs, and who was looked upon as a wonder, but always treated with the greatest consideration and respect. The wild Bedouin would bring a present of camel's milk or truffles, and the boys caught jerboas and other small animals for the Frank lady. During the whole of our journey she was never exposed to annoyance, although wearing, with the exception of the red Turkish cap and an Arab cloak, the European dress.

After we had enjoyed all the luxuries of an Arab feast,

---

[*] I have already mentioned the changes in the colours of the desert. Almost in as many days white had succeeded to a pale straw colour, red to white, blue to red, lilac to blue, and now the face of the country was as described in the text.

visited the women's compartments, where most of the ladies of the tribe had assembled to greet us, examined the 'chetab,' or camel saddle, used by the wives of the chiefs, and inquired into various details of the harem, we returned as we came, through the flowers and long grass, to our tents at Arban.

CHAPTER VI.

Leave Arban—The banks of the Khabour—Artificial mounds—Mijwell—The cadi of the Bedouins—The 'thar,' or blood revenge—Caution of Arabs—A natural cavern—An extinct volcano—The confluents of the Khabour—Suleiman Agha—Encampment at Um-Jerjeh—Mohammed Emin leaves us—Visit to the Milli Kurds—Arab love-making—The Dakheel—Bedouin poets and poetry—Leave the Khabour—Arab sagacity—The Hol—Khatouniyah—Return of Suttum—Ferhan—Sinjar villages—Eski Mosul—Departure of Suttum.

THE hot weather was rapidly drawing near. The discoveries in the mound of Arban, and the ruins near the river, were not of sufficient importance to induce me to remain much longer on the Khabour. I wished, however, to explore the stream, as far as I was able, towards its principal source, and to visit Suleiman Agha, the Turkish commander, who was now encamped on its banks. He had urged me to bring Mohammed Emin with me, pledging himself to place no restraint whatever on the perfect liberty of the Arab chief. With such a guarantee, I ventured to invite the Sheikh to accompany me. After much hesitation, arising from a very natural fear of treachery, he consented to do so.

On the 19th of April we crossed the Khabour, and encamped for the night on its southern bank. On the following morning we commenced our journey to the eastward. Mohammed Emin was still in doubt as to whether he should go with me or not: but at last, after more than once turning back, he took a desperate resolution, and pushed his mare boldly forward. His children commended him, with tears, to my protection, and then left our caravan for their tents.

We rode from bend to bend of the river, without following its tortuous course. Its banks are belted with poplars, tamarisks, and brushwood, the retreat of wild boars, francolins, and other game, and studded with artificial mounds, the remains of ancient settlements. This deserted, though rich and fertile, district must, at one time, have been the seat of a dense population. It is only under such a government as that of Turkey that it could remain a wilderness.

After a short day's journey of four hours and a half we raised our tents for the night amongst luxuriant herbage, which afforded abundant pasture for our horses and camels. The spot was called Nahab. The river, divided into two branches by a string of small wooded islands, is fordable except during the freshes. Near our encampment was a large mound named Mehlaibiyah, and in the stream I observed fragments of stone masonry, probably the remains of ancient dams for irrigation.

Next morning Suttum returned to his tents with Rathaiyah, leaving us under the care of his younger brother, Mijwell. After I had visited the Turkish commander, whom he did not appear over anxious to meet, he was to join us in the desert, and accompany me to Mosul. Mijwell was even of a more amiable disposition than his brother; was less given to diplomacy, and troubled himself little with the politics of the tribes. A pleasant smile lighted up his features, and a fund of quaint and original humour made him at all times an agreeable companion. Although he could neither read nor write, he was one of the cadis or judges of the Shammar, an office hereditary in the family of the Saadi. Disputes of all kinds are referred to these recognised judges. Their decrees are obeyed with readiness, and the other members of the tribe are rarely called upon to enforce them. They administer rude justice; and, although pretending to follow the words of the Prophet, are rather guided by ancient custom than by the law of the Koran, which binds the rest of the Mohammedan world. The most common source of litigation is, of course, stolen property. They receive for their decrees, payment in money or in kind; and he who gains the suit has to pay the fee. Amongst the Shammar, if the dispute relates to a deloul, the cadi gets two gazees, about eight shillings; if to a mare, a deloul; if to a man, a mare.

Various ordeals, such as licking a red-hot iron, are in use, to prove a man's innocence. If the accused's tongue is burnt, no doubt exists as to his guilt.

One of the most remarkable laws in force amongst the wandering Arabs, and one probably of the highest antiquity, is the law of blood, called the Thar, prescribing the degrees of consanguinity within which it is lawful to revenge a murder or homicide. Although a law, rendering a man responsible for blood shed by any one related to him within the fifth degree, may appear to members of a civilised community one of extraordinary rigour, and involving manifest injustice, it must nevertheless be admitted, that no power vested in any one individual, and no punishment however severe, could tend more to the maintenance of order and the prevention of bloodshed amongst the wild tribes of the desert. As Burckhardt has justly remarked, 'this salutary institution has contributed in a greater degree than any other circumstance, to prevent the warlike tribes of Arabia from exterminating one another.'

If a man commit a murder or accidental homicide, the cadi endeavours to prevail upon the family of the victim to accept a compensation for the blood in money or in kind, the amount being regulated according to custom in different tribes. Should the offer of 'blood-money' be refused, the 'Thar' comes into operation, and any person within the 'khomse,' or the fifth degree of blood of the homicide, may be legally killed by any one within the same degree of consanguinity to the victim.

This law is enforced between tribes remote from each other, as well as between families, and to the blood revenge may be attributed many of the bitter feuds which exist amongst the Arab clans. It affects, in many respects, their social condition, and has a marked influence upon their habits, and even upon their manners. Thus an Arab will never tell his name, especially if it be an uncommon one, to a stranger, nor mention that of his father, or of his tribe, if his own name be ascertained, lest there should be Thar between them. Even children are taught to observe this custom, that they may not fall victims to the blood revenge.

Hence the suspicion with which a Bedouin regards a stranger, and his caution in disclosing anything relating to the movements, or dwelling-place, of his friends. In most encampments are found refugees, sometimes whole families, who have left their tribe on account of a homicide for which they are amenable. In case, after a murder, persons within the 'Thar' take to flight, three days and four hours are by immemorial custom allowed to the fugitives before they can be pursued. Frequently they never return to their friends, but remain with those who give them protection, and become incorporated into the tribe by which they are adopted. Frequently the homicide himself will wander from tent to tent over the desert, or even rove through the towns and villages on its borders, with a chain round his neck and in rags, begging contributions from the charitable to enable him to pay the apportioned blood-money. I have frequently met such unfortunate persons who have spent years in collecting a small sum.

Leaving the caravan to pursue the direct road, I struck across the country to the hill of Koukab, accompanied by Mohammed Emin and Mijwell. This remarkable cone, rising in the midst of the plain, had been visible from our furthest point on the Khabour. As we drew near to it, the plain was covered with angular fragments of black basalt, and crossed by dykes of the same volcanic rock. Mohammed Emin led us first to the mouth of a cave in a rocky ravine not far from the foot of the hill. It was so choked with stones that we could scarcely squeeze ourselves through the opening, but it became wider, and led to a descending passage, the bottom of which was lost in the gloom. We advanced cautiously, but not without setting in motion an avalanche of loose stones, which, increasing as it rolled onwards, by its loud noise disturbed swarms of bats that hung to the sides and ceiling of the cavern. Flying towards the light, these noisome beasts almost compelled us to retreat. They clung to our clothes, and our hands could scarcely prevent them settling on our faces. The rustling of their wings was like the noise of a great wind, and an abominable stench arose from the recesses of the cave. At length they settled again to their daily sleep, and we were able to go forward.

After descending some fifty feet, we found ourselves on the margin of a pond of fresh water. The pitchy darkness prevented our ascertaining its size, which could not have been very great. The cave is frequently a place of refuge for the wandering Arabs, and the Bedouins encamp near it in summer to drink the cool water of this natural reservoir. Mohammed Emin told me that, in the previous year, he had found a lion in it, who, on being disturbed, merely rushed out and fled across the plain.

Volcanic Cone of Koukab.

Leaving the cavern and issuing from the ravine, we came to the edge of a wide crater, in the centre of which rose the remarkable cone of Koukab. To the left of us was a second crater, whose lips were formed by the jagged edges of basaltic rocks, and in the plain around were several others smaller in size. They were all evidently the remains of an extinct volcano, which had been active within a comparatively recent geological period, even perhaps within the time of history or tradition, as the name of the mound, Koukab, means in Arabic a star and a jet of flame.

I ascended the cone, which is about 300 feet high, and composed entirely of loose lava, scoria, and ashes, thus resembling the cone rising in the crater of Vesuvius. It is steep and difficult of ascent, except on one side, where the summit is easily reached even by horses. Within, for it is hollow, it resembles an enormous funnel, broken away at one edge, as if a stream of molten lava had burst through it. Anemonies and poppies, of the brighest scarlet hue, covered its side; although the dry lava and loose ashes scarcely seemed to have collected sufficient soil to nourish their roots. It would be difficult to describe the richness and brilliancy of this mass of flowers, the cone from a distance having the appearance of a huge inverted cup of burnished copper, over which poured streams of blood.

From the summit of Koukab I gazed upon a scene as varied as extensive. Beneath me the two principal branches of the Khabour united their waters. I could trace them for many miles by the dark line of their wooded banks, as they wound through the golden plains. To the left, or the west, was the true Khabour, the Chaboras of the ancients; a name it bears from its source at Ras-al-Ain (*i. e.* the head of the spring). The second stream, that to the east, is called by the Arabs the Jerujer (a name, as uttered by the Bedouins, equally difficult to pronounce and to write), and is the ancient Mygdonius, flowing through Nisibin. The lake of Khatouniyah was just visible, backed by the solitary hill of the Sinjar. The Kurdish mountains bounded the view to the east. In the plain, and on the banks of the rivers, rose many artificial mounds; whilst in the extreme distance to the north, could be distinguished the flocks and black tents of a large wandering tribe. They were those of the Chichi and Milli Kurds, encamped with the Turkish commander, Suleiman Agha.

On some fragments of basaltic rock projecting from the summit of the cone, were numerous rudely-cut signs, the devices of the Shammar, carved there on the visit of different Sheikhs. Each tribe, and, indeed, each subdivision and family, has its peculiar mark, to be placed upon its property and burnt upon its camels. In little recesses, carefully sheltered by heaped-up stones, were hung miniature cradles, like those commonly suspended to the poles of a Bedouin tent. They had been placed there as ex-votos by Shammar women who wished to become mothers.

After I had examined the second large crater, we rode towards the Jerujer, on whose banks the caravan was to await us. The plain was still covered with innumerable fragments of basalt embedded in scarlet poppies. We found our companions near the junction of the rivers, where a raft had been constructed to enable us to cross the smaller stream.

We had scarcely crossed the river before a large body of horsemen were seen approaching us. As they drew nigh I recognised in the Turkish commander an old friend, 'the Topal,' or lame, Suleiman Agha, as he was generally called in the country. He had been Kiayah, or lieutenant-governor, to the celebrated Injeh Bairakdar Mohammed Pasha, and, like his former master, possessed considerable intelligence, energy, and activity. From his long connection with the tribes of the desert, his knowledge of their manners, and his skill in detecting and devising treacheries and stratagems, he was generally chosen to lead expeditions against the Arabs. He was now endeavouring to recover the government treasure plundered by the Hamoud Bedouins.

He was surrounded by Hyta-Bashis, or commanders of irregular cavalry, glittering with gold and silver-mounted arms, and rich in embroidered jackets and silken robes, by Aghas of the Chichi and Milli Kurds, and by several Arab chiefs. About five hundred horsemen, preceded by their small kettle-drums, crowded behind him. His tents were about six miles distant; and, after exchanging the usual salutations, we turned towards them. Many fair speeches could scarcely calm the fears of the timid Jebour Sheikh. Mijwell, on the other hand, rode boldly along, casting contemptuous glances at the irregular cavalry, as they galloped to and fro in mimic combat.

The delta, formed by the two streams, was covered with tents. We wended our way through crowds of sheep, horses, cattle, and camels. The Chichi and Milli Kurds, who encamp during the spring at the foot of the mountains of Mardin, had now sought, under the protection of the Turkish soldiery, the rich pastures of the Khabour.

Suleiman Agha lived under the spacious canvas of the Chichi chief. The tents of the Kurdish tribes are remarkable for their size and the richness of their carpets and furniture. They are often divided into as many as four or five distinct compartments, by screens of light cane or reeds, bound together with many-coloured woollen threads, disposed in elegant patterns and devices. Carpets hung above these screens complete the divisions. In that set aside for the women a smaller partition encloses a kind of private room for the head of the family and his wives. The rest of the harem is filled with piles of carpets, cushions, domestic furniture, cooking utensils, skins for making butter, and all the necessaries of a wandering life. Here the handmaidens prepare the dinner for their master and his guests. In the tents of the great chiefs there is a separate compartment for the servants, and one for the mares and colts.

I sat a short time with Suleiman Agha, drank coffee, smoked, and then adjourned to my own tents, which had been pitched upon the banks of the river opposite a well-wooded island, and near a ledge of rocks forming one of those beautiful falls of water so frequent in this part of the Khabour. Around us were the pavilions of the Hytas, those of the chiefs marked by their scarlet standards. At a short distance from the stream the tents of the Kurds were pitched in parallel lines forming regular streets, and not scattered, like those of the Bedouins, without order over the plain. Between us and them were picketed the horses of the cavalry, and as far as the eye could reach beyond, grazed the innumerable flocks and herds of the assembled tribes. We were encamped near the foot of a large artificial Tel called Umjerjeh; and on the opposite side of the Khabour were other mounds of the same name. My Jebour workmen began at once to excavate in these ruins.

Two days after my arrival Mohammed Emin left us. Suleiman Agha had already invested him with a robe of honour, and had prevailed upon him to join with Ferhan in taking measures for the recovery of the plundered treasure. The scarlet cloak and civil treatment had conciliated the Jebour chief, and when he parted with the Turkish commander in my tent there was an unusual display of mutual compliments and pledges of eternal friendship. Mijwell looked on with indignant contempt, swearing between his teeth that all Jebours were but degenerate, ploughing Arabs, and cursing the whole order of *temminahs*.*

We were detained at Umjerjeh several days by the severe illness of Mr. Hormuzd Rassam. I took the opportunity to visit the tents of the Milli, whose chief, Mousa Agha, had

The Tent of the Milli Chief.

invited us to a feast. On our way thither we passed several encampments of the tribes of Chichi, Sherrabeen, and Harb, the men and women running out and pressing us to stop and eat bread. The spacious tent of Mousa Agha was divided by

---

* The form of salutation used by the Turks, consisting of raising the hand from the breast, or sometimes from the ground, to the forehead.

partitions of reeds tastefully interwoven with coloured wool. The coolest part of the salamlik had been prepared for our reception, and was spread with fine carpets and silken cushions. The men of the tribe, amongst whom were many tall and handsome youths, were dressed in clean and becoming garments. They assembled in great numbers, but left the top of the tent entirely to us, seating themselves, or standing at the sides and bottom, which was wide enough to admit twenty-four men crouched together in a row. The chief and his brothers, followed by their servants bearing trays loaded with cups, presented the coffee to their guests.

After some conversation we went to the harem, and were received by his mother, a venerable lady, with long silvery locks and a dignified countenance and demeanour. Her dress was of the purest white and scrupulously clean. She was almost the only comely old woman I had seen amongst Eastern tribes. The wives and daughters of the chiefs, with a crowd of women, were collected in the tent. Amongst them were many distinguished by their handsome features. They had not the rich olive complexion or graceful carriage of the Bedouin girls, nor their piercing eyes and long black eyelashes. Their beauty was more European, some having even light hair and blue eyes. It was evident, at a glance, that they were of a different race from the wandering tribes of the desert.

The principal ladies led us into the private compartment, divided by coloured screens from the rest of the tent. It was furnished with more than usual luxury. The cushions were of the choicest silk, and the carpets (in the manufacture of which the Milli excel) of the finest fabric. Sweetmeats and coffee had been prepared for us, and the women did not object to partake of them at the same time. Mousa Agha's mother described the various marriage ceremonies of the tribe. Our account of similar matters in Europe excited great amusement amongst the ladies. The Milli girls are highly prized by the Kurds. Twenty purses, nearly 100*l.*, we were boastingly told, had been given for one of unusual attractions. The chief pointed out one of his own wives who had cost him that sum. Other members of the same establishment had deserved a less extravagant investiture of money. The prettiest girls were called before us, and the old lady appraised each, amidst the loud laughter of their companions, who no doubt rejoiced to see their friends valued at their true worth. They were all tatooed on the arms, and on other parts of the body, but less so than the Bedouin ladies. The operation is performed by Arab women, who wander from tent to tent for the purpose. Several were present, and wished to give us an immediate proof of their skill upon ourselves. We declined, however. It is usually

Women of the Milli Tribe.

done at the age of six or seven: the punctures are made by a needle, and the blue colour is produced by a mixture of gunpowder and indigo rubbed into the wounds. The process is tedious and painful, as the designs are frequently most elaborate, covering the whole body. The Kurdish ladies do not, like the Mussulman women of the towns, conceal their faces; nor do they object to mingle, or even eat, with the men. During my stay at Umjerjeh I invited the harem of the Chichi chief, and their friends, to a feast in my tent—an invitation they accepted with every sign of satisfaction.

We had an excellent dinner in the salamlik, varied by many savoury dishes and delicacies sent from the harem: such as truffles, dressed in different ways, several preparations of milk and cream, honey, curds, &c. After we had retired, the other guests were called to the feast by relays. The chief, however, always remained seated before the dishes, eating a little with all, and leaving his brothers to summon those who were invited, such being the custom amongst these Kurds.

Mijwell, during our visit, had been seated in a corner, his eyes wandering from the tent and its furniture to the horses and mares picketed without, and to the flocks pasturing around. He cast, every now and then, significant glances towards me, which said plainly enough, 'All this ought to belong to the Bedouins. These people and their property were made for *ghazous*.' As we rode away I accused him of evil intentions. 'Billah, ya Bej!' said he, 'there is, indeed, enough to make a man's heart grow white with envy: but I have now eaten his bread under your shadow, and should even his stick, wherewith he drives his camel, fall into my hand, I would send it to him.' He entertained me, as we returned home, with an account of his domestic affairs. Although already married to one wife, and betrothed to Maizi, whom he would soon be able to claim, he was projecting a third marriage. His heart had been stolen by an unseen damsel, whose beauties and virtues had been the theme of some wandering Arab rhymers, and she was of the Fedhan Aneyza, the mortal enemies of the Shammar. Her father was the Sheikh of the tribe, and his tents were on the other side of the Euphrates. The difficulties and dangers of the courtship served only to excite still more the ardent mind of the Bedouin. His romantic imagination had pictured a perfection of loveliness; his whole thoughts were now occupied in devising the means of possessing this treasure.[*] He had already apprised the girl of his love by a trusty messenger, one of her own tribe, living with the Shammar. His con-

---

[*] Burckhardt remarks that 'Bedouins are, perhaps, the only people of the East that can be entitled true lovers.' (Notes on Bedouins, p. 155.)

fidant had extolled the graces, prowess, and wealth of the young Sheikh, with all the eloquence of a Bedouin poet, and had elicited a favourable reply. More than one interchange of sentiments had, by such means, since passed between them. The damsel had, at last, promised him her hand, if he could claim her in her own tent. Mijwell had now planned a scheme which he was eager to put into execution. Waiting until the Fedhan were so encamped that he could approach them without being previously seen, he would mount his deloul, and leading his best mare, ride to the tent of the girl's father. Bread would, of course, be laid before him, and having eaten he would be the guest, and under the protection, of the Sheikh. On the following morning he would present his mare, describing her race and qualities, to his host, and ask his daughter; offering, at the same time, to add any other gift that might be thought worthy of her. The father, who would probably not be ignorant of what had passed between the lovers, would at once consent to their union, and give back the mare to his future son-in-law. The marriage would shortly afterwards be solemnised, and an alliance would thus be formed between the two tribes. Such was Mijwell's plan, and it was one not unfrequently adopted by Bedouins under similar circumstances.

A Bedouin will never ask money or value in kind for his daughter, as fathers do amongst the sedentary tribes and in towns, where girls are literally sold to their husbands, but he will consult her wishes, and she may, as she thinks fit, accept or reject a suitor, so long as he be not her cousin. Presents are frequently made by the lover to the damsel herself before marriage, but rarely to the parents.

I talked with Mijwell about the peculiar customs of the Arab tribes. None are more religiously respected by the true Bedouin than those regulating the mutual relations of the protected and protector, called the Dakheel. A violation of Dakheel would be considered a disgrace not only upon the individual but upon his family, and even upon his tribe, which never could be wiped out. No greater insult can be offered to a man, or to his clan, than to say that he has broken the Dakheel. A disregard of this sacred obligation is the first symptom of degeneracy in an Arab tribe; and when once it exists, the treachery and vices of the Turk rapidly succeed to the honesty and fidelity of the true Arab character. The relations between the Dakheel and the Dakhal (or the protector and protected), arise from a variety of circumstances, the principal of which are, eating a man's bread and salt, and claiming his protection by doing certain acts, or repeating a certain formula of words. Amongst the Shammar, if a man can seize the end of a string or thread, the other end of which is held by his enemy, he immediately becomes his Dakheel.* If he touch the canvas of a tent, or can even throw his mace towards it, he is the Dakheel of its owner. If he can spit upon a man, or touch any article belonging to him with his teeth, he is Dakhal, unless, of course, in case of theft, it be the person who caught him. A woman can protect any number of persons, or even of tents. If a horseman ride into a tent, he and his horse are Dakhal. A stranger who has eaten with a Shammar, can give Dakheel to his enemy; for instance, I could protect an Aneyza, though there is blood between his tribe and the Shammar. According to Mijwell, any person, by previously calling out 'Nuffa' (I renounce), may reject an application for Dakheel.

The Shammar never plunder a caravan within sight of their encampment, for as long as a stranger can see their tents they consider him their Dakhal. If a man who has eaten bread and slept in a tent, steal his host's horse, he is dishonoured, and his tribe also, unless they send back the stolen animal. Should the horse die, the thief himself should be delivered up, to be treated as the owner of the stolen property thinks fit. If two enemies meet and exchange the

* For the very singular customs as to the confinement and liberation of a *haramy*, or robber, and of the relation between a *rabat* and his *rabiet*, or the captor and the captive, see Burckhardt's 'Notes on the Bedouins,' p. 89. I can bear witness to the truth and accuracy of his account, having, during my early wanderings amongst the Bedouins, witnessed nearly everything he describes. The English reader can have no correct idea of the habits and manners of the tribes of the desert, habits and manners probably dating from the remotest antiquity, and consequently of the highest interest, without reading the truthful descriptions of this admirable traveller.

'*Salam aleikum*' (Peace be with you) even by mistake, there is peace between them, and they will not fight. It is disgraceful to rob a woman of her clothes; and if a female be found amongst a party of plundered Arabs, even the enemy of her tribe will give her a horse to ride back to her tents. If a man be pursued by an enemy, or even be on the ground, he can save his life by calling out 'Dakheel,' unless there be blood between them. It would be considered cowardly and unworthy of a Shammar to deprive an enemy of his camel or horse where he could neither reach water nor an encampment. When Bedouins meet persons in the midst of the desert, they will frequently take them within a certain distance of tents, and, first pointing out their site, then rob them of their property.

An Arab who has given his protection to another, whether formally, or by an act which confers the privilege of Dakheel, is bound to protect his Dakhal under all circumstances, even to the risk of his own property and life. I could relate many instances of the greatest sacrifices having been made by individuals, and even of whole tribes having been involved in war with powerful enemies by whom they have been almost utterly destroyed, in defence of this most sacred obligation. Even the Turkish rulers respect a law to which they may one day owe their safety, and more than one haughty Pasha of Baghdad has found refuge and protection in the tent of a poor Arab Sheikh, whom, during the days of his prosperity, he had subjected to every injury and wrong, and yet who would then defy the government itself, and risk his very life, rather than surrender his guest. The essence of Arab virtue is a respect for the laws of hospitality, of which the Dakheel in all its various forms is but a part.

Amongst the Bedouins who watched our camels was one Saoud, a poet of renown amongst the tribes. With the exception of a few ballads that he had formerly composed in honour of Sofuk, and other celebrated Shammar Sheikhs, he chiefly recited extemporary stanzas on passing events, or on persons who were present. He would sit in my tent of an evening, and sing his verses in a wild, though plaintive, strain, to the great delight of the assembled guests, and particularly of Mijwell, who, like a true Bedouin, was easily affected by poetry, especially with such as might touch his own passion for the unknown lady. The Arab chief would sway his body to and fro, keeping time with the measure, sobbing aloud as the poet sang the death of his companions in war, breaking out into loud laughter when the burden of the ditty was a satire upon his friends, and making extraordinary noises and grimaces to show his feelings, more like a drunken man than a sober Bedouin. But when the bard improvised an amatory ditty, the young chief's excitement was almost beyond control. The other Bedouins were scarcely less moved by these rude measures, which have the same kind of effect on the wild tribes of the Persian mountains. Such verses, chanted by their self-taught poets, or by the girls of their encampment, will drive warriors to the combat, fearless of death, or prove an ample reward on their return from the dangers of the *ghazou* or the fight. The excitement they produce exceeds that of the grape. He who would understand the influence of the Homeric ballads in the heroic ages, should witness the effect which similar compositions have upon the wild nomades of the East. Amongst the Kurds and Lours I have not met with bards who chanted extempory verses. Episodes from the great historical epics of Persia, and odes from their favourite poets, are recited during war or in the tents of their chiefs. But the art of improvising seems innate in the Bedouin. Although his metre and mode of recitation are rude to European ears, his rich and sonorous language lends itself to this species of poetry, whilst his exuberant imagination furnishes him with endless beautiful and appropriate allegories. The wars between the tribes, their *ghazous*, and their struggles with the Turks, are inexhaustible themes for verse, and in an Arab tent there is little else to afford excitement or amusement. The Bedouins have no books; even a Koran is seldom seen amongst them: it is equally rare to find a wandering Arab who can read. They have no written literature, and their traditional history consists of little more than the tales of a few storytellers, who wander from encampment to encampment, and earn their bread by chanting verses to the monotonous tones of a one-stringed fiddle made of a gourd covered with sheep-skin.

The extemporary odes which Saoud sung before us were chiefly in praise of those present, or a good-natured satire upon some of our party.

We left the encampment of Suleiman Agha on the 29th of April, on our return to Mosul. We again visited the remarkable volcanic cone of Koukab. As we drew near to it, Mijwell detected, in the loose soil, the footprints of two men, which he immediately pronounced to be those of Shammar thieves returning from the Kurdish encampments. The sagacity of the Bedouin in determining from such marks, whether of man or beast, and, from similar indications, the tribe, time of passing, and business, of those who may have left them, with many other particulars, is well known. In this respect he resembles the American Indian, though the circumstances differ under which the two are called upon to exercise this peculiar faculty. The one seeks or avoids his enemy in vast plains, which, for three-fourths of the year, are without any vegetation; the other tracks his prey through thick woods and high grass. This quickness of perception is the result of continual observation and of caution encouraged from earliest youth. When the warriors of a tribe are engaged in distant forays or in war, their tents and flocks are frequently left to the care of a mere child. He must receive strangers, amongst whom may be those having claims of blood upon his family, and must guard against marauders, who may be lurking about the encampment. Every unknown sign and mark must be examined and accounted for. If he should see the track of a horseman he must ask himself why one so near the dwellings did not stop to eat bread or drink water? was he a spy; one of a party meditating an attack, or a traveller, who did not know the site of the tents? When did he pass? From whence did he come? Whilst the child in a civilised country is still under the care of its nurse, the Bedouin boy is compelled to exercise his highest faculties, and on his prudence and sagacity may sometimes depend the safety of his tribe.

The expert Bedouin can draw conclusions from the footprints and dung of animals that would excite the astonishment of an European. He will tell whether the camel was loaded or unloaded, whether recently fed or suffering from hunger, whether fatigued or fresh, the time when it passed by, whether the owner was a man of the desert or the town, whether a friend or foe, and sometimes even the name of his tribe. I have frequently been cautioned by my Bedouin companions, not to dismount from my dromedary, that my footsteps might not be recognised as those of a stranger; and my deloul has even been led by my guide to prevent those who might cross our path detecting that it was ridden by one not thoroughly accustomed to the management of the animal.

We encamped for the night near the mound of Thenenir, and resumed our journey on the following morning. Bidding farewell to the pleasant banks of the Khabour, we struck into the desert in the direction of the Sinjar. Extensive strata of the gypsum, or alabaster, used in the Assyrian edifices, formed for some miles the surface of the plain.

We soon approached a dense mass of reeds and rank herbage, covering a swamp called the Hol, which extends from the Lake of Khatouniyah to within a short distance of the Khabour. This jungle is the hiding-place of many kinds of wild beasts: lions lurk in it, and in the thick cover the Bedouins find their cubs. As we drew near to the first spring that feeds the marsh, about eight miles from Thenenir, we saw a leopard stealing from the high grass. When pursued, the animal turned and entered the thickets before the horseman could approach it. When we reached the head spring of the Hol, the Jebours fired the jungle, and the flames soon spread far and wide. Long after we had left the marsh we could hear the crackling of the burning reeds, and until nightfall the sky was darkened by thick volumes of smoke.

After a six hours' ride we found ourselves upon the margin of a small lake, whose quiet surface reflected the deep blue of the cloudless sky. To the south of it rose a line of low undulating hills, and to the east the furrowed mountain of the Sinjar. On all other sides was the desert, in which this solitary sheet of water lay like a mirage. In the midst of the lake was a peninsula, joined to the mainland by a narrow causeway, and beyond it a small island. On the former were the ruins of a town, whose falling walls and towers were doubled in the clear waters. It would be difficult to imagine a scene more calm, more fair, or more unlooked for in the midst of a wilderness. It was like fairy-land.

Town and Lake of Khatouniyah.

The small town of Khatouniyah was, until recently, inhabited by a tribe of Arabs, but had been deserted on account of a feud, arising out of the rival pretensions of two chiefs. The lake may be about six miles in circumference. The water, although brackish, like nearly all the springs in this part of the desert, is not only drinkable, but, according to the Bedouins, exceedingly wholesome for man and beast. It abounds in fish, some of which are said to be of very considerable size. As we approached, the Bairakdar seeing something struggling in a shallow rode to it, and captured a kind of barbel, weighing above twenty pounds. Waterfowl and waders, of various kinds, congregate on the shores. The stately crane and the graceful egret, with its snow-white plumage and feathery crest, stand lazily on its margin; and thousands of ducks and teal eddy on its surface round the unwieldy pelican.

Our tents were pitched on the very water's edge. At sunset a few clouds which lingered in the western sky were touched with the golden rays of the setting sun. The glowing tints of the heavens, and the clear blue shadows of the Sinjar hills, mirrored in the motionless lake, imparted a calm to the scene which well matched the solitude around.

We had scarcely resumed our march in the morning when we spied Suttum and Khoraif coming towards us, and urging their fleet mares to the top of their speed. A Jebour, leaving our encampment at Umjerjeh, when Hormuzd was dangerously ill, had spread a report in the desert that he was actually dead. To give additional authenticity to his tale he had minutely described the process by which my companion's body had been first salted, and then sent to Frankistan (Europe) in a box on a camel. Suttum, as we met, showed the most lively signs of grief; but when he saw the dead man himself restored to life, his joy and his embraces knew no bounds.

We rode over a low undulating country, at the foot of the Sinjar hills, every dell and ravine being a bed of flowers. About five miles from Khatouniyah we passed a small reedy stream, called Suffeyra, on which the Boraij (Suttum's tribe) had been encamped on the previous day. They had now moved further into the plain, and we stopped at their watering-place, a brackish rivulet called Sayhel, their tents being about three miles distant from us in the desert. We pitched on a rising ground immediately above the stream. Beneath us was the golden plain, swarming with moving objects. The Khorusseh, and all the tribes under Ferhan, had now congregated to the north of the Sinjar previous to their summer migration to the pastures of the Khabour. Their mares, camels, and sheep came to Sayhel for water, and during the whole day there was one endless line of animals passing to and fro before our encampment. I sat watching them from my tent. As each mare and horse stopped to drink at the troubled stream, Suttum named its owner and its breed, and described its exploits. The mares were generally followed by two or three colts, who are suffered, even in their third year, to run loose after their dams, and to gambol unrestrained over the plain. It is to their perfect freedom whilst young that the horses of the desert owe their speed and the suppleness of their limbs.

In the evening, as I was seated before my tent, I observed a large party of horsemen and riders on delouls approaching our encampment. They stopped at the entrance of the large pavilion reserved for guests, and picketing their mares, and

Arab Camels.

turning loose their dromedaries adorned with gay trappings, seated themselves on the carpets. The chiefs were our old friends, Mohammed Emin and Ferhan, the great Shammar Sheikh. We cordially embraced after the Bedouin fashion. I had not seen Ferhan since the treacherous murder of his father by Nejib Pasha of Baghdad,* to which he alluded

* Nineveh and its Remains, p. 78.

with touching expressions of grief, bewailing his own incompetency to fill Sofuk's place, and to govern the divided tribe. He was now on his way with the Jebour Sheikh to recover, if possible, the government treasure, plundered by the Hamoud, for which, as head of the Shammar, he was held responsible by the Porte. After they had eaten of the feast we were able to prepare for them, they departed about sunset for the tents of the Jebours.

On the 4th of May we made a short day's journey of five hours to a beautiful stream issuing from the Sinjar hill, beneath the village of Khersa. Leaving the plain, which was speckled as far as the eye could reach with the flocks and tents of the Bedouins, we skirted the very foot of the Sinjar range. Khersa had been deserted by its inhabitants, who had rebuilt their village higher up on the side of the hill.

Next day we made but little progress, encamping near a spring under the village of Aldina, whose chief, Murad, had now returned from his captivity. Grateful for my intercession in his behalf, he brought us sheep and other provisions, and met us with his people as we entered the valley. The Mutesellim was in his village collecting the revenues, but the inhabitants of Nogray had refused to contribute the share assigned to them, or to receive the governor. He begged me to visit the rebellious Yezidis, and the whole day was spent in devising schemes for a general peace. At length the chiefs consented to accompany me to Aldina, and, after some reduction in the salian, to pay the taxes.

We rode on the following day for about an hour along the foot of the Sinjar hill, which suddenly subsides into a low undulating country. The narrow valleys and ravines were blood-red with gigantic poppies. The Bedouins adorned the camels and horses with the scarlet flowers, and twisted them into their own head-dresses and long garments. Even the Tiyari dressed themselves up in the gaudy trappings of nature, and as we journeyed chanting an Arab war-song, we resembled the return of a festive procession from some sacrifice of old. During our weary marches under a burning sun, it required some such episodes to keep up the drooping spirits of the men, who toiled on foot by our sides. Poetry and flowers are the wine and spirits of the Arab; a couplet is equal to a bottle, and a rose to a dram, without the evil effects of either. Would that in more civilised climes the sources of excitement were equally harmless!

About nine miles from our last encamping place we crossed a stream of sweet water named Aththenir, and stopped soon after for the day in the bosom of the hills, near some reedy ponds, called Fukka, formed by several springs. As this was a well-known place of rendezvous for the Bedouins when out on the ghazou, Suttum displayed more than usual caution in choosing the place for our tents, ascending with Khoraif a neighbouring peak to survey the country and scan the plain below.

In the afternoon the camels had wandered from the encampment in search of grass, and we were reposing in the shade of our tents, when we were roused by the cry that a large body of men were to be seen in the distance. The Bedouins immediately sought to drive back their beasts. Suttum unplatting his long hair, and shaking it in hideous disorder over his head and face, and baring his arms to the shoulder, leapt with his quivering spear into the saddle. Having first placed the camp in the best posture of defence I was able, I rode out with him to reconnoitre. But our alarm was soon quieted. The supposed enemy proved to be a party of poor Yezidis, who, taking advantage of our caravan, were going to Mosul to seek employment during the summer.

In the evening Suttum inveighed bitterly against the habit of some travellers of continually taking notes before strangers. I endeavoured to explain the object and to remove his fears. 'It is all very well,' said the Sheikh, 'and I can understand, and am willing to believe, all you tell me. But supposing the Turks, or any body else, should hereafter come against us, there are many foolish and suspicious men in the tribe, and I have enemies, who would say that I had brought them, for I have shown you everything. You know what would be the consequences to me of such a report. As for you, you are in this place to-day, and a hundred days' journey off to-morrow, but I am always here. There is not a plot of grass nor a spring that that man (alluding to one of our party) does not write down.' Suttum's complaints were not unreasonable, and travellers cannot be too cautious in this respect, when amongst independent tribes, for even if they do not bring difficulties upon themselves, they may do so upon others.

We had a seven hours' ride on the delouls, leaving the caravan to follow, to the large ruin of Abou Maria. My workmen had excavated for some time in these remarkable mounds, and had discovered chambers and several enormous slabs of Mosul marble, but no remains whatever of sculpture. They had, however, dug out several bricks bearing the name of Sardanapalus, the founder of the north-west palace at Nimroud. A short ride of three hours brought us to Eski (old) Mosul, on the banks of the Tigris. According to tradition this is the original site of the city. There are mounds, and the remains of walls, which are probably Assyrian. Mosul was still nine caravan hours distant, and we encamped the next night at Hamaydat, where many of our friends came out to meet us. On the 10th of May we were again within the walls of the town, our desert trip having been accomplished without any mishap or accident whatever.

Suttum left us two days after for his tents, fearing lest he should be too late to join the warriors of the Khorusseh, who had planned a grand *ghazou* into Nedjd. They were to be away for thirty days, and expected to bring back a great spoil of mares, dromedaries, and camels. As for three days they would meet with no wells, they could only ride their delouls, each animal carrying a spearman and a musketeer, with their skins of water and a scanty stock of provisions. They generally contrive to return from these expeditions with considerable booty. Suttum urged me to accompany them; but I had long renounced such evil habits, and other occupations kept me in Mosul. Finding that I was not to be persuaded, and that the time was at length come for us to part, he embraced me, crammed the presents we had made to himself and his wives into his saddle-bags, and, mounting his deloul, rode off with Mijwell towards the desert.

CHAPTER VII.

*Discoveries at Kouyunjik—Procession of figures bearing fruit and game—
Locusts—Led horses—An Assyrian campaign—Dagon, or the fish-
god—The chambers of records—Inscribed clay tablets—Return to Nimroud—Effects of the flood—Discoveries—Small temple under high
mound—The Evil Spirit—Fish-god—Fine bas-relief of the king—Great
inscribed monolith—Cedar beams—Second temple.*

DURING my absence in the desert, the excavations at
Kouyunjik had been actively carried on under the superintendence of Toma Shishman. I hastened to the ruins,
crossing in a rude ferry-boat the river, now swollen by the
spring rains to more than double its usual size.*

The earth had been completely removed from the sides of
the long gallery, on the walls of which were sculptured the
transport of the large stone and of the winged bulls.† An
outlet was discovered near its western end, opening into a
narrow descending passage; an entrance, it would appear,
into the palace from the river side.‡ Its length was ninety-
six feet, its breadth not more than thirteen. The walls were
panelled with sculptured slabs about six feet high.§ Those
to the right, in descending, represented a procession of servants carrying fruit, flowers, game, and supplies for a banquet,
preceded by mace-bearers. The first servant bore an object
which I should identify with the pineapple, unless there were
every reason to believe that the Assyrians were unacquainted
with that fruit. The leaves sprouting from the top proved
that it was not the cone of a pine or fir tree.

The attendants who followed carried clusters of ripe dates
and flat baskets of osier-work, filled with pomegranates,

---

* The flood nearly reached the mounds of Kouyunjik and Nebbi
Yunus.
† No. XLIX. Plan I. p. 4.   ‡ No. LI. same Plan.
§ The figures were about 4¼ feet in height.

Attendants carrying Pomegranates and Locusts. (Kouyunjik.)

apples, and bunches of grapes. They raised in one hand boughs to drive away the flies. Then came men bearing hares, partridges, and dried locusts fastened on rods. The locust has ever been an article of food in the East, and is still sold in the markets of many towns in Arabia.

The locust-bearers were followed by a man with strings of pomegranates; then came, two by two, attendants carrying on their shoulders low tables, such as are still used in the East at feasts, loaded with baskets of cakes and fruits of various kinds. The procession was finished by a long line of servants bearing vases full of flowers.

These figures were dressed in a short tunic, confined at the waist by a shawl or girdle. They wore no head-gear, their hair falling in curls on their shoulders.

On the opposite walls of the passage were fourteen horses without trappings, each led by a groom holding a halter twisted round the lower jaw. The animals and men were designed with considerable truth and spirit. The procession was marshalled by a staff-bearer, or chamberlain. The grooms wore a short tunic and an embroidered belt, and to this was attached that ornament of fur, or coloured fringe, peculiar to the costumes of the warriors of the later Assyrian period.*

This passage may have led to the banqueting hall, where royal feasts were held, and was therefore adorned with appropriate subjects. At its western end the gallery turned abruptly to the north, its walls being there built of solid stone-masonry. I lost all further traces of it, as the workmen were unable, at that time, to carry on the tunnel beneath a mass of earth and rubbish about forty feet high. I did not, consequently, ascertain its western outlet. We had, however, nearly reached the edge of the mound; and as there was no space left for a chamber of any size beyond, this passage may have opened on a flight of steps, or on an incline leading from the river, and forming a private entrance or postern into the palace.

The workmen had returned to the chamber already de-

---

* Specimens of the led horses, and of the figures bearing locusts, are now in the British Museum. See Plates 7, 8, and 9 of the 2nd series of the 'Monuments of Nineveh' for the entire series.

scribed as containing bas-reliefs representing the sack of a city in the mountains, and as opening into the broad gallery on whose walls were depictured the various processes employed by the Assyrians in moving their colossal figures.* From this chamber branched to the south a narrow passage,† whose sculptured panels had been purposely destroyed. It led into a great hall or court, which the workmen did not then explore.‡ They continued for a few feet along its western side, and then turning through a doorway, discovered a chamber, from which again, always following the line of wall, they entered a spacious apartment,§ completely surrounded with bas-reliefs, representing one continuous subject. The Assyrian army was seen fording a broad stream amidst wooded mountains. Rivulets flowed from the hills to the river, irrigating in their course vineyards and orchards. The king in his chariot was followed by warriors on foot and on horses richly caparisoned, by led horses with even gayer trappings, and by men bearing on their shoulders his second chariot, which had a yoke ornamented with bosses and carvings. He was preceded by his army, the variously accoutred spearmen and the bowmen forming separate regiments or divisions. After crossing the river they attacked the enemy's strongholds, which they captured, putting to death or carrying into captivity their inhabitants. Unfortunately, the bas-reliefs describing the general result of the campaign, and probably the taking of the principal city, had been destroyed. The captives wore a kind of turban wrapped in several folds round the head, and a short tunic confined at the waist by a broad belt. From the nature of the country it may be conjectured that the sculptures represented the invasion and conquest of some part of Armenia, and the river may perhaps be identified with the Euphrates, near whose head waters, as we learn from the inscriptions, Sennacherib waged one of his most important wars.

* No. XLVIII. Plan I. p. 4.
† No. XLII. same Plan; 72 feet long, and 11 broad.
§ No. XIX. same Plan.   ‡ Nos. XXIX. and XXXVIII. same Plan.

On the north side of the chamber were two doorways leading into separate apartments. Each entrance was formed by two colossal bas-reliefs of the fish-god. These figures combine the human shape with that of the fish. The head of the fish forms a kind of mitre for the head of the man, whilst its scaly back and fan like tail fall behind, leaving the human limbs and feet exposed. They wear a fringed tunic, and bear the two sacred emblems, the basket and the cone.

The god Dagon of the Philistines and of the inhabitants of the Phœnician coast appears to have been worshipped under nearly the same form. When the ark of the Lord was brought into the great temple of the idol at Ashdod, and the statue fell a second time, 'the head of Dagon and both the palms of his hands were cut off upon the threshold; only the *fishy* part of Dagon

Assyrian Cylinder, with Dagon, or the Fish-god.

was left to him.'* His worship appears to have extended over Syria, as well as Mesopotamia and Chaldæa. He had many temples, as we learn from the Bible, in the country of the Philistines, and it was under the ruins of one of them that Sampson buried the people of Gaza who had 'gathered them together for to offer a great sacrifice unto Dagon their god, and to rejoice.'†

The first doorway, guarded by the fish-gods, led into two small chambers opening into each other, and once panelled with bas-reliefs, the greater part of which had been destroyed.‡ On a few fragments, still standing against the walls, could be traced a city on a sea whose waters were covered with galleys. I shall call these chambers 'the chambers of records,' for they appear to have contained the decrees of the Assyrian kings and the archives of the empire.

The historical records and public documents of the Assy-

---

* 1 Sam. v. 6. † Judges, xvi. 23.
‡ Nos. XL. and XLI. Plan I. p. 4.

rians were kept on tablets and cylinders of baked clay. Many specimens have been brought to this country. On a large hexagonal cylinder presented by me to the British Museum are the chronicles of Esarhaddon: on a similar cylinder discovered in the mound of Nebbi Yunus, are eight years of the annals of Sennacherib: on a barrel-shaped cylinder, known as Bellino's, we have part of the records of the same king; and other cylinders have been found with the annals of earlier and later monarchs. The importance of such relics will be readily understood. They present, in a small compass, an abridgment, or recapitulation, of the inscriptions on the great monuments and palace walls, giving in a chronological series the events of each monarch's reign. The writing is so minute, and the letters are so close one to another, that it requires considerable experience to separate and transcribe them.

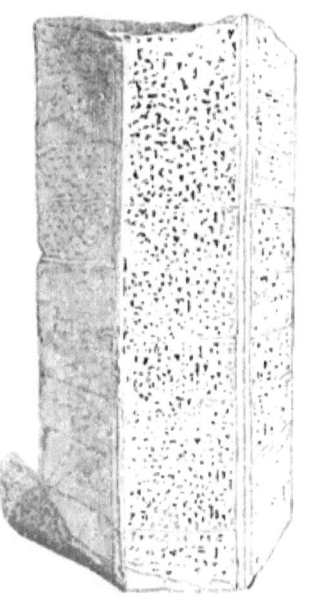

Cylinder with Assyrian Records.

The chambers I am describing appear to have been a depository for such documents. To the height of a foot or more from the floor they were entirely filled with them; some entire, but the greater part broken into fragments. They were of different sizes; the largest tablets were flat, and measured about 9 inches by 6½ inches; the smaller were slightly convex, and some were not more than an inch long, with but one or two lines of writing. The cuneiform characters on most of them were singularly sharp and well-defined, but so minute in some instances as to be almost illegible without a magnifying glass. They had been impressed by an instrument on the moist clay, which had been afterwards baked. These documents appear to be of various kinds, principally historical records of wars, and distant expeditions undertaken by the Assyrians; royal decrees

Clay Tablet with Cylinder impressed. (From Kouyunjik.)

stamped with the king's name; lists of the gods, and probably a register of offerings made in their temples; prayers; tables of the value of certain cuneiform letters, expressed by different alphabetical signs; trilingual and bilingual vocabularies of the Assyrian and of an ancient language once spoken in the country; grammatical phrases; calendars; lists of sacred days; astronomical calculations; lists of animals, birds, and various objects, &c. &c. Many are sealed with seals, and prove to be legal contracts or conveyances of land. Others bear rolled impressions of engraved cylinders. On some tablets are found Phœnician, or cursive Assyrian characters and other signs.

The adjoining chambers contained similar relics, but in far smaller numbers. Many cases were filled with these tablets, which are deposited in the British Museum. We cannot overrate their value. They furnish us with materials for the complete decipherment of the cuneiform character, for restoring the language and history of Assyria, and for inquiring into the customs, sciences, and, it may perhaps even be added, literature of its people. The documents that have thus been discovered at Nineveh probably exceed all that have yet been afforded by the monuments of Egypt. But years must elapse before the innumerable fragments can be put together, and the inscriptions transcribed. A considerable number have already been published by the Trustees of the British Museum.*

Inscribed Tablet, with Inscription at one end in Cursive Characters.

Together with these tablets were discovered a number of pieces of fine clay, bearing the impressions of seals, which had evidently been attached, like modern official seals of wax, to documents written on leather, papyrus, or parch-

* A selection from the inscriptions on these cylinders and tablets is now in course of publication by the Trustees of the British Museum. Two volumes have already appeared, edited by Sir H. Rawlinson and Mr. Norris.

ment. The documents themselves had perished. In the clay seals may still be seen the holes for the string, or strips of skin, by which the seal was fastened to them. In some

Piece of Clay with Impressions of Seals.

Impression of a Seal on Clay.

Back of the same Seal, showing the Marks of the String and the Fingers.

instances the very ashes remained, and the marks of the thumb and finger which had been used to mould the clay, can still be traced.

The greater part of these seals are Assyrian, but amongst them are some bearing Egyptian, Phœnician, and other symbols and characters. Sometimes several impressions of the same seal are found on one piece of clay. The Assyrian devices are of various kinds, the most common is that of a king slaying a lion with his sword or dagger. This would appear to be a royal signet. It is frequently surrounded by an inscription, or by an ornamental border.

But the most important and remarkable discovery was that of a piece of clay bearing the impression of two royal signets, one Assyrian, the other Egyptian. The Egyptian represents the king slaying his enemies. The name, written in hieroglyphics and enclosed in the usual royal cartouche, is that of Sabaco the Second, the Ethiopian, of the twenty-fifth Egyptian dynasty. This king reigned in Egypt at the end of the seventh century B.C., about the time when Sennacherib ascended the Assyrian throne. He was, it is believed, the So, mentioned in the second book of Kings (xvii. 4) as

Impressions of the Signets of the Kings of Assyria and Egypt (Original Size.)

Part of Cartouche of Sabaco, enlarged from the Impression of his Signet.

having received ambassadors from Hoshea, king of Israel, who, by entering into a league with the Egyptians, called down the vengeance of Shalmaneser, whose tributary he was, which led to the first great captivity of the people of Samaria. Shalmaneser was the immediate predecessor of Sennacherib, and Tirakah, the Egyptian king, who was defeated by the

Assyrians near Lachish, was the immediate successor of Sabaco.

We may conjecture that these seals were attached to a treaty of peace concluded between the Assyrian and Egyptian kings, and deposited in the royal archives at Nineveh; and that the document itself, probably written on papyrus or parchment, has perished. This singular proof of the alliance between the two monarchs is still preserved with the remains of the state documents of the Assyrian empire; furnishing one of the most remarkable instances of corroborative evidence on record, whether we regard it as verifying the general accuracy of the interpretation of the cuneiform inscriptions, or as an illustration of Scripture history.*

The signet cylinder of Sennacherib himself was afterwards discovered at the foot of the great bulls forming an entrance to his palace, and is now in the British Museum. It is engraved with wonderful minuteness and delicacy, on a cylinder of translucent green felspar, called amazon stone. The king stands in front of the sacred tree, bearing acorns instead of flowers. Above

Royal Cylinder of Sennacherib.

is the winged emblem of Ashur, here represented as a triad with three heads, a very remarkable and interesting mode of portraying the supreme deity.

The second entrance formed by the fish-gods opened into a small chamber, whose sides had been panelled with bas-reliefs representing the siege of a castle, in a country wooded with fir trees, amongst which were long lines of warriors on foot, on horseback, and in chariots.† But there were no remains of inscription, and no peculiarity of costume to identify the conquered people.

A few days after my return to Mosul, I floated down the

---

* These seals, and others found at Kouyunjik, are in the British Museum.
† No. xxxix. Plan I. p. 4.

river on a raft to Nimroud. The flood, which had spread over the plain during my absence in the desert, had destroyed a part of the village. The mud walls of my house were falling in, and the rooms with their furniture were deep in mud and silt. The stables and outhouses had become a heap of ruins, and the enclosure wall with Ibrahim Agha's loopholes had completely disappeared. The centre of the plain of Nimroud was now a large lake, and the cultivated fields were overspread with slime. The Shemutti gathered round me as I arrived, and told me of crops destroyed, and of houses swept away.

The workmen had not been idle during my absence, and discoveries of considerable interest and importance had been made in the high mound on the level of the artificial platform. The first trenches had been opened in the side of the ravine between the ruins of the tower and those of the north-west palace. A pavement of large square bricks, bearing the usual superscription of the early Nimroud king, was soon uncovered. It led to a wall of sun-dried bricks, coated with plaster, which proved to be part of a small temple built by Sardanapalus, the founder of the north-west palace, and dedicated to the Assyrian Hercules, whose name is read Mir or Bar.

I have already mentioned * that a superstructure of bricks rested upon the stone basement-wall of the tower, at the north-west corner of the mound. It was against the eastern and southern faces of this superstructure that the newly discovered temple abutted. Four of its chambers were explored, chiefly by means of tunnels carried through the enormous mass of earth and rubbish in which the ruins were buried. The great entrances were to the east. The principal portal † was formed by two colossal human headed lions, sixteen feet and a half high and fifteen feet long. They were flanked by three small winged figures, one above the other, divided by an ornamental cornice, and between them was an inscribed pavement slab of alabaster. In front of each was a square stone, apparently the pedestal of an altar, and the walls on both sides were adorned with enamelled bricks.

* Page 37. † Entrance 1, B, Plan II. p. 34.

Entrance to small Temple (Nimroud)

COLOSSAL HUMAN FIGURES.

About thirty feet to the right of this gateway was a second,* formed by two singular figures. One was that of a monster, whose head, of fanciful and hideous form, had long pointed ears and extended jaws, armed with huge teeth. Its body was covered with feathers, its fore-feet were those of a lion, its hind legs ended in the talons of an eagle, and it had spreading wings and the tail of a bird. Behind this strange image was a winged man, whose dress consisted of an upper garment with a skirt of skin or fur, an under robe fringed with tassels, and the sacred horned hat. A long sword was suspended from his shoulders by an embossed belt; sandals, armlets, and bracelets, completed his attire.† He hurled an object resembling the thunderbolt of the Greek Jove against the monster, who turned furiously towards him. This group appears to represent the bad spirit driven out by a good deity.

Fish-God at Entrance to small Temple. (Nimroud.)

On the slabs at right angles to these sculptures, forming the outer part of the entrance, were two colossal human figures, without wings, wearing garlands on their heads, and bearing branches ending in three flowers. Within the temple, at right angles to the entrance, were sculptured fish-gods, somewhat differing in form from those at Kouyunjik. The

* Entrance 2, B, Plan II. p. 34.
† Plate 5, of 2nd series of the 'Monuments of Nineveh.'

fish's head formed part of the three-horned cap usually worn by the winged figures. The tail only reached a little below the waist of the man, who was dressed in a tunic and long furred robe.*

At this entrance to the temple stood a tablet with the figure of Sardanapalus, the founder of the north-west palace, in high relief, carved out of a solid block of limestone, which had been cut into the shape of an arched frame, resembling the rock tablets of Bavian and the Nahr-el-Kelb. The monarch wore his sacrificial robes, and carried the sacred mace in his left hand. Round his neck were hung the four sacred symbols, the crescent, the star or sun, the trident, and the cross. His waist was encircled by the knotted cord, and in his girdle were three daggers. Above his head were other mythic symbols of Assyrian worship, the winged globe, the crescent, the star, the bident, and the horned cap. The entire slab, 8 ft. 8. in. high, by 4 ft.

Effigy of King.

6 in. broad, and 1 ft. 3 in. thick, was covered, on all sides, except where the sculpture intervened, with an inscription, in small arrow-headed characters. It was fixed on a plain square pedestal and stood isolated from the building. In front of it was an altar of stone, supported on lions' feet, very much resembling in shape the tripod of the Greeks.†

* Specimens of all these figures are now in the British Museum.
† The figure and altar are now in the British Museum. The inscrip-

The lion entrance led into a chamber 46 ft. by 19 ft. Its walls of sundried bricks were coated with plaster, on which the remains of figures and ornaments in colour could still be traced.* Nearly opposite to the entrance was a doorway† panelled with slabs sculptured with winged figures carrying maces. Flanking it on the four sides were priests wearing garlands.

The inner door opened into a chamber 47 ft. by 31 ft.,‡ ending in a recess paved with one enormous alabaster slab, no less than 21 ft. by 16 ft. 7 in., and 1 ft. 1 in. thick. This monolith had been broken into several pieces, probably by the falling in of the roof, and had in several places been reduced to lime by fire. The whole of its surface, as well as the side facing the chamber, was occupied by one inscription, 325 lines in length, divided into two parallel columns, and carved with the greatest care. The back of the slab, resting on a solid mass of sundried bricks, was also covered with cuneiform writing, occupying three columns. It is difficult to understand why so much labour should have been thrown away upon an inscription which was not seen. Still more curious is the fact, that whilst this inscription contained all the historical details of that on the upper side, the records of two or three more years were added. It is possible that the builders of the temple had determined that if their enemies should deface their annals, there should still remain another record, inaccessible and unknown, which would preserve the history of their greatness and glory unto all time.

The inscriptions on the monolith are, for the most part, similar to that on the tablet with the figure of the king discovered at the entrance to the temple. They record the campaigns and victories of Sardanapalus, chiefly in the mountainous country to the east and north-west of Assyria, and in Syria and Mount Lebanon. The order of his marches is described with great geographical minuteness. Some few names of cities, such as Tyre, Sidon, and one or two others on the

---

tion contains the usual genealogical list of royal names, an invocation to various gods, and an account of the wars and conquests of the king.

* Chamber *a*, Plan II. p. 34.   † Entrance 3, *b*, same Plan.
‡ Chamber *b*, same Plan.

Phœnician coast, may be identified, but the greater number of places mentioned are unknown to us. Sardanapalus boasts that he carried his arms further than any of his predecessors. In addition to the records of his wars, the inscription appears to contain an account of the building of his great palace at Nimroud (Calah), a city founded by one of his forefathers, which will probably prove highly interesting and valuable when it can be satisfactorily deciphered.

Opening into the recess paved with the inscribed stone was a small closet, 13 feet by 3, which may have been used to keep the sacrificial utensils and the garments of the priests. The entrance formed by the good spirit driving out the evil principle led into a chamber * connected by separate door ways with the two rooms last described. The walls were simply plastered.

Standing one day on the mound, I smelt the sweet smell of burning cedar. The Arab workmen, excavating in the small temple, had dug out a beam, and, the weather being cold, had made a fire with it to warm themselves. The wood was cedar; probably one of the very beams mentioned in the inscriptions as having been brought from the forests of Lebanon by Sardanapalus. After a lapse of nearly three thousand years, it had retained its original fragrance. Many other such beams were discovered.† The whole superstructure, as well as the roof and floor of the building, like those of the temple and palace of Solomon, may have been of this precious material.

About one hundred feet to the east of the building last described, and on the very edge of the artificial platform, I discovered a second temple, apparently dedicated to the Assyrian goddess, Beltis. Its principal entrance faced the south, and was on the same level as the north-west palace. This gateway was formed by two colossal lions with extended jaws, gathered-up lips and nostrils, and flowing manes. The heads, though to a certain extent conventional in form, were designed with that vigour and spirit so remarkably displayed by the Assyrian sculptor in the delineation of animals. The

* Chamber *c*, Plan II. p. 34.
† Several specimens are now in the British Museum.

Entrance to a small Temple dedicated to Beltis. (Nimroud.)

limbs conveyed the idea of strength and power, the veins and muscles were accurately portrayed, and the outline of the body was not deficient in truth. But the forepart of the animal, which was in full, was narrow and cramped, and unequal in dignity to the side. In the general treatment the sculpture resembles the archaic monuments of Greece, and it is on this account peculiarly interesting. In it, indeed, we may perhaps trace those conventional forms from which the Greek artist first derived his ideal lion.*

Statue of King from Temple. Nimroud.

This gateway, about eight feet wide, was paved with one slab, on which was a part of the usual inscription containing the annals of Sardanapalus. The height of the lions was about 8 feet, and their length thirteen. An inscription was carved across them. In front of them, in the corners formed by walls projecting at right angles with the entrance, were two altars, hollow at the top, and ornamented with gradines resembling the battlements of a castle.† The exterior walls appeared to have been adorned with enamelled bricks, many of which still remained.

* Plate 2, 2nd series of 'Monuments of Nineveh.' One of these lions is now in the British Museum.
† An altar nearly similar in shape is seen on the top of a hill, in a bas-relief at Khorsabad, Botta, plate 16.

The lion portal led into a chamber 57 feet by 25.* At one end was a recess similar to that in the opposite temple, and also paved with one great alabaster slab, 19½ ft. by 12 ft., inscribed on both sides. The inscriptions were nearly the same as those on both monoliths.

Above the great inscribed slab was found an interesting figure of the king, attired as high priest in his sacrificial robes, 3 feet 4 inches high, and cut in a hard, compact limestone.† In his right hand he held an instrument resembling a sickle, and in his left the sacred mace. On his breast was an inscription with his name and titles, and describing him as the conqueror from the river Tigris to Mount Lebanon and the Great Sea.

* C, Plan II. p. 34. † Now in the British Museum.

CHAPTER VIII.

The summer—Encampment at Kouyunjik—Mode of life—Departure for the mountains—Akra—Rock-tablets at Gunduk—District of Zibari—Namet Agha—District of Shirwan—of Baradost—of Gherdi—of Shemdina—Moussa Bey—Nestorian bishop—Convent of Mar Hananisho—District and plain of Ghaour—Dizza—An Albanian friend—Bash-Kalah—Izzet Pasha—A Jewish encampment—High mountain pass—Mahmoudiyah—First view of Wan.

THE difficulties and delay in crossing the Tigris, now swollen by the melting of the mountain snows, induced me to pitch

Landing Place with Ferryboats on the Tigris at Mosul.

my tents on the mound of Kouyunjik, and to reside there with all my party, instead of daily passing to and fro in the rude ferry-boats to the ruins.

During the day, when not otherwise occupied, I made drawings of the bas-reliefs discovered. I went below into the subterranean passages soon after the sun had risen, and remained there, without again seeking the open air, until it was far down in the western horizon. The temperature in the dark tunnels was cool and agreeable, nearly twenty degrees of Fahrenheit lower than that in the shade above; but I found it unwholesome, the sudden change and consequent chill bringing on attacks of ague.

After the sun had set we dined outside the tents, and afterwards reclined on our carpets to enjoy the cool balmy air of an Eastern night. The broad silver river wound through the plain, the great ruin cast its dark shadows in the moonlight, the lights of 'the lodges in the gardens of cucumbers'* flickered at our feet, and the deep silence was only broken by the sharp report of a rifle fired by the watchful guards to frighten away the wild boars that lurked in the melon beds. Around us were the tents of the Jebour workmen; their chiefs and the overseers generally sat with us to talk over the topics of the day until the night was far spent. We slept under the open sky, making our beds in the field.

July had set in, and we were now in 'the eye of the summer.' My companions had been unable to resist its heat. One by one we dropped off with fever. Mr. Hormuzd Rassam and myself struggled on the longest, but at length we also gave way. Fortunately our ague attacks did not coincide. We were prostrate alternate days, and were, therefore, able to take charge alternately of the works. By the 11th of July I had sent to Busrah the first collection of sculptures from Kouyunjik, and on that day, in the middle of the hot stage of fever, and half delirious, I left Mosul for the mountains. There were still parts of central Kurdistan unvisited by the European traveller. The districts belonging to the Zibari Kurds, between Rahwandiz and the Nestorian valleys, had but recently made a tardy and partial submission to the Porte, and, still unoccupied by Turkish troops, acknowledged

---

* Isaiah, i. 8. These temporary huts are raised in the gardens and plantations of melons, cucumbers, and other fruit, by the men who watch day and night to protect them against thieves and wild animals.

only their own hereditary chiefs. The tribes inhabiting them are renowned for their lawlessness.

I determined, therefore, to visit these districts on my way to Wan, to devote some days to the examination of the ruins and cuneiform inscriptions in and near that city, and then to return to Mosul through the unexplored uplands to the south of the lake of Wan, and by such of the Nestorian valleys as I had not seen during my former journey in the mountains. I should thus spend the hottest part of the summer in the cool regions of Kurdistan, and be again at Nineveh by September, when the heats begin to decline.

Few European travellers can brave the perpendicular rays of an Assyrian sun. Even the well-seasoned Arab seeks the shade during the day, and journeys by night. As we had no motive for neglecting the usual precautions, we struck our tents late in the afternoon, and got upon our horses at the foot of the mound of Kouyunjik as the sun went down.

Five hours' ride over the plain brought us to the small Turcoman village of Bir Hillan (the well of stone), which stands on the south-eastern spur of the Makloub hills. After two hours' rest we continued our journey, and crossed this spur before morning dawned. The Gebel Makloub is here divided into two distinct ranges by a deep valley. The southern ridge, rocky and furrowed like the northern, is called the Gebel Ain-es-sufra (the hill of the yellow spring), from a discoloured fountain in one of its ravines, a place of pilgrimage of the Yezidis. We descended into a broad plain, stretching from it to the first Kurdish range, and soon found ourselves on the banks of the Ghazir, here a clear sparkling stream clothed with tall oleanders, now bending under their rosy blossoms. We sought the shade of some spreading walnut-trees, during the heat of the day, near the small Kurdish village of Kaimawa.

We were again on our way in the afternoon. Instead of striking for the mountains by the direct path across the plain of Navkur, we rode along the foot of a range of low hills, forming its western boundary, to the large Kurdish village of Bardaresh. Having rested for a few hours, we descended in the middle of the night into a plain receiving the drainage of the surrounding highlands, and during the rainy season almost impassable from mud. In the summer the broad fissures and deep crevices, formed by the heat of the sun, render it scarcely less difficult to beasts of burden. Scattered over it are many flourishing villages, inhabited almost entirely by Kurds. Artificial mounds, the remains of ancient civilisation, but of small size when compared with the great ruins of Assyria, rise amongst the hovels of the Kurdish peasants.

After we had crossed the parched and burning plain we entered a valley in the Kurdish hills, watered by a stream called Melik or Gherasin. We had to climb over much broken ground—rocky ridge and ravine—before reaching the slope of the mountain covered with the gardens and orchards of Akra. We tarried for a moment at a cool spring rising in a natural grotto, and collected into two large basins. As such places usually are, it was, if not a sacred, a genial spot to the Mussulmans, and they had chosen a small open terrace near for a burial-ground. Saints abound amongst the Kurds, as amongst all ignorant people, and there are few grave-yards without a large supply of their tombs: that near the fountain of Akra appeared to be particularly favoured, and the place of mourning was made gay by the many-coloured remnants of old garments, which fluttered like streamers from the tall head-stones.*

Although Akra stands on the mountain-side, it is still within the region of the great heats, and the inhabitants pass the summer-nights beneath the sky. During this season they leave their dwellings, and encamp in the gardens. The town contains nearly six hundred families, and the whole district about three hundred villages and hamlets, furnishing a considerable part of the revenues of the pashalic of Mosul.

Some days elapsed before my companions, who were suffering from fever, were able to journey. I took advantage of the delay to visit two rock tablets near the village of

---

* The custom of placing *ex-voto* offerings on or near the tomb of a holy person—generally pieces torn from the garments—prevails throughout the East. Frequently the branches of a neighbouring tree, and the iron grating of the windows of the resting-place of a saint, are completely covered with such relics.

Gunduk. They have been carved at the mouth of a spacious natural cavern, whose roof is fretted with stalactites, and down whose sides trickles cool clear water, and hang dank ferns and creeping plants. It is called Guppa d'Mar Yohanna, or the cave of St. John, and near it is an ancient Nestorian church dedicated to Saint Audishio. The bas-reliefs are Assyrian. The upper represents a man slaying a wild goat with a spear. In the lower, as far as I could distinguish the sculpture, which is high on the rock and much injured, are two women facing each other, and seated on stools. Each holds a child above a kind of basin or circular vessel, as if in the act of baptizing it. Behind the seated female to the left, a figure bears a third child, and is followed by a woman. On the opposite side is a group of three persons, apparently sacrificing an animal. There are no traces of inscriptions on or near the tablets.

On the 17th July my companions were able to move to the higher mountains. We all longed for a cooler climate, and we rejoiced as at sunrise we left our garden. The town, through which we passed, contains a few well-built stone houses, rising one above the other on the hill side, a mosque, a bath, and a ruined castle; and was formerly the stronghold of an independent chief, who enjoyed the title of pasha, and boasted, like his relation of Amadiyah, a descent from the Abbasside caliphs. The last, Mohammed Seyyid Pasha, has long been a kind of political prisoner at Mosul.

A precipitous and difficult path leads up the mountain. From the summit of the pass, the eye wanders over the plains of Navkur and Sheikhan, the broken hill country around Arbil, and the windings of the Zab and the Ghazir. On the opposite side is a deep valley dividing the Akra hills from a second and loftier range. We now entered the region of dwarf oaks, and stopped, after a short day's journey, at the Kurdish hamlet of Hashtgah, surrounded by gigantic trees and watered by numerous streams.

Through the valley ran a broad clear stream, one of the confluents of the Zab. We rode along its banks for nearly an hour, and then struck into a narrow gorge thickly wooded with oak. Another stony and precipitous pass was between us and the principal district of Zibari. From its summit the main stream of the Zab is seen winding through a rich valley, beyond which rise the more central and loftier mountains of Kurdistan, with their snowy peaks. Descending into the low country we rode by the village of Birikapra, the residence of Mustafa Agha, the former head of the Zibari tribes. The present chief, Namet Agha, dwells at Heren, about two miles beyond. He had lately been at Mosul to receive from the Pasha his cloak of investiture, and during his visit had been my guest. His abilities and acquirements were above the ordinary Kurdish standard, which indeed is low enough; for, as the Arab proverb declares, 'Be the Kurd a Kurd or a prophet, he will still be a bear.' He spoke Persian with fluency, and was not ignorant of Arabic. As he was well acquainted with the geography of Kurdistan, I learnt from him many interesting particulars relating to the less-known districts of the mountains.

The Kurds belong to a sect of Mussulmans notoriously strict in the observance of their religious duties. The Agha had feasted all night, and was now sleeping through his daily fast. He was stretched on a rich carpet beneath a cluster of trees, and near a reservoir of water, outside the walls of his small mud castle. A thin white cloak, embroidered with silk and golden threads, was thrown over him, and whilst one attendant fanned his head, a second gently kneaded his naked feet. I begged that he should not be disturbed, and we proceeded to settle ourselves for the day under the trees. The unusual stir, however, soon awoke the chief. He welcomed me with friendly warmth; and, although forbidden to eat himself, he did not leave his guests uncared for. The breakfast brought to us from his harem comprised a variety of sweetmeats and savoury dishes, which did credit to the skill of the Kurdish ladies.

There are about fifty Catholic Chaldæan families, recent converts from Nestorianism, in Heren. They have a church, and had no cause to complain of their Kurdish masters, especially during the government of the present chief.

Namet Agha placed me under the protection of his cousin, Mullah Agha, who was ordered to escort me to the borders of the pashalic of Hakkiari, now occupied by the Turkish troops. Our guide was a tall, sinewy mountaineer, dressed in the many-coloured loose garments, and huge red and black turban folded round the high conical felt cap, which give a peculiar and ungainly appearance to the inhabitants of central Kurdistan. He was accompanied by three attendants,

A Kurd.

and all were on foot, the precipitous and rocky pathways of the mountains being scarcely practicable for horses, which are rarely kept but by the chiefs. They carried their long rifles across their shoulders, and enormous daggers in their girdles.

We left Heren early on the morning of the 19th, and soon reaching the Zab rode for two hours along its banks, to a spot where a small raft had been made ready for us to cross the stream. Many villages were scattered through the valley on both sides of the river, and the soil is not ill cultivated. We passed the night in Rizan, near the ferry.

We now entered the tract which has probably been followed for ages by the mountain clans in their periodical migrations. Besides the sedentary population of these districts, there are certain nomade Kurdish tribes called Kochers, who subsist entirely by their flocks. As they do not engage in agriculture, but rely upon the rich pastures of Assyria, they change their encamping grounds according to the season of the year, gradually ascending from the plains watered by the Tigris and Zab towards the highest peaks in summer, and returning to the low country as the winter draws nigh. They are notorious thieves and robbers, and during their annual migrations commit serious depredations upon the settled inhabitants of the districts on their way, and more especially upon the Christians. As they possess vast flocks of sheep and herds of cattle, their track has in most places the appearance of a beaten road.

The country to the east of the Zab is broken into a number of parallel ranges of wooded hills, divided by narrow ravines. Small villages are scattered here and there on the mountain sides, in the midst of terraces cultivated with wheat and planted with fruit trees. The scenery occasionally assumes a character of beauty and grandeur, as the deep green valleys open beneath the traveller's feet, and the lofty snow-capped peaks of Rahwandiz rise majestically in the clear blue sky. Our first night's encampment, after leaving the Zab, was near the small hamlet of Bani. Crossing a high ridge, we left the district of Zibari, and entered that of Shirwan, whose chief, Miran Bey, came out to meet us at the head of his armed retainers. He led us to the large village of Bersiyah, situated beneath a bold and lofty peak called Piran. A feast had been prepared for us, and we rested under a walnut-tree. Through the valley beneath ran a considerable confluent of the Zab, dividing the districts of Shirwan and Gherdi. During the afternoon, we rode for three hours along this stream, through open valleys and narrow gorges, until we reached Harouni, in the district of Baradost. Most of the villages in these mountains have small mud forts, with four or six towers,—the places of refuge and defence of the numerous petty chiefs during their frequent broils and blood-feuds. We met a few Jewish families who wander from village to village. The men are pedlars and goldsmiths, and are not unwelcome guests, even in the intolerant families of the Kurds, as they make and refashion the ornaments of the ladies.

On one of the many peaks towering above Harouni, is the large village of Khan-i-resh, with its orchards and gardens, the residence of the chief of the district of Baradost. We reached it by a very rapid ascent, and were received by the Mir, Fezullah Bey, in a spacious chamber, supported by wooden pillars, and completely open on the side facing the valley, over which it commanded an extensive and beautiful prospect. The turban of the chief, a Cashmere shawl striped red and white, vied in size with the largest headgear we had seen in Kurdistan. His robes were of silk richly embroidered, and his dark eyes were rendered more lustrous by a profuse besmearing of *kohl* over the eyelids. He was surrounded by a crowd of well-armed and well-dressed attendants, and received us as if he had been the petty sovereign of the hills. Although he had condescended for the last two years to contribute some eight purses (35*l.*) towards the Turkish revenues, he still boasted an entire independence, and submitted with evident ill-will to the control of the Agha of Zibari, under whom his tribes had been placed by the Pasha of Mosul.* He received Mullah Agha, however, with civility, and read the letters of introduction from Namet Agha, of which I was the bearer. Like most of the mountain chiefs, he spoke Persian, the language used in Kurdistan for all written communications, and in books, except the Koran and a few pious works, which are in Arabic. The Kurdish dialects are mere corruptions of the Persian, and are not, with rare exceptions, employed in writing.

The Mir pressed me to pass the night with him as his guest; but, after partaking of his breakfast, I continued my journey, and reached, by sunset, the small turreted stronghold of Beygishni.

The next morning we crossed one of the shoulders of the lofty peak of Ser-i-Resh, into the valley of Chappata.† It

---

* It was this chief, or one of his dependants, I believe, who plundered and was about to murder two American missionaries, who attempted to cross the mountains the year after my visit.

† Or Chapnaia, in Chaldæan.

was necessary to visit the Mir of Gherdi, through whose territories we were now travelling, and whose protection we consequently required. He was away from his castle. After having rested and eaten bread there, we left the bold upland upon which the village stands, and entered a wild and narrow gorge. A very steep pathway led us to the summit of the northern shoulder of the Ser-i-Resh, from whence we gazed over a sea of mountain ranges, whose higher peaks were white with eternal snow. As we wound down a rugged track on the opposite side of the pass, we came upon a party of gaily dressed Kurds, crouching in a circle round a bubbling spring. They were Iahya Bey, the Mir, and his people, who had come from Rua to meet me. The chief, after the usual exchange of civilities, insisted upon returning to that village with us, and mounted his fine white mare, whose tail was dyed bright red with henna to match his own capacious scarlet trowsers. I could scarcely refuse his offer of hospitality, although our day's journey was thereby much shortened, and we rode together down the mountain until, turning into a valley, we found the chief's carpets spread beneath the trees, with the repast that he had prepared for us.

We had now left the naked hills which skirt the Assyrian plains, and had entered the wooded districts of Kurdistan. On the following day we journeyed through a valley thick with walnuts and other large trees, and followed the windings of one of the principal confluents of the Zab. We crossed it, backwards and forwards, by wicker suspension bridges, until we ascended, through a forest of orchards watered by innumerable streamlets, to Nera, the village of Mousa Bey, the chief of Shemdeena.

The solitude of the place was only broken by a few boys who were bathing in a brawling stream. The chief himself and the inhabitants were still slumbering after their night's observance of the Ramazan. We pitched our tents near some springs on an open lawn, and waited the return of an aged servant who had been disturbed by the noise of our caravan, and had undertaken to announce our arrival to his master.

We had evidently to deal with a man of civilisation and luxury, for the old Kurd shortly returned followed by numerous attendants, bearing sherbets and various Persian delicacies, in china bowls. Mousa Bey himself came to us in the afternoon, and his manners and conversation confirmed the impression that his breakfast had produced. Intercourse with Persia, beyond whose frontiers his own tribe sometimes wandered, had taught him the manners and language of his neighbours. He was somewhat proud of his acquirements; and when he found that he could exhibit them before the crowd of armed followers that respectfully surrounded him, by talking to me in a learned tongue, a bond of friendship was immediately established between us. He told me that he was descended from one of the most ancient of Kurdish families, whose records for many hundred years still exist; and he boasted that Sheikh Tahar, the great saint, had deemed him the only chief worthy, from his independence of the infidel government of the Sultan, to receive so holy a personage as himself after the downfall of Beder Khan Bey. This Sheikh Tahar, who as the main instigator of many atrocious massacres of the Christians, and especially of the Nestorians, ought to have been pursued into the uttermost parts of the mountains by the Turkish troops, and hanged as a public example, was now suffering from fever. He sent to me for medicine; but as his sanctity would not permit him to see, face to face, an unbelieving Frank, and as he wished to have a remedy without going through the usual form of an interview with the doctor, I declined giving him any help.

In Nera are many Jewish families, who make a livelihood by weaving the coloured woollen stuffs worn by the Kurds. The Bishop of Shemisden (or Shemdeena), hearing of my arrival, sent one of his brothers to meet me. He came to us in the evening, and inveighed against the fanaticism and tyranny of the Bey, who, he declared, had driven many Christians from their villages into Persia.

We rose early on the following day, and left Nera long before the population was stirring, by a very steep pathway, winding over the face of a precipice, and completely overhanging the village. Reaching the top of the pass we came upon a natural carpet of Alpine flowers of every hue, spread over the eastern declivity of the mountain, and cooled and moistened by the snows and glaciers which fringed the deep basin. The valley at our feet was the Nestorian district of Shemisden, thickly set with Christian villages, the first of which, Bedewi, we reached, after passing a few cultivated patches cleared from the forest of oaks. The inhabitants who flocked out to see us were miserably poor, the children starved and naked, the men and women scarcely half-covered with rags. Leaving the caravan to proceed to our night's resting-place, I turned down the valley to visit the bishop at Mar Hananisho.

A ride of three-quarters of an hour brought us to the episcopal residence. Mar Isho, the bishop, met me at some distance from it. He was shabbily dressed, and not of prepossessing appearance; but he appeared to be good-natured, and to have a fair stock of common sense. After we had exchanged the common salutations, seated on a bank of wild thyme, he led the way to the porch of the church. Ragged carpets and felts had been spread in the dark vestibule, in the midst of sacks of corn, bourghoul, and other provisions for the bishop's establishment. Various rude agricultural instruments, and spinning-wheels, almost filled up the rest of the room; for these primitive Christians rely on the sanctity of their places of worship for the protection of their temporal stores.

The church itself was entered by a low doorway, through which a man of moderate size could scarcely squeeze himself, and was even darker than the anteroom. It is an ancient building, and the bishop knew nothing of the date of its foundation. Although service is occasionally performed, the communion is not administered in it. One or two tattered parchment folios, whose title-pages were unfortunately wanting, but which were evidently of an early period, were heaped up in a corner with a few modern manuscripts on paper, the prey of mildew and insects. The title of the bishop is 'Metropolitan of Roustak,' a name of which I could not learn the origin. His jurisdiction extends over many Nestorian villages, chiefly in the valley of Shemisden. Half of this district is within the Persian territories, and from the convent we could see the frontier dominions of the Shah. It is in the high road of the periodical migrations of the great tribe of Herki, who pass like a locust cloud twice a year over the settlements of the unfortunate Christians, driving before them the flocks, spoiling the granaries, and carrying away even the miserable furniture of the hovels. It is in vain that the sufferers carry their complaints to their Kurdish master; he takes from them double the lawful taxes and tithes. The Turkish government has in this part of the mountains no power, if it had the inclination, to protect its Christian subjects.

After we had partaken of the frugal breakfast of milk, honey, and fruit prepared for us by the bishop, we turned again into the high road to Bash-Kalah. We had another pass to cross before descending into the valley of Harouna, where our caravan had encamped for the night. On the mountain top were several Nestorian families crouching, half naked, for shelter beneath a projecting rock. They seized the bridles of our horses as we rode by, beseeching us to help them to recover their little property, which, but a few hours before, had been swept away by a party of Herki Kurds. I could do nothing for these poor people, who seemed in the last stage of misery. On the other side of the valley we spied the black tents of the robbers, and their vast flocks of sheep and herds of horses roving over the green pastures. Their encampments were scattered over the uplands even to the borders of the snow, and to the feet of the bare perpendicular peaks forming the highest crests of the mountains. We were not certain what our own fate might be, were we to fall in with a band of these notorious marauders.

From the summit of the pass we looked down into two deep and well-wooded valleys, hemmed in by mountains of singularly picturesque form. We descended into the more northern valley, and passing the miserable Nestorian hamlet of Sourasor, and the ruined church and deserted Christian village of Tellana, reached our tents about sunset. They were pitched near Harouna, whose Nestorian inhabitants were too poor to furnish us with even the common coarse black bread of barley.

A low ridge separated us from the district of Ghaour or

Ghiaver, a remarkable plain of considerable extent; the basin, it would seem, of some ancient lake, and now a vast morass, receiving the drainage of the great mountains which surround it. To the west it is bounded by a perfect wall of rock, from which spring the lofty snow-clad peaks of Jelu, the highest of central Kurdistan. To the east, a line of hills forms the frontier limits of Turkey and Persia. We had now quitted the semi-independent Kurdish valleys, and had entered the newly created province of Hakkiari, governed by a Pasha, who resides at Bash-Kalah. The plain of Ghaour is, however, exposed to the depredations of the Herki Kurds, who, when pursued by the Turkish troops, seek a secure retreat in their rocky fastnesses, beyond the limits of the pashalic. The district contains many villages, inhabited by a hardy and industrious race of Nestorian Christians, and is a Nestorian bishopric.

We were obliged to follow a track over the low hills skirting the plains in order to avoid the marsh. On its very edge we passed several Kurdish villages, the houses being mere holes in the earth, almost hidden by heaps of dry dung collected for fuel. The snow lies deep in this elevated region during more than half the year, and all communication is cut off with the rest of the world, except to the adventurous footman who dares brave the dangers of the mountain storm. During the summer the moist earth brings forth an abundance of flowers, and the plain was now chequered with many-coloured patches. Here and there were small fields of grain, which had just time to ripen between the snows of the long winters. The husbandman with his rude plough, drawn sometimes by ten buffaloes, was even now preparing the heavy soil for the seed. The cold is too great for the cultivation of barley, of fruits, and even of most vegetables, and there is not a solitary tree in the plain. The supplies of the inhabitants are chiefly derived from Persia.

A ride of six hours and a-half brought us to the large village of Dizza, the chief place of the district, and the residence of a Turkish Mudir, or petty governor. This office was filled by one Adel Bey, the brother of Izzet, the Pasha of the province. A small force of regular and irregular troops was quartered, with him, on the inhabitants, and he had two guns to awe the Kurds of the neighbourhood. Soon after my arrival I called on him. Seated near him on the divan I found my old friend Ismail Agha of Tepelin, who had shown me hospitality three years before in the ruined castle of Amadiyah.* He was now in command of the Albanian troops forming part of the garrison. A change had come over him since we last met. The jacket and arms which had once glittered with gold, were now greasy and dull. His face was as worn as his garments. After a cordial greeting he made me a long speech on his fortunes, and on that of Albanian irregulars in general. 'Ah! Bey,' said he, 'the power and wealth of the Osmanlis is at an end. The Sultan has no longer any authority. The accursed Tanzimat (Reform) has been the ruin of all good men. Why, see Bey, I am obliged to live upon my pay; I cannot eat from the treasury, nor can I squeeze a piastre—what do I say, a piastre? not a miserable half-starved fowl, out of the villagers, even though they be Christians. Forsooth they must talk to me about reform, and ask for money! The Albanian's occupation is gone. Even Tafil-Bousi (a celebrated Albanian condottiere) smokes his pipe, and becomes fat like a Turk. It is the will of God. I have foresworn raki, I believe in the Koran, and I keep Ramazan.'

The night was exceedingly cold. The change from the heat of the plains to the cool nights of the mountains had made havoc amongst our party. Nearly all of us were laid up with fever. I could not, however, delay, and on the following morning our sickly caravan was again toiling over the hills. We had now entered the Armenian districts. The Christian inhabitants of Dizza are of that race and faith. From the elevated plain of Ghaour a series of valleys leads to Bash-Kalah, and the stream which winds through them joins the head-waters of the Zab. We encamped for the night at the Kurdish village of Perauniss.

Next day, near the village of Charderrah (the four valleys), we passed some ponds of muddy water, bubbling with gaseous

---

* Nineveh and its Remains, p. 122.

exhalations of a sulphurous smell, and reached in the afternoon Antiss, inhabited by Armenians and Nestorians.

The branch of the Zab, which we had seen gradually swollen by small mountain rills, had become a considerable stream. We forded it near the ruins of a fine bridge, apparently of early Turkish masonry, and beneath an old deserted castle called Kalianon. We now entered the valley of this great confluent of the Tigris, its principal source being but a few miles to the north of us, near the frontiers of Persia. The land is so heavy, that the rude plough of the country requires frequently as many as eight pairs of oxen. The Armenian ploughmen sit on the yokes, and whilst guiding or urging the beasts with a long iron-pointed goad, chant a monotonous ditty, to which the animals appear so well accustomed, that when the driver ceases from his dirge, they also stop from their labours.

A dell near our path was pointed out to me as the spot where the unfortunate traveller Schulz was murdered by Nur-Ullah Bey, the Kurdish chief of Hakkiari.* Turning up a narrow valley towards the high mountains, we suddenly came in sight of the castle of Bash-Kalah, one of the ancient strongholds of Kurdistan. Its position is remarkably picturesque. It stands on a lofty rock, jutting out from the mountains which rise in a perpendicular wall behind it. At its foot are grouped the houses of a village.

We were met on the outskirts of the village by the Muhrdar, or seal-bearer, of the Pasha, with an escort of cawasses. He led us to a convenient spot for our tents, near a spring, and

* I subsequently met in the Nestorian district of Baz, a Christian, who was in the service of Nur-Ullah Bey at the time of the murder, and was employed to bury the body. According to him, Schulz, who passed by the name of Yohanan, was taken by the guides, furnished him by a Persian prince, to Nur-Ullah Bey, instead of to Mar Shamoun, whom he intended to visit. He was described in a letter sent to the Kurdish chief as a dangerous man, who was spying out the country; an impression which was confirmed by his habit of making notes continually and openly. He remained ten days with the Bey, and then continued his journey accompanied by Kurdish guards, who killed him by their master's orders beside a stream called Av Spiresa, near the castle of Pisa, close to Bash-Kalah. Two of his Christian servants were murdered with him; his two Persian attendants were taken to Nur Ullah Bey, and also put to death.

shortly after brought provisions for ourselves and horses, sent by the governor, who, it being early in the afternoon, was still in bed after his night's vigils. It was not until long after dark that I visited Izzet Pasha. I found him encamped at a considerable elevation in a rocky ravine, which we reached, guided by cawasses carrying huge glass lanterns, by a very precipitous and difficult track. A small rivulet had been dammed up in front of his tents, and formed a reservoir which mirrored the red light of a number of torches.

Bash-Kalah was formerly the dwelling-place of Nur-Ullah Bey. He joined Beder Khan Bey in the great massacres of the Nestorians, and for many years sorely vexed those Christians who were within his rule. After a long resistance to the troops of the Sultan, he was captured about two years before my visit, and banished for life to the island of Candia.

On resuming our journey, after a day's rest, we took a direct though difficult track to Wan, only open in the middle of summer. Following a small stream, we entered a ravine leading into the very heart of the mountains. Three hours' ride, always rapidly ascending along the banks of the rivulet, brought us to a large encampment. The flocks had been driven down from the higher pastures, and were gathered together to be milked before the black tents. The women were crouching round their sheep. Their long hair was platted in tresses ending in tassels mingled with gold coins. From a high turban of gay colours, also adorned with coins, a thin white veil fell over their shoulders, and their flowing garments were of bright silk. The children ran to and fro with wooden bowls, and a girl standing near sang a plaintive air, beating the measure on a tambourine. The features of the women and of the men, who came out of their tents as we rode up, as well as the tongue in which they addressed one another, showed at once that they were not Kurds. They were Jews, shepherds and wanderers, of the stock, may be, of those who, with their high priest Hyrcanus, were carried away captive from Jerusalem by Tigranes in the second century of our era, and placed in the city and neighbourhood of Wan. Their descendants, two hundred years after, were already so numerous that Shapour (Sapores) II. destroyed no less than 10,000 families in Wan alone.*

We encamped near the Jewish nomades, and I visited their tents, but could learn nothing of their history. They fed their flocks, as their fathers had done before them, in these hills, and paid taxes to the governor of Bash-Kalah. There are many other families, keepers of sheep like themselves, scattered over the mountains.

We had now reached the higher regions of Kurdistan. Next morning we soon left the narrow flowery valley and the brawling stream, and entered an undulating upland covered with deep snow, more than ten thousand feet above the level of the sea. On all sides of us were towering peaks, and to the west a perfect sea of mountains, including the lofty ranges of Hakkiari and Bohtan. Far away to the north was the azure basin of Lake Wan, and beyond it rose the solitary white cone of the Subhan Dagh. A light wind drove a few fleecy clouds across the sunny landscape, now veiling some distant hill, now hiding in shadow the deep valleys. A covey of large birds sailed with a rapid swoop, and with the whistling sound peculiar to the partridge kind, from an opposite height, and alighted within a few yards of me. They were the Kabk-i-dereh, or the Our-kaklik, as they are called by the Turks; a gigantic partridge, almost the size of a small turkey, only found in the highest regions of Armenia and Kurdistan.

Descending rapidly, and passing, near the foot of the mountain, one or two miserable, half-deserted Kurdish hamlets, we entered a long narrow ravine, shut in by perpendicular cliffs of sandstone and conglomerate. This outlet of the mountain streams opens into the valley of Mahmoudiyah, in the centre of which rises an isolated rock crowned by the picturesque castle of Kosh-Ab.

We pitched our tents on a green lawn, near the bank of the foaming stream which sweeps round the foot of the castellated rock. Soon after our arrival a Kurdish Bey, of venerable appearance, a descendant of the hereditary chiefs of

* Moses of Chorene, l. ii. c. 19. St. Martin, 'Mém. sur l'Arménie,' vol. i. p. 139.

Mahmoudiyah, called upon me. He had once been the owner of the castle, but had been driven from it by an adventurer of some celebrity in this part of Kurdistan. This marauder had recently been captured by the Turks, who had seized his property, but had not restored it to its rightful owner. The village, once a town, whose ruined mosques, baths, and bridges still remain, was named Mahmoudiyah, after a certain Mahmoud Bey, who was of the noble Kurdish family claiming lineal descent from the Abbasside caliphs,

The Castle of Mahmoudiyah.

of which the Bey of Jezirah, or Bohtan, is the acknowledged head. The castle, built in the fifteenth century, is called Nerin, or more generally Kosh-Ab, 'the sweet water,' from the pure stream flowing beneath it.

We rose early next morning, and went up to the castle. As it was still Ramazan, the small garrison of regular troops and undisciplined Albanians had feasted during the night and were now sleeping. We knocked at the iron-bound gate for some time without arousing the slumberers. At length a slip-shod sentinel, who appeared to have been fast asleep at his post, drew back the rusty bolts. He would not, however, admit us, until he had received orders from the officer in command, who, with much good-nature, slipt on a threadbare uniform, turned out the scarcely-awakened guard, and received us with military honours. The castle is falling into ruins, though its towers still rise boldly from the edge of the precipice, overhanging at a giddy height the valley below. In them, open to the cool breezes of the mountain, are the dwelling-rooms of the old Kurdish chiefs, adorned with tasteful lattice-work, and with painted panellings and gilded cornices. They were tenanted by the Turkish troops, whose bright arms and highly-polished kitchen utensils hung on the gaudy walls. A few long brass guns richly embossed, the work of the early Turkish conquerors of Kurdistan, lie, upset from their carriages, on the crumbling battlements. After drinking coffee and smoking pipes with the captain of the guard, we walked down the narrow pathway leading to the valley, and, mounting our horses, joined the caravan, which had preceded us on the road to Wan.

We stopped, after a ride of about fourteen miles, at the Armenian village of Hindostan, situated in a rich but thinly peopled valley called Khawassan. On the following morning we crossed this valley to Nourtchouk, at the outskirts of which I was met by the priest at the head of the inhabitants. A range of low hills now separated us from the plain and lake of Wan. We soon reached their crest, and a landscape of surpassing beauty was before us. At our feet, intensely blue and sparkling in the rays of the sun, was the inland sea, with the sublime peak of the Subhan Dagh, mirrored in its transparent waters. The city, with its castle-crowned rock and its embattled walls and towers, lay embowered in orchards and gardens. To our right a rugged snow-capped mountain opened midway into an amphitheatre, in which, amidst lofty trees, stood the Armenian convent of Yedi Klissia (the seven churches). To the west of the lake was the Nimroud Dagh, and the highlands nourishing the sources of the great rivers of Mesopotamia. The hills forming the foreground of our picture were carpeted with the brightest flowers, over which wandered the flocks, whilst the gaily dressed shepherds gathered around us as we halted to contemplate the enchanting scene.

We now descended rapidly towards Wan, and as we issued into the plain, a party of horsemen galloped towards us. I soon recognised amongst them my friend Mr. Bowen;* with him were the Cawass-Bashi and a troop of irregular cavalry, sent out by the Pasha to escort me into the city. Nor did the governor's kindness end with this display of welcome. After winding for nearly an hour through orchards and gardens, whose trees were bending under the weight of fruit, and then through the narrow and crowded streets, we were led to his serai or palace, which, such as it was, had been made ready for our use, and where his treasurer was waiting to receive us. Notwithstanding the fast, an abundant breakfast of various meats and sweet messes, cooked after the Turkish fashion, had been prepared for us, and we soon found repose upon a spacious divan, surrounded by all the luxuries of Eastern life.

* The Rev. Mr. Bowen, who died Bishop of Sierra Leone.

CHAPTER IX.

Mehemet Pasha—Description of Wan—Its history—Improvement in its condition—The Armenian bishop—The cuneiform inscriptions—The caves of Khorkhor—The Meher Kapousi—A tradition—The Bairam—An Armenian school—Amikh—The convent of Yedi Klissia—Leave Wan—The Armenian patriarch—The island of Akhtamar—An Armenian church—History of the convent—Pass into Mukus—The district of Mukus—Of Shattak—Of Nourdooz—A Nestorian village—Encampments—Mount Ararat—Mar Shamoun—Jula-Merik—Valley of Dez—Pass into Jelu—Nestorian district of Jelu—An ancient church—The bishop—District of Baz—Of T'khoma—Return to Mosul.

MEHEMET PASHA was living during the fast of Ramazan in a kiosk in one of the gardens outside the city walls. We had scarcely eaten, before he came himself to welcome me to Wan. He was the son of the last Bostandji-Bashi of Constantinople, and having been brought up from a child in the imperial palace, was a man of pleasing and dignified manners, and of considerable information. His rule was mild and conciliating, and he possessed those qualities so rare in a Turkish governor, yet so indispensable to the civilisation and well-being of the empire,—a strict honesty in the administration of the revenues of his province, and a sense of justice beyond the reach of bribes. From Christians and Kurds we had received, during our journey through his pashalic, the highest testimony to his tolerance and integrity.

I remained a week at Wan, chiefly engaged in copying cuneiform inscriptions, and in examining its numerous remarkable monuments of antiquity. The city is of very ancient date. It stands on the borders of a large and beautiful lake, a site eminently suited to a prosperous community. The lofty mountains bordering the inland sea to the east, here recede, in the form of an amphitheatre, leaving a rich plain five or six miles in breadth, in the midst of which rises an isolated, calcareous rock. To the summit of this natural stronghold there is no approach, except on the western side, where a gradual but narrow ascent is defended by walls and bastions. From the earliest ages it has consequently been the acropolis of the city, and no position could have been stronger before the discovery of the engines of modern warfare. The fortifications and castle, of a comparatively recent date, are now in ruins, and are scarcely defensible, with their few rusty guns, against the attacks of the neighbouring Kurds.

The modern town of Wan stands at the foot, and to the south of, the isolated rock. Its streets and bazaars are small, narrow, and dirty, but its houses are not ill built. It is surrounded by fruitful gardens and orchards, irrigated by artificial rivulets derived from the streams rising in the Yedi Klissia mountains. It may contain between twelve and fifteen thousand inhabitants.

According to Armenian history, the Assyrian queen Semiramis founded the city, which, after her, was originally named Schamiramjerd. Here, in the delicious gardens which she had planted in the fertile plain, and which she had watered with a thousand rills, she sought refuge from the intolerable heats of a Mesopotamian summer, returning again, on the approach of winter, to her palaces at Nineveh.

The first city having fallen to decay, it is said to have been rebuilt, shortly before the invasion of Alexander the Great, by an Armenian king named Wan, after whom it was subsequently called. It appears to have been again abandoned, for we find that it was once more raised from its foundations in the second century B.C. by Vagharschag, the first king of the Arsacian dynasty of Armenia, who made it the strongest city in the kingdom. In the eleventh century it was ceded by the royal family of the Ardzrounis to the Greek emperors, from whom it was taken by the Seljuk Turks. It fell, in 1392, into the hands of Timourlane, who, according to his custom, gave the inhabitants over to the sword. Even in his day, the great monuments of solid stone, raised by the Assyrian queen, were still shown to the stranger.

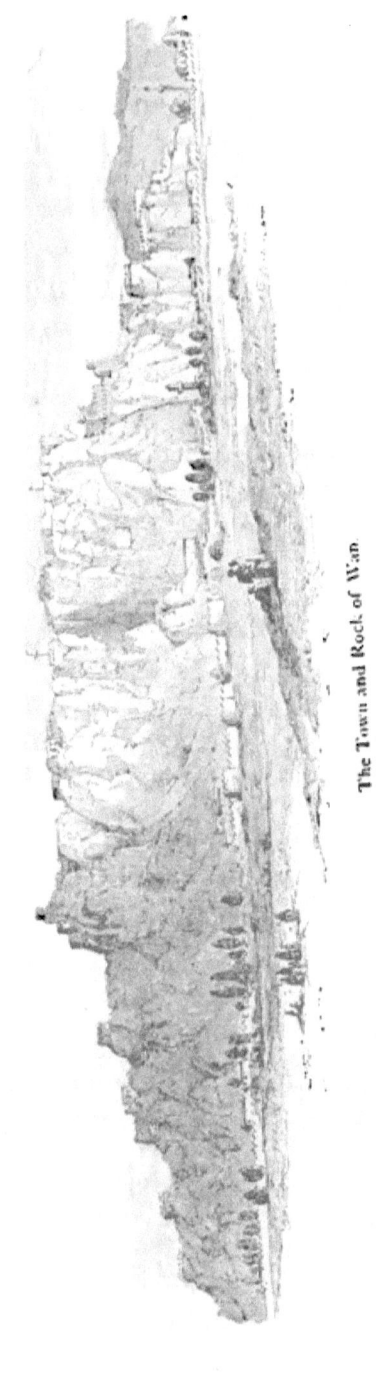

The Town and Rock of Wan.

The city had been seized, sometime previous to my visit, by a rebel Kurdish chief, Khan Mahmoud, who massacred the Turkish garrison, inflicted large fines upon the Christians, and grievously oppressed the dependent villages. After the troops of the Sultan had made many vain attempts to recover the place, it finally yielded two years before my journey. Under the mild rule of Mehemet Pasha it was rapidly rising to prosperity. The protection he had given to the Armenians had encouraged that enterprising and industrious people to enlarge their commerce, and to build warehouses for trade. Two handsome khans, with bazaars attached, were nearly finished. Shops for the sale of European articles of clothing and of luxury had been opened; and, what was of still more importance, several native schools had already been established. These improvements were chiefly due to one Sharân, an Armenian merchant, and a man of liberal and enlightened views, who had seconded with energy and liberality the desire of the Pasha to ameliorate the social condition of the Christian population.

Shortly after my arrival, the Armenian bishop called upon me. He was dressed in the peculiar costume of his order,—long black robes and a capacious black hood almost concealing his head,—and was accompanied by the priests and principal laymen of his diocese. On his breast he wore the rich diamond crescent and star of the Turkish order of merit, of which he was justly proud. It had been asked for him of the Sultan by the Pasha, as an encouragement to the Christians, and as a proof of the spirit of tolerance which animated the government. If such principles were fully carried out in Turkey, there would be good hope for the empire.

The inscriptions of Wan are of two distinct periods, though all in the cuneiform writing. The most ancient are in a character identical with that on the oldest monuments of Assyria. The only one not entirely in this Assyrian character is on the southern face of the rock, inaccessible, but easily legible, on account of the size and distinctness of its letters, by a glass from below. It is a trilingual tablet carved by Xerxes, the son of Darius, very nearly word for word the same as those of the same king at Hamadan (Ecbatana) and Persepolis.

The most important inscriptions at Wan are on the southern face of the isolated rock, round the entrance to a set of excavated chambers, probably once serving as tombs,

Tombs in the Rock at Wan.

which, unlike the artificial caves at Bavian and Malthaiyah, may be referred to the same period as the inscriptions. They appear to record the victories and deeds of a king, and it is highly probable that they were placed over royal sepulchres.

They are contained in eight parallel columns, and divided into above 300 lines and thirteen consecutive paragraphs. The letters are large and admirably carved, and the writing is divided by horizontal lines. They are defective in many places, partly from natural decay, but mainly from wilful injury: the obliterated characters may to a great extent be restored by a comparison of the several inscriptions which contain corresponding passages.

The remaining inscriptions are on the northern face of the rock. They are five in number. The longest and most important contains twenty-nine lines, and is on the side wall to the left on entering an artificial vaulted recess. It has been partly destroyed by a rude cross cut by the Armenians across the tablet. The cave is called the 'Khazana Kapousi,' or the treasure gate, and is held to be a sacred spot by Christians and Mussulmans. Beneath it, according to tradition, an iron gate, guarded by genii armed with swords of flame, closes the entrance to a vast hall filled with all manner of riches. The magic words that can alone open this portal are contained in the inscription, which is guarded at night by a serpent, who retires at break of day into a hole near the cave.

An inscription of seventeen lines is carved at the entrance to a second chamber, and on tablets cut in the rock are three more, each of nineteen lines, word for word alike, but with orthographical variations in the royal name.

The Pasha had kindly placed the 'Mimar Bashi,' or architect in chief of the town, an intelligent and honest Armenian, named Nikoos, under my orders during my researches at Wan. I also found in the place a half-crazy Cawass, who had been all the way to Constantinople to obtain a firman for leave to dig for treasure beneath the inscribed tablets. The imperial document had been granted, with a clause, however, that a share of the riches discovered should be paid into the Sultan's treasury. His search had hitherto been vain, although his purse had been emptied; but he knew all the old stones and inscriptions in the neighbourhood. With the aid of these two men I carried on excavations for a short time at the foot of the northern face of the rock, without other results than clearing away the earth from one or two half-buried tablets, and laying bare the artificially smoothed rock.

About a mile and a half to the east of the town, near a small village in the gardens, is a recess in the rock containing a long cuneiform inscription. It is called Meher Kapousi, which, according to the people of Wan, means the Shepherd's Gate, from a tradition that a shepherd, having fallen asleep beneath it, was told in a dream the magic word that opened the portal. He awoke and straightway tried the talisman. The stone doors flew apart, disclosing to his wondering eyes a vast hall filled with inexhaustible treasures; but as he entered they shut again behind him. He filled with gold the bag in which, as he tended his flocks, he carried his daily food. After repeating the magic summons, he was permitted to issue into the open air. But he had left his crook, and must return for it. The doors were once more unclosed at his bidding. After securing his crook, he sought to retrace his steps, but had forgotten the talisman. His faithful dog waited outside until nightfall. As its master did not come back, it took up the bag of gold, and, carrying it to the shepherd's wife, led her to the gates of the cave. She could hear the cries of her husband, and they are heard to this day, but none can give him help.

The inscription of the Meher Kapousi originally consisted of ninety-five lines, comprising the same record twice repeated. Only about sixty are now legible.

Near the Shepherd's Gate the rocks are excavated into a vast number of caves. In some places long flights of steps lead nowhere, but finish abruptly in the face of the perpendicular precipice; in others the cliff is scarped to a great height without any apparent object. A singular shaft, with stairs, leading into a cavern, is called Zimzim. It is difficult to account for the use and origin of these singular excavations: their height from the plain and their inaccessible position almost preclude the idea of their having been quarries.

All these cuneiform inscriptions, together with a few fragments of inscribed stones in the churches of Wan, belong to a dynasty which appears to have reigned in Armenia from about the middle of the eighth century B.C. to the end of the seventh. Six royal names of this dynasty are found in them. The language of two of the inscriptions is Assyrian, the remainder are in a dialect which is believed to be of Turanian or Tatar origin.[*]

At sunrise, on the 8th August, the roaring of cannon, echoed by the lofty rock, announced the end of Ramazan, and the beginning of the periodical festivities of the Bairam. Early in the morning the Pasha, glittering with gold and jewels, and surrounded by the members of his household, the officers of the garrison, and the gaily-dressed chiefs of the irregular troops, rode in procession through the streets of the town. As it is customary, he received in the palace the visits

---

[*] A further account of the inscriptions at Wan will be found in the unabridged edition of my 'Nineveh and Babylon.'

of the cadi, the mollahs, and the principal Mussulman inhabitants of Wan, as well as of the bishop, clergy, and elders of the Armenian church. The population, rejoicing at their release from a fast almost intolerable in summer, decked them-

Kurds of Wan.

selves in holiday garments, and made merry in the houses and highways. The sounds of music and revelry issued from the coffee-houses and places of public resort. The children repaired to swings, merry-go-rounds, and stalls of sweetmeats, which had been raised in the open spaces within the walls. The Christians add this feast to their own festivals, already too numerous,* and, like their Mussulman neighbours, pay visits of compliment and ceremony. Their women, who are said to be handsome, but are even more rigidly concealed than the Mohammedan ladies, crept through the streets in their long white veils.

I called in the evening on the bishop, and next morning,

* The Mussulmans have only two great annual feasts in which labour gives way to rejoicings and festivities; the Christians of all sects have little else but fasts and festivals throughout the year. A lazy Christian will add to his own holidays the Friday of the Mohammedans and the Saturday of the Jews.

at his invitation, visited the principal schools. Five have been established since the fall of the Kurdish Beys, and the enjoyment of comparative protection by the Christian population. Only one had been opened within the walls; the rest were in the gardens, which are thickly inhabited by Armenians, and form extensive suburbs to Wan. The school in the town was held in a spacious building newly erected, and at that time scarcely finished. More than two hundred children of all ages were assembled. They went through their exercises and devotions at the sound of a bell with great order and precision, alternately standing and squatting on their hams on small cushions placed in rows across the hall. An outer room held basins and towels for washing, and the cloaks and shoes taken off on entering. Books were scarce. There were not more than a score in the whole school. The first class, which had made some progress, had a few elementary works on astronomy and history, published by the Armenian press at Constantinople and Smyrna, but only one copy of each. The boys, at my request, sang and chanted their prayers, and repeated their simple lessons.

Such schools, imperfect though they be, are proofs of a great and increasing improvement in the Christian communities of Turkey.[*] A change of considerable importance, and which, it is to be hoped, may lead to the most beneficial results, is now taking place in the Armenian Church. It is undoubtedly to be attributed to the judicious, earnest, and zealous exertions of the American missionaries; their establishments, scattered over nearly the whole Turkish empire, have awakened amongst the Christians, and especially amongst the Armenians, a spirit of inquiry and a desire for the reform of abuses, and for mental culture, which must ultimately tend to raise their political, as well as their social, position.

[*] The desire of a large number of the Armenians to improve their institutions, and to adopt the manners of Europe, is a highly interesting, and indeed important, fact. I was amused, after having contributed a trifle to the funds of the school, at having presented to me a neatly printed and ornamented receipt, with the amount of my donation duly filled up in the blank space left for the purpose, the document being signed by the head of the school.

Schools in opposition to the American establishments have been opened in the capital, and in most of the large towns of Asia Minor, by the Armenians themselves; and elementary and theological works, of a far more liberal character than any hitherto published in Turkey, have been printed by Armenian printing-presses in Constantinople and Smyrna, or introduced into the country from the well-known Mechitarist convent at Venice. This is another, though an indirect, result of their labours, which the American missionaries may justly contemplate with satisfaction.

I left Wan on the 10th August, for the village of Amikh, where, according to my Armenian guide, Nikoos, an inscription was engraved on the rocks. We struck into a fine undulating corn country, abounding in Christian villages. The soil is well cultivated, though by dint of much labour. Eight, or even ten, pairs of oxen are frequently yoked to a plough, which differs from that seen in any other part of Turkey; and having two wheels, one larger than the other, more resembles those in common use in England. The landscape was richly tinted by large plots of bright yellow thistles, cultivated for the oil expressed from the seeds, to be used by the Armenians during their numerous fasts. We reached at sunset a deep bay hemmed in by gardens and orchards, and sheltered from the wind by an amphitheatre of low rocky hills. I pitched my tent about a mile from the village, near a transparent spring, in a small glade shelving to the water's edge, and embowered in white roses.

Early next morning I sought the inscriptions, which I had been assured were graven on the rocks near an old castle, standing on a bold projecting promontory above the lake. After climbing up a dangerous precipice by the help of two or three poles, in which large nails had been inserted to afford a footing, I reached a small natural cavern. A few crosses and ancient Armenian letters were rudely cut near its entrance. There was nothing else, and I had to return as I best could, disappointed, as many a traveller has been, under similar circumstances, before me.

From Amikh I rode across the country to the monastery of Yedi Klissia, whose gardens on the side of the lofty mountain of Wurrak are visible from most parts of the plain. I stopped for an hour at the church of Kormawor before ascending to the convent. An aged priest, with beard white as snow, and wearing a meion-shaped cap, and long black robes, was the guardian of the place. He led me into an arcade surrounding the inner court of the building. Seeing that I was a Frank, he guessed at once that I was searching for inscriptions, and pointed to a circular stone, the base of a wooden column. It bore three imperfect lines of cuneiform writing, part of an inscription belonging to one of the Wan kings. A second inscription on a black stone, and several fragments with the same royal name, were built into the walls.

Eight hours' ride brought me to the large Armenian convent of Yedi Klissia, or the seven churches, built of substantial stone masonry, and enclosing a spacious courtyard planted with trees. It has more the appearance of a caravanserai than that of a place of religious retreat, and is beautifully situated near the mouth of a wooded ravine, halfway up a bold mountain, which ends in snowy peaks. Spread beneath it is the blue lake and smiling plain, and the city, with its bold castellated rock, and its turreted walls half hid in gardens and orchards.

The church, a substantial modern edifice, stands within the courtyard. Its walls are covered with pictures as primitive in design as in execution. There is a victorious St. George blowing out the brains of a formidable dragon with a bright brass blunderbuss, and saints, attired in the traditionary garments of Europe, performing extravagant miracles. The intelligence of the good priest at the head of the convent was pretty well on a par with his illustrated church history. He was a specimen of the Armenian clergy of Asia Minor. As he described each subject to me, he spoke of the Nestorians as heretics, because they were allowed, by the canons of their church, to marry their mothers and grandmothers; of the Protestants as freemasons or atheists; and of the great nations of Europe as the Portuguese, the Inglese, the Muscovs, and the Abbash (Abyssinians).

I found two short cuneiform inscriptions; one on a stone amongst the ruins of the old church, the other built into the walls of the new. They contain the name and titles of a king.

Sickness having overcome both Dr. Sandwith and Mr. Cooper, they left me at Yedi Klissia, and returned to Europe.

In the afternoon of the 12th August I left the gates of the convent with Mr. Hormuzd Rassam. Once more I was alone with my faithful friend, and we trod together the winding pathway which led down the mountain side. We had both been suffering from fever, but we still had strength to meet its attacks, and to bear cheerfully, now unhindered, the difficulties and anxieties of our wandering life.

We made a short journey of three and a half hours to the pleasant village of Artamit or Adremit, and encamped beneath its fruit trees in a garden near the lake. Our path on the following day led through a hilly district, sometimes edging a deep bay, then again winding over a rocky promontory. We crossed by a bridge the large stream which we had seen at Mahmoudiyah, and which here discharges itself into the lake. The feast of St. George had been celebrated during the previous day at the church of Narek, and we passed, as we rode along, merry groups of Armenians returning from their pilgrimage. The women, seated with their children on the backs of mules and asses, and no longer fearing the glances of haughty Kurds, had lifted their veils from their ruddy faces. They were dressed in scarlet cloaks, which half concealed their festive robes. To their plaited hair was attached a square black pad of silk hung with tassels, and sometimes with coins. Most of the men carried umbrellas to protect themselves from the rays of the sun. In the midst of them, surrounded by a crowd of adherents, was the Patriarch of Akhtamar, once the head of the Armenian Church, but now only recognised by a small section of Christians living in the province of Wan. He rode a mule, and was dressed in long black robes, with a silken cowl hanging over his head. Several youthful priests, some carrying silver-headed wands, followed close behind him. He was on his way to the city, and I thus lost the opportunity of seeing him at his residence on the sacred island.

On the shores of the lake were several encampments of gipsies; the men to be distinguished by their swarthy countenances, the women and children by their taste for begging.

We passed through Vastan, in the eleventh century the residence of the royal Armenian family of Ardzrouni, but now a mere village. Not far from it we found the convent boat on the beach. Four sturdy monks were about to row it back to the island of Akhtamar. As they offered to take me with them, I left the caravan, and, with Mr. Rassam and the Bairakdar, was soon gliding over the calm surface of the lake.

In the absence of the Patriarch we were received at the convent by an intelligent and courteous monk named Kirikor. His hair, as well as his beard, had never known the scissors, and fell in long luxuriant curls over his shoulders. It was of jetty black, for he was still a young man, although he had already passed twenty years of a monastic life. He led us through an arched doorway into the spacious courtyard of the convent, and thence into an upper room furnished with comfortable divans for the reception of guests. Tea was brought to us after the Persian fashion, and afterwards a more substantial breakfast, in which the dried fish of the lake formed the principal dish.

The church, which is within the convent walls, is built of a fine red sandstone. Like other religious edifices of the same period and of the same nation, it is in the form of a cross, with a small hexagonal tower, ending in a conical roof, rising above the centre. The first monastery was founded by a Prince Theodore in A.D. 653; and the church is attributed to the Armenian king Kakhik, of the family of Ardzrouni, who reigned in the tenth century; but the island appears from a very remote date to have contained a castle of the Armenian kings. The entrance and vestibule of the church are of a different style from the rest of the building, being a bad imitation of modern Italian architecture. They were added about one hundred years ago by a patriarch, whose tomb is in the courtyard. The interior is simple. A few rude pictures of saints and miracles adorn the walls, and a gilded throne for the Patriarch stands near the altar. The exterior, however, is elaborately ornamented with friezes and broad bands of sculptured figures and scroll work, the upper part being almost covered with bas-reliefs, giving to the whole building a very striking and original appearance. The conical roof of the tower, rising over the centre of the cross, rests upon a frieze of hares, foxes, and other animals. Above arched windows are bands of rich foliage, and beneath them, at the base of the tower, a row of small vaulted recesses. The roof of the transept is supported by human heads. Beneath is a frieze, quite Assyrian in its character, consisting of lions springing upon stags, and figures of wild goats, hares, and deer. Under the projecting roof of the aisle is another frieze, formed of bunches of grapes mingled with grotesque forms of men, animals, and birds. Next is a row of heads, projecting in high relief from the wall. They are succeeded by bas-reliefs representing Scripture stories from the Old and New Testaments, divided into separate subjects by medallions with images of Armenian saints. An elaborate border of scroll work completes the exterior decoration about half way up the building. The human form is rudely portrayed in these sculptures; but the general design is far from inelegant, and the ornaments are rich and appropriate. I know of no similar specimen of Armenian architecture, and I regret that time would not allow me to make detailed drawings of the edifice.

In a grave-yard outside the church are several most elaborately carved tombstones belonging to the early Armenian patriarchs. That of Zachariah, who died in the fourteenth century, and who was for one year patriarch at Echmiadsin, and for nine years at Akhtamar, is especially worthy of notice for the richness and elegance of its ornaments. In the portico is a circular black stone, like a millstone, with short cuneiform inscriptions, containing a royal name, on the two flat sides. A library of manuscripts, said to have been once preserved in the convent, no longer exists.

The patriarchate of Akhtamar, or Aghthamar, was founded in 1113 by an archbishop of the island, who declared himself independent of the universal Patriarch, residing at Echmiadsin. Its jurisdiction does not extend far beyond the immediate neighbourhood of Wan, and the ecclesiastic who fills the office is generally even more ignorant than other dignitaries of the Armenian Church.

The convent and church are built on a small rocky island about five miles from the shore. On an adjacent islet are the ruined walls of a castle partly under water. Intercourse with the main land is carried on by the one crank boat, which, whenever the weather permits, goes backwards and forwards daily for such provisions as are required by the inmates of the monastery.

Late in the afternoon, accompanied by the monk Kirikor, I was rowed to the farm and garden belonging to the convent, near the village of Ashayansk. A few monks live there, and tend the property of the convent, supplying the Patriarch with the produce of the dairy and orchards. They received us very hospitably. Kirikor rode with me on the following morning as far as the large Armenian village of Narek, in which there is a church dedicated to St. George, much frequented by pilgrims from Wan and the surrounding country.

We had now left the lake, and our track led up a deep ravine, which gradually became more narrow as we drew nigh to the high mountains that separated us from the unexplored districts of Mukus and Bohtan. We passed a large Armenian village named Pagwantz, near which, on the summit of a precipitous rock, stands the ruined castle of Khan Mahmoud, the rebel chief. He was the eldest of seven brothers, all of whom governed under him different districts on the borders of the lake, and sorely oppressed the Christian inhabitants. Five were captured by the Turks, and are in banishment.

On both sides of the ravine were villages and ruined castles. Numerous streams from the hill-sides irrigated plots of cultivated ground. Ere long we entered a rocky barren tract, patched here and there with fragrant Alpine flowers. After climbing up a steep declivity of loose stones like the moraine of a Swiss glacier, and dragging our horses with much difficulty after us, we found ourselves amidst eternal snow, over which we toiled for nearly two hours, until we reached the crest of the mountain, and looked down into the deep valley of Mukus. This is considered one of the highest passes in Kurdistan, and one of the most difficult for beasts of burden. The flocks of the nomade Kurds of Bohtan were feeding in the gullies. The descent was even more rapid and precipitous than the ascent, and we could scarcely prevent our weary horses from rolling down into the ravine with the stones which we put into motion at every step. At the foot of the pass is a small Armenian church called Khorous Klissia, or 'the church of the cock,' because a black cock is said to warn the traveller when the snowdrifts hide the mountain tracts.

There was no other pathway down the rocky ravine than the dry bed of the torrent. As we approached the widening valleys the springs began to collect together and to form a considerable stream, through which we had to wade as we best could. A track followed by the shepherds in their periodical migrations to the uplands, had been carried here and there over the foaming water by trunks of trees. But these simple bridges had been washed away during a recent storm. Leaving the laden horses to find their way over the stones and through the torrent, I rode onwards with Hormuzd. We passed soon after a deep natural cavern, from which burst, white with foam and struggling through a bed of pink flowers, a most abundant spring. This was one of the principal sources of the eastern branch of the Tigris, here called the river of Mukus, which, according to an Armenian tradition, only issued from the rock about five hundred years ago.

A ride of eight hours brought us to the large scattered village of Mukus, the principal place of the district of the same name. We were met, as we drew near, by the Mudir or governor, an active bustling Turk, who had already chosen, with the usual taste of an Eastern, the prettiest spot, a lawn on the banks of the river, for our tents, and had collected provisions for ourselves and our horses. The good Pasha of Wan had sent to the different chiefs on our way, and had ordered preparations to be everywhere made for our reception. The Tigris is here a deep stream, and is crossed by a stone bridge. The houses are built without order, on the slopes of the mountain, each family choosing some open place more free from stones than the usual rocky declivities to cultivate a small plot of ground. The place may contain altogether about two thousand inhabitants.

The district of Mukus, anciently Mogkh, and one of the provinces of the Armenian kingdom, had only lately been brought under the authority of the Sultan. Like the rest of this part of Kurdistan, it had long maintained its independence under hereditary chiefs, the last of whom, Abdal Bey, after several times defeating the Turkish troops sent against him, was at length captured as he was flying into Persia.

The Mudir showed the greatest anxiety for our welfare during the night, continually visiting our tents to see that the Albanians he had placed as guards over our property did not sleep, as the village swarmed with Bohtan thieves.

The principal Armenians of Mukus and their priests knew of no ruins or inscriptions in the district, and I found them even more ignorant than their fellow-countrymen of the districts around Wan, whose stupidity has passed into a Turkish proverb. Long subjection to the Kurds and a constant intercourse with Mussulmans, have led them to adopt their manners and dress; their religion, at the same time, consists of mere outward profession, and the punctual performance of a few ceremonies and fasts.

We left Mukus early in the afternoon, accompanied by the Mudir. The path following the course of the river leads to Sert, Jezirah, and the Assyrian plains. We soon turned from it, and entered a valley running eastwards. On the mountain-sides were many villages, buried, like those of Tiyari, in orchards and groves of walnut trees. We forced our way through thickets and through matted climbing plants, the track being continually lost in rivulets or in watercourses for irrigation. The valley soon narrowed into a wild gorge. The ravine ended at length in the gardens of Aurenj. We chose amongst them a sheltered nook for our night's resting-place.

Next day we crossed a high mountain ridge covered in some places with snow, separating the district of Mukus from that of Shattak. Its northern and western slopes are the summer pastures of the Miran Kurds, whose flocks were still feeding on the green lawns and in the flowery glens. On the opposite side of the pass we found an encampment of Hartushi Kurds, under one Omar Agha, a noble old chieftain, who welcomed us with unbounded hospitality, and set before me every luxury that he possessed. I could scarcely resist his entreaties that we should pass the night under his tent. I had honoured it, he declared, by entering into it. All that it contained, his children, his wives, and his flocks, were, upon his head, no longer his but my property. I had no wish to profit by his generosity, and at length we parted. Resuming our journey we descended by a precipitous pathway into a deep valley. A broad stream, another arm of the eastern Tigris, wound through it; its glittering waters had been just visible amidst the gardens of Shattak, from the mountain-top.

Here again the Mudir had been apprised of our coming, and was ready to receive us. He had collected provisions for ourselves and horses in an open space on the river bank. Shattak is a small town, rather than a village. It is chiefly inhabited by Armenians, an industrious and hardy race, cultivating the sides of the mountains, on which are built their villages, and weaving in considerable quantities the gay-coloured woollen stuffs so much esteemed by the Kurds. In nearly every house was a loom, and the rattle of the shuttle was heard at almost every door. The large and flourishing Armenian communities inhabiting the valleys between lake Wan and the district of Jezirah, appear to be unknown to modern geographers, and are unnoticed in our best maps. The difficulties and dangers of the road have hitherto deterred travellers from entering their mountains. The existence of this people in the very heart of Kurdistan might, if taken advantage of by the Porte, be the means of establishing an important trade, and of quieting and civilising a country but recently brought under its rule. The mountains produce galls, wool (some of which has the same silky texture as that of Angora), the small under-wool of the goat called *tiftik* (a valuable article of export), and minerals. In the bazaar at Shattak I saw a few English prints, and other European wares, brought for sale from Wan.

The priests and principal Armenians of the place came to me soon after my arrival, and I learnt from them that efforts had already been made to improve the condition of the Christian community, now that the oppressive rule of the Kurdish hereditary chiefs had been succeeded by the more tolerant government of the Sultan. A school had been opened, chiefly by the help of Sheran, the active and liberal Armenian banker of Wan.

The town itself is called by the Armenians Tauk, by the Kurds Shokh, and when spoken of together with the numerous villages that surround it, Shattak. It stands near the junction of two considerable streams, forming one of the head-waters of the eastern Tigris, and uniting with the Bohtan-Su. The largest comes from the district of Albagh. These streams, as well as that of Mukus, abound in trout of the most delicious flavour. The entire district contains fifty villages and numerous *mezras* or hamlets. The revenues are about the same as those of Mukus. A few Mussulmans live on the right bank of the stream opposite Shokh, round the ruins of an old castle, medresseh (college), and mosque, all apparently at one time handsome and well-built edifices.

We left Shokh on the 17th August, by a bridge crossing the principal stream. After a long and difficult ascent we came to a broad green platform called Tagu, the pastures of the people of Shattak, and now covered with their tents and flocks. This high ground overlooked the deep valleys, through which wound the two streams, and on whose sides were many smiling gardens and villages. We stopped at an encampment of Miran Kurds, a large and wealthy tribe, pasturing their flocks far and wide over the mountains and ravines of Shattak and Nourdooz. Their chief had died five days before. We had passed on the road his son, a boy covered with embroidery and gold, and surrounded by armed servants. He was on his way to Wan to receive a cloak of investiture from the Pasha, who had recognised him as lord of the clan.

Crossing a high mountain pass, on which the snow still lingered, we descended into a deep valley like that of Shattak, chiefly cultivated by Armenians. We crossed a small stream, and ascended on the opposite side to Ashkaun, in the district of Nourdooz. The inhabitants were outside the village, near a clear spring, washing and shearing their sheep.

Our ride on the following day was over upland pastures of great richness, and through narrow valleys watered by numerous streams. Here and there were villages inhabited by Kurds and Armenians. We were now approaching the Nestorian districts. The first man of the tribe we met was an aged buffalo-keeper, who, in answer to a question in Kurdish, spoke to me in the Chaldee dialect of the mountains. Hormuzd and my servants rejoiced at the prospect of leaving the Armenian settlements, whose inhabitants, they declared, were for stupidity worse than Kurds, and for rapacity worse than Jews. Chilghiri was the first Nestorian village on our way. The men, with their handsome wives and healthful children, came

A Nestorian Family.

out to meet us. We continued our journey to Merwanen, which we found deserted by its inhabitants for the Zomas, or summer pastures. The Kiayah, or chief, however, with one or two of his people, had ridden down to examine the state of the crops, and turning his horse he led us up the steep pathway to his tents. They were huddled up in a little rocky nook, high on the mountain, and in the midst of snow. Unlike the Kurds, the Nestorians do not shift their encampments, but remain on one spot during the whole time they are in the Zomas. They thus live for some months in the midst of the dung of animals and filth of all kinds, whilst vermin abounds as plentifully as in their wretched villages. The cattle and flocks are kept during the night in folds, formed by a circular wall four or five feet high, built of loose stones. The dwellings, indeed, consist of little more than such rude inclosures, with coarse black goat-hair canvas stretched over them. As the nights are cold, and protection from the high winds is necessary in these lofty regions, a shallow pit is dug in the centre of the hut, in which the family crouches for warmth when not engaged in out-door occupations. Although poor and needy, the people of Merwanen were not less hospitable than other Nestorians I had met with. They brought us as the sun went down smoking messes of millet boiled in sour milk and mixed with mountain herbs.

The Nestorian Christians of these Kurdish districts dress like their Mussulman neighbours, and can scarcely be distinguished from them. They still go armed, and are less exposed to oppression than the suffering tribes of Tiyari. The Kiayah and a party of musketeers escorted us next day to a large encampment of Hartushi Kurds, near the outlet of a green valley, watered by many streams, forming the most easterly sources of the Tigris. Abd-ur-Rahman, the chief, was absent from his tents collecting the annual taxes of the tribe. In his absence we were received under his capacious goat-hair tent by a conceited mollah, who, being the spiritual adviser of its master, considered himself also the joint owner of his personal property. He did the honours, as if we were his guests, in a very patronising fashion. A scene of activity rarely witnessed in a Kurdish community reigned around. The banks of a small stream running through the midst of the camp were crowded with sheep: some being washed in the pure water, others being under the scissors of the shearers. Groups of boys and women were already beating and pressing the newly cut wool into felt, a manufacture of the Hartushi Kurds much prized for its close yet soft texture. In the tents girls were seated before the long warps stretched over the green-sward for the woof of their beautiful carpets. I was not unknown to these mountaineers, who wander during the winter in the plains to the east of the Tigris, below Jezirah, and frequently come into Mosul to trade. A group of chiefs, gaily dressed in the striped cloth of Bohtan, soon collected round us. The wives of Abd ur-Rahman Agha did not suffer their husband's good name for hospitality to be forfeited. Although Hormuzd and myself were the only partakers of the feast, a primitive table-cloth formed of the skins of the wild goat was spread before us, and covered with a great pile of the white and delicate mountain bread.

The mountain rising above us was the boundary between the pashalics of Wan and Hakkiari, and is the watershed of the Tigris and Zab. On the opposite side the streams uniting their waters flow towards the latter river. The first district we entered was that of Lewen, inhabited chiefly by Nestorians. The whole population with their flocks had deserted their villages for the Zomas. We ascended to the encampment of the people of Billi, a wretched assemblage of dirty hovels, half tent and half cabin, built of stones and black canvas. Behind it towered, amidst eternal snows, a bold and majestic peak, called Karnessa-ou-Daoleh. Round the base of this mountain, over loose stones and sharp rocks, and through ravines deep in snow, we dragged our weary horses next day.

After a fatiguing and indeed dangerous ride, we found ourselves on a snowy platform variegated with Alpine plants. The tiny streams which trickled through the ice were edged with forget-me-nots of the tenderest blue, and with many well-remembered English flowers. I climbed up a solitary rock to take bearings of the principal peaks around us. A sight as magnificent as unexpected awaited me. Far to the north, and high above the dark mountain ranges which spread like a troubled sea beneath my feet, rose one solitary cone of unspotted white sparkling in the rays of the sun. Its form could not be mistaken; it was Mount Ararat. My Nestorian guide knew no more of this stately mountain, to him a kind of mythic land far beyond the reach of human travel, than that it was within the territories of the Muscovites, and that the Christians called it Bashut-tamahamda. From this point alone was it visible, although nearly 150 miles distant, and we saw it no more during our journey.

We descended rapidly by a difficult track, passing here and there encampments of Kurds and the tents and flocks of the people of Julamerik. To the green pastures succeeded the region of cultivated fields, and we seemed to approach more settled habitations. We suddenly spied an aged man with long robes, black turban, and a white beard which fell almost to his girdle; he was following a precipitous pathway, and was mounted on a tall and sturdy mule. A few lusty mountaineers, in the striped dress and conical felt cap of the Nestorians, walked by his side and supported him on the animal, which with difficulty scrambled over the loose stones. We at once recognised the features of Mar Shamoun, the Patriarch of the Nestorians, or, as he proudly terms himself, 'of the Chaldæans of the East.' He had not known of our coming, and he shed tears of joy as he embraced us. Kochhannes, his residence, was not far distant, and he turned back with us to the village. Since I had seen him misfortune and grief, more than age, had worn deep furrows in his brow, and had turned his hair and beard to silvery grey. We had last met at Mosul, the day previous to his escape from confinement into Persia. Since that time he had been wandering on the confines of the two border countries, but had now sought repose once more in the old seat of the patriarchs of the mountain tribes.

We soon reached his dwelling. It was solidly built of hewn stone, and stood on the very edge of a precipice overhanging a ravine, through which wound a branch of the Zab. A dark vaulted passage led us into a room, scarcely better lighted by a small window closed by a greased sheet of coarse paper. The tattered remains of a felt carpet, spread in a corner, was the whole of its furniture. The garments of the Patriarch were hardly less worn and ragged. Even the miserable allowance of 300 piastres (about 2*l.* 10*s.*), which the Porte had promised to pay him monthly on his return to the mountains was long in arrears, and he was supported entirely by the contributions of his faithful but poverty-stricken flock. Kochhanes was, moreover, still a heap of ruins. At the time of the massacre Mar Shamoun scarcely saved himself by a precipitous flight before the ferocious Kurds of Beder Khan Bey entered the village and slew those who still lingered in it, and were from age or infirmities unable to escape.

My tents were pitched on a lawn near Mar Shamoun's dwelling. Near to us was a small church, built about 150 years ago, on an isolated rock. The only entrance to it is by a low door, high up from the ground, and reached by a ladder. The interior consists of a yard in which service is performed during summer, and an inner chamber for winter. Mar Shamoun officiated every evening about sunset in the open air, reading the whole service himself, dressed in his usual robes. A few persons from the ruined village attended, and formed his congregation.

We remained a day with the Patriarch, and then took the road to Julamerik, three caravan hours distant from Kochhannes. Its castle, strongly built and defended by towers and bastions, is picturesquely situated upon a bold rock, overlooking the valley of the Zab. The town and bazaars are below it. They were almost deserted, their inhabitants, as is the custom of the country, living in tents with their flocks amid the summer pastures on the mountains.

Near Julamerik we met many poor Nestorians flying, with their wives and children, they knew not whither, from the oppression of the Turkish governors.

The direct road by Tiyari to Mosul is carried along the river Zab, through ravines scarcely practicable to beasts of burden. It issues into the lower valleys near the village of Lizan. Intead, however, of descending the stream, we turned to the north, in order to cross it higher up by a bridge leading into Diz. I had not yet visited this Nestorian district. Mar Shamoun, as well as the people of Julamerik, declared that the mountain pathways could not be followed by our baggage mules; but a man of Taal offering to show us a track open to horsemen, we placed ourselves under his guidance. On the banks of the Zab, I found the remains of an ancient road, cut in many places in the solid rock. From the greatness of the work, I am inclined to attribute it to the Assyrians.

At length, after many falls, and more than once turning back from the polished rocks, across which our track was carried, we found ourselves before a wicker suspension bridge. This primitive structure had been almost washed away by recent floods, and now hung from the tottering piers by a slender rope of twisted osiers. It seemed scarcely able to bear the weight of a man. But some Nestorians, who, seeing us from the opposite side of the river, had come to our help, undertook to carry our baggage across, and then to lead the horses over one by one. After some delay this dangerous passage was effected without accident, and we entered the valley of Diz. But there was another stream between us and the first Nestorian village. We had to ford an impetuous torrent boiling and foaming over smooth rocks, and reaching above our saddle-girths. One of the baggage mules lost its footing. The eddying waters hurried it along and soon hurled it into the midst of the Zab. The animal having, at length, relieved itself from its burden, swam to the bank. Unfortunately it bore my trunks; my notes and inscriptions, the fruits of my labours at Wan, together with the little property I possessed, were carried far away by the stream. After the men from the village had long searched in vain, the lost load was found about midnight, stopped by a rock some miles down the river.

We passed the night in the miserable village of Rabban Audishio. Only two families dwelt in it; the other inhabitants had been slain in the massacre. On the opposite side of the valley, but high in the mountains, was the village of Seranius. The pathway to it being precipitous, and inaccessible even to mules, we turned to Madis, the residence of the Melek, or chief, of the district of Diz. We crossed the stream by a rude bridge consisting of two poles, resting on opposite rocks. The Melek was abroad collecting the taxes, which he had been summoned to pay to the governor of Julamerik. The villages of Diz, like those of the Nestorian valleys in general, stand in the midst of orchards and cultivated terraces. They were laid waste, and the houses burnt, during the first massacre. Diz was the first Christian district attacked by Beder Khan Bey. The inhabitants made a long and determined resistance, but were at length overpowered by numbers. Those who fell into the hands of the Kurdish chieftain were put to death without mercy, none being spared, as in Tiyari, for slaves. The trees were cut down, and the villages reduced to their present state of misery and desolation. They might slowly have recovered had not the Turks, by an unjust and oppressive system of government and taxation, checked all the efforts of these poor but industrious people to cultivate their lands, and rebuild their ruined dwellings.

We continued our journey through a deep and narrow valley hemmed in by high mountains and by perpendicular cliffs. The Melek met us on the road near the village of Chericherch, or Klissa. The old man turning back with me, I dismounted and sat with him beneath a walnut tree. He had little to tell but the usual tale of misery and distress. The Turkish governor had called upon the district to pay about 150*l.*, a small sum certainly, but more than he could collect by seizing the little property of the inhabitants. Even the seed for their next harvest had been taken from them, as well as the very millet with which they made their coarse bread. The valley produces nothing but a little rice, garas (a kind of millet), and barley, a few walnut and apple trees and hemp. Scarcely any wheat is raised, and the taxes levied on mills almost prevent its being ground into flour.

Leaving the Melek to pursue his tax-gathering, we rode through a magnificent valley, now narrowing into a wild gorge walled with precipitous cliffs then opening into an amphitheatre of rocks encircling a village embedded in trees. At length it was abruptly closed by the towering peaks and precipices of the Jelu mountain. At its foot is the village of Khouresin, where we encamped for the night. The inhabitants were, for the most part, in the summer pastures.

The next morning, after with difficulty dragging our weary

beasts up a steep and dangerous mountain track, we found the Nestorian families with their flocks at the very base of those cliffs of naked rock, which, rising far above the surrounding mountains of Hakkiari, form the peak of Jelu, and are visible even from Mosul. On all sides of them was snow; but the small recess in which they had built their miserable hovels of loose stones, mud, and dried grass, was carpeted with Alpine herbs and flowers. These poor people were in extreme wretchedness and want; even their clothing had been taken for taxes.

We were still separated from the valley of Jelu by a shoulder jutting from the lofty Soppa-Durek mountain. Before reaching this rocky ridge we had to cross a broad tract of deep snow, over which we had much difficulty in dragging our heavily-laden mules. When on the crest of the pass we found ourselves surrounded on all sides by rugged peaks, the highest being that known as the Toura Jelu, of which we had scarcely lost sight from the day we had left Mosul. It is probably the highest mountain in central Kurdistan, and may be about 15,000 feet. On its precipitous sides the snow cannot rest; but around it are eternal glaciers.

These mountains abound in bears, leopards, wolves, chamois, wild goats, and sheep, of which I was assured there are three distinct varieties. The large yellow partridge, as well as the red-legged, are also found in great numbers.

From the top of the pass we looked down into a deep abyss. The flocks of the Jelu villagers had worn a small pathway in its almost perpendicular sides during their periodical migrations to and from the Zomas; but frequently it was only marked by a polished line across flat, slippery rocks of enormous breadth, or by a faint streak over the loose stones. Down this terrible descent we had to drag our jaded horses, leaving our track marked in blood. I have had some experience in bad mountain passes, but I do not remember to have seen any much worse than that leading into Jelu. After numerous accidents and great labour we left a rocky gully, and found ourselves on a slope ending, at a dizzy depth, in a torrent scarcely visible from our path. The yielding soil offered even a more difficult footing for our beasts than the polished rocks. One of our mules soon fell, and rolled over and over with an avalanche of stones for two or three hundred feet. We fully expected to find the animal dashed to pieces; but breaking away from the broad pack-saddle, it contrived to check its rapid course and to regain its legs. Its load, however, was hurled into the valley, and we watched it as it bounded from rock to rock, until it was lost to sight in the depths below. We continued our journey, and it was an hour or two before the active mountaineers succeeded in recovering it.

The wild mountain ravine was now changed for the smiling valley of Jelu. Villages, embowered in trees, filled every nook and sheltered place. We descended to Zerin or Zerayni, the principal settlement, and the residence of the Melek. To our left were two other villages, Alzan and Meedee.

As my large caravan descended the hill-side, the inhabitants of Zerin took us for Turks, and we lacked that hospitable reception which two or three years before would have awaited a stranger in these Christian communities. Wherever the Osmanli has placed his foot, he has bred fear and distrust. His visit has ever been one of oppression and rapine. The scarlet cap, and the well-known garb of a Turkish irregular, are the signals for a general panic. The women hide in the innermost recesses to save themselves from insult; the men slink into their houses, and offer a vain protest against the seizure of their property. In many parts of Turkey the new system and the better discipline of the army have placed a check upon these scenes of injustice and violence, and the villager may hope to get some, if not adequate, pay for the supplies he furnishes to those who quarter themselves upon him. But in the Nestorian valleys the old habits were still in vigour, and the appearance of a stranger caused a general hiding and dismay. When, at last, we had satisfied the trembling people of Zerin that we were not Mussulmans, they insisted upon our being Americans, of whom they had, at that moment, for certain religious reasons, almost as great a distrust. At length they made out that I was the consul of Mosul, and the Melek arriving at this crisis we were received with due hospitality. Our baggage was carried to the roof of a house, and provisions were brought to us without delay.

Although, during his expedition into Tiyari, Beder Khan Bey had seized the flocks of the people of Jelu, and had compelled them, moreover, to pay large contributions in money and in kind, he had not been able to enter their deep and well-guarded valleys. The blackened walls, the roofless houses, the plundered church, and the neglected vineyards, which marked in other parts of the mountains the once flourishing villages of the Nestorian tribes, did not disfigure the smiling district of Jelu. Its inhabitants, too, still maintained to a certain extent the appearance of their former prosperity, notwithstanding the rapacity and injustice of their new masters. Both men and women were gaily dressed in the many-coloured garments usually worn by their Mussulman neighbours.

The Nestorians of Jelu have no trade to add to their wealth. Shut out from all intercourse with the rest of the world, during six months of the year, by the deep snows of the lofty mountains that surround them, it is only in summer that they are able to exchange a few loads of fruit and a little honey and wax in the districts about Amadiyah for such supplies of corn as may serve for their immediate wants. Many of the men, however, wander during the winter into Asia Minor, and even into Syria and Palestine, following the trade of basket-making, in which they are very expert. Thus they save money, and are able in the summer to cultivate the land around their villages. There was only one priest in Zerin, and there appeared to be in Jelu less of that earnest religious feeling so peculiar to the Nestorians than in any other Tiyari district I had visited. The travels of the men, and their intercourse with the rest of the Christian world, have not improved their morals, their habits, or their faith.

The district of Jelu is under a bishop whose spiritual jurisdiction also extends over Baz. He resides at Martha d'Umra (the village of the church), separated by a bold rocky ridge from Zerin. It was Sunday as we descended through orchards, by a precipitous pathway, to his dwelling. The bishop was away. He had gone lower down the valley to celebrate divine service for a distant congregation. The inhabitants of the village were gathered round the church in their holiday attire, and received us kindly and hospitably. From a belfry issued the silvery tones of a bell, which echoed through the valley, and gave an inexpressible charm to the scene. It is not often that such sounds break upon the traveller's ear in the far East, to awaken a thousand pleasant thoughts of home, and to recall to memory many a happy hour.

This church is said to be the oldest in the Nestorian mountains, and is a plain, substantial, square building, with a very small entrance. To me it was peculiarly interesting, as having been the only one that had escaped the ravages of the Kurds, and as containing, therefore, its ancient furniture and ornaments. Both the church and the dark vestibule were so thickly hung with relics of the most singular and motley description, that the ceiling was completely concealed by them. Amongst the objects which first attracted my attention were numerous China bowls and jars of elegant form and richly coloured, but black with the dust of ages. They were suspended, like the other relics, by cords from the roof. I was assured that they had been there from time out of mind, and had been brought from the distant empire of Cathay by those early missionaries of the Chaldæan Church, who bore the tidings of the gospel to the shores of the Yellow Sea. If such were really the case, some of them might date so far back as the sixth or seventh centuries, when the Nestorian Church flourished in China, and its missions were spread over the whole of central Asia. The villagers would not, in the absence of their bishop, allow me to move any of these sacred relics. The sister of the Patriarch, they said, had endeavoured to wash one some years before, and it had been broken. Hung with the China vases was the strangest collection of objects that could well be imagined: innumerable bells, of all forms and sizes, many probably Chinese, suspended in long lines from one side to the other of the church, making a loud and discordant jingle when set in motion; porcelain birds and animals, grotesque figures in bronze, remains of glass chandeliers, two or three pairs of old bullion epaulets, and a variety of other things, all brought at various periods by adventurous inhabitants of the village, who had wandered into distant lands, and had returned to their homes with some evidence of their travels to place in their native church. The walls were dressed with silks of every colour and texture, and with common Manchester prints. Notwithstanding the undoubted antiquity of the church, and its escape from plunder, I searched in vain for ancient manuscripts.

We followed the valley to the village of Nara, where the bishop was resting after his morning duties. A young man of lofty stature and handsome countenance, dressed in the red-striped loose garments of the Kurds, and only distinguished by a turban of black silk from those around him, came out to meet us. A less episcopal figure could scarcely be imagined; but, although he seemed some Kurdish hunter or warrior, he gave us his benediction as he drew near. We seated ourselves together beneath the shade of a gigantic tree; and whilst the good people of the village were preparing a simple repast of yaghourt and garas, we discussed the affairs of the church and the political condition of the tribe.

A broad and rapid torrent crossed by a bridge, and a steep mountain wooded with oak, over which we climbed by a rugged pathway, separate the districts of Jelu and Baz. The first village we came to was Shouwa, but we rested for the night at Martha Akhtayiah,* adjoining Ergub, the furthest limits of my journey to the Nestorian districts in 1846. We were at once recognised by the villagers. The men and women crowded round us, vieing with each other in offers of hospitality. We alighted at the clean and spacious house of the Melek, who was, however, away at the time of our arrival. The inhabitants had been shamefully ill-used and over-taxed by the Turkish authorities, and were driven to a state of despair. I had, as usual, to listen to sad tales of misery and misfortune, without having it in my power to offer either consolation or relief.

* *I. e.* The lower village, corrupted into Makhtaiyah.

We were now in the track I had followed during my former visit to the mountains.* Crossing the precipitous pass to the west of Baz, which, since my first visit, had been the scene of one of the bloodiest episodes of the Nestorian massacre, we entered the long narrow ravine leading into the valley of Tkhoma. We stopped at Gunduktha, where, four years before, I had taken leave of the good priest Bodaca, who had been amongst the first victims of the fury of the Kurdish invaders. The Priest, the Rais, and the principal inhabitants, came to us as we stopped in the churchyard. But they were no longer the gaily dressed and well-armed men who had welcomed me on my first journey. Their garments were tattered and worn, and their countenances haggard and wan. The church, too, was in ruins; around were the charred remains of the burnt cottages, and the neglected orchards overgrown with weeds. A body of Turkish troops had lately visited the village, and had destroyed the little that had been restored since the Kurdish invasion. The same taxes had been collected three times, and even four times, over. The relations of those who had ran away to escape from these exactions had been compelled to pay for the fugitives. The chief had been thrown, with his arms tied behind his back, on a heap of burning straw, and compelled to disclose where a little money that had been saved by the villagers had been buried. The priest had been torn from the altar, and beaten before his congregation. Men showed me the marks of torture on their body, and of iron fetters round their limbs. For the sake of wringing a few piastres from this poverty-stricken people, all these deeds of violence had been committed by officers sent by the Porte to protect the Christian subjects of the Sultan, whom they pretended to have released from the misrule of the Kurdish chiefs.

The smiling villages described in the account of my previous journey were now a heap of ruins. From four of them alone 770 persons had been slain. Beder Khan Bey had driven off, according to the returns made by the Meleks,

---

* Nineveh and its Remains, p. 157.

24,000 sheep, 300 mules, and 10,000 head of cattle; and the confederate chiefs had each taken a proportionate share of the property of the Christians. No flocks were left by which they might raise money wherewith to pay the taxes now levied upon them, and even the beasts of burden, which could have carried to the markets of more wealthy districts the produce of their valley, had been taken away.

We remained a night in Tkhoma to see the Meleks who came to us from Tkhoma Gowaia. On the following morning, it being the Feast of the Virgin, the people assembled for prayers—a crowd of miserable, half-naked men, women, and children. Leaving the valley, we crossed the high mountain inclosing Tkhoma to the south, and passed through Pinianish into Chaal, a district inhabited by Mussulmans, and which had consequently not suffered from the ravages of the Kurdish chiefs. It presented, with its still flourishing villages surrounded by gardens and vineyards, a vivid contrast to the unfortunate Christian valley we had just left.

A rapid descent through a rocky gorge brought us to the Zab, over which there were still the remains of a bridge, consisting of two poles fastened together by osier bands placed across the stone piers. It almost required the steady foot and practised head of a mountaineer to cross the roaring stream by this perilous structure. The horses and mules were, with much trouble and delay, driven into the river, and after buffeting with the whirlpools and eddies reached, almost exhausted, the opposite bank.

We now entered the valley of Berwari, and, crossing the pass of Amadiyah, took the road to Mosul, through a country I had already more than once visited. Leaving the caravan and our jaded horses, I hastened onwards with Hormuzd, and travelling through the night reached Mosul in the afternoon of the 30th of August, after an absence of seven weeks.

CHAPTER X.

Discoveries at Kouyunjik during the summer—Description of the sculptures—Capture of cities on a great river—Alabaster pavement—Conquest of tribes inhabiting a marsh—Their wealth—Chambers with sculptures belonging to a new king—Conquest of the people of Susiana—Portrait of the king—His guards and attendants—The city of Shushan—Captive prince—Musicians—Captives put to the torture—An inclined passage—Two small chambers—Colossal figures.

WHILST I had been absent in the mountains the excavations had been continued at Kouyunjik, notwithstanding the summer heats.

A great hall, or rather open court, connected by a passage with the chamber in which was represented the moving of the winged bulls,* had been fully explored. It was not quite square; the longest sides, those from west to east, being rather more than 140 feet, and the others 126 feet. It had four grand entrances, formed by colossal human-headed bulls, one on each side.†

The sculptures panelling the western wall were for the most part still entire. They recorded a campaign and a victory, in a country traversed by a great river, filled with crabs and fish of various kinds, and lined with date-bearing palms.‡ On one side of the stream was the king in his chariot, surrounded by his bodyguard and followed by his led horses. On the opposite bank the Assyrian army laid siege to a de-

---

* No. XIX. Plan I. p. 4.

† It is to be observed that neither of these entrances are exactly in the middle of the sides of the hall. Those opposite to each other, however, correspond.

‡ From the size of the river, it may be conjectured that it represents the Euphrates in Babylonia. No fragment of inscription remains by which this conquered country might be identified.

tached fort, forming an outwork to a city surrounded by high battlemented walls, and defended by lofty towers rising one above the other. Five square gateways opened upon a small

Arabs and Nestorians moving a Slab at Kouyunjik.

stream or canal. The city walls seemed deserted by the inhabitants, but the fort was defended by archers. Drawn up before it were warriors variously armed, and cavalry discharging their arrows without dismounting from their horses. A kneeling Assyrian, protecting himself by a broad wicker shield, was forcing the stones from the lower part of the fortifications with an instrument probably of iron.

Assyrian warriors were bringing human heads to the registrars, to show the numbers of the slain. The spoil, consisting of furniture, arms, and vessels of elegant form, was being registered by the scribes, to be divided amongst the victorious troops. The captive women with their children were seen riding in carts drawn by oxen. The dress of the male prisoners consisted of a short tunic encircled at the waist by a broad belt, that of the women of an inner shirt and an outer fringed robe falling to the ankles. The hair of both was confined by a simple band or fillet round the temples.

Next came the siege and capture of a city standing on the opposite bank of the same great river, and surrounded by a ditch edged with lofty reeds. The Assyrian footmen and cavalry had already crossed this dike, and were closely pressing the besieged, who, no longer seeking to defend themselves, were asking for quarter. A warrior, covering himself with his large circular shield, was attempting to set fire to one of the gates with a torch. Part of the city had already been taken, and the conquerors were driving away captives and cattle. Carts drawn by oxen were laden with furniture and large metal vessels. On the other side of the river Sennacherib in his gorgeous war chariot, and surrounded by his guards, received the captives, the heads of the slain, and the spoil. It is remarkable that this was one of the few figures of the king which had escaped mutilation by those who overthrew the Assyrian empire, burned its palaces, and levelled its cities with the dust.*

The captives, bearing skins probably containing water and flour to nourish them during a long and distressing march, were fettered in pairs, and urged onwards by their guards. Some of the women were on foot, others with their children on mules and in carts drawn by oxen. Mothers were represented holding the water-skins for their young ones to quench their thirst, whilst in some instances fathers had placed their weary children on their shoulders, for they were marching during the heat of a Mesopotamian summer, as the sculptor had shown by introducing large clusters of dates on the palms. Thus were driven the inhabitants of Samaria through the desert to Halah and Habor, by the river of Gozan and

* This bas-relief is now in the British Museum.

X.] *DESCRIPTION OF THE SCULPTURES.* 241

the cities of the Medes,* and we may see in these bas-reliefs a picture of the hardships and sufferings to which the captive people of Israel were exposed when their cities fell into the hands of the Assyrian king, and their inhabitants were sent to colonise the distant provinces of his empire.†

On the south side of the court, the sculptures on parts of four slabs only had been preserved. They graphically depicted the passage of the river by the great king. His led horses had been partly stripped of their costly furniture, and the grooms were taking them to the water's edge. One horse had already been detached from the royal chariot, and a groom was removing the yoke from the second. A charioteer still held the reins, and an eunuch raised a parasol above the monarch's head. Men were making ready skins to form a raft for the king to cross the stream. Some carried such as had already been inflated, others were blowing up those that were still empty, and tying up the orifice after they had been filled. The bas-relief represented a scene that may still be daily witnessed on the banks of the Tigris.

Many warriors, supporting their spears and heavy shields on their backs by cords, had already commenced crossing the stream on skins, and horses led by their grooms were swimming to the opposite bank.‡

On the south side of the court a centre portal flanked by winged bulls, and two small entrances, formed by gigantic figures, opened into a long chamber, § whose sculptured walls had been burnt to lime. On the calcined slabs, however, could still be traced Assyrian warriors mounting by ladders to the assault of cities, battering rams, long lines of archers, slingers, and spearmen, a sea with double-banked galleys, and a fortified camp, containing pavilions and tents, in which were men engaged in various domestic occupations. The

---

* 2 Kings, xvii. 6.
† See 2nd series of the 'Monuments of Nineveh,' Plates 42 and 43, for drawings of some of the bas-reliefs described in the text.
‡ Plate 41 of 2nd series of the 'Monuments of Nineveh.' These interesting bas-reliefs were unfortunately on the raft, which, after my return to Europe, was plundered by the Arabs on its passage to Baghdad, and were consequently lost.
§ No. XXIV. Plan I., 98 by 27 feet.

R

king, as usual, superintended the operations from his chariot. At both ends of the chamber, doors, guarded by colossal figures, led into smaller apartments, in which the bas-reliefs had been almost entirely destroyed.* Facing the great portal was a corresponding, but still wider, entrance, formed by a pair of human-headed lions. Between them was an enormous alabaster pavement slab, sculptured in relief, with an elegant design, consisting of a border of alternate tulips or lotus flowers and cones, enclosing similar ornaments arranged in squares and surrounded by rosettes.†

On either side of this grand portal were doors, guarded by colossal figures, amongst which was the fish-god.

On the walls of the chamber into which these three entrances led,‡ a few fragments, with part of a procession of captives and warriors, only remained. We were now upon the very brink of the southern side of the mound, and had consequently reached the furthest chamber in this part of the palace. There were no traces of an exterior wall.

Returning to the great hall we found an entrance formed by colossal figures leading into a long narrow chamber,§ about 70 feet by 12, whose walls had partly escaped the general wreck. It appeared to be the remains of an entrance into the palace, like that on the western face, or a gallery leading to the outer terrace, which probably surrounded the building. On its walls were sculptured the conquest of some of those tribes which have inhabited, from the remotest period, the vast marshes formed by the Euphrates and Tigris in southern Babylonia.

In these bas-reliefs the swamps with the jungles of lofty reeds, the narrow passages cut through them like streets, and the shallow stagnant water abounding in fish, such as are still seen in the marshes in Southern Mesopotamia,∥ were faithfully, though rudely, portrayed. Men and women, seated on rafts, were hiding themselves in the thick brakes, whilst the Assyrian warriors followed the fugitives in light boats of

---

* Nos. xxv. and xxvi. Plan I. p. 4.
† Plate 56, 2nd series of the 'Monuments of Nineveh.'
‡ No. xxvii. Plan I.   § No. xxviii. same Plan.
∥ See chapter xii.

wicker work, such as are used to this day. Some had overtaken and were killing their enemies. Others were returning to the banks with captives, and with the heads of the slain. In the water were the bodies of the dead already food for the fishes. The fighting men of the conquered tribes were armed with bows, and wore short tunics; the women had long fringed robes; the hair of both was confined round the temples by a fillet.

Although the people represented in these bas-reliefs dwelt in the swampy districts of Chaldæa, unless, indeed, they had only taken refuge in them to escape the vengeance of the Assyrian king, they appear to have been as rich, if not richer, than any others conquered by Sennacherib. With the exception of three slabs and part of a fourth, containing the battle in the marsh, the entire walls of the chamber were sculptured with the captives and spoil brought by the victorious troops to their king. Unfortunately the image of Sennacherib himself in his chariot, which, to judge from a fragment or two found in the rubbish, must have exceeded all others in the palace, in the finish and richness of the details, had been entirely destroyed. Women and children on foot, on asses, and in carts drawn by oxen, waggons laden with furniture, cauldrons and vessels in metal, oxen mules, camels, sheep and goats, vases and jars of the most elegant forms, spears, swords, and shields, curiously carved couches, chairs, and tables, were included in the booty with which the Assyrian conquerors returned in triumph to Nineveh. The country through which they passed abounded in the date-bearing palm. The Assyrian warriors, hungry after their long march, were represented before a fire roasting the limbs of a sheep.*

Returning to the great hall, from which this gallery led, I found on its western side three other entrances, corresponding with those on the southern, the centre formed by a pair of winged bulls in a fossiliferous limestone.† They led into

* Drawings from this highly interesting series of bas-reliefs, which so fully illustrate the wars of the Assyrians, will be found in the 2nd series of my work on the 'Monuments of Nineveh,' Plates 25, 26, and 35.
† No. XXIX. Plan I. p. 4.

a chamber 58 feet by 34, panelled with unsculptured slabs of the same material. Three similar doorways opened into a parallel chamber of the same length, though rather narrower.* Its walls had been ornamented with carved alabaster slabs, of which a few fragments remained. A fortified camp, containing the usual pavilions and tents; priests sacrificing a sheep before a fire altar; a castle on the seashore; double-banked galleys hung round with shields; and long lines of captives (the women wearing hoods fitting close over their heads, and falling to their feet behind; the men, turbans of several folds, such as are frequently represented at Khorsabad); were amongst the bas-reliefs still preserved.

Three doorways on the western side of this chamber, similar to those on the eastern, led into as many distinct rooms, unconnected with each other. There were thus three magnificent portals, one behind the other, each formed by winged bulls facing the same way, and all looking towards the great hall or court, the largest bulls, those in front, being above 18 feet high, and the smallest, those leading into the inner chamber, about 12.† It would be difficult to conceive any interior architectural arrangement more imposing than this triple group of gigantic forms as seen in perspective by those who stood in the centre of the court, dimly lighted from above, and harmoniously coloured or overlaid, like the cherubims in the temple of Solomon, with gold.

At the southern ends of the two parallel chambers just described were entrances opening into a room, 82 feet by 24, whose walls were of the same unsculptured limestone.‡ From it a portal, formed by winged lions in the same material, led into an apartment 76 feet by 26, standing on the edge of the mound, and consequently one of the last on this side of the palace.§ Only six slabs, neither of them entire, remained against its walls. These slabs, like the bulls, were of a limestone abounding in fossils, probably

---

* No. XXXIV. Plan I. p. 4.   About 29 feet wide.
† These were entrances to Chambers, No. XXIX. and No. XXXVI. same Plan.
‡ No. XXX. same Plan.   § No. XXXIII. same Plan.

'the polished stone, full of shells,' noticed by Zenophon in the plinth of the walls of Mespila,* and were covered from top to bottom with small figures, most elaborately carved, and designed with great spirit. Although bearing a general resemblance to the bas-reliefs of Kouyunjik, there was sufficient in the style of art and in the details to show that they were not of exactly the same period. Fortunately several epigraphs still remained over the principal groups, and enable us to determine the name of the monarch who caused these sculptures to be carved, and to identify the events and incidents they portray.

The three slabs to the right of the winged lions on entering were occupied by a highly curious representation of a battle. The Assyrians, having besieged and captured some great city, appeared to be pursuing the flying enemy. On the first slab was part of a mound, on which a castle was probably built. Down the side of this artificial elevation ran the defeated warriors, no longer attempting defence, but giving themselves up to despair. One was plucking out his beard, a common action amongst Easterns to denote grief; some were tearing their hair, and others turning round to ask for quarter from their pursuers. On the sides of the mound lay the dead and dying, and the bows and quivers of the slain. A wounded mule was falling to the ground, whilst his rider, pierced by an arrow, raised his hands to implore for mercy. An Assyrian soldier, or ally, distinguished by a low round cap, and a kind of belt or shawl twisted round his breast, was dragging a body towards him, probably with the intention of cutting off the head. Beneath the mound a horseman was piercing with his spear a flying enemy, and two warriors in a car drawn by a mule, were hastening from the battlefield.

The remainder of the subject was divided by horizontal parallel lines, into six parts; of which, however, only three were entire. In the lowest compartment, archers and spearmen, some on horses, were represented in close combat with the enemy, whose armies, like those of the Assyrians,

* Anab. c. iii. lib. 4.

were composed of footmen and cavalry. The battle field was strewn with the slain, and with their scattered arms; but, as usual, the sculptor, to flatter the vanity of his countrymen, had not portrayed a single Assyrian either dead or wounded. In the second frieze the enemy were seen fighting in carts drawn by mules. In the next compartment were Assyrian warriors bearing the heads of the slain, and leaving the field of battle in a cart captured from the foe. Above this group was an epigraph, unfortunately much mutilated, which recorded the slaughter of a king, who appears, from other inscriptions on the same sculptures, to have reigned over Elam or Susiana.

Assyrian Warriors in a Cart, captured from the Elamites. (Kouyunjik.)

Behind the cart with the Assyrian warriors was the tent of the registrar, to which had been led a captive chief and his two attendants. Within was collected a heap of human heads, and warriors were bringing more of these bloody trophies to the appointed scribes. In another part of the battle was seen the chariot of one of the princes of the Elamites. Four spirited horses, wounded by arrows, were plunging and rearing, and the chief and his charioteer were falling from the overturned chariot. Beneath was an Assyrian warrior holding his horse by the bridle, and advancing towards a fallen enemy, who, turning towards his conqueror, placed one hand upon his throat, a gesture either of entreaty, or to indicate his approaching fate. He appears, from an inscription above his head, to have been a general of the Susianian king. Around these groups, Assyrians, armed with battle-axes and maces, were slaying the unresisting foe. In this part of the bas-relief were two short epigraphs, which are believed to state that the slaughtered warriors were sons of the king of Elam. These princes were distinguished by a peculiar round cap, to which was attached a long feather falling down the back, a head-dress subsequently worn by Persian kings. They were clothed in embroidered and fringed robes, and their chariots were drawn by four horses.

Crows and vultures were represented feasting upon the slain. Adjoining the field of battle was a broad river, into which the Assyrians were driving the retreating enemy: it was filled with the dead bodies of men and horses, and with bows and quivers. Above the battle scenes were the conquerors torturing, and leading into captivity their prisoners. They were divided into three rows, but parts of two only had been preserved. Some of the captives, with their hands manacled in iron fetters, knelt over an object which might be a chafing-dish with hot coals, or a vessel to receive their blood. One of the torturers held his victim by a collar round his neck; whilst a second, seizing the unfortunate prisoner by the hair, was about to strike him with an iron-headed mace.

The epigraphs declare that the war recorded by these sculptures was undertaken by an Assyrian king, whose image was represented on a slab not yet described, against the people of Elam or Susiana. It is of considerable importance thus to identify the conquered people, and to be able to ascertain the costume, the arms, and the mode of warfare of a nation well known in ancient history. The Elamites, we find from these bas-reliefs, used even in war, besides chariots, a kind of cart drawn by mules, and consisting of a flat stage raised upon lofty wheels, which had as many as twelve and even sixteen spokes. The largest of these cars could hold five or six persons, and they were adorned with a fringed or embroidered cloth or cushion. The smallest, it would appear, contained only one warrior and the charioteer, who sat on a kind of raised seat. Such carts are probably alluded to by the prophet Ezekiel when he speaks of 'the chariots, waggons, and wheels,' belonging to 'the Babylonians, and all the Chaldæans, Pekod, and Shoa, and Koa, and all the Assyrians, who should come up against Jerusalem.* The harness of the mules consisted of a simple band round the chest, hung with rosettes and tassels, probably of coloured wool. They were guided either by reins, or by a long rod held by the charioteer in his right hand. Mules were also, it would seem, ridden by this people in battle, and were then caparisoned like horses.† The dress of the fighting men consisted chiefly of a tunic, or single shirt, falling to the knee, and bound at the waist by a narrow girdle. Some of them had round their shoulders a kind of band knotted in front. This appears to have been a contrivance to support the quiver suspended at the back. Their hair was long, and was confined by a fillet, tied behind the head in a kind of bow. The captive chief and his attendants in the tent wore robes falling to the knee in front, and to the ankles behind. Those who fought on foot were armed with the bow, but the cavalry used the spear. The archers carried at their backs quivers of peculiar form, and ornamented at the sides and on the top with rosettes. I have already described the peculiar dress of the princes; it was completed by high boots or greaves laced up in front, and probably of yellow leather.

Amongst the captives were men clothed in fringed robes

---

* Ezek. xxiii. 23, 24.

† Susiana is still celebrated for its mules. These animals were evidently much esteemed by the ancients. They were even used by kings. When David sent for Solomon to be anointed king over Israel he caused him to ride on his mule. (1 Kings, i. 33.) They were also noted for their swiftness and endurance (2 Sam. xiii. 2), were used for posts (Esther, viii. 10), and were amongst objects of tribute and spoil, as we see them represented in the sculptures. (1 Kings, x. 25, 2 Chron. ix. 24.)

and a short under-tunic ; these were probably the lords of the land. The women wore their hair in curls, falling on their shoulders, and bound above the temples by a band or fillet. Some had one long ringlet on each side of the face. Their children were either naked or clothed in simple shirts.

The Assyrian troops were divided into cavalry and foot. The horsemen carried the bow and spear, and wore coats of mail, high greaves, and the usual pointed helmet. Their horses were covered with clothes, and even, it would seem, with a kind of leather armour, reaching from the head to the tail, to protect them from the arrows of the enemy. It consisted of several separate pieces fastened together by buttons or loops. Over it was thrown an ornamental saddle-cloth or leopard's skin, upon which the rider sat. Under the neck of the horse was hung a bell or a tassel. Between its ears was an arched crest, and the different parts of the harness were richly embroidered and ornamented with rosettes. The costumes of the footmen varied according to their arms. The archers, probably auxiliaries from different tribes in alliance with the Assyrians, were dressed in very short tunics. A broad belt, with the fringed ornament peculiar to the later Assyrian period, encircled their waist, and over their shoulders they wore a cross belt, of chequered cloth, to support the quiver. Their hair, confined by a plain fillet, was rolled up behind in one large curl. All the spearmen had the pointed helmet; but some wore coats of mail and metal greaves, and others a simple tunic, without any covering to their legs. Their shields protected nearly the whole person, and were rounded at the top and straight at the bottom. Some appear to have been faced with small square pieces of leather, others to have been made entirely of metal, with embossed edges. For the first time we see in these bas-reliefs, the Assyrians using the battle-axe and the mace.

The three slabs on the opposite side were better preserved than those I have just described. They formed part of the same subject, which had evidently been carried round the four walls of the chamber. They represented the triumph of the Assyrian king, and, like the battle scenes, were divided by horizontal lines into several bands. The monarch stood in his chariot, surrounded by his bodyguard. Unfortunately his face, with those of the charioteer and the eunuch bearing the parasol, had been purposely defaced. The royal robes were profusely adorned with rosettes and fringes; the attendant eunuch was dressed in a chequered garment resembling a Scotch plaid. The chariot was most elaborately decorated. The body was carved with an elegant pattern of intersecting circles and rosettes, and edged by a tasteful border. In a circular panel was a kneeling figure drawing a bow, probably the protecting deity of the Assyrian king. In the fore part was a case to receive the arrows and bow. The chariot was more lofty than that seen in earlier Assyrian sculptures. The wheels were unusually large, and had eight spokes, encircled by an ornamental border. The harness of the horses consisted of a band under the chest, with rosettes and tassels, a cluster of large tassels hanging over the shoulder from the yoke, an embroidered or ivory-studded breast-band, and head-pieces similarly adorned. Two lofty plumes rose between their ears.

In front of the chariot were two warriors or guards in embroidered robes and greaves. Their long hair was bound by a fillet, whose tasseled ends fell loose behind. They were preceded by two remarkable figures, both eunuchs, and probably intended for portraits of some well-known officers of the royal household. One was old and corpulent: his forehead high and ample; his nose curved and small, and his chin round and double. The wrinkles of the brow, the shaggy eyebrows, and the bloated cheeks, with the stubble beard peculiar to beings of his class, were very faithfully represented. His short hair was tied with a fillet. His companion was younger, and had not the same marked features. He carried before him a square object resembling a closed box or book, perhaps a clay tablet containing some decree or register, such as were discovered in the ruins. Both wore long plain shirts, and round their waists a simple cord, in which was fixed a whip, probably a sign of their office.

Above this remarkable group was an inscription in eight lines, fortunately almost entire. From it we learn that the king, whose deeds were thus recorded, was the son of Esar-haddon, and the grandson of Sennacherib, and that the conquered people represented in the sculptures were the Elamites, or inhabitants of the ancient Susiana. His name has been read 'Asshur-bani-pal;' and there is reason to believe that he is no other than the Sardanapalus whose history has been partly handed down to us by the Greek and Roman historians.*

Above the royal chariot was a row of trees, and beneath a procession of mace-bearers and led horses, richly caparisoned. A lower compartment contained a curious ground-plan of a city, probably the capital of the country—Susa, or Shushan the palace, mentioned in the book of Daniel. It was surrounded by a wall, with equidistant towers and gateways. The houses were flat-roofed, and some had one tower or upper chamber, and others two. They had no exterior windows, and their doors were square; thus, in general form, closely resembling the common dwellings of the ancient Egyptians, of which a model found in a tomb is preserved in the British Museum. Nor were they unlike the meaner houses of the modern town of Shushter, the representative of ancient Susa. Unfortunately, part of the slab containing the city had been destroyed, and the representations of many of the more important edifices were probably wanting. Outside the walls were groves of palms and other trees, and a kind of suburb of houses scattered amongst the gardens as around Baghdad. On the river bank stood two forts with towers, one raised on an artificial mound. Near the large river, at the bottom of the slab, was either a pond in the midst of palm trees, or the source of a rivulet which fell into the main stream.

The adjoining slab was divided into eight bands, and the next into seven. On both were represented the Assyrian army returning from its victorious campaign, and bringing to the king the captives and the spoil. The prisoners were being cruelly tortured in his presence. The eunuch general, or Tartan, led a chief or prince of the conquered people, grasping his captive by the wrist, and raising in one hand

---

* It is probable that there were several Assyrian kings whose names could be converted into the Greek Sardanapalus. We have seen that the royal founder of the north-west palace at Nimroud was one of them.

a long and massy spear. At his back was hung a quiver and
bow, and an embossed belt encircled his mailed vest. The
prisoner wore a simple robe falling to his ankles, and a
knotted fillet round his head. Above him was an inscription
unfortunately much mutilated, but apparently stating that he
was a son of the king of the Elamites. In this inscription
the name of the capital is written 'Shushan,' as in the Bible.

Before the captive prince were gathered those who had
surrendered to the Assyrian general, for they still carried their
arms. Some of them knelt, some bowed to the ground, and
others, stretched at full length, rubbed their heads in the
dust—signs of grief and submission still practised in the
East. They were followed by a led horse, and by a cart
drawn by a mule. Another Tartan of the Assyrian army,
holding his war-horse and carrying his spear, also received
the homage of the conquered Susianians. The Assyrian
generals were welcomed by men and women, dancing, singing, and playing on instruments of music. Thus, 'when

Singers coming out to meet the Conquerors. (Kouyunjik.)

David was returned from the slaughter of the Philistines,
the women came out of all the cities of Israel, singing
and dancing to meet Saul, with tabrets, with joy, and
with instruments of music.'* We find from various
passages in the Scriptures, that the instruments of music
chiefly used on such triumphant occasions were the harp
(one with ten strings) the tabor, and the pipe,† precisely

---

* 1 Sam. xviii. 6.
† Isaiah, v. 12. In Daniel, iii. 5, according to the received translation, the 'cornet, flute, harp, sackbut, psaltery, and dulcimer,' are men-

those represented in the bas-reliefs. First came five men; three carried harps of many strings, which they struck with both hands, dancing at the same time to the measure; a fourth played on the double-pipes, such as are seen on the monuments of Egypt,* and were used by the Greeks and Romans. The fifth carried an instrument not unlike the modern santour of the East, consisting of a number of strings stretched over a sounding board. The strings, pressed with the fingers of the left hand to produce the notes, were struck with a small wand or hammer held in the right. The men were followed by six female musicians, four playing on harps, one on the double-pipes, and the sixth on a kind of drum beaten with both hands, resembling the *tabbul* still used by Eastern dancing girls.

The musicians were accompanied by women and boys and girls, singing and clapping their hands to the measure. The women wore various head-dresses. Some

---

tioned; but it is scarcely possible to determine what the instruments really were: they probably resembled those represented in the bas-reliefs described in the text. The instrument of ten strings mentioned in Psalm xxxiii. 2, xlii. 3, and cxliv. 9, may have been the harp of the sculptures, and the psaltery the smaller stringed instrument.

* Wilkinson's 'Ancient Egyptians,' vol. ii. p. 232—234. &c.

had their hair in long ringlets, some platted or braided, and others confined in a net.* One held her hands to her throat, as the Arab and Persian women still do when they make those shrill and vibrating sounds peculiar to the vocal music of the East. The whole scene, indeed, was curiously illustrative of modern Eastern customs.

Behind the two Assyrian generals were cavalry, chariots, led horses, and armed warriors.

Assyrians flaying their Prisoners alive, and carrying away Heads of the Slain (Kouyunjik).

A long line of warriors, some bearing maces, bows, spears, and shields, and others crossing their hands before them in the common Eastern attitude of respect, were the attendants and bodyguard of the king, and were represented of different heights, being probably picked men formed into companies or regiments according to their size and strength. They walked in front of a row of trees.

Above the Assyrian warriors were captives being tortured, who differed in costume from the Susianian fighting-men represented in the adjoining bas-reliefs. They were distinguished by the smallness of their stature, and by a very

---

* The modern fashion appears, therefore, to be but a revival of a very ancient one. Isaiah includes 'the caps of network' amongst the various articles of dress of the Jewish women (ch. iii. v. 8, Rev. Mr. Jones's version).

marked Jewish countenance—a sharp hooked nose, short bushy beard, and long narrow eyes. Could they have belonged to the Hebrew tribes who were carried away from Samaria and Jerusalem, and placed by Shalmaneser, Sennacherib, or Esarhaddon, in the distant regions of Elam, and who, having become powerful in their new settlements, had revolted against their Assyrian rulers, and were once again subdued? They wore a kind of conical cap, with tails or ribands, an inner garment reaching a little below the knee, a fringed robe falling down the back to the ankles, and boots turned up at the toes and laced in front. Some in iron fetters were being led before the king, for judgment or pardon. Others had been condemned to the torture, and were already in the hands of the executioners. Two were fastened naked at full length on the ground, and were being flayed alive. Other unfortunate victims were undergoing no less horrible punishments. The brains of one were being beaten out with an iron mace, whilst an officer held him by the beard. A torturer was wrenching the tongue out of the mouth of another who had been pinioned to the ground. The bleeding heads of the slain were tied round the necks of the living, who seemed reserved for still more barbarous tortures.*

The only spoil represented in these bas-reliefs as carried away by the Assyrians consisted of horses and bundles of precious woods. At the top of each slab was a line of warriors drawn up in array, and at the bottom a broad river filled with those killed in the fight, and horses, mules, chariots, carts, bows, and quivers.†

Although these bas-reliefs were carved, as shown by the inscriptions upon them, by a later king, the chamber itself, like the rest of the edifice, was built by Sennacherib, and on the back of each slab were inscribed his name and usual titles. The inscriptions behind the winged lions at the entrance also contained his name. The slabs round the room

---

* A short inscription above the torturers appears to declare that the victims having spoken blasphemies against Ashur, the great god of the Assyrians, their tongues had been pulled out.

† These six bas-reliefs are now in the British Museum. Drawings of them are given in the 2nd series of my 'Monuments of Nineveh,' Plates 45 to 49.

appear, therefore, to have been originally plain, as in the adjoining chambers, and to have been subsequently sculptured by order of the son and successor of Esarhaddon.

Assyrians torturing their Captives. (Kouyunjik.)

These bas-reliefs prove that many changes had taken place in the arts and dress of the people of Assyria between the reign of Sennacherib and that of his grandson. The later sculptures are principally distinguished by their minute finish, the sharpness of the outline, and the very correct delineation of animals. We now approach the period of the fall of the Assyrian empire and of the rise of the kingdoms of Babylon and Persia. The arts passed from Assyria to the sister nations, and thence to Ionia and Greece. There is much in the bas-reliefs I have just described to remind us of the early works of the Greeks executed immediately after the Persian war.

X.] *DESCRIPTION OF THE CHAMBERS.* 257

The chamber containing these sculptures had an entrance opening upon the edge of the mound. Of this doorway there only remained, on each side, a block of plain limestone, which may, however, have been the base of a sphinx or other figure. The outer walls to which it led * had been panelled with the usual alabaster slabs. Upon them were bas-reliefs of a campaign in a country already represented in another part of the palace,† and distinguished by a deep valley watered by a river, vineyards, and wooded mountains.

It is doubtful whether these walls belonged to a chamber, or formed part of the southern face of the palace, as they were on the very brink of the platform. At right angles to them, to the west, a pair of winged bulls opened upon another wall, of which there were scarcely any remains, and midway between the two entrances was a deep doorway,‡ flanked on both sides by four colossal mythic figures, amongst which were the fish-god and the deity with the lion's head and eagle's feet. It led to an ascending passage, between nine and ten feet wide, and forty-four feet in length, paved with hard lime or plaster about an inch and a half thick, the walls of which were built of the finest sun-dried bricks, admirably fitted together. Three rows of square projections, each formed by

Colossal Figures at an Entrance.   (Kouyunjik.)

two bricks, were carried along both sides of this passage. Here and there were circular holes purposely cut into the brickwork. These projections may have supported shelves on which the archives and other public documents were de-

* No. LX. Plan I.
† In No. XXXVIII. same Plan. See page 166.
‡ Entrance *b*, No. LX.

S

posited, for it was in this passage that were discovered the detached seals described in a former chapter.

This inclined way probably led to the upper chambers of the palace, or to the galleries which may have been carried round the principal chambers and halls.

I have only to describe two more rooms discovered in this part of the ruins during the summer.* They opened into the chamber parallel with that containing the sculptured records of the son of Esarhaddon. The entrances to both were formed by two pairs of colossal figures in bold relief, each

Cases containing Sculptures ready for Embarkation.

pair consisting of a man wearing the horned cap surmounted by a fleur-de-lis, and a lion-headed and eagle-footed human figure raising a dagger in one hand, and holding a mace in the other. The bas-reliefs on the walls recorded a campaign against a nation dwelling amidst a wooded and mountainous country, and in strongly fortified cities, which the Assyrians took by assault, with battering rams and scaling ladders, carrying away a vast amount of spoil and captives.

* No. XXXI., 26 by 14 feet, and No. XXXII., 22 by 20 feet.

The prisoners had short bushy hair and beards, and wore an inner garment reaching to the knee, an outer cloak of skins or fur, and gaiters laced in front. The robes of the women were short; their hair hung low down their backs, and was then gathered up into one large curl.*

I was engaged until the middle of October in moving and packing bas-reliefs from Kouyunjik ; a task demanding much time and labour, as the slabs, split into fragments by the fire, had to be taken to pieces, and then arranged and numbered, with a view to their future restoration. Nearly a hundred cases containing these remains were at length dragged to the river side, to await the construction of the rafts by which they were to be forwarded to Busrah, where a vessel was shortly expected to transport them to England.

* Plates 19 and 31 of the 'Monuments of Nineveh,' 2nd series

CHAPTER XI.

Departure for Babylon — The Awai — Descent of the river — Tekrit — The plain of Dura — The Naharwan — Samarrah — Kadesia — Palm groves — Kathimain — Approach to Baghdad — The city — Arrival — Modern Baghdad — Departure for Babylon — Abde Pasha's camp — Approach to Babylon — The ruins — Arrival at Hillah — The chiefs of Hillah — Present of lions — Description of the town — The ruins of Babylon — The walls — Visit to the Birs Nimroud — Description of the ruin — View from it — Excavations and discoveries in the Mound of Babel — In the Mujelibe or Kasr — The tree Athelé — Excavations in the ruin of Amran — Bowls, with inscriptions in Hebrew and Syriac characters — The Jews of Babylonia.

The winter was now drawing near, and the season was favourable for examining the remains of ancient cities in Babylonia. As the operations at Nimroud were suspended, I determined to employ fewer men at Kouyunjik, and to devote myself, during the cold weather, to researches amongst the great mounds of Southern Mesopotamia. I selected about thirty of the most skilful Arabs who had been employed at Nineveh, to accompany me.

Having entrusted Toma Shisman with the superintendence of the excavations, I quitted Mosul on the 18th of October, accompanied by Hormuzd Rassam and Mr. Romaine, an English traveller, on his way to India. There were cases enough containing sculptures from Kouyunjik to load a raft of considerable size. My Jebours, armed with guns, went with them for defence, as the banks of the Tigris were swarming with Bedouins, who had nearly interrupted all intercourse both by the river and high road between Mosul and Baghdad. I occupied a smaller raft.

We stopped for the first night beneath the mound of Hammum Ali. On the following morning we crossed the foaming rapids of the Awai, or great dam. During the previous three years the river had gained much ground to the eastward, washing away the alluvial soil of the plain, and gradually seeking its ancient bed at the foot of the mound. The stonework which, on my first visit to Nimroud, was only just visible in the high bank,* now stood, like a tower, almost in

A Kellek, or Raft of Skins, on the Tigris.

the centre of the Tigris, dividing the impetuous stream into two roaring cataracts. Solid masonry beneath the level of the river connected this isolated mass with the opposite bank. I endeavoured to trace it inland, but after digging for some days without coming to the end, I relinquished the attempt. The result of this experiment shows that the Awai may possibly be the remains of a wall now covered by the deposits of the river, and not an ancient dam. It would have required time and labour to trace its course, and to determine its original object, deeply buried as it is beneath the soil.

The navigation of the Tigris as far as Kalah Sherghat was so insecure, that I deemed it prudent, in order to avoid a collision with the Arabs, to engage a Bedouin chief, named Awaythe, a Sheikh of the Fedagha Shammar, to accompany us. Placing one of his sons on his mare, and ordering him to follow us along the banks of the river, he stepped upon

* Nineveh and its Remains, p. 5.

my raft, where he spent his time in giving us accounts of wars and ghazous, smoking his pipe and pounding coffee.

We reached Tekrit in three days without accident or adventure. Bedouin tents and moving swarms of men and camels were occasionally seen on the river banks, but under the protection of our Sheikh we met with no hindrance. Tekrit is almost the only permanent settlement of any importance between Mosul and Baghdad. It is now a small town, but was once a place of some size and strength. The remains of an ancient castle crown a high sandstone rock rising from the river, and amidst crumbling hovels are seen the ruins of mosques, baths, and well-built houses, and that labyrinth of tombs which invariably marks the site of an ancient Mohammedan city. Tekrit is chiefly famous as the birthplace of Saleh-ed-din, better known to the English reader as Saladin, the hero of the Crusades, and the magnanimous enemy of our Richard Cœur-de-Lion. His father, Ayub, a chief of a Kurdish tribe of Rahwandiz, was governor of its castle for the Seljukian monarchs of Persia. Tekrit is now inhabited by a few Arabs, who carry on, as raftsmen, the traffic of the river between Mosul and Baghdad.

Between this place and Baghdad, although the country is now almost a desert, there is much to interest the traveller who, for the first time, floats down a river winding through the great alluvial plains of Chaldæa. Leaving Tekrit, we first pass a small whitewashed Mussulman tomb, rising on the left or eastern bank of the Tigris, in a plain that still bears the name of Dura. It was here, as some believe, 'that Nebuchadnezzar the king made an image of gold, whose height was threescore cubits and breadth six cubits, and called together the princes, the governors, and the captains, the judges, the treasurers, the counsellors, the sheriffs, and all the rulers of the provinces to its dedication, and that certain Jews would not serve his gods, nor fall down and worship the golden image that he had set up.'[*] It is now a wilderness, with here and there a shapeless mound, the remains of some ancient habitation. It was here also that,

---

[*] Daniel, iii.

after the death of the Emperor Julian, his successor Jovian concluded a disgraceful peace with the Persian king Sapores (Shapour), and saved the Roman army by yielding to the enemy the five great provinces to the east of the Tigris. It was here, too, that he crossed the river, a broad and deep stream, and commenced his disastrous retreat through Mesopotamia.

Not far below, and on the same side of the river, the great canal of the Naharwan, the wonder of Arab geographers, robbed the Tigris of a large portion of its waters. Its innumerable arms once spread fertility over many districts, rich in villages and gardens. Lofty banks, all that remain of this mighty work, may still be traced, stretching, like natural hills, far across the plains, here crossed by the remains of a richly-decorated bridge, there losing themselves amidst a confused heap of mounds, marking the site of some ancient city.

Below the Naharwan, ruins, walls, and dwellings, built chiefly of large pebbles, united by a strong cement, a mode of construction peculiar to the Sassanian and early Arab periods, stand on the alluvial cliffs. They are called Eski, or old, Baghdad. On the opposite side of the Tigris, another mass of falling masonry, named Ashek, crowns a projecting ridge.

A tower, about two hundred feet high, now rises above the eastern bank of the river. An ascending way winds round it on the outside like the spiral of a screw, reminding the traveller of the common ideal pictures of the Tower of Babel. It marks the site of the ancient city of Samarrah, where the Roman army under Jovian rested after marching and fighting a long summer's day.* It subsequently became the capital of Motassem Billah, the eighth caliph of the Abbasside dynasty. A half-ruined mosque is now a place of pilgrimage to Mussulmans of the Sheeah sect, for it is said to cover the tombs of the last Imaums of the race of Ali, and to be the hiding-place of the twelfth prophet, Mehdi, who is to appear at the second coming of Christ. The modern town, inhabited by Arabs, consists of a few falling houses surrounded by a mud wall, and defended by bastions and towers.

* Gibbon's 'Decline and Fall,' chap. xxiv.

On both sides of the river, as the raft is carried gently along by the now sluggish current, the traveller sees huge masses of brick work jutting out from the falling banks, or overhanging the precipice of earth which hems in the stream. Here and there are walls of the solid masonry of the Sassanian period, and cupolas fretted with the elegant tracery of early Arab architecture. These are the remains of the palaces and castles of the last Persian kings and of the first Caliphs. The place is still called Gadesia or Kadesia, and near it was fought that great battle between the fire-worshippers of Persia and the followers of Mahomet, which gave to the new nation, issuing from the wilds of Arabia, the dominion of the Eastern world.[*]

Remains of an earlier period are not wanting. A huge mound on the west bank of the river, within sight of Samarrah, is known to the Arabs as the Sidd-ul-Nimroud, the wall or rampart of Nimroud. By some it is believed to be part of the Median wall which, in the days of old, guarded Babylon against invasion from the north. A few heaps of earth on an angle formed by the junction of the Naharwan and another great canal derived from the Tigris, may represent the ancient Chaldæan city of Opis.

The current becomes more gentle at every broad reach, until the raft scarcely glides past the low banks. The water has lost its clearness and its purity; tinged by the rich alluvial soil it has turned to a pale yellow colour. The river at length widens into a noble stream. Pelicans of snowy plumage and coloured wildfowl float lazily on the waters, and white herons stand motionless on the margin. A dark line now bounds the southern horizon. It gradually breaks into vast groves of the feathery palm. The loud creaking of waterwheels disturbs the silence which has hitherto reigned over the deserted waters, and groups of half-naked Arabs gather together on the banks to gaze on the travellers.

We are now amidst the date groves. If it be autumn, clusters of golden fruit hang beneath the fan-like leaves; if spring, the odour of orange blossoms fills the air. The coo-

---

[*] Gibbon's 'Decline and Fall,' chap. li.

ing of the doves that flutter amongst the branches begets a pleasing melancholy, and a feeling of listlessness and repose.

The raft creeps round a projecting bank, and two gilded domes and four stately minarets, all glittering in the rays of an eastern sun, suddenly rise high above the dense bed of palms. They are of the mosque of Kathimain, which covers the tombs of two of the Imaums or saints of the Sheeah sect.

The low banks swarm with Arabs,—men, women, and naked children. Mud hovels screened by yellow mats, and groaning waterwheels worked by the patient ox, are seen beneath the palms. The Tigris becomes wider and wider, and the stream is almost motionless. Circular boats, of reeds coated with bitumen, skim over the water. Horsemen, and riders on white asses,[*] hurry along the river side. Turks in flowing robes and broad turbans, Persians in high black caps and close-fitting tunics, the Bokhara pilgrim in his white head-dress and wayworn garments, the Bedouin chief in his tasselled keffieh and striped aba, Baghdad ladies with their scarlet and white draperies fretted with threads of gold, and their black horsehair veils, concealing even their wanton eyes, Persian women wrapped in their unsightly garments, and Arab girls in their simple blue shirts, are all mingled together in one motley crowd, and flow in a busy stream without ceasing, from the gates of the western suburb of Baghdad to the sacred precincts of Kathimain.

A pine-shaped cone of snowy whiteness rises to the right; near it are one or two drooping palms, that seem fast falling to decay, like the building over which they can no longer throw their shade. This is the tomb of Zobeide, the lovely queen of Haroun-al-Reshid, a name that raises many a pleasant association, and recalls to memory a thousand romantic dreams of early youth.

A mosque cut in two, a singular object, next appears on the eastern bank. The river has gradually undermined and

---

[*] The white ass of Baghdad is much esteemed in the East. Some are of considerable size, and fancifully dyed with henna, their tails and ears bright red, and their bodies spotted, like an heraldic talbot, with the same colour, they bear the chief priests and the men of the law, as they appear to have done from the earliest times. (Judges, v. 10.)

carried away the other part, leaving the innermost recesses
of its dome, of which exactly half remains, its places of
prayer, and its chapel-like chambers open to the air. Coloured cupolas and minarets rise on all sides above the
palms, until the trees are succeeded by a long line of mud-
built houses. We pass the palace of the governor, an edifice
of mean materials and proportions. At its windows the
Pasha himself and the various officers of his household may
be seen reclining on their divans, amidst wreaths of smoke.
A crazy bridge of boats crosses the stream, and appears to
bar all further progress. At length the chains are loosened,
two or three of the rude vessels are withdrawn, and the rafts
glide gently through. A few minutes more, and we are
anchored beneath the spreading folds of the British flag,
opposite a handsome building, not crumbling into ruins like
its neighbours, but kept in repair with European neatness.
A small iron steamer floats motionless before it. We have
arrived at the dwelling of the English Consul-general and
political agent of the East India Company at Baghdad.

It was early in the morning of the 26th October that I
landed at the well-remembered quay of the British residency.
In the absence of Colonel (now Sir Henry) Rawlinson, then
in England, his political duties had been confided to Captain
Kemball, who received me with great kindness. I acknowledge with gratitude the hospitality and effective assistance I
invariably experienced from him during my sojourn at Baghdad, and my researches in Babylonia.

Baghdad, with its long vaulted bazaars rich with the produce and merchandise of every clime, its mixed population
of Turks, Arabs, Persians, Indians, and men of all Eastern
nations, its palm groves and gardens, its painted palaces and
unsightly hovels, its present misery and its former magnificence, have been so frequently described, that I will not
detain the reader with any minute account of this celebrated
city. Tyranny, disease, and inundations have brought it
very low. Nearly half of the space enclosed within its walls
is now covered by heaps of ruins, and the population is daily
decreasing, without the hope of change. During my residence in Baghdad no one could go far beyond the gates

without the risk of falling into the hands of wandering Arabs, who prowled unchecked over the plains, keeping the city itself almost in a continual state of siege. Notwithstanding these drawbacks, the importance of its position is so great, that Baghdad must at all times command a considerable trade. It is a link between the East and the West; it is the storehouse from which the tribes of the desert obtain their clothing and their food; and it is the key to the holy places annually sought by thousands upon thousands of Persian pilgrims of the Sheeah sect.

It is remarkable that, with the exception of the ruins of an ancient college, and of some other buildings, there is scarcely a trace to be found in Baghdad of that magnificent city, 'the Abode of Peace,' on which the Caliphs lavished every resource of Eastern wealth and taste. The stranger will now seek in vain for the palaces and gardens of Haroun-al-Reshid, and the universities and mosques of Al Mamoun. Even the very names of those great princes, the glory of Islam, are almost forgotten, or are only heard in the coffee-house, where the Arab storyteller relates his fanciful tale.

The only remains of the Babylonian period hitherto discovered within the city walls are the ruins of an enormous drain or subterranean passage, built of large square bricks bearing the name of Nebuchadnezzar. A lofty pile of sun-dried bricks, intermixed with layers of reeds, called Akker-Kuf, rises in the midst of a marsh to the west of the Tigris, about four or five miles from the city gates. During my visit to Baghdad it was not easy to reach this ruin on account of the swamp, and as it is merely a solid mass of mud masonry, excavations in it would scarcely have led to results of any interest.*

It was not until the 5th of December that I was able to leave Baghdad. I had been struggling with my old enemy, intermittent fever, and the surrounding country was still in the hands of the Arabs, two reasons for remaining within

* There is, I believe, some doubt as to whether Akker-Kuf is a pure Babylonian ruin.

the gates. At length Abde Pasha, the governor of the province, placed himself at the head of his troops, and marched against the rebellious tribes. Before going to Babylon I determined to visit him, and to make acquaintance with several Sheikhs of the southern tribes friendly to the Turkish government who were in his camp.

The marshes formed by the Saklawiyah, a great canal derived from the Euphrates, had reached almost to the very walls of the western suburb of Baghdad, interrupting communication by land, and spreading disease through the city. To get into the highway to Hillah, we were obliged to make a circuit of some miles, fording ditches, wading through water and deep mud, and crossing wide streams by crazy bridges of boats. We had been nearly three hours on horseback before we rode through the vaulted gateway of the Khan-i-Zad, the first habitable caravanserai on the road.

The plains between Khan-i-Zad and the Euphrates are covered with a perfect network of ancient canals and watercourses; but 'a drought is upon the waters of Babylon, and they were dried.'* Their lofty embankments, stretching on every side in long lines until they are lost in the hazy distance, or magnified by the mirage into mountains, still defy the hand of time, and seem rather the work of nature than of man. The face of the country, too, is dotted with mounds and shapeless heaps, the remains of ancient towns and villages. A long ride of ten hours through this scene of solitude and desolation brought us to the tents of the Pasha of Baghdad, pitched on the western bank of the Euphrates, below the village of Musseiyib, and on the inlet of the Hindiyah canal. A bridge of boats had been placed across the river to connect the camp of the governor with Baghdad. As we approached we heard the loud hum of human voices; but the whole encampment was concealed by dense clouds of dust. Once over the bridge we found ourselves in the midst of a crowd of Turkish soldiers, Arabs and workmen of every kind hurrying to and fro in wild disorder; some bearing earth and mud in baskets, or in their

---

* Jeremiah, l. 38.

cloaks, others bending under the weight of bundles of brushwood, mats, and ropes. Women and girls were mingled with the men, and as they laboured they chanted in a monotonous tone verses on the Pasha and their chiefs, improvised for the occasion. This busy throng was building up the dam which was to shut out the waters of the Euphrates from the canal, dry the marshes, and bring the rebellious tribes to obedience.

Before leaving the camp I obtained letters to the principal chiefs of the southern tribes from the Pasha as well as from Wadi, the Sheikh of the Zobeide, and other influential Sheikhs. The town of Hillah was about eighteen miles from the Turkish tents further down the Euphrates. We were obliged to take the longest road by the eastern bank of the river, as the Arabs infested the country to the west. Between Musseiyib and the ruins of Babylon the country abounds in dry canals and ancient mounds. A few villages, surrounded by palm groves, stand on the banks of the Euphrates and on the channels, which still carry the waters of the river into the heart of Mesopotamia. After riding about four hours we perceived a huge hill to the south. As we drew nearer its flat table-like top and perpendicular sides, rising abruptly from an alluvial plain, showed that it was the work of man, and not a natural elevation. At length we could plainly distinguish around it great embankments, the remains of walls and canals. Gradually, as the caravan slowly advanced, the ruin assumed a definite shape. It was the mound of Babel.

This is the first great ruin seen on approaching ancient Babylon from the north. Beyond it long lines of palms hem in the Euphrates, which now winds through the midst of the ancient city. To the vast mound of Babel succeed long undulating heaps of earth, bricks, and pottery. A solitary mass of brick-work, rising from the summit of the largest mound, marks the remains known to the Arabs as the 'Mujelibé,' or the 'overturned.'*

Other shapeless heaps of rubbish cover for many an acre the face of the land. The lofty banks of ancient canals fret

---

* This is the Kasr of Rich and subsequent travellers.

the country like natural ridges of hills. Some have long been choked with sand; others still carry the waters of the river to distant villages and palm groves. On all sides, fragments of glass, marble, pottery, and inscribed brick are mingled with that peculiar nitrous and blanched soil, which, bred from the remains of ancient habitations, checks or destroys vegetation, and renders the site of Babylon a naked and hideous waste. Owls start from the scanty thickets, and the foul jackal skulks through the furrows. Truly 'the glory of kingdoms and the beauty of the Chaldee's excellency is as when God overthrew Sodom and Gomorrah. Wild beasts of the desert lie there; and their houses are full of doleful creatures; and owls dwell there, and satyrs dance there. And the wild beasts of the islands cry in their desolate houses, and dragons in her pleasant palaces, for her day has come.'*

A few black tents and flocks of sheep and camels were scattered over the yellow plain. They belonged chiefly to the Zobeide, an ancient tribe, renowned in the history of the conquering Arabs under their first caliphs, and now pasturing their flocks in the wilds of Babylonia.† From Amran, the last of the great mounds, a broad and well-trodden track winds through thick groves of palms. About an hour's ride beneath pleasant shade brings the traveller to the falling gateway of the town of Hillah. A mean bazaar crowded with Arabs, camels, and asses, leads to a bridge of boats across the Euphrates. The principal part of the town, containing the fort and the residence of the governor, is on the opposite side of the river. We turned off, however, to the left, as our quarters had been made ready on the western bank. A party of irregular troops sent out to meet me, conducted my caravan to a spacious house standing on the very edge of the stream, and belonging to one of the principal families of the place. It had once contained rich furniture, and handsomely

---

* Isaiah, xiii. 19-22, and compare Jeremiah, l. 39: 'therefore the wild beasts of the desert with the wild beasts of the island shall dwell there, and the *owls* shall dwell therein.' A large grey owl is found in great numbers, frequently in flocks of nearly a hundred, in the low shrubs among the ruins of Babylon.

† From this tribe was the celebrated lady of Haroun-al-Reshid, 'the Zobeide,' as she was called from her origin.

decorated rooms in the Persian style, but was now fast falling into utter ruin. The cold wind whistled through the rotten wooden panels of the windows, for there was no glass, and the crumbling ceiling and floor threatened to give way together. In this frail dwelling we prepared to pass a part of our winter in Babylonia.

My first care on arriving at Hillah was to establish friendly relations with the principal inhabitants of the town as well as with the Turkish officer in command of the small garrison that guarded its mud fort. Osman Pasha, the general, received me with courtesy and kindness, and during the remainder of my stay gave me all the help I could require. On my first visit he presented me with two lions. One was nearly of full size, and was well known in the bazaars and thoroughfares of Hillah, through which he was allowed to wander unrestrained. The inhabitants could accuse him of no other objectionable habit than that of taking possession of the stalls of the butchers, who, on his approach, made a hasty retreat, leaving him in undisturbed possession of their stores, until he had satisfied his hunger and deemed it time to depart. He would also wait the coming of the kuffas, or wicker boats, of the fishermen, and, driving away their owners, would help himself to a kind of large barbel, for which he appeared to have a decided relish. For these acts of depredation the beast was perhaps less to be blamed than the Pasha, who rather encouraged a mode of obtaining daily rations, which, although of questionable honesty, relieved him from butchers' bills. When no longer hungry he would stretch himself in the sun, and allow the Arab boys to take such liberties with him as in their mischief they might devise. He was taller and larger than a St. Bernard dog, and, like the lion generally found on the banks of the rivers of Mesopotamia, was without the dark and shaggy mane of the African species.* The other lion was but a cub, and had recently been found by an Arab in the Hindiyah marshes.

* I have, however, seen lions on the river Karoon, with a long black mane. The inhabitants of the country make a distinction between them and the common maneless lion; the former are Kafir, or infidels, the others Mussulmans. By a proper remonstrance, and at the same time

Unfortunately it fell ill of the mange, to which the animal when confined is very liable, and soon after died. The other was too old to be sent to England by land, and I was thus unable to procure specimens for this country of the Babylonian lion, which had not then, I believe, been seen alive in Europe.

The Mudir, or governor of Hillah, was Shabib Agha, the head of one of the principal families of the town. He claimed a kind of hereditary right to this office. He was aged and infirm, suffering from asthma, and little able to manage public affairs, which were chiefly confided to his youngest and favourite son, a boy of about twelve years old. It was with this child that, in common with the inhabitants of Hillah, I transacted business. He received and paid visits with wonderful dignity and decorum. His notes and his inquiries after my health and wants were couched in the most eloquent and suitable terms. He showed a warm and affectionate interest in my welfare, and in the success of my undertakings, which was quite touching. Every morning he crossed the river with a crowd of secretaries, slaves, and attendants, to ascertain, by personal inspection, whether I needed any help. His salutations were expressed with the greatest gravity. 'We trust that it has pleased God to preserve your Excellency's health. Our town is yours as well as our house. Our harem begs your Excellency's acceptance of sour milk and francolins. May we show that we are your slaves, by ordering the irregular troops to accompany you on your ride; your person is more precious to us than our eyes; and there are evil men, enemies of our Lord the Sultan, abroad in the desert,' and so on. He then gave me his usual report on the political state of the country, and related the successes of the Pasha or of the rebels; I am afraid his sympathies were more with the latter than with the legitimate power. At the same time he issued orders for rations to be collected for the troops, dictated letters to be sent to the Turkish authorities, summoned levies from the Arab tribes, and settled disputes amongst the inhabitants of the town,

pronouncing the profession of faith, a true believer may induce the one to spare his life, but the unbelieving lion is inexorable.

occasionally diverting himself with a peep into a kaleidoscope, in which he took great delight, and which I afterwards presented to him. He was a noble boy, with black sparkling eyes, and a bright olive complexion. He wore the long silken robes of a town Arab, with the fringed keffieh or striped head-kerchief of the Bedouin falling over his shoulders. On the whole, he made as good and active a governor as I have often met with in an Eastern town, and was an instance of that precocity which is frequently seen in Eastern children. A cordial friendship was soon established between us, and during my stay at Hillah, Azeez Agha, for such was his name, was my constant guest.

From the principal people of Hillah, as well as from Shabib Agha (the father of Azeez), I received every help. The day after my arrival they sent me presents of francolins, gazelles, and other game, and during my stay were unremitting in their attentions. Hillah, like most towns in this part of Turkey, is peopled by Arabs once belonging to different tribes, but now forgetting their clanships in a sedentary life. They maintain, however, a friendly intercourse with the Bedouins and with the wild inhabitants of the marshes, being always ready to unite with them in attempting to throw off their allegiance to the Sultan. As several families divide the authority and have their private feuds, which lead to constant broils and bloodshed, the town, thus weakened, falls an easy prey to the Turks, when regular troops are sent against it.

At the time of my visit, its inhabitants were anxiously awaiting the result of the expedition of Abde Pasha against the rebellious tribes. Their allegiance to the Turkish governor and the consequent payment of taxes depended upon its success. If the Pasha were beaten they would declare openly in favour of the Arabs, with whom, it was suspected, they were already in communication. The Hindiyah marshes are within sight of the town, and the Kazail (the tribe that dwells in them) ravaged the country to its gates. I was consequently unable to do more than visit the celebrated ruin of the Birs Nimroud. To excavate in it in the then disturbed state of the country was impossible.

Hillah may contain about eight or nine thousand inhabitants. A few half-ruined mosques and public baths are its principal buildings. Its bazaar supplies the Bedouins with articles of clothing, arms, dates, coffee, and corn, and contains a few common Manchester goods and English cutlery and hardware. The Euphrates flows through the town, and is about two hundred yards wide and fifteen feet deep; a noble stream, with a gentle current, admirably fitted for steam navigation. The houses, chiefly built of bricks taken from the ruins of ancient Babylon, are small and mean. Around the town, and above and below it for some miles, are groves of palm trees, forming a broad belt on both sides of the river. In the plain beyond them a few canals bear water to plots cultivated with wheat, barley, and rice.

Plan of Part of the Ruins of Babylon on the Eastern Bank of the Euphrates.

The ruins of Babylon have been so frequently described, that I prefer giving a general sketch of them to entering into accurate details of measurements and distances; at the same time referring my reader to the accompanying plan, which will enable him to understand the position of the principal mounds.

The road from Baghdad to Hillah crosses, near the village of Mohawill, a wide and deep canal. On its southern bank is a line of earthen ramparts, which are generally believed to be the most northern remains of the ancient city of Babylon. From their summit the traveller scans a boundless plain, through which winds the Euphrates, with its dark belt of evergreen palms. Rising in the distance, high above all surrounding objects, is the one square mound, in form and size more like a natural hill than the work of men's hands. This is the first great ruin to the east of the river, and the Arab names it 'Babel.'

The traveller, before reaching this ruin, still about four miles distant, follows a beaten track winding amidst low mounds, and crossing the embankments of canals long since dry. Some have here traced the lines of the streets, and the divisions between the inhabited quarters of ancient Babylon. They believe them to correspond with the descriptions of ancient authors, who declare that the city was divided into a number of equal squares by parallel thoroughfares. But no traces whatever have been discovered of that great wall of earth rising, according to Herodotus, to the height of two hundred royal cubits, and no less than fifty cubits broad; nor of the ditch that encompassed it. The mounds seem to be scattered without order, and to be gradually lost in the vast plains to the eastward.

But southward of Babel, for the distance of nearly three miles, there is almost an uninterrupted line of mounds, the ruins of vast edifices, collected together as in the heart of a great city. They are inclosed by earthen ramparts, the remains of a line of walls which, leaving the foot of Babel, stretch inland about two miles and a half from the present bed of the Euphrates, and then turning nearly at right angles are continued to the eastern bank of the river.*

It is evident that the space inclosed within this continuous rampart could not have contained the whole of that mighty city, whose magnificence and extent were the wonder of the ancient world. The walls of Babylon, according to Herodotus, measured 120 stadia on each side, and formed a perfect

* The plan in the text gives a correct idea of the position of the principal ruins. Very elaborate and careful surveys of the site of Babylon have been made by Captain Jones.

square of 480 stadia, or nearly sixty miles. Several later writers have repeated his statement. Strabo and Diodorus Siculus have, however, reduced the circuit of the city to 385 and 360 stadia; and such, according to Clitarchus, were its dimensions, when it yielded to Alexander.

It is difficult to explain the total absence of all traces of the external wall and ditch so fully and minutely described by Herodotus and other ancient writers, and, according to their concurrent accounts, of such enormous dimensions. If a vast line of fortifications, with its gates, and equidistant towers, all of stupendous height and thickness, did once exist, it is scarcely to be believed that no part whatever of them should now remain. Darius and other conquerors are said to have pulled down and destroyed these defences; but it is surely impossible that any human labour could have obliterated their very traces, had they been of stone or brick.

But Herodotus states that, in the midst of each division of the city, there was a circular space surrounded by a lofty wall: one contained the royal palace; the other, the temple of Belus. There can be little difficulty in admitting that the mounds within the earthen rampart on the eastern bank of the river might represent the first of these fortified inclosures, which we know to have been on that side of the Euphrates. It is not impossible, as Rich has suggested, that the Birs Nimroud, around which—as it will be seen—there are still the traces of a regular wall, may be the remains of the temple of Belus, unless the ruins of it have been entirely obliterated by the changes which have taken place in the course of the river.

It may be inferred, I think, from the descriptions of Herodotus and Diodorus Siculus,* that Babylon was built on the same general plan as Nineveh. More than one fortified inclosure, formed by lofty walls and towers, and containing the royal palaces and the temples with their numerous dependent buildings, courtyards, and gardens, rose in different quarters of the city. They were so built and guarded as to be able to resist an enemy and stand a protracted siege.

---

* Diodorus Siculus particularly describes, after Ctesias, the two fortified palaces (l. ii. c. 8).

Around them were the common dwellings of the people, with their palm groves, their orchards, and their small plots of corn-land.

If the exterior fortifications were mere ramparts of mud and brushwood, such as are still raised round modern Eastern cities, they would, when once neglected, have fallen to dust, and have left no traces behind. I confess that I can see no other way of accounting for their entire disappearance.

I will now describe the results of my researches amongst the ruins near Hillah. Parties of workmen were placed at once on the two most important mounds, the Babel of the Arabs (the Mujelibé of Rich) and the Mujelibé (the Kasr of the same traveller). I was compelled, as I have stated, to abandon my plan of excavating in the Birs Nimroud. This great pile of masonry is about six miles to the south-west of Hillah. It stands on the very edge of the vast marsh formed by the waters of the Hindiyah canal, and by the periodical floods of the Euphrates. The plain between it and the town is, in times of quiet, under cultivation, and is irrigated by a canal derived from the Euphrates near the village of Anana. This year, however, in consequence of the rebellion of the tribes of Al Khazail and Al Maidan, who inhabit the morasses, the land had been left unsown. Shortly after my arrival at Hillah I visited the Birs, accompanied by one Sheikh Zaid, and a party of well-armed Agayls.

The Birs Nimroud, 'the palace of Nimrod' of the Arabs, and 'the prison of Nebuchadnezzar' of the Jews; by old travellers believed to be the very ruins of the tower of Babel; by some, again, supposed to represent the temple of Belus, the wonder of the ancient world; and, by others, to mark the site of Borsippa, a city celebrated as the highplace of the Chaldæan worship, is a vast heap of bricks, slag, and broken pottery. The dry nitrous earth of the parched plain, driven before the furious south wind, has thrown over the huge mass a thin covering of soil in which no herb or green thing can find nourishment or take root. It rises to the height of 153 feet, and has on its summit a compact mass of brickwork, 37 feet high by 28 broad. Neither the original form nor object of the edifice, of which it is the ruin, had, previous to my visit, been determined. On one side of it, beneath the crowning masonry, lie huge fragments torn from the pile itself. The calcined and vitreous surface of the bricks fused into rock-like masses, show that their fall may have been caused by lightning; and, as the ruin is rent almost from top to bottom,

The Birs Nimroud, or Tower of Babel of early Travellers.

early Christian travellers, as well as some of more recent date, have not hesitated to recognise in them proofs of that divine vengeance, which, according to tradition, arrested by fire from heaven the impious attempt of the first descendants of Noah.

Even the Jews, it would appear, at one time identified the

Birs Nimroud with the Tower of Babel. Benjamin of Tudela, who saw it in the twelfth century, gives the following curious account of the ruin. 'The tower built by the dispersed generation is four miles from Hillah. It is constructed of bricks, called Al-ajur (the word still used by the Arabs for kiln-burnt bricks); the base measures two miles, the breadth 240 yards, and the height about 100 canna. A spiral passage, built into the tower (from ten to ten yards), leads up to the summit, from which there is a prospect of twenty miles, the country being one wide plain, and quite level. The heavenly fire which struck the tower, split it to its very foundation.'* No traces whatever now remain of the spiral passage spoken of by the Jewish traveller.

Whatever may have been the original edifice, of which the Birs Nimroud is the ruin, or whoever its founder, it is certain that as yet no remains have been discovered there more ancient than of the time of Nebuchadnezzar. Every inscribed brick taken from it—and there are thousands and tens of thousands—bear the name of this king. It must, however, be remembered, that this fact is no proof that he actually founded the building. He may have merely added to, or rebuilt, an earlier edifice. It is not impossible that, at some future time, more ancient remains may be discovered at the Birs.

The ruins are divided into two distinct parts, undoubtedly the remains of two different buildings. A wall, the remains of which are marked by mounds of earth, appears to have inclosed both of them. To the west of the high mound, topped by the tower-like pile of masonry, is a second, which is larger but lower, and in shape more like the ruins on the eastern bank of the Euphrates. It is traversed by ravines and watercourses, and strewed over it are the usual fragments of stone, brick, and pottery. Upon its summit are two small Mohammedan chapels, one of which, the Arabs declare, is built over the spot where Nimrod cast the patriarch Abraham into the fiery furnace, according to the common Eastern tradition.

Travellers, as far as I am aware, have hitherto failed in

* Asher's Transl. p. 107.

suggesting any satisfactory restoration of the Birs. It is generally represented, without sufficient accuracy, as a mere shapeless mass. But it examined from the summit of the adjoining mound, its outline would at once strike any one acquainted with the ruins to the west of Mosul, described in a former part of this work.* The similarity between them will be recognised, and it will be seen that they are all the remains of edifices built upon very nearly, if not precisely, the same plan. It will be perceived that the mound rises abruptly from the plain on one face, the western, and falls to its level by a series of gradations on the opposite side. The brickwork, still visible in the lower parts of the mound, as well as in the upper, shows the sides of several distinct stages or terraces. I believe the isolated mass of masonry to be the remains of one of the highest terraces, if not the highest, and the whole edifice to have consisted, on the eastern or south-eastern side, of a series of stages rising one above the other, and, on the western or north-western, of one solid perpendicular wall. The annexed sketch shows how far the proposed restoration suits with the actual form of the ruin; but it must be borne in mind that the number and size of the terraces is merely conjectural.†

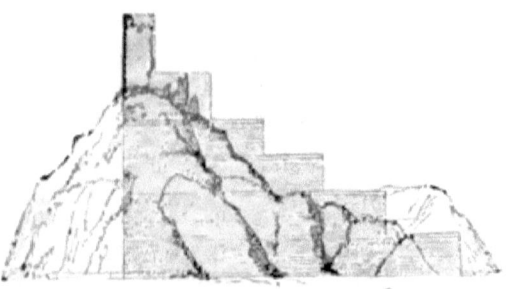

Eastern Face of the Birs Nimroud with proposed Restoration.

It is probable that the ascents from terrace to terrace consisted of broad flights of steps, or of inclined ways, carried up the centre of each stage. A step may still be traced

* Chap. iv. pp. 88, 89.
† Sir H. Rawlinson, who subsequently made some excavations in the Birs Nimroud, believes it to be the ruin of a temple of Nebo, erected by Nebuchadnezzar at Borsippa, and built in seven stages, representing the seven planetary spheres, each stage being distinguished by a typical colour. In the foundations at two of the angles he found clay cylinders with annals of Nebuchadnezzar.

around the foot of the ruin, probably part of the basement or first platform, and as the whole is surrounded by the remains of a quadrangular inclosure, it is in every respect like those in the desert to the west of Mosul. Around the Birs are heaps of rubbish marking the sites of ancient buildings.

The edifice, of which this remarkable ruin is the remains, was built of kiln-burnt bricks. Fragments of stone, marble, and basalt, scattered amongst the rubbish, show that it was adorned with other materials. The cement is of so tenacious a quality, that it is almost impossible to detach one brick from the mass entire. The ruin is a specimen of the perfection of Babylonian masonry.

From the summit of the Birs Nimroud I gazed over a vast marsh, for Babylon is made 'a possession for the bittern and pools of water.'* In the midst of the swamps could be faintly distinguished the mat huts of the Kazail, forming villages on the small islands. The green morass was spotted with herds of black buffalos. The Arab settlements showed the activity of a hive of bees. Light boats were skimming to and fro over the shallow water, whilst men and women urged onwards their flocks and laden cattle. The booming of the cannon of the Turkish army, directed against the fort of Hawaina, resounded in the distance; and the inhabitants of the marsh were already hurrying with their property to safer retreats, in anticipation of the fall of their stronghold.

To the south-west, in the extreme distance, rose the palm trees of Kifil, casting their scanty shade over a small dome, covering the tomb of Ezekiel. To this spot annually flock in crowds, as their forefathers have done for centuries, the Jews of Baghdad, Hillah, and other cities of Chaldæa, the descendants of the captives of Jerusalem, who still linger in the land of their exile. Although tradition alone may place in the neighbourhood of Babylon the tomb of the prophet, yet from a very early period the spot appears to have been sought in pilrimage by the pious Hebrew. I visited the edifice some years ago. It is now but a plain building, despoiled of the ornaments and manuscripts which it once appears to have

---

* Isaiah, xiv. 23.

contained. The description given by Benjamin of Tudela of this place is so curious, that I cannot forbear transcribing it. 'On the banks of the Euphrates stands the synagogue of the prophet Ezekiel, who rests in peace. The place of the synagogue is fronted by sixty towers, the room between every two of which is also occupied by a synagogue; in the court of the largest stands the ark, and behind it is the sepulchre of Ezekiel, the son of Busi, the Cohen. This monument is covered by a large cupola, and the building is very handsome; it was erected by Jeconiah, king of Judah, and the 35,000 Jews who went along with him, when Evil Merodach released him from the prison, which was situated between the river Chaboras and another river. The name of Jeconiah, and of all those who came with him, are inscribed on the wall, the king's name first, that of Ezekiel last.

'This place is considered holy unto the present day, and is one of those to which people resort from remote countries in order to pray, particularly at the season of the new year and atonement day. Great rejoicings take place there about this time, which are attended even by the Prince of the Captivity and the presidents of the Colleges of Baghdad. The assembly is so large, that their temporary abodes cover twenty miles of open ground, and attracts many Arabian merchants, who keep a market or fair.

'On the day of atonement, the proper lesson of the day is read from a very large manuscript Pentateuch of Ezekiel's own handwriting.

'A lamp burns night and day on the sepulchre of the prophet, and has always been kept burning since the day that he lighted it himself; and the oil and wicks are renewed as often as necessary. A large house belonging to the sanctuary contains a very numerous collection of books, some of them as ancient as the second, some even coeval with the first temple, it being customary that whoever dies childless bequeaths his books to the sanctuary. Even in time of war neither Jew nor Mohammedan ventures to despoil and profanate the sepulchre of Ezekiel.'*

* Asher's translation. On the Tigris, near its junction with the Euphrates, is the traditionary tomb of Ezra. The Jews, from the first

I remained in Hillah until the 19th December, riding every day to the ruins on the eastern bank of the river, to superintend the excavations. The first trenches were opened in the great mound of Babel, about five miles from the gate of Hillah, and three-quarters of a mile from the river.* I sought the subterranean passage opened and described by Mr. Rich, and on removing the rubbish I soon came to 'the quadran-

Mound of Babel: Ruins of Babylon.

gular funnel, about thirteen feet square, of burnt brick and bitumen,' which he had discovered. After the lapse of forty years, it had been again filled with earth. The workmen

centuries of the Christian æra, also appear to have visited this spot as the place of sepulture of the prophet. Benjamin of Tudela says of it, 'The sepulchre of Ezra, the priest and scribe, is in this place (name lost), where he died on his journey from Jerusalem to King Artaxerxes.' In the early part of the 13th century, a celebrated Jewish poet, named Jehuda Charisi ben Salomo, described both tombs in verse. (Dr. Zunt's Essay in 2nd volume of Asher's ed. of Benjamin of Tudela.)

* The dimensions of the mound, as given by Rich, are, the northern face, 200 yards in length; the southern, 219; the eastern, 182; and the western, 136. The elevation at the N.E. angle, 141 feet.

entered the underground chamber in which Mr. Rich found a coffin of wood, containing a skeleton still well preserved. The entrance to other galleries, which he had not explored, were still closed by large burnt bricks, amongst which were a few square stones, inscribed with two lines of cuneiform characters, containing the name and titles of Nebuchadnezzar, king of the Chaldees.

Beneath this masonry were found several coffins, similar to that discovered by Mr. Rich. They still held skeletons, which fell to pieces as soon as exposed to the air. No relic or ornament had been buried with the bodies. The wood of the coffins was in the last stage of decay, and could only be taken out piecemeal. A foul and unbearable stench issued from these loathsome remains, and from the passages which had become the dens of wild beasts, who had worked their way into them from above. It was almost impossible to stay for many minutes underground. Even the Arabs were compelled to leave their work after a few days.

On the northern side of the mound, above these places of sepulture, are the remains of a massive wall of sundried brick. The masonry is not united by bituminous cement, as in the vaults, but apparently by simple mud, as in modern Arab buildings; and between each course of bricks are spread thin layers of reeds still perfectly preserved.

The coffins discovered at Babel are of a comparatively recent period, and are not pure Babylonian. They may be of the time of the Seleucidæ, but I am inclined to think that they are even of a still later date. It is evident that they were buried after the destruction of the edifice covered by the mound. Upon that great heap, over the fallen palace or temple, was probably raised one of those citadels built long after the destruction of the Babylonian empire and its magnificent capital, and which resisted the arms of Demetrius Poliorcetes.* Of that stronghold the thick wall of sundried brick on the northern side is probably the remains.

Deep trenches opened on the surface of the mound, and several tunnels carried into its sides at different levels, led to

---

* Diod. Sic. l. xix. s. 100.

no other discovery than that of relics such as are found in large numbers amongst all Babylonian ruins, especially after heavy rains, and which belong to different periods, extending from the earliest times to the sixth or seventh century of the Christian era. The most interesting were arrow-heads in bronze and iron, small glass bottles (some coloured, others ribbed, and otherwise ornamented), and vases of earthenware of various forms and sizes, sometimes glazed with a rich blue colour.

At a little depth beneath the soil were numerous bricks, bearing the usual superscription of Nebuchadnezzar.

It was evident that the remains of the original edifice were to be sought far beneath the surface, and I accordingly opened tunnels at the very foot of the mound nearly on a level with the plain. On the eastern side the workmen soon reached solid piers and walls of brick masonry, buried under an enormous mass of loose bricks, earth, and rubbish. We uncovered eight or ten piers and several walls branching in various directions, but I failed to trace any plan, or to discover any remains whatever of sculptured stone or painted plaster.

During the remainder of my stay in Babylonia workmen continued to excavate in this part of the mound, discovering nothing but a confused heap of ruin and standing masonry. The enormous accumulation of loose rubbish above them, not a hard compact mass, as at Nineveh, but continually crumbling and falling in, exposed the men to a risk scarcely warranted by the results of their labours.

On the western and southern sides of the mound were also discovered, at the very base, remains of solid masonry. The bricks bore the usual superscription of Nebuchadnezzar, and were firmly cemented together with fine white mortar. It is thus evident that a vast edifice once stood either on the level of the plain, or raised upon enormous piers and buttresses of brickwork; and that the tombs, and any remains of building that may exist on or near the present surface of the mound, are of a comparatively recent period. I will not attempt to decide whether Babel be the ruins of a great palace of Nebuchadnezzar, of the celebrated hanging gardens, or of a temple. The Jews, in the time of Benjamin of Tudela, appear to have believed it to be the ruins of the palace, and near it was pointed out the site of the fiery furnace in which Chananiah, Mishael, and Asariah (Shadrach, Meshach, and Abednego) were thrown by command of the king.* The ruin is not without its Mohammedan traditions. Within it are suspended by the heels, until the day of judgment, the two fallen angels, Harut and Marut, and the Arabs relate endless tales of the evil spirits which haunt the place.

The only remains of Babylonian building not covered by soil and sand, but still standing above ground, are about one

The Mujelibé, or Kasr: Ruins of Babylon. (From Rich.)

mile to the south of the mound last described. It is the Kasr, or Palace, of Rich; a name by which it is now generally known to travellers, but the Arabs call it the Mujelibé, or the 'overturned.' It rises on the river bank, and is about seven

* Benjamin of Tudela, vol. i. p. 106, ed. Asher.

hundred yards square. The principal part of this great ruin consists of loose bricks, tiles, and fragments of stone; but nearly in the centre a solid mass of masonry, still entire, and even retaining remains of architectural ornament, protrudes from the confused heap of rubbish. Piers, buttresses, and pilasters may be traced; but the work of destruction has been too complete to allow us to determine whether they belong to the interior or exterior of a palace. I sought in vain for some clue to the general plan of the edifice. The bricks are of a pale yellow colour, and are not exceeded in quality by any found in the ruins of Babylonia. They are as firmly bound together by a fine lime cement, as those at the Birs Nimroud. Upon nearly every brick is clearly and deeply stamped the name and titles of Nebuchadnezzar, and the inscribed face is always placed downwards. This wonderful piece of masonry is so perfect, and so fresh in colour, that it seems but the work of yesterday, although it is undoubtedly part of a building which stood in the midst of old Babylon.

This ruin has for ages been the mine from which the

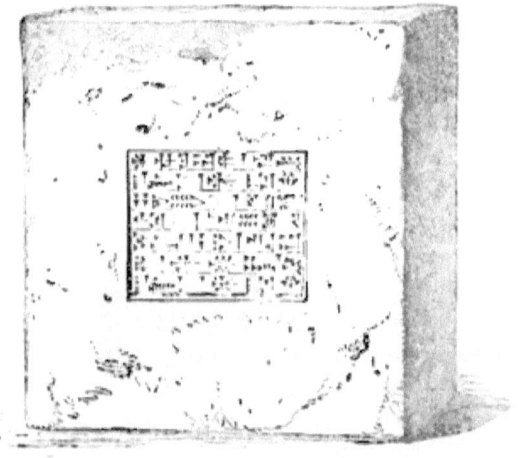

Babylonian Brick.

builders of cities rising after the fall of Babylon have obtained their materials. To this day there are men who have no other trade than that of gathering bricks from this vast heap and taking them for sale to the neighbouring towns and villages, and even to Baghdad. There is scarcely a house in Hillah which is not almost entirely built with them; and as the traveller passes through the narrow streets, he sees in the walls of every hovel a record of the glory and power of Nebuchadnezzar. Those who had been engaged from childhood in this brick-trade, assured me that no sculptures or inscribed slabs had been discovered in their time, and that no remains of stone walls existed in any part of the mound.

Many bricks found in this ruin are covered with a thick enamel or glaze. The colours have resisted the effects of time, and preserve their original brightness. Parts of figures and ornaments may still be traced on some of them. The principal colours are a brilliant blue, red, a deep yellow, white and black. We learn from ancient authors that the walls of the palaces of Babylon were painted with the figures of men and animals, and there can be no doubt that these enamelled bricks are from the walls of an edifice. Fragments of glass, Babylonian gems and cylinders, small bronze figures, and other relics of this nature are occasionally found on the mound by the Arabs, and are bought by the Jews of Hillah, who sell them again to European travellers.

The huge lion described by Rich still exists half buried in the rubbish. It stands over a man with outstretched arms, and some imaginative travellers see in the group a representation of Daniel in the lions' den. The figures are in black basalt, either so barbarously executed as to show very little progress in art, or left unfinished by the sculptor.

Near the northern edge of the ruin is the solitary tree Athelé, well-known to the Arabs, and with which are connected various traditions. It is said to have stood in the hanging gardens of Babylon, and to have been saved by God from the general destruction which overwhelmed the impious city, that Ali might tie his horse to its trunk after the defeat of the enemies of the Prophet in the great battle of Hillah. No other tree of the same kind exists, according to the same tradition, in the whole world. It is, however, a species of tamarisk, of no great rarity, I believe, whose long feathery branches tremble in the breeze with a melancholy murmur well suited to the desolate heap over which it may have waved for a thousand years.

The only relic of any interest I was fortunate enough to discover in this ruin was a fragment of limestone, on which were sculptured in relief parts of two figures, undoubtedly those of gods. The name of one is given in Babylonian charac-

Fragment from the Mujelibé. (Babylon.)

ters. The fragment is interesting, as showing that the Babylonians portrayed their divinities in the same manner as the Assyrians. They wear the same high head-dress ornamented with feathers and rosettes, the elaborately curled hair and beard, and the embroidered garments, and they hold the same staff with a ring as the gods in the rock sculptures of Bavian.

Excavations were carried on for some days in the smaller mounds scattered over the plain between Babel and the ruin last described, but without any results, except the discovery of the remains of brick masonry, of a few earthen vases, and of fragments of glass.

The last ruin I examined was a mound of great extent, sometimes called by the Arabs, **Jumjuma**, from a neighbouring village of that name, and sometimes, as stated by Rich, **Amran ben Ali**, from a small domed tomb of a Mohammedan saint on its summit. No masonry is here seen as in the Mujelibé. All remains of buildings, if there be any still existing, are deeply buried beneath the loose nitrous earth. It is traversed by innumerable ravines, and its form and level are equally irregular.* I opened trenches in various parts, but could find no traces of an edifice of any kind. Some small objects of considerable interest were, however, discovered.

The mound of Amran, like nearly all those in Babylonia, was used as a place of burial for the dead long after the destruction of the great edifices whose ruins it covers. Some specimens of glass, and several terracotta figures, lamps, and jars, evidently of the time of the Seleucidæ, or of the Greek occupation, were dug out of it. With these relics were five cups or bowls of earthenware, and fragments of others, covered on the inner surface with letters written in a kind of ink. Similar objects had already been found in other Babylonian ruins.

They are to be referred, it is believed, to the Jews of the Captivity in Babylon, and are consequently of great interest to Oriental scholars, and especially to biblical students. The inscriptions upon them are in the ancient Chaldæan language, and are written in characters previously unknown. The letters appear to be a mixture of the Syriac and Palmyrine, and in some instances resemble the ancient Phœnician. The subjects of these inscriptions are amulets or charms against evil spirits, diseases, and every kind of misfortune. They must have been written long prior to any existing manuscripts in the ancient Hebrew and Chaldæan languages that we now know of, there being no divisions between words (except in one instance, where the forms of the letters

---

* Rich gives its dimensions as 1,100 yards by 800.

would seem to indicate a later date), nor are there any vowel points. But the most remarkable circumstance connected with them is, that the characters used on one bowl answer precisely to the description given of the most ancient Hebrew letters in the Babylonian Talmud, which contains an account of the nature and origin of the letters used by the Jews.

Inscribed earthen Bowls, from Babylon.

The orthography of the inscriptions is very defective, and sometimes pure Hebrew sentences are found mixed with the Chaldee. The words 'Halleluiah' and 'Selah' occur in nearly every one of them. All this tends to confirm the opinion that the writers were Jews: for it is well known that the early Christians were utterly ignorant of Hebrew, nor is there any proof that it was cultivated at Babylon; on the contrary, it was at Babylon that the Hebrew ceased to be a spoken language, the Jews being compelled, by their lengthened captivity, to adopt the Chaldæan, whilst at the same time they were corrupted by the idolatry and superstitions of the Babylonians. The Chaldæans were formerly famous for divination, astrology, and witchcraft, and there is no doubt but that the Jews were not only led away by these practices, but brought them into their own country; for we find that the Jewish captives taken to Rome by Titus Vespasian, immediately after the destruction of Jerusalem, were acquainted with astrology, casting nativities, and magic. We are told this by Juvenal, the Roman satirist.* It is customary in many parts of the East at the present day, when a person is ill whose malady baffles the skill of the ordinary physician, to send for a magician, who frequently attempts to cure the patient by writing a charm on some convenient utensil, such as a bowl, plate, or bason, and commanding the sick person to put water into the vessel containing the charm, and to drink it up. It seems highly probable that the bowls from Babylon, now in the British Museum, have been used for a similar purpose; one, it would seem, contained some substance like soup, and had never been entirely washed out! †

Little doubt can exist as to the Jewish origin of these bowls; and such being the case, there is no reason to question their having belonged to the descendants of those Jews who were carried captive by Nebuchadnezzar to Babylon and the surrounding cities. These strangers appear to have clung with a tenacity peculiar to their race to the land of their exile. We can trace them about Babylon from almost the time of their deportation down to the twelfth century of the Christian era, when the Hebrew traveller, Benjamin of Tudela, wandered over the regions of the East and among the cities of the Captivity to seek the remnant of his ancient nation. During the Persian dominion in Mesopotamia we find them enduring tortures and persecution rather than help to rebuild a temple dedicated to a false god.‡ In the time of the Roman supremacy in the East they appear to have been a turbulent race, rebelling against their rulers, and waging civil war amongst themselves.§ They had celebrated schools in many cities of Assyria and Chaldæa.

As early as the third century Hebrew travellers visited Babylon, and some of them have left records of the state

---

* See Sat. iii. v. 13 *et seq.*, Sat. vi. vv. 541—546.

† The inscriptions on these bowls were first translated by the late Mr. Thomas Ellis of the British Museum. For the translations and a full description of the bowls see the complete edition of my 'Nineveh and Babylon,' ch. xxii.

‡ Josephus against Appian, l. i. cviii.

§ They were subdued by Lusius Quietus during the reign of the emperor Trajan.

of their countrymen. The Babylonian Talmud, compiled in the beginning of the sixth century, contains many valuable notices of the condition of the Jewish colonies in Babylonia, and enumerates more than two hundred Babylonian towns then under the Persian rule, inhabited by Jewish families. In manuscripts of the eighth and ninth centuries we have further mention of these colonies.*

Benjamin of Tudela found no less than twenty thousand Jews dwelling within twenty miles of Babylon, and worshipping in the synagogue, built, according to tradition, by the prophet Daniel himself. In Hillah alone were ten thousand persons and four synagogues, and he gives the number of families and of their places of worship in every town he visited, keeping during his journey an exact daily itinerary, which includes nearly all the stations on the modern caravan routes. Allowing for some exaggeration on the part of this traveller, it is still evident that a very considerable Jewish population lived in his time in the cities of Babylonia.

According to their own tradition, these Hebrew families were descended from the Jews of the Captivity. They still preserved their pedigrees, and traced their lineage to the princes and prophets of Judah. Their chief resided at Baghdad, and his title was 'Lord Prince of the Captivity.' He was lineally descended, according to his people, from king David himself. Even Mohammedans acknowledged his claim to this noble birth, and called him 'Our Lord, the son of David.' His authority extended over the countries of the East as far as Thibet and Hindostan. He was treated on all occasions with the greatest honour and respect, and when he appeared in public he wore robes of embroidered silk, and a white turban encircled by a diadem of gold.†

A few Jewish families still linger at Hillah, and in Baghdad the principal native trade and money transactions are carried on by Jews, who are the bankers and brokers of the governors of the city, as they no doubt anciently were of the Abbasside Caliphs.

* See Dr. Zunz's valuable essay on the 'Geographical Literature of the Jews,' in the 2nd volume of Asher's 'Itinerary of Benjamin of Tudela.'
† Benjamin of Tudela's Travels; and see Milman's 'History of the Jews,' book xix. &c.

CHAPTER XII.

State of the ruins of Babylon—Cause of the disappearance of buildings—Nature of original edifices—Babylonian bricks—The history of Babylon—Its commerce—Canals and rivers—The arts—Engraved gems—Fall of the city—The mounds of El Hymer—of Anana—Ruins in Southern Mesopotamia—Departure from Hillah—Sand-hills—Villages in the Jezirah—Sheikh Karboul—Ruins—First view of Niffer—The marshes—Arab boats—Arrive at Souk-El-Afaij—Sheikh Agab—Town of the Afaij—Description of the ruins of Niffer—Excavations in the mounds—Discovery of coffins—Of various relics—Mr. Loftus' discoveries at Wurka—The Arab tribes—Wild beasts—Lions—Customs of the Afaij—Leave the marshes—Return to Baghdad—A mirage.

THE discoveries amongst the ruins of ancient Babylon were far less numerous and important than I could have anticipated. No sculptures or inscribed slabs, the panelling of the walls of palaces, appear to exist beneath them as in those of Nineveh. Scarcely a detached figure in stone, or a solitary tablet, has been dug out of the vast heaps of rubbish. 'Babylon is fallen, is fallen; and all the graven images of her gods he hath broken unto the ground.'*

The complete absence of such remains is to be explained by the nature of the materials used in the erection of even the most costly edifices of Babylon. In the vicinity there were no quarries of alabaster, or of limestone, such as existed near Nineveh. The city was built in the midst of an alluvial country, far removed from the hills. The deposits of the mighty rivers which have gradually formed the Mesopotamian plains consist of a rich clay. Consequently stone for building purposes could only be obtained from a distance. The black basalt, a favourite material amongst the Babylonians for carving detached figures, and for architectural ornaments, as appears from fragments found amongst the

* Isaiah, xxi. 9.

ruins, came from the Kurdish mountains, or from the north of Mesopotamia.

The Babylonians were content to avail themselves of the building materials which they found on the spot. With the tenacious mud of their alluvial plains, mixed with chopped straw, they made bricks, whilst bitumen and other substances collected from the immediate neighbourhood furnished them with an excellent cement. A knowledge of the art of manufacturing glaze, and colours, enabled them to cover their bricks with a rich enamel, thereby rendering them equally ornamental for the exterior and interior of their edifices. The walls of their palaces and temples were also coated, as we learn from several passages in the Bible, with mortar and plaster, which, judging from their cement, must have been of very fine quality. The fingers of the man's hand wrote the words of condemnation of the Babylonian empire 'upon the plaster of the wall of the king's palace.' Upon those walls were painted historical and religious subjects, and various ornaments, and, according to Diodorus Siculus, the bricks were enamelled with the figures of men and animals. Images of stone were no doubt introduced into the buildings. We learn from the Bible that figures of the gods in this material, as well as in metal, were kept in the Babylonian temples. But such sculptures were not common, otherwise more remains of them must have been discovered in the ruins.*

It may be conjectured that, in their general plan, the Babylonian palaces and temples resembled those of Assyria. We know that the arts, the religion, the customs, and the laws of the two kindred people were nearly identical. They spoke, also, the same language, and used, very nearly, the same written characters. One appears to have borrowed from the other; and, without attempting to decide the question of the priority of the independent existence as a nation and of the civilisation of either people, it can be admitted that they

* The great inscription of Nebuchadnezzar, engraved on a black stone, and divided into ten columns, in the museum formed by the East India Company, appears to contain some interesting details as to the mode of construction and architecture of the Babylonian palaces and temples.

had to a certain extent a common origin, and that they maintained for many centuries an intimate connection. We find no remains of columns at Babylon, as none have been found at Nineveh. If such architectural ornaments were used, they must have been either of wood or of brick.

Although the building materials used in the great edifices of Babylon may seem extremely mean when compared with those employed in the stupendous palace-temples of Egypt, and even in the less massive edifices of Assyria, yet the Babylonians appear to have raised, with them alone, structures which excited the wonder and admiration of the most famous travellers of antiquity. The profuse use of colour, and the taste displayed in its combination, and in the ornamental designs, together with the solidity and vastness of the immense substructure upon which the buildings proudly stood, may have chiefly contributed to produce this effect upon the minds of strangers. The palaces and temples, like those of Nineveh, were erected upon lofty platforms of brickwork. The bricks, as in Assyria, were either simply baked in the sun, or were burnt in the kiln. The latter are of more than one shape and quality. Some are square; others are oblong.* Those from the Birs Nimroud are generally of a dark red colour, whilst those from the Mujelibé are mostly of a light yellow. A large number of them have inscriptions in a complex cuneiform character peculiar to Babylon. These superscriptions have been impressed upon them by a stamp, on which the whole inscription was cut in relief. Each character was not made singly, as on the Assyrian bricks, and this is the distinction between them. Almost all the bricks brought from the ruins of Babylon bear the same inscription, with the exception of one or two unimportant words, and record the building of the city by Nebuchadnezzar, the son of Nabubaluchun (?). We owe the interpretation of these names to the late Dr. Hincks.

It may not be out of place to add a few remarks upon the

* The usual dimensions of the Babylonian bricks are as nearly as possible one foot square, by three and a half inches thick. Mr. Birch has conjectured that they may represent multiples of some Babylonian measure, perhaps the cubit.

history of Babylon. The time of the foundation of this celebrated city is still a question which does not admit of a satisfactory determination, and into which I will not enter. Some believe it to have taken place at a comparatively recent date; but if, as Egyptian scholars assert, the name of Babylon is found on monuments of the eighteenth Egyptian dynasty, we have positive evidence of its existence at least in the fifteenth century before Christ.* After the rise of the Assyrian empire, it appears to have been sometimes under the direct rule of the kings of Nineveh, and at other times to have been governed by its own independent chiefs. Expeditions against Babylonia are recorded in the earliest inscriptions yet discovered in Assyria; and as it has been seen, even in the time of Sennacherib and his immediate predecessors, large armies were still frequently sent against its rebellious inhabitants. The Babylonian kingdom was, however, almost absorbed in that of Assyria, the dominant power of the East. When this great empire began to decline, Babylon rose for the last time. Media and Persia were equally ready to throw off the Assyrian yoke, and at length the allied armies of Cyaxares and the father of Nebuchadnezzar captured and destroyed the capital of the Eastern world.

Babylon now rapidly succeeded to that proud position so long held by Nineveh. Under Nebuchadnezzar she acquired the power forfeited by her rival. The bounds of the city were extended; buildings of extraordinary size and magnificence were erected; her victorious armies conquered Syria and Palestine, and penetrated into Egypt. Her commerce, too, had now spread far and wide, from the east to the west, and she became 'a land of traffic and a city of merchants.'†

But her greatness as an independent nation was short-lived. The neighbouring kingdoms of Media and Persia, united under one monarch, had profited, no less than Babylon, by the ruin of the Assyrian empire, and were ready to dispute with her the dominion of Asia. Scarcely half a century had elapsed from the fall of Nineveh, when 'Belshazzar,

---

* Mr. Birch has found more than one notice of Babylon on Egyptian monuments of the time of Thothmes III.

† Ezekiel, xvii. 4.

the king of the Chaldæans, was slain, and Darius, the Median, took the kingdom.'* From that time Babylonia sank into a mere province of Persia. It still, however, retained much of its former power and trade, and, as we learn from the inscriptions of Bisutun, as well as from ancient authors, struggled more than once to regain its ancient independence.

After the defeat of Darius and the overthrow of the Persian supremacy, Babylon opened its gates to Alexander, who deemed the city not unworthy to become the capital of his mighty empire. On his return from India, he wished to rebuild the temple of Belus, which had fallen into ruins, and in that great work he had intended to employ his army, now no longer needed for war. The priests however, who had appropriated the revenues of this sacred shrine, and feared lest they would have again to apply them to their rightful purposes, appear to have prevented him from carrying out his design.†

The last blow to the prosperity and even existence of Babylon was given by Seleucus when he laid the foundation of his new capital on the banks of the Tigris (B.C. 322). Already Patrocles, his general, had compelled a large number of the inhabitants to abandon their homes, and to take refuge in the desert, and in the province of Susiana.‡ The city, exhausted by the neighbourhood of Seleucia, returned to its ancient solitude.* According to some authors, neither the walls nor the temple of Belus existed any longer, and

---

* Daniel, v. 30, 31. This event took place B.C. 538. Whether the Darius of the book of Daniel be Cyrus himself, or a Median who commanded the armies of that monarch, and was afterwards appointed viceroy of Babylon, is one of the many disputed points of ancient history.
† Arrian, Exp. Alex. l. vii. c. 17. See Jeremy's Epistle in the Apocryphal book of Baruch, vi. 10, 11, and 28, for instances of the cupidity of the Babylonian priests. They had even stripped the idols of their robes and ornaments to adorn their wives and children. This epistle contains a very curious account of the idol worship of the Babylonians.
‡ Diod. Sic. xix. 100.
§ 'Cæterò ad solitudinem rediit exhausta vicinitate Seleuciæ.' (Pliny, l. vi. c. 30.) Strabo states that part of the city was destroyed by the Persians, and part by time, and that the rest perished in consequence of the neglect of the Macedonians. It had become, he declares, a vast solitude (lib. xvi. p. 2049).

only a few Chaldæans continued to dwell around the ruins of their sacred edifices.*

Still, however, a part of the population appears to have returned to their former seats, for, in the early part of the second century of the Christian æra, we find the Parthian king, Evemerus, sending numerous families from Babylon into Media to be sold as slaves, and burning many great and beautiful edifices still standing in the city.†

In the time of Augustus, the city is said to have been entirely deserted, except by a few Jews who still lingered amongst the ruins.‡ St. Cyril, of Alexandria, declares, that in his day, about the beginning of the fifth century, in consequence of the choking up of the great canals derived from the Euphrates, Babylon had become a vast marsh; and fifty years later the river is described as having changed its course, leaving only a small channel to mark its ancient bed. Then were verified the prophecies of Isaiah and Jeremiah, that the mighty Babylon should be but 'pools of water,' that the sea should come upon her, and that she should be covered with the multitude of the waves thereof.'§

In the beginning of the seventh century, at the time of the Arab invasion, the ancient cities of Babylonia were ' a desolation, a dry land, and a wilderness.' Amidst the heaps that alone marked the site of Babylon there rose the small town of Hillah.

Long before Babylon had overcome her rival Nineveh she was famous for the extent and importance of her commerce. No position could have been more favourable than hers for carrying on a trade with all the regions of the known world. She stood upon a navigable stream that brought to her quays the produce of the temperate highlands of Armenia, approached in one part of its course within almost one hundred

---

* Pausanias, Attic. c. 16. But, according to Pliny, the temple of Belus still existed in his day (lib. vi. c. 30).
† B.C. 127. Diod. Sic. Fragm. l. xxxiv. c. 21. Justin, l. xlii. c. 1. Athenæus, l. xi. p. 463.
‡ And yet Trajan is said to have visited the house in Babylon in which Alexander died, and to have performed religious ceremonies to the memory of the hero. (Dio in Excerpt. p. 785.)
§ Isaiah, xiv. 23; Jeremiah, li. 42.

miles of the Mediterranean Sea, and emptied its waters into a gulf of the Indian Ocean. Parallel with this great river was one scarcely inferior in size and importance. The Tigris, too, came from the Armenian hills, flowed through the fertile districts of Assyria, and carried their varied produce to the Babylonian cities. Moderate skill and enterprise could scarcely fail to make Babylon, not only the emporium of the Eastern world, but the main link of commercial intercourse between the East and the West.

The inhabitants did not neglect the advantages bestowed upon them by nature. A system of navigable canals that may excite the admiration of even the modern engineer, connected together the Euphrates and Tigris, those great arteries of her commerce. With a skill, showing no common knowledge of the art of surveying, and of the principles of hydraulics, the Babylonians took advantage of the different levels in the plains, and of the periodical rises in the two rivers, to complete the water communication between all parts of the province, and to fertilise, by artificial irrigation, an otherwise barren and unproductive soil. Alexander, after he had transferred the seat of his empire to the East, so fully understood the importance of these great works, that he ordered them to be cleansed and repaired, and superintended the work in person, steering his boat with his own hand through the channels. I have so frequently had occasion to mention them, and to describe their actual remains, that I will not weary the reader with a further account of them.

High-roads and causeways across the desert united Syria and Palestine with Babylonia. Fortified stations protected the merchant from the wandering tribes of Arabia, walled cities served as resting-places and storehouses, and wells at regular intervals gave an abundant supply of water during the hottest season of the year. One of those highways was carried through the centre of Mesopotamia, and crossing the Euphrates near the town of Anthemusia led into central Syria.* A second appears to have left Babylon by the west-

---

* Strabo, lib. xvi. p. 1061. Oxf. ed.

ern quarter of the city, and entered Idumæa, after passing through the country of the Nabathæans. Others branched off to Tadmor, and to cities which were built in the midst of the desert almost solely for purposes of trade.

To the east of Babylonia was the celebrated military and commercial road described by Herodotus.* It led from Sardis to Susa in ninety days' journey, and was furnished, at intervals of about fifteen miles, with stations and public hostelries, probably resembling the modern caravanserais of Persia.

Merchandise and travellers descended the rivers upon rafts of skins, as well as in boats built of reeds coated with bitumen, or of more solid materials. The land trade was no doubt principally carried on, as at the present day, by caravans of merchants, who loaded their goods on the backs of camels, horses, and asses. The Assyrian sculptures show that waggons and carts drawn by mules and oxen were not unknown, and as the roads appear to have been carefully kept in repair, this more convenient and cheaper mode of transporting merchandise was probably not neglected.

It is difficult to determine how far the Babylonians may have navigated in vessels the Indian Ocean.† Of the various articles of merchandise stored in Babylon, the produce of the islands and shores of the Persian Gulf, and even of India, formed no inconsiderable part. Pearls, from the fisheries of Bahrein, which still supply Arabia, Persia, and Turkey, and perhaps even from Ceylon; cotton, spices, frankincense, precious stones, ivory, ebony, silks, and dyes, were amongst the objects of trade brought to her markets. They could only have been obtained from the southern coasts of Arabia, and directly or indirectly from the Indian peninsula. We learn from the Kouyunjik inscriptions, that the people inhabiting the country at the mouths of the united waters of the Tigris and Euphrates possessed vessels in which, when defeated by the Assyrians, they took refuge on

* L. v. c. 52 and 53.
† Heeren, with his usual critical skill, has investigated the subject in his essay on the commerce of the Babylonians, in the 2d vol. of his 'Historical Researches.'

the sea. The prophet Isaiah also alludes to the ships of the Chaldæans.* Timber for ship-building could have been floated with ease from the mountains of Armenia to the very quays of Babylon, or to her ports at the head of the Persian Gulf. We have seen that Sennacherib sent down the Tigris the materials for the construction of the vessels required in the siege of the cities of southern Chaldæa, and that he employed Phœnician mariners to build and navigate them.

Terracotta Tablet from Babylon, representing a Dog.

But although a coasting trade might have existed along the shores of the Persian Gulf and of the ocean as far as India, yet a very considerable trade was also carried on by land with the same country through Media, Hyrcania, and

* Chap. xliii. 14.

the centre of Asia. It was by this road that gold and various precious stones were probably supplied to Babylon and Nineveh.

A race of dogs too, much prized by the Babylonians, was brought from India. A satrap of Babylon is declared to have devoted the revenues of four cities * to the support of a number of these animals. On a small terracotta tablet in the British Museum, from Colonel Rawlinson's collection, obtained, I believe, at Baghdad, but probably found in some ancient ruin in the neighbourhood, is the figure of a man leading a large and powerful dog, which has been identified with a species still existing in Thibet.

Tin, cedar-wood, and various articles were brought from Phœnicia and other parts of Syria, which were in return supplied with the produce of India and the Persian Gulf, through Babylon.†

Whilst the Babylonians imported the produce of the East and West, they also supplied foreign countries with many valuable articles of trade. Corn, which according to tradition first grew wild in Mesopotamia, and was there first eaten by man, was cultivated to a great extent, and was sent to distant provinces. The Babylonian carpets, silks, and woollen fabrics, woven or embroidered with figures of mythic animals and with exquisite designs, were not less famous for the beauty of their texture and workmanship, than for the richness and variety of their colours. The much-prized Sindones, or flowing garments, were the work of the looms of Babylon even long after she had ceased to be a city.‡

---

* Herod. l. i. c. 192.   † Ezekiel, xxvii. 15.

‡ Of the early reputation of the looms of Babylon we may form an idea from the fact of 'a goodly Babylonish garment' (i.e. garment of Shinar) being mentioned in the book of Joshua (vii. 21) amongst the objects buried by Achan in his tent. In a curious decree of the time of Diocletian, regulating the maximum value of articles of clothing and food throughout the Roman empire, several objects from Babylon are specified. Babylonian skins of the first quality are rated at 500 denarii; of the second quality at 40; Babylonian shoes, called mullai, at 120 denarii per pair; and a Babylonian girdle at 100. Plain Babylonian socks are also mentioned, but the amount at which they were valued is wanting. This decree was discovered at Eski Hissar, the ancient Stratoniccia, in Asia Minor. (See Leake's Asia Minor.)

The engraved gems and cylinders discovered in the ruins bear ample witness to the skill of the Babylonian lapidaries. Many of these relics exist in European collections, and, during my residence at Hillah, I was able to obtain several

Babylonian Cylinder in Sienite (Size of the Original).

interesting specimens from the Arabs, who usually pick them up on the mounds after rain. The most remarkable of them is a cylinder of spotted sienite, upon which are incised seven figures, and a few Babylonian characters. The figures are cut with delicacy and spirit. Six appear to represent foreign captives. They are led by a warrior, armed with bow and arrows, and having on his back a quiver ending in a sharp point like the head of a spear. The prisoners are clothed in robes of skin or fur. One wears a flat projecting cap, and two of them carry weapons in the form of a pickaxe. The fourth figure seems to be that of a woman, and the last two are smaller in size than the others. One

Engraved Gem from Babylon.

bears on his shoulders a table or stool, the other a bag hanging on a hooked stick. The letters of the inscription are rudely formed, and have not yet been deciphered.

Another interesting gem found by me at Babylon is an agate cone, upon the base of which is engraved a winged priest or deity, standing in an attitude of prayer before a cock on an altar. Above this group is the crescent moon. The Hebrew commentators* conjecture that Ner-

---

* Selden, De Dis Syris, p. 251.

gal, the idol of the men of Cuth, had the form of a cock.* On a cylinder in the British Museum there is a subject almost similar. A priest, wearing the sacrificial dress, stands at a table, before an altar bearing a crescent, and a smaller altar on which stands a cock. It would appear, therefore, that this bird was either worshipped by the Babylonians, or by some neighbouring nation; or that it was sacrificed, as in Greece, on the celebration of certain religious ceremonies.†

Cylinder in the British Museum.

The vast trade that rendered Babylon the gathering-place of men from all parts of the known world, and supplied her with luxuries from the remotest climes, had the effect of corrupting the manners of her people, and producing that general profligacy and those effeminate customs which mainly contributed to her fall. The description given by Herodotus of the state of the population of the city when under the dominion of the Persian kings, is quite sufficient to explain the cause of her speedy decay and ultimate ruin. The account of the Greek historian fully tallies with the denunciations of the Hebrew prophets against the sin and wickedness of Babylon. Her inhabitants had gradually lost their warlike character. When the Persian broke into their city they were revelling in debauchery and lust; and when

* 'And the men of Cuth made Nergal,' in Samaria, where they had been transplanted after the first captivity. (2 Kings, xvii. 30.) The country of the Cuthites was probably in the neighbourhood of Babylon, though the commentators have not agreed upon its exact site. Josephus says that it was in Persia (Antiq. ix. 14).

† Can this image have any connection with the brazen figure of the bird which I have described in a former part of this work as belonging to the Yezidis?

the Macedonian conqueror appeared at their gates, they received with indifference the yoke of a new master.

It is not difficult to account for the rapid decay of the country around Babylon. As the inhabitants deserted the city the canals were neglected. When once those great sources of fertility were choked up, the plains became a wilderness. Upon the waters conveyed by their channels to the innermost parts of Mesopotamia depended not only the harvests, the gardens, and the palm groves, but the very existence of the towns and villages which were far removed from the river banks. They soon turned to mere heaps of earth and rubbish when those waters no longer reached them. Vegetation ceased, and the plains, parched by the burning heat of the sun, were ere long once again a vast arid waste.

Such were the causes of the fall of Babylon. Her career was equally short and splendid; and although she has thus perished from the face of the earth, her ruins are still classic, indeed sacred, ground. The traveller visits, with no common emotion, those shapeless heaps, the scene of so many great and solemn events. In this plain, according to tradition, the primitive families of our race first found a resting-place. Here Nebuchadnezzar boasted of the glories of his city, and was punished for his pride. To these deserted halls were brought the captives of Judæa. In them Daniel, undazzled by the glories around him, remained steadfast to his faith, rose to be a governor amongst his rulers, and prophesied the downfall of the kingdom. There was held Belshazzar's feast, and was seen the writing upon the wall. Between those crumbling mounds Cyrus entered the neglected gates. Those massive ruins cover the spot where Alexander died.

About two hours and a half, or eight miles to the northeast of Hillah, a mound, scarcely inferior in size to those of Babylon, rises in the plain. It is called El Hymer, meaning, according to the Arabs, 'the red,' from its colour. The ruin has assumed a pyramidal form, but it is evidently the remains of a solid square structure, consisting, like the Birs Nimroud, of a series of terraces or platforms. It may be conjectured, therefore, that it was a sacred edifice built upon the same general plan as all the temples of Babylonia and

Assyria. The basement or substructure appears to have been of sundried brick; the upper part, and probably the casing of the lower, of bricks burnt in the kiln, many of which are inscribed with the name and titles of Nebuchadnezzar. Although the masonry is solid and firmly bound together, it is not united by a white cement like that of the Mujelibé. The same tenacious mud that was used for making the bricks has been daubed, as far as I could ascertain, between each layer. The ruin is pierced, like the Birs, by square holes to admit air.

Around the centre structure are scattered smaller mounds and heaps of rubbish, covered with the usual fragments of pottery, glass, and bricks.

Opposite to the Mujelibé (or Kasr), on the western bank of the Euphrates, is a village called Anana, and near it a quadrangle of earthen ramparts, like the remains of a fortified inclosure. A large mass of brick masonry is still seen in the river bed when the stream is low. The inhabitants of the village brought me a fragment of black stone with a rosette ornament upon it, very Assyrian in character. With the exception of these remains, and the Birs Nimroud, there are scarcely any ruins of ancient buildings on the Arabian side of the Euphrates.

On the eastern bank low mounds, covered with broken pottery and glass, are found in almost every direction. One resembles another, and there is nothing either in their appearance, or in their contents, as far as they have hitherto been ascertained, deserving of particular description. They only prove how vast and thriving the population of this part of Mesopotamia must at one time have been, and how complete is the destruction that has fallen upon this devoted land.

The south of Mesopotamia abounds in extensive and important ruins, of which little is known. The country around them is inhabited by Arabs of the tribes of Rubbiyah and Ahl Maidan, notorious for their lawlessness, and scarcely more intelligent or human than the buffaloes which they tend. These ruins are best reached from Hillah. The Sheikhs of the Arab tribes living near them are usually in friendly communication with the principal people of that town. To visit these districts of Mesopotamia it is, however, necessary to travel under the protection of some powerful chief. I was, therefore, compelled to send a special messenger to Agab, the Sheikh of the Afaij, to inform him of my intention to enter his territories, and to ask for men to conduct me. Some days elapsed before I received an answer to my letter. At length, one evening, two horsemen rode to my door, and having tethered their mares announced that they were come to lead me to the village of their chief.

The Afaij dwell in the midst of extensive marshes formed by the Euphrates, about fifty miles below Hillah. On the eastern border of these swamps rise the great ruins of Niffer, which I was first desirous of examining. Although Agab's horsemen could protect us when we were once amongst their own Arabs, yet there were hostile tribes on our way who little respected their master's authority. Various plans were consequently suggested for our journey. It was finally settled that we should keep as much as possible in the centre of Mesopotamia, and thus avoid the neighbourhood of the Euphrates, as the Arabs were now congregated along the banks of the river. Having hired mules and laid in a proper stock of provisions, tools, and packing cases to hold any antiquities that might be discovered, and accompanied by my Jebour workmen, I started on my journey on Wednesday, the 15th of January.

The weather was bright and intensely cold. The sky was cloudless, but a biting north wind swept across the plain. It was the middle of the Babylonian winter, and a hard frost daily whitened the ground. We left Hillah by the Baghdad gate. The Bairakdar was with me, with the rest of my Mosul servants. My huntsman, old Seyyid Jasim, wrapt up in his thick Arab cloak, bore his favourite hawk on his wrist. He was followed, as usual, by the greyhounds. The Jebours went partly on foot, riding by turns on the baggage horses. Mr. Hormuzd Rassam was wanting to complete our party. He had been kept in Baghdad by severe illness almost since our arrival, and for the first time during my wanderings in Mesopotamia he was not with me.

We followed a track leading towards the centre of the Mesopotamian desert. The long belt of feathery palms bordering the Euphrates for many and many a mile, and broken here and there by a dome or a minaret, became gradually less distinct, until it was but a faint black line edging the horizon. Our course was nearly due east. About six miles from the town we found ourselves amidst moving sand-hills, extending far and wide on all sides. They were just high enough to shut out the view of the surrounding country. The fine sand shifts with every breeze, and the wrinkled heaps are like the rippled surface of a lake. When the furious southerly wind sweeps over them, it raises a dense suffocating dust, blinding the wayfaring Arab, and leaving him to perish in the trackless labyrinth.

The sand issues from the earth like water from springs, and the Arabs call the sources, of which we passed two or three, 'Aioun-er-rummel' (the sand springs). The banks of ancient canals, still rising among the moving heaps, showed that the soil had once been under cultivation. The sand is now fast spreading over the face of the country, and threatens ere long to overwhelm several small Arab settlements.

After four hours' ride we left the sand-heaps, and again came in sight of the black belt of palm-trees. We found ourselves near the village of Hamza, whose mud hovels are built round a tomb, covered by a white dome, and shaded by a few slender palms. After stopping to drink water, we proceeded to a small hamlet called Allak, and took up our quarters for the night in the museef of its Sheikh. The inhabitants were of the tribe of Sherayfaut from Mecca. They had been attacked and plundered two days before our visit by the Maidan Arabs from the other side of the Euphrates. Even the very doors of the huts had been torn from their hinges, and dragged away. Notwithstanding his poverty the poor Sheikh received us very hospitably. He related to me how from the numerous artificial mounds in the surrounding plains were frequently taken, after rain had washed away the soil, earthen jars and coffins, containing ornaments of gold and silver.

As we continued our journey during the following day, still

keeping in the desert, we passed one or two small encampments of the Zobeide tribe. The Arabs, alarmed at the approach of so large a party, and believing us to be horsemen on a foray, sallied forth to meet us at some distance from their tents, flourishing their weapons and chanting their wild war-cry. The plain, although now without any stationary population, was once thickly inhabited. The white domed tombs rising to the right and left of our track marked where former villages had stood, whilst the embankments of innumerable canals, long deserted by their waters, crossed our path, bearing witness to the skill and industry which once turned these barren plains into one vast garden. The lion, the hyena, the wolf, the jackal, the wild boar, the fox, and the porcupine now alone break the solitude of a wilderness once the seat of the most luxurious and civilised nation of the East.

We had scarcely passed a ruin called Haroun, when a party of Arabs on horseback and on foot suddenly came forth from behind the lofty banks of a dry canal. They had seen our caravan from afar, and had waylaid us. After they had followed us for some distance they turned back to their tribe, deeming it prudent not to venture on an attack, as we were fully prepared for them.

Shortly after their departure, a gazelle rose from a thicket, and bounded across the plain. Seyyid Jasim unloosed his hawk, and I pursued with the dogs. The sight of horsemen galloping to and fro alarmed an Arab settlement gathered round a small mud fort belonging to a chief called Karboul. The men armed themselves and came out against us. Our Afaij guides, however, soon made themselves known to them, and they then escorted us to their tents, dancing a wild dance, shouting their war cries, singing war-songs, and firing their matchlocks. Most of them had no other clothing than the shirt taken off their shoulders and tied round their loins. Their countenances were singularly ferocious, their bright eyes and white teeth making them even more hideous. Long black matted hair was scattered over their heads in horrid confusion, and their bodies were tanned by the burning sun to the colour and substance of old leather.

Their Sheikh, Karboul, was scarcely less savage in his appearance, though somewhat better clothed. He led me with words of welcome to his spacious tent. His followers, excited by the late alarm, and now full of warlike enthusiasm, were not, however, to be dismissed until they had satisfied themselves by performing various warlike dances. They did so in circles before the tent, raising a few tattered flags, and deafening me by their shouts and barbarous songs.

These wild beings, little better than mere beasts, lived in hovels made of mats and brushwood. They fed large herds of buffaloes; but the greater part of their sheep and cattle had been driven away by the Bedouins. Their tribe was the Shabanch, a branch of the Ahl Ukra.

Next morning Karboul sent his son and a party of horsemen to escort us for some distance on our road. We soon came to the borders of those marshes which have now spread over the lower part of the Mesopotamian plains. As we ascended the lofty banks of ancient canals, over which our track continually led, we saw a boundless expanse of dark green. It seemed as if the parched desert had been suddenly turned into pastures and fields of young corn. But we only gazed upon a vast bed of tall reeds bred by the wide-spreading swamps, no less a sign of desolation, neglect, and decay, than the yellow wilderness.

We had now to make a considerable circuit to the east to avoid the marsh. We passed numerous artificial mounds, covered with fragments of bricks, pottery, glazed tiles, richly-coloured glass and other relics that mark the site of Babylonian ruins. The dry beds of canals everywhere crossed our path, and limited our view. The parched soil outside the swamp has become fine sand, amidst which small tufts of the hardy tamarisk form the only vegetation. These bushes, thus standing alone, were turned by the mirage into forests, whilst the embankments of the old watercourses seemed like ranges of hills.

After two hours' ride we emerged from the labyrinth of dry canals, and ascending a heap of rubbish covering some ancient ruin, we beheld, looming on the horizon like distant mountains, the principal object of my journey—the mounds of Niffer. They were still nearly ten miles from us. Magnified as they were by the mirage they appeared far to exceed in size and height any artificial elevation that I had hitherto seen. To the east of us rose another great ruin, called Zibbliyah, a lofty, square mass, apparently of sundried brick.

Heads of Arab Delouls.

We rode along the dry bed of a wide canal, passing here and there the former sites of Bedouin encampments, marked by the heaps of dry camels' dung, the blackened stones on which the cauldron had been heated, and the narrow trenches dug to carry off the winter rain. The tents lately pitched on these spots belonged to the Shammar Arabs, who had wandered thus far to the south, and after having plundered all the tribes not strong enough to resist them, were now on their way back to the spring pastures in northern Mesopotamia. The Bedouins cannot, it is said, remain to the south of Baghdad after the month of February, as their camels would be destroyed by eating a poisonous herb which at that season of the year begins to grow plentifully in the desert. We saw many tracks of lions in the sand, some not many hours old. Flocks of pelicans whitened the plain;

we startled innumerable waterfowl from the reeds; and the pheasant-like francolin sprang with a loud whirring noise from almost every thicket.

After a journey of five hours we reached the ruins of Niffer. The irregular heaps, crossed by numerous deep ravines, are divided into two principal parts by a broad gully, apparently the dry bed of a canal. I could not trace it to the south of the ruins. The mounds cover altogether a very considerable area of ground, and stand on the edge of the marsh, which is gradually encroaching upon them, and which occasionally, during high floods of the Euphrates, completely surrounds them. They are strewed with fragments of brick, glazed and unglazed pottery, and glass, and covered with a loose nitrous soil, into which the feet sink above the ankles. In the ravines large earthen jars and portions of brick masonry are occasionally uncovered by the rains. Commencing my search after antiquities as soon as we had reached the summit of the principal mound, it was not long before I discovered, in one of these newly-formed ruts, a perfect vase, about five feet high, containing human remains. Other objects of the same kind were found by the Arabs who were with me.

The caravan had continued its journey along the western foot of the mound, and my tents were pitched about two miles beyond the ruins on the margin of the marsh. In front of the encampment was a small space, from which the reeds seemed to have been carefully cleared. From it branched several narrow lanes, which, losing themselves in the thick forest of lofty canes, appeared to lead into the interior of the morass. From the top of Niffer I had faintly distinguished in the distance the mat hovels forming the settlements of the Afaij Arabs, and the great herd of buffaloes pasturing in the swamps; but from our tents the view was bounded within a few yards of us by the dense vegetation springing from the stagnant water.

We had sent one of our Afaij guides to inform Sheikh Agab of our approach. I had not been long seated in my tent when suddenly a number of black boats, each bearing a party of Arabs, darted from the reeds and approached the shore.

They were of various sizes. In the bottom of some, eight or ten persons sat crouched on their hams; in others, only one or two. Men standing at the head and stern with long bamboo poles of great lightness guided and impelled them. The largest were built of teak wood, but the others consisted simply of a very narrow framework of rushes covered with bitumen.

The tiradas, for so these boats are called by the Arabs, drew up along the bank before our tents. The largest contained three chiefs, who landed and advanced towards me. They were the sons of the Sheikh of the Afaij. Their father had sent them to welcome me to his territories. They brought with them provisions for my party, as their village, they said, was still far distant, and it would be impossible to transport our baggage and lead our horses thither before nightfall. The young men were handsome, well-dressed, and well-armed, and very courteous. My tent was soon filled by their companions and followers. Each man wore a long white shirt, a black abba or cloak, and a bright yellow and scarlet keffieh over his head. They all carried rifles of great length and weight. The charges of ball and powder were contained in pieces of hollow reed cut to equal lengths and fastened across their breasts to broad leather bands ornamented with small shells and glass beads. Each was, moreover, armed with a sword and a large curved Persian dagger. The complexion of these marsh Arabs, from constant exposure to the intense heat of the sun, is almost black, with the usual contrast of eyes of extraordinary brilliancy, and teeth of the whiteness of pearls. They wear their hair in long, well-greased plaits.

The young Sheikhs had been ordered by their father to remain with me during the night, and to place a proper guard round the tents, as the outskirts of the marsh were infested, we were assured, by roving Bedouins and midnight thieves. I gained, as other travellers have done before me, some credit for wisdom and superhuman knowledge by predicting, through the aid of an almanack, a partial eclipse of the moon. It duly took place to the great dismay of my guests, who well nigh knocked out the bottoms of all my kitchen utensils in their endeavour to frighten away the Jins who had thus laid hold of the planet.*

Soon after sunrise next morning the Sheikh's own tirada issued from the reeds into the open space. It had been spread with carpets and silken cushions for my reception. The baggage was placed in other boats, but the unfortunate horses, under the guidance of a party of naked Arabs, had to swim the streams, and to struggle through the swamps as they best could. The armed men entered their various vessels, and we all left the shore together.

The tirada in which I sat was skilfully managed by two Arabs with long bamboo-poles. It skimmed rapidly over the small lake, and then turned into a broad street cut through green reeds rising fourteen or fifteen feet on both sides of us. We passed the entrances to many lanes branching off to the right and to the left. From them came black boats filled with Arab men and women carrying the produce of their buffalo herds to the Souk or market. As we glided along we occasionally disturbed flocks of waterfowl, and large kingfishers of the most brilliant plumage, seated on the bending rushes watching their prey.

Herds of buffaloes here and there struggled and splashed amongst the reeds, their unwieldy bodies completely concealed under water, and their hideous heads just visible upon the surface. Occasionally a small plot of ground, but little above the level of the marsh, and itself half a swamp, was covered with huts built of reeds, canes, and bright yellow mats. These were the dwellings of the Afaij, and, as we passed by, troops of half-naked men, women, and children issued from them, and stood on the bank to gaze at the strangers.

The lanes now became more crowded with tiradas. The boatmen, however, darted by the heavier vessels, turned the sharp corners, and managed their frail barks with great skill

---

* The common notion amongst ignorant Mohammedans is, that an eclipse is caused by some evil spirit catching hold of the sun or moon. On such occasions, in Eastern towns, the whole population assembles with pots, pans, and other equally rude instruments of music, and, with the aid of their lungs, make a din and turmoil which might suffice to drive away a whole army of evil spirits, even at so great a distance.

and ease. The openings in the reeds began to be more numerous, and it required a perfect knowledge of the various windings and streets to follow the right way. This singular scene recalled vividly to my mind the sculptures at Kouyunjik representing the Assyrian wars in marshes of the same nature, and probably formed by the waters of the same river. The streets through the reeds, and the tiradas or boats of rushes smeared with bitumen, are faithfully delineated in the bas-reliefs, showing how little the barbarous inhabitants of these great swamps have changed after the lapse of nearly three thousand years.*

After an hour's journey we left the reeds and came to a swampy plain. A mud-built edifice rose about half a mile beyond. It was the watchtower and landmark of the Souk-el-Afaij, or market-place of the tribe, and near it was the residence of the Sheikh. Scattered over the open ground were buffaloes, oxen, and mat-covered cabins.

We entered a narrow canal and stopped at length near some larger and better built huts than any we had yet seen. Before them, at the water's edge, and waiting to receive us, were drawn up a number of armed men, at the head of whom stood a tall, handsome Arab. He was attired in a long robe of scarlet silk of Damascus, over which he wore one of those cloaks richly embroidered in gold thread down the back and one arm, peculiar to Baghdad. This was Agab, Sheikh of the Afaij. As I stepped out of the tirada he threw his arms round my neck, and gave me the usual embrace of welcome.

The chief led us at once to the museef. The guest-house was built of the same materials as the smaller cabins, but they were far more tastefully put together. It resembled in shape the boiler of some enormous steam-engine. Reeds bound together were bent into arches at regular intervals, and formed a series of ribs, upon which were stretched the choicest mats. About fifty persons could conveniently sit in this hut. In the centre was the usual array of bright pots and tiny cups ranged in circular trays, round a smouldering

---

* See woodcut p. 336, and Plates 25, 27, and 18, 2nd series, of the 'Monuments of Nineveh.'

fire. A hideous black slave, crouching upon his haunches, was roasting coffee and pounding the fragrant beans in an iron mortar. Down both sides were spread carpets and mats; soft cushions of figured silk were especially prepared for the European guest.

The museef stood at a short distance from the other huts, and in a corner formed by two water-streets branching off at right angles. In front of it was the harem of the Sheikh. It consisted of several cabins in an inclosure formed entirely by walls of reeds and mats. Beyond was a great collection of huts, and in the middle of them the bazaars, consisting of double rows of shops, all of the same frail materials.

Agab received me in the most friendly manner, and entered at once into my plans for excavating, describing the ruins existing in the neighbourhood. He ordered his people to raise a hut for my servants and the Jebour workmen, and to pitch my tents in the open space opposite the museef. Building is not a lengthy or difficult process where the materials are so simple. Within an hour the mats had been dragged from the harem, the bundles of reeds turned into graceful arches, and the cabin duly covered in. As a dwelling-place, however, the small island on which the Sheikh of the Afaij had thought fit to erect his movable capital was not perhaps the most desirable in the world. Had the Euphrates risen by any sudden flood we should have been completely under water. Indeed, the place was little better than a swamp, and we appeared to be actually below the level of the streams that encompassed us. We were, at the same time, far distant from the ruins, and much time would be lost in going backwards and forwards every day. I proposed, therefore, to the Sheikh to encamp under the mound of Niffer itself, and to live there during the excavations. But Agab would not listen for one moment to this suggestion. He declared that we should be stripped of every thing within twenty-four hours, and perhaps be killed, in the bargain, by the Bedouins who were wandering over the desert, or by the neighbouring tribes, who were all in open rebellion against the Sultan. If even by a miracle we escaped these enemies, it would be utterly impossible to avoid a still greater danger in the Jins and evil spirits who swarmed after dark amongst the ruins. No Arab would pass a night on the mounds of Niffer. To complete the list of perils, there were wild beasts without number. Our horses first, and then we ourselves, would be devoured by the lions, which leave the marsh after sunset in search of prey. It was useless to contend against this array of evils, and the only real source of apprehension, that from the Arab tribes, not being without foundation, I made up my mind to remain at the Souk.

To please the Sheikh I engaged some of his Arabs as workmen, and he placed his son Mohammed over them, ordering him to accompany me daily to the ruins, and to protect me during my visits to them. I hired, at the same time, two large boats to take the excavators every morning to the mounds and to bring them back at night. The Sheikh himself, with a number of his armed followers, frequently accompanied us, ostensibly to guard me against any marauders who might pass that way, but really to be at hand in case of the discovery of treasure. He believed, of course, that I was searching after gold. Agab knew so many authentic instances of enormous wealth having been dug up at Niffer, that it was useless to argue with him upon the subject. He related to me, in the usual expressive manner of the Arabs, the following story :—In the time of Hatab, the uncle of Wadi, Sheikh of the Zobeide, a cameleer of that tribe chanced to be at Damascus with his camels. As he was walking one day in the bazaar, an aged man accosted him. 'O Sheikh of the Caravan,' said he, 'I know that thou art from the southern Jezirah, and from the land of the Zobeide. God be praised for sending thee to me! Now there is in that country a great mound, that marks the site of an ancient city of the Unbelievers, called Niffer. Go, dig in the dry bed of the Shat-el-Neel, in the midst of the ruins, and thou wilt find a stone white as milk; bring it to me, and thou shalt have for a reward double the usual hire for thy camels both there and back.' The cameleer was at a loss to guess how the old man knew of the stone, but he did as he had been asked, and in the place described to him he found the white stone, which was just a camel's burden. He took it to Damascus, and gave it to the Sheikh, who first paid him his just reward, and then broke the stone into pieces before him. It was, of course, full of gold, and the philosopher had learnt where it was to be found in the books of the Infidels.

Being thus compelled to remain at the Souk, I fitted up my tent and cabins as well as I was able. The weather was intensely cold, and it was the middle of the rainy season. By the help of mats we were able to keep out the water to a certain extent. The excavations were carried on until the 3rd of February, and I will describe at once their general results.

Niffer consists rather of a collection of mounds of unequal height and irregular form, than of one compact platform, like the principal ruins of Assyria. The mounds may be divided into four distinct groups, each surrounded and separated from the others by deep ravines, which have the appearance of ancient streets. A high cone at the north-east corner is probably the remains of a square tower constructed entirely of large sundried bricks. It is called by the Arabs the Bint-el-Ameer, 'the daughter of the prince.' I could not ascertain the origin of the name, which must be connected with some ancient tradition. The Afaij say that within it is still preserved a ship of gold filled with the same precious metal. Beneath the cone, masonry of sun-dried and kiln-burnt bricks protrudes from the sides of the ravines. The bricks are generally smaller in dimensions than those from Babylon, and long and narrow in shape. Many of them are stamped with inscriptions in the Babylonian character, containing the name of a king and of the city.

My workmen were divided into gangs, and were placed in different parts of the ruins. The only discovery of any interest made during the first day was that of a series of small recesses, or cells of brickwork, six feet deep, and about three feet wide. They contained human remains, and were sepulchres, built above the ancient ruins.

During the two subsequent days we found many vases and jars of earthenware, some glazed and others plain. With these relics was a bowl, unfortunately much broken, covered with ancient Hebrew characters, similar to those discovered at Babylon. Fragments of similar vessels were afterwards dug out of the ruins.

On the fourth day of the excavations we uncovered a coffin or sarcophagus, of highly glazed blue pottery. Within it were human remains, which crumbled to dust almost as soon as exposed to the air. The earthenware was so ill-burnt, and had suffered so much from age, that I was unable to remove this coffin entire. It fell to pieces as soon as I endeavoured to detach it from the soil by which it was surrounded. But beneath it was found a second, and subsequently scarcely a day elapsed without the discovery of four or five similar coffins. The largest were about six feet long; some, containing the remains of children, scarcely exceeded three. They were all of nearly the same shape; an oval, about two feet wide, for the head and shoulders of the corpse, ending in a narrow box for the legs and feet. The oval was closed by a detached flat lid; the rest of the coffin was covered, and there was a small hole at the end. The body must, consequently, have been forced into the sarcophagus from the top or open part.

Lid of Glazed Coffin.

Some of these coffins were ornamented with scroll work and other designs; others, with rude figures of men and animals in relief. They were all of the same fragile material. The clay, moreover, having been only partially burnt, had been exposed to the action of the nitre so abundant in the soil. Without considerable care it was impossible to remove any entire, although the surrounding earth was easily detached from them.

Human remains, more or less perfect, were found in all these sarcophagi. Sometimes, as the lid was carefully removed, I could almost distinguish the body, wrapped in its graveclothes, and still lying in its narrow resting-place. But no sooner did the outer air reach the empty crust of humanity than it fell away into dust, leaving only the skull and one or two bones. Small cups or vases in the same glazed pottery, and a few beads and engraved gems, were occasionally gathered from the crumbling remains; but no ornaments of gold or silver were discovered at Niffer, though it appears that the Arabs frequently find them in similar coffins from other ruins in southern Mesopotamia.

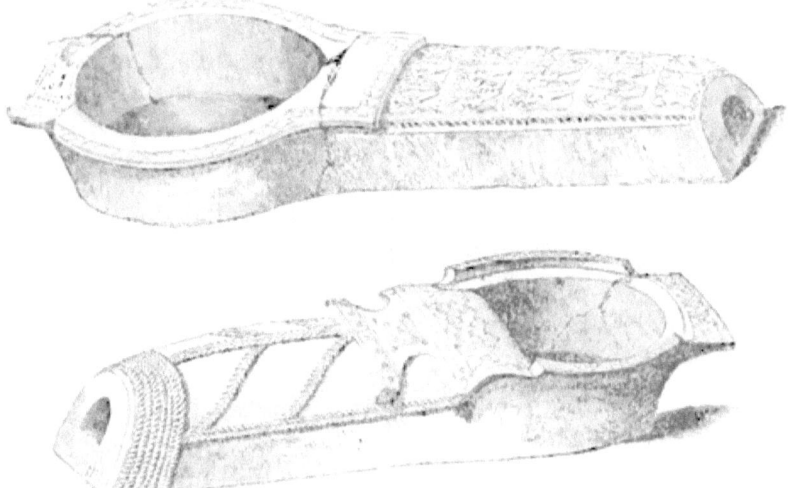

Glazed Coffins from Babylonia, in the British Museum.

From a curious relic in terracotta, discovered and sent to this country by Mr. Loftus, we learn the manner in which the dead were placed in these singular coffins. It represents the corpse of a man in one of the sarcophagi I have described. The body and extremities are swathed in linen, the bands of which are very clearly shown in the clay figure. They were probably smeared over with bitumen to preserve them; the head and hands were left uncovered. The man represented in the model wears a kind of flat turban, and his hair falls in ringlets on his shoulders. His beard is elaborately curled, like that of the ancient Assyrians. In each hand he holds a kind of mace with a circular top, probably some religious

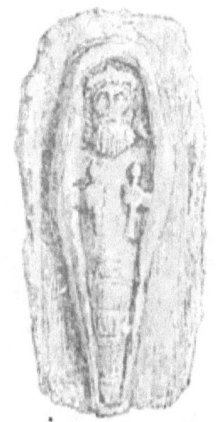

Terracotta Model of a Body in a Coffin.

V

emblem, which may be compared with one of similar form, frequently seen in the hand of the king in the bas-reliefs of Nineveh. The coffin in this relic is open and not partly closed, but it may have been so made in the model to show the manner in which the body was prepared and placed within it.

It is impossible to estimate the number of these earthen coffins; the upper part of the mound in some places appeared to consist almost entirely of them. They generally rested one upon the other, but in some cases were separated by a layer of flat bricks or tiles. As fast as the fragments of one were removed a second appeared beneath it; and, notwithstanding the number thus taken away, I did not penetrate many feet beneath the surface. In the lower part of Mesopotamia are many ruins in which similar remains are equally abundant. According to Mr. Loftus, the vast mound of Wurka is built almost entirely of such coffins, piled one above the other, and consequently hundreds of thousands of them must exist in it alone.

It is difficult to arrive at a very satisfactory conclusion as to the precise date of these remains. My own impression is, that they do not belong to a very early time, but are to be attributed to a period subsequent to the fall of the Babylonian empire, extending from the second or first century before the Christian æra to even the time of the Arab invasion.

In one part of the mound, in a kind of recess or small chamber of brick masonry, was discovered a heap of pottery of a yellow colour, very thin and fragile, much resembling that still made at Baghdad to hold water in hot weather. Many vases and cups were still entire. With them were fragments of glass bottles, jars, and other vessels, and several highly glazed or enamelled dishes. These relics appeared to be of the same period as the sarcophagi. A large number of coarse jars or urns, some nearly six feet high, were dug out of various parts of the mound. They contained bones of men and animals, and their mouths had been carefully closed by a tile or brick plastered with bitumen.*

* The Rev. Mr. Rawlinson, in his 'Ancient Monarchies' (v. i. ch. v.), has assumed that the vases, terracotta coffins, and other objects found in the mounds to the south of Babylon, are of Chaldæan origin, and belong

Although many deep trenches were opened in the ruins, and in the conical mound at the north-east corner, no other remains or relics were discovered. The Arabs have a story that a great black stone exists somewhere at Niffer. After I had searched in vain for it, I was assured that it was near some mounds several miles to the east. I sent a party of workmen to the spot, but with no better success. On the whole, I am much inclined to question whether extensive excavations carried on at Niffer would produce any very important or interesting results.

The marshes and jungles about Niffer are the retreats of many kinds of wild animals. Lions abound. I have seen them frequently, and during the excavations we found fresh traces of their footsteps almost daily amongst the ruins. The Maidan Arabs boast of capturing them in the following manner, and Arabs have assured me that they have seen the feat performed. A man, having bound his right arm with strips of tamarisk, and holding in his hand a strong piece of the same wood, about a foot or more in length, hardened in the fire and sharpened at both ends, will advance boldly into the animal's lair. When the lion springs upon him, he forces the wood into the animal's extended jaws, which will then be held open whilst he can dispatch the astonished beast at his leisure with the pistol that he holds in his left hand!

In the jungles are also found leopards, lynxes, wild cats, wolves, hyenas, jackals, deer, porcupines, boars in vast numbers, and other animals. Wildfowl, cranes, and bustards abound, and that beautiful game-bird the francolin, or black partridge, swarms in the low brushwood. The Arabs shoot them with ball. The marshes are full of fish, which attain a considerable size. They are chiefly, I believe, a kind of barbel. Their flesh is coarse and full of bones, but they afford the Arabs a constant supply of food. They are generally taken by the spear.

Although the Afaij and other inhabitants of the marshes

---

to a very ancient period, even preceding the foundation of the Assyrian empire, and has built some of his theories about a primitive Chaldæan kingdom upon this assumption. I believe them to be of comparatively recent date, probably not earlier than the Parthian period.

recognise some of the laws of the Bedouins, they are wanting in many of the virtues of the Arabs of the desert. They have, however, several customs relating to the duties of hospitality, which are rigidly adhered to. To say of a man 'that he has sold bread,' is to offer him the greatest of insults. To part with a loaf for money is accounted an act bringing disgrace not only upon the perpetrator of the act, but upon his whole family. I found this peculiar custom exceedingly inconvenient during my residence amongst the Afaij. Sheikh Agab insisted upon giving daily to my large party their supplies of bread, and it was impossible to obtain it in any other manner. Even its sale in the public market was forbidden. I was, at length, compelled to send to a considerable distance for flour, and then to employ my own workmen in baking it. The same scruples do not exist with regard to other articles of food. They are sold in the bazaar, as in all Eastern towns.

Every encampment and collection of huts, however small, belonging to the Afaij and other Arabs of the Jezirah, has a museef, or guest-house. It is generally kept up by the Sheikh of the community, and is the resort of the men of the tribe, who meet in it during the day to discuss public affairs, or to listen to storytellers and gossip-mongers. Here the traveller is hospitably entertained, and is supplied with food for himself and his horse without any return whatever being expected. It would, indeed, be considered an insult to offer payment to the owner of the museef. Even in their intercourse with Europeans these Arabs have not yet learned to receive money from travellers; and although a cloak, a silk dress, a pair of boots, or any present of this kind is readily accepted by the entertainer, it is rather looked upon as a mark of honour and favour conferred upon him, than as an acknowledgment for his hospitality. In encampments of comparatively wealthy tribes, almost every person of any substance has his museef always open for the reception of strangers, and even in the Souk of the Afaij, a coffee-house, or place of public entertainment, is unknown. A stranger, according to custom, may remain three days as a guest without being asked any questions. After that time, unless invited to continue, he must leave the museef, but he can take up his abode in another for the same period, and thus stop in the encampment until he has visited all those who receive guests. On arriving, the traveller is immediately offered coffee, and during his stay he receives two meals a-day; a breakfast in the morning about ten o'clock, and dinner soon after sunset. All those who happen to be in the museef are invited to eat at the same time. At night he is generally supplied with a carpet or mat to sleep upon, and sometimes with a coverlet. The museefs of the great chiefs are usually crowded with guests and strangers.

Unfortunately the state of Mesopotamia was such that I could not visit the ruins of Wurka, and even disturbances were to be apprehended amongst the Afaij, as Agab, their Sheikh, was threatened by a rival chief. The dampness of the soil upon which my tent was pitched, and the unwholesome air of the surrounding marshes, had brought on a severe attack of pleurisy and fever. I was soon unable to move from my bed, and was reduced at length to a state of extreme weakness. Fortunately it occurred to me to use a blistering fluid given to me for an injured horse, or I should probably not again have left the Afaij swamps. Notwithstanding the severity of the remedy it gave me immediate relief, and when Hormuzd joined me on the 28th of January, I resolved to make an attempt, without further delay, to reach Baghdad, where I could obtain medical aid. To add to our misfortunes, the rain fell in unceasing torrents for four days, and of course soon made its way through our tents. The waters of the marsh began to rise perceptibly, and the Afaij were preparing to abandon their mat huts, and to seek, in their light tiradas, a safer retreat.

I determined to strike once more into the desert, where we were less likely to meet with hostile Arabs than in the beaten tracks, and to make a forced march to some village in the neighbourhood of Hillah.

On the 2d of February, I took leave of Agab, and pitched my tents for the night beneath the mounds of Niffer. Before dawn on the following morning we were urging our horses over the desert plains of the centre of Mesopotamia.

Two armed adherents of the Sheikh were with us, rather to act as guides than to protect us from enemies. We travelled without any cause for alarm as far as the great ruin of Zibbliyah. A large body of horsemen then suddenly appeared in the distance. We ascended the mound, and prepared to defend ourselves from this elevated position. But either the Arabs did not perceive us, or were bent upon some warlike expedition which did not admit of delay, for they passed onwards, and left us to continue our journey.

Zibbliyah rises from a heap of rubbish in the centre of the desert, and consists of a solid mass of large, crumbling, sundried bricks, between the courses of which, at intervals, are layers of reeds as in many pure Babylonian buildings. It is apparently the remains of a tower. I could find no fragments of inscribed bricks or pottery.

We saw no human habitation until long after nightfall, when we reached the small Arab hamlet of Bashayi. It was surrounded, for defence, by a low mud wall, and some time was spent in a parley and explanation before the timid inhabitants would open their gates. I could hardly remain in my saddle until we were admitted within the inclosure. I tottered into a wretched hovel, thick with smoke, and sank down exhausted, after a ride of fourteen hours and a fortnight's abstinence from food.

My poor Jebour workmen being on foot had been unable to keep up with the caravan during our forced march. They did not reach the village until daybreak, and then in a very sorry plight, for they were stripped to the skin. They had approached, in search of water, the tents of some Arabs, and falling in with a plundering party had been robbed of everything and left naked in the desert.

In the morning I had scarcely strength to mount my horse. But with the caravan I made another forced march in the beaten track to Baghdad, and reached the khan of Iskanderiyah at nightfall.

I quitted the khan with the Bairakdar before dawn to canter into Baghdad. As the sun rose from the sea-like plain, the great ruin of Ctesiphon appeared above the eastern horizon. The remains of this famous palace of the Persian kings have often been described. A vaulted hall, exceeding 150 feet in depth and about 106 feet high, forms the centre of the building. It is completely open at one end to the air, but on both sides of it are wings, divided into several floors, each containing dwelling apartments. Such is the

Throne-room, Teheran.

plan of most modern Persian houses, in which a great Iwan, or open hall for summer residence, is flanked by sleeping and other rooms, in two or three stories. The exterior of the palace of Ctesiphon is ornamented with pilasters, cornices, and arches of brickwork, now fast falling to decay, but probably once covered with fine plaster, or partly cased with stone. The architecture is peculiar to the time of the Parthian and Sassanian dynasties, being a mixture of Western and Eastern forms and decoration, resulting from the long connection between the Persian and Roman empires.

This ruin, with a few mounds and heaps of rubbish scattered around it, is all that now remains of the capital of the Parthian empire. On the opposite bank of the Tigris long lines of earthen ramparts, forming a quadrangle, and enclosing the usual signs of former habitations, mark the site of the city built by Seleucus after the fall of Babylon.

I did not visit Ctesiphon on this occasion; the river separated me from the ruins, and I only mention them in this place to describe a remarkable effect of mirage which I witnessed as I rode towards Baghdad. As the quivering sun rose in unclouded splendour, the palace was transformed into a vast arcade of arches resting upon columns and masses of masonry. Gradually this arcade was, as it were, compressed like the slides of a telescope, but the building gained in height what it lost in length, and one arch slowly appeared above the other, until the ruin assumed the shape of a tower reaching to the sky, and pierced from the base to the summit by innumerable arches. In a few minutes this strange edifice began to melt away into air, and I saw a magnified, though perfect image of the palace; but upon it was its exact counterpart upside down. Other equally singular changes succeeded until the sun was high in the heavens, and the ruin at length disappeared in the distance. The small bushes of camel-thorn scattered over the desert were during this time turned into forest trees, and a transparent lake imaged in its counterfeit waters the varying forms of the edifice. Although I have seen many extraordinary effects of mirage during my wanderings in the East, I scarcely remember to have witnessed one more striking or more beautiful than that near the ruins of Ctesiphon.*

I had but just strength left me to reach the gates of Baghdad. Once in the city, under the friendly care of Dr. Hyslop, I soon recovered my health, and was ready to start on fresh adventures.

---

* I witnessed another very remarkable effect of mirage in the early spring of 1840, when riding one morning over the plains near Bir, on the Euphrates. Suddenly, as if by enchantment, a magnificent city, standing on the borders of a lake, rose before me. Palaces, domes, towers, and the spires of Gothic cathedrals were reflected in the blue waters. The deception was so complete, the appearance so real, that I could scarcely believe that some mighty capital had not been by magic transported into the desert. There was scarcely a stone or a bush to account for this singular phenomenon.

CHAPTER XIII.

Departure from Baghdad—Journey through Mesopotamia—Early Arab remains—The Median wall—Tekrit—Horses stolen—Instance of Bedouin honesty—Excavations at Kalah Sherghat—Reach Mosul—Discoveries during absence—New chambers at Kouyunjik—Description of bas-reliefs—Extent of the ruins explored—Bases of pillars—Small objects—Absence of Assyrian tombs—Assyrian relics—Remains beneath the tomb of Jonah—Discoveries at Shereef-Khan—at Nimroud—Engraved cylinders.

THERE was no hope of improvement in the state of the country round Baghdad, I therefore determined to return to Mosul. On the 27th of February, bidding adieu to my friends, I crossed the Tigris by the crazy bridge of boats, and took the crowded road to Kathimain. There I passed the night beneath the hospitable roof of the Nawab of Oude. At daybreak on the following morning, under the guidance of Sahiman, the brother of Suttum, who had agreed to escort me to Mosul, and accompanied by Hormuzd, the Jebours, and my servants, I left the sacred suburb, and followed a beaten track leading to the desert. In order to avoid the windings of the river, we struck across the barren plain. The low houses of Kathimain soon disappeared from our sight, but for some miles we watched the gilded domes and minarets of the tombs of the Imaums, rising above the dark belt of palms, and glittering in the rays of the morning sun. At last they too vanished, and I had looked for the last time upon Baghdad. We were now in as complete a wilderness as if we had been wandering in the midst of Arabia, and not within a few miles of a great city. Not a living creature broke the solitude. Here and there we saw the sites of former encampments, but the Arabs had long since left them, either to move further into the desert, or to seek security from an enemy amongst the date groves on the banks of the river.

We travelled with speed over the plain, and in four hours and a half passed the ruins of a large caravanserai, called Tarmiyah. After a ride of nine hours we found ourselves in the midst of the palm trees of a village called Summaichah, formerly a town of some importance, and still watered by the Dujail, a wide and deep canal of the time of the Caliphs, derived from the Tigris. The inhabitants seeing horsemen in the distance armed themselves hastily, anticipating an attack. They met us at some distance from their dwellings, firing their guns, brandishing their naked scimitars, and shouting their war-cry. Finding that we were travellers and friends they escorted us to the house of their Sheikh, Hashem, who immediately slew a sheep, and made other preparations for our entertainment.

The plain on all sides is intersected by the remains of innumerable canals and watercourses, derived from the Tigris and the Dujail. Their lofty banks narrow the view, and it was only as we passed over them, after quitting Summaichah, that we saw the distant palm groves of the large village of Belled. Scouts had been stationed on the higher mounds, far and near, to give notice to the inhabitants of the approach of Bedouins, that the flocks might be driven within the walls. They had quickly spread the alarm when they saw us drawing near, and a body of armed men appeared in the distance ready to meet the supposed robbers. We left them and their village to the right, and passed through the ruins of an Arab town of the time of the Caliphs. Beyond it we crossed the Dujail, by a falling bridge of four large arches, with a small arch between each. The beauty of the masonry, the ornamental inscriptions, and rich tracery of this ruin, showed that it was of the best period of Arab architecture.

To the north of the Dujail we wound through a perfect maze of ancient canals now dry. It required the practised eye of the Bedouin to follow the sand-covered track. About eight miles beyond the bridge the embankments suddenly ceased. A high rampart of earth then stretched as far as the eye could see, to the right and to the left. At certain distances were mounds, forming square inclosures, like ruined outworks. A few hundred yards in advance was a second rampart, much lower and narrower than the first. We had reached what some believe to be the famous Median wall, one of the many wonders of Babylonia, built by the Babylonians across Mesopotamia, from river to river, to guard their wealthy city and thickly peopled provinces against invasion from the north.

Beyond the Median wall we entered upon undulating gravelly downs, furrowed by deep ravines, and occasionally rising into low hills. With the rich alluvial soil of Babylonia, we had left the boundaries of the ancient province. The banks of the Tigris are here, in general, too high, and the face of the country too unequal, to admit of artificial irrigation being carried far inland by watercourses derived from the river.

The spiral tower, the dome, and the minarets of Samarrah at length appeared above the eastern horizon. After nine hours and a half's journey we encamped for the night on the Tigris opposite to the town. As the sun went down we watched the women who, on the other side of the river, came to fetch their evening supplies of water, and gracefully bearing their pitchers on their heads returned to the gates. But on our bank the solitude was only broken by a lonely hyæna coming to drink at the stream, and the hungry jackals that prowled round our tents. The ruins of an early Arab town, called Ashik, stood on a hill in the distance, and near our camping place were the deserted walls of a more recent settlement.

On the third day of our journey another ride of nine hours and a half, along the banks of the Tigris, brought us to Tekrit, whose inhabitants bear a notoriously bad character. Next day our halting-place, after crossing for seven hours and a half the same undulating gravelly downs, was near the ruins of a fine old khan, called Karnaineh, once standing on the bank of the river, but now nearly a mile from it. Next morning we struck inland, in order to avoid the precipitous hills of Makhoul, at whose feet sweeps the Tigris.

Our tract led through a perfect wilderness. We found no

water, nor saw any moving thing. When after a long ride of about eleven hours we reached some brackish springs, called Belaliss, the complete solitude lulled us into a feeling of security, and we all slept without keeping the accustomed watch. I was awoke in the middle of the night by an unusal noise close to my tent. I immediately gave the alarm, but it was too late. Two of our horses had been stolen, and in the darkness we could not pursue the thieves. Sahiman broke out in reproaches of himself as the cause of our mishap, and wandered about until dawn in search of some clue to the authors of the theft. At length he tracked them, declared unhesitatingly that they were of the Shammar, pointed out from marks almost imperceptible to any eye but to that of a Bedouin, that they were four in number, had left their delouls at some distance from our tents, and had already journeyed far before they had been drawn by our fires to the encampment. These indications were enough. He swore an oath that he would follow and bring back our stolen horses wherever they might be, for it was a shame upon him and his tribe that, whilst under his protection in the desert, we had lost any thing belonging to us. And he religiously kept his oath. When we parted at the end of our journey, he began at once to trace the animals. After six weeks' search, during which he went as far as Ana on the Euphrates, where one had been sold to an Arab of the town, he brought them to Mosul. I was away at the time, but he left them with Mr. Rassam, and returned to the desert without asking a reward for performing an act of duty imperative on a Bedouin. Such instances of honesty and good faith are not uncommon amongst the wandering Arabs, as I can bear witness from personal experience.

Mr. Rassam had, at my request, sent a party of Jebours to excavate at Kalah Sherghat. The springs of Belaliss are separated from the shoulder of the Gebel Makhoul, which overhangs these ruins, by a wild rocky valley, called Wadi Jehannem, the Valley of Hell. We crossed it and the hills in about three hours and a half, and came suddenly upon the workmen, who, of course, took us for Bedouin plunderers, and prepared to defend themselves. They had opened trenches in various parts of the great mound, but had made no discoveries of any importance, and I am inclined to doubt whether an edifice panelled with sculptured slabs ever existed on the platform. Fragments of a winged bull in the alabaster of the Nineveh palaces, part of a statue in black stone with a few cuneiform characters, pieces of an inscribed tablet of copper, and the fragments of a large inscribed cylinder in baked clay, were, it is true, found in the ruins; but these remains were scarcely sufficient to warrant the continuation of the excavations on a spot so difficult of access, and exposed to so much risk from the Bedouins.

We encamped in the jungle to the north of the ruins, and galloped the following day into Mosul.

I will now describe the sculptures uncovered whilst I was at Baghdad and after my return to Mosul, previous to my departure for England.

To the north of the great centre hall or court* at Kouyunjik, four new chambers had been discovered.† The first was 96 feet by 23. On its walls were represented the return of an Assyrian army from war, with their spoil of captives and cattle. The prisoners were distinguished by a cap turned back at the top, not unlike the Phrygian bonnet reversed, short tunics, and a broad belt. The women had long curls falling over their shoulders, and were clothed in fringed robes. The fighting-men of the conquered tribe wore a simple fillet round their short hair; a tunic, falling in front to the knee, and behind to the calf of the leg; a wavy girdle,

Loading a Camel. (Kouyunjik.)

and a cross-belt round their breasts, ending in two large tassels. At their backs they carried a quiver topped by a circular ornament. The captives bore ingots of gold, or

---

* No XIX. Plan I. p. 4. † No. XLIII. same Plan.

some other metal. Their beasts of burden were laden with the same objects. A kneeling camel, receiving its load, was designed with considerable truth and spirit. One man puts his foot on the neck of the animal to prevent it from rising,

Captives in a Cart. (Kouyunjik.)

as is still the custom. The camel saddle nearly resembled that still used by the Arabs. The women rode on mules, and in carts drawn by these animals and sometimes by men. Asses and waggons bore cauldrons and sacks, probably containing corn. One bas-relief represented captives resting; two unharnessed mules stood eating their barley in front of

Captives resting. (Kouyunjik.)

the loaded cart; a woman seated on a stone held her child upon her knees, whilst her husband drank water from a cup.

This chamber opened at one end into a small room,* 23 feet by 13. On its walls were represented captives

* No. XLIV. Plan I. p. 4.

dressed in short tunics with skins falling from their shoulders, boots laced up in front, and cross-bands round their legs; they had short, bushy hair and beards.

In the outer chamber two doorways opposite the grand entrances into the great court, led into a parallel apartment, 62 feet by 16 feet.* On its walls were represented the conquest of the same people. There were long lines of prisoners; some in carts, others on foot. The fighting men, armed with bows and quivers, were made to bear part of the spoil. In the costumes of the warriors and captives, and in the forms of the waggons and war-carts, these bas-reliefs bore a striking resemblance to the sculptures of the son of Esarhaddon, described in a previous chapter.† It may, therefore, be inferred that the conquest of the same nation was celebrated in both, and that on these walls we have recorded the successful wars of Sennacherib in the country of Susiana or Elam.‡

This chamber, like the one parallel to it, led at one end into a small room 17 feet square.§ On its walls, the campaign recorded in the adjoining chamber had been continued. The bas-reliefs still preserved represented the king in his chariot receiving the captives; musicians playing on harps before him; mountains and forests, and a castle.

These rooms completed the discoveries on the southern side of the palace. On the northern side of the same edifice and on the river-face of the platform, one wall of a third great hall or court had been uncovered; the other walls had not been excavated at the time of my departure from Mosul. From the very ruinous state of this part of the building, and from the small accumulation of earth above the level of the foundations, it is doubtful whether any sculptures now exist in it. In the wall still standing were three entrances,‖ the centre formed by winged lions, and the others by fish gods. Of the bas-reliefs only fragments remained. On some were represented the conquest of a tribe dwelling in the marshes of

---

* No. XLVI. same Plan. † See chapter x.
‡ See Plates 33 and 34, of the 2nd series of the 'Monuments of Nineveh' for drawings of several of the bas-reliefs in the two chambers.
§ No. XLVII. Plan I. p. 4. ‖ No. LXIV. Plan I.

336   NINEVEH AND BABYLON.   [CHAP.

Southern Mesopotamia. The Assyrians pursued their enemies in wicker boats, such as I have described in my account of the Afaij Arabs; and, on the islands formed by the small streams flowing through the morass, were Assyrian warriors

Battle in a Marsh in Southern Mesopotamia.   (Kouyunjik.)

on horseback. It will be seen by the accompanying woodcut how closely the country resembled that now inhabited by the Afaij tribes. The captive women wore long robes fringed and embroidered. The palm-tree flourished on the dry land outside the swamps.*

On the same side of the court was represented the conquest of a people clothed in long garments, the women wearing turbans, with veils falling to their feet. The Assyrians had plundered their temples, and were seen carrying away their idols.† 'Of a truth, Lord, the kings of Assyria have laid waste all the nations and their countries, and have cast their gods into the fire; for they were no gods, but the work of men's hands, wood and stone; therefore they have destroyed them.'‡

The three entrances led into one chamber, 86 feet by 24.§ On its calcined walls were only the faint traces of bas-reliefs. I could distinguish a line of chariots in a ravine between mountains, warriors throwing logs on a great burning pile of wood, castles on the tops of hills, Assyrians carrying away spoil, amongst which was a royal umbrella, and the king on his throne receiving his army on their return from battle with the captives and booty. The walls of a small room ‖ opening into the northern end of this chamber had almost entirely disappeared. The fragments found in the rubbish showed that they had also been covered with sculptures.

Opposite to and corresponding with the three entrances into the court were three other doorways leading into a parallel chamber of somewhat smaller dimensions.¶ Parts of four slabs were the only sculptures sufficiently well preserved to be drawn: they represented the siege of a great city, whose many-towered walls were defended by slingers, archers, and spearmen. The king himself in his chariot was present at the attack. Around him were his warriors and his led-horses.

Three more chambers were discovered in this part of the

---

* See also Plate 27 of the 2nd series of the 'Monuments of Nineveh.'
† Plate 30 of the 2nd series of the 'Monuments of Nineveh.'
‡ Isaiah, xxxvii. 18, 19.   § No. LXV. Plan I. p. 4.
‖ No. LXVI. same Plan, 26 feet by 19.
¶ No. LXVII. same Plan. Its length was about 82 feet, and its breadth 16.

building. They were on the very edge of the river-face of the mound. The walls of the outer room* had been almost entirely destroyed. An entrance, formed by colossal winged figures, led from it into a second chamber, about 24 feet square, in which the sculptures were still partly preserved. Amongst the bas-reliefs was another battle in a marsh. The Assyrian warriors were seen fighting in boats, and bringing their captives to the shore, one of the vessels being towed by

Assyrians cutting down the Palm Trees belonging to a captured City.
(Kouyunjik.)

a man swimming on an inflated skin.† Sennacherib himself, in his chariot, in the midst of a grove of palm-trees, received the prisoners, and the heads of the slain.

The third chamber,‡ entered from that last described through a doorway guarded by colossal eagle-footed figures, contained the sculptured records of the conquest of part of Babylonia, or of some other district to the south of it. Long lines of chariots, horsemen, and warriors, divided into com-

---

* No. LXXI. Plan I. p. 4.   † No. LXX. same Plan.
‡ No. LXIX. Plan I.   About 23 feet by 19.

panies according to their arms and their costumes, accompanied the king. The Assyrians cut down the palm-trees within and without the walls of the captured cities. Men beating drums, such as are still seen in the same country, and women clapping their hands in cadence to their song, came out to greet the conquerors. Beneath the walls was represented a great cauldron, which appears to have been supported upon oxen; perhaps a vessel resembling the brazen sea of the temple of Solomon.*

Such were the discoveries in the ruined palace of Sennacherib at the time of my departure for Europe. In this magnificent edifice I had opened no less than seventy-one halls, chambers, and passages, whose walls, almost without an exception, had been panelled with slabs of sculptured alabaster recording the wars, the triumphs, and the other great deeds of the Assyrian king. By a rough calculation, about 9,880 feet, or nearly two miles, of bas-reliefs, with twenty-seven portals, formed by colossal winged bulls and lion-sphinxes, had been uncovered in that part alone of the building explored during my researches. The greatest length of the excavations was about 720 feet, the greatest breadth about 600 feet.† The pavement of the chambers was from 20 to 35 feet below the surface of the mound.

Deep trenches and tunnels were opened, and experimental shafts sunk in various parts of the mound of Kouyunjik. Enormous walls and foundations of brick masonry, fragments of sculptured and unsculptured alabaster, inscribed bricks, numerous small objects, and various other remains, were discovered. To the north of the ruins of Sennacherib's palace, on the same level, and resting upon a pavement of limestone slabs, were found four circular pedestals. They appeared to form part of a double line of similar objects, extending from the edge of the platform to an entrance to

* 1 Kings, vii. 23–25. The brazen sea of Solomon stood upon twelve oxen, three facing each cardinal point. It must be borne in mind that the Assyrian sculptor frequently represented only one figure to signify many, and that more than one ox probably supported the vessel portrayed in this bas-relief.

† These measurements merely include that part of the palace actually excavated.

the palace, and may have supported the wooden columns of a covered way, or have served as bases to an avenue of statues. The earth not having been sufficiently cleared away around them, I was unable to ascertain whether there was more than a double row. They were amongst the very few

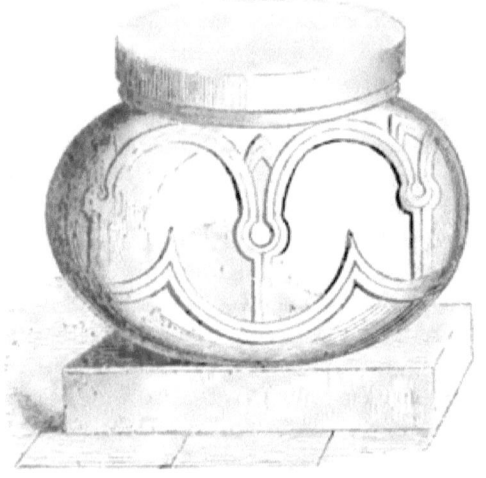

Assyrian Pedestal, from Kouyunjik.

architectural remains dug out at Nineveh. The ornament upon them is not inelegant, and is somewhat Saracenic in its character.

It is remarkable that, notwithstanding the most careful search in all parts of the country round Mosul, I have been unable to find one undoubted Assyrian tomb, nor can I conjecture how or where the people of Nineveh buried their dead.* The sepulchral chambers in the hills, so frequently described in these pages, are unquestionably of a compara-

* The tombs discovered above the ruins, as I have already stated, are probably Roman or Parthian. Mr. Rassam found in one of them, after my departure, a thin mask of gold, which had been moulded upon the features of the deceased, and a gold coin of the Emperor Maximinus. Mr. Loftus discovered a tomb rudely constructed of stone, seventeen feet beneath the foundations of the south-east palace at Nimroud. It contained the remains of three human bodies, a copper hatchet, a knife blade, and a spear head. These objects are in the British Museum. It is very doubtful whether they are Assyrian.

tively late period. The rocky gullies outside and between the inclosure walls of Kouyunjik have been examined over and over again with the greatest care for traces of tombs, but in vain. In the numerous isolated conical mounds scattered over the face of the country, I have detected nothing to show that they were places of sepulture. The only Assyrian sepulchre hitherto discovered is probably the vaulted chamber in the high mound of Nimroud, which may have once contained the remains of the royal builder of the north-west palace. Did the Assyrians, like the fire-worshippers of Persia, expose their dead till nought remained but the bleached bones; or did they burn them and then scatter their ashes to the winds? Not a clue is given to their customs in this matter by any bas-relief or monument hitherto discovered. The Assyrians, unlike the Egyptians, appear to have avoided all allusions to their dead and to their funeral rites.

I had long been desirous of making some experiments in the mound on which stands the so-called tomb of the prophet Jonah, and which forms part of the great group of ruins opposite Mosul. But the sanctity of the place prevented any attempt to excavate openly, and it was necessary to carry on my researches without exciting the suspicion of the Mussulman inhabitants of the neighbourhood.

A village has risen round the mosque containing the tomb. The rest of the mound is occupied by a burying-ground, thickly set with Mussulman gravestones. True believers from the surrounding country bring their dead to this sacred spot, and to disturb a grave on Nebbi Yunus would have caused a tumult which might have led to no agreeable results. The pretended tomb is in a dark inner room. None but Mussulmans should be admitted within the holy precincts, but I have more than once visited the shrine, with the sanction of my good friend, Mullah Sultan, a guardian of the mosque. A square plaster or wooden sarcophagus, covered by a green cloth embroidered with sentences from the Koran, stands in the centre of an apartment spread with a common European carpet. A few ostrich eggs and coloured tassels, such as are seen in similar Mohammedan buildings, hang from the ceiling. A small grated window looks into the hall, where the true believers assemble for prayer. It is needless to repeat that the tradition which places the tomb on this spot is a mere fable.*

The village of Nebbi Yunus is inhabited by Turcomans. Hearing that the owner of a house wished to make underground apartments for summer, I offered to dig them for him, on condition that I should have all the relics and sculptures discovered during the excavations. By these means I was able to examine a small part of the mound.

After a few days' labour, the workmen came to the walls of a chamber panelled with inscribed, but unsculptured, alabaster slabs. The inscriptions upon them contained the name, titles, and genealogy of Esar-haddon, like those on the bulls of the south-west palace at Nimroud. Several bricks and fragments of stone bore the same inscription. No remains of an earlier period were then discovered. After my return to England, a pair of colossal human-headed bulls, and two figures of the Assyrian Hercules slaying the lion, similar to those in the Louvre, were uncovered.

Three miles to the north of the inclosure of Kouyunjik, and on the bank of the Tigris, is a village called Shereef Khan. Near it are several mounds. The largest, though much inferior in size to the great ruins of Assyria, is distinguished, like those of Nimroud and Khorsabad, by a conical elevation at one corner. Near it are the remains of a canal, which once led water from the Tigris into a rich alluvial plain. These embankments might be mistaken for a wall or rampart. I carried on, for some time, excavations in this mound, and discoveries of interest were made in it. At a small depth beneath the surface of the soil were the remains of a building, and a broad flight of alabaster steps. The walls of the chambers were of sundried bricks, but several slabs of alabaster and painted and inscribed bricks were found in the ruins.

The inscriptions upon the bricks contain the names of Sargon and Sennacherib. From two inscribed limestone

---

* Benjamin of Tudela places the tomb of Jonah at Ain Japhata, to the south of Babylon.

slabs, also found in the ruins, we learn that a palace was erected on the spot by Esar-haddon for his son.*

At Nimroud the excavations had been almost suspended. A few Arabs, still working in the centre of the mound, had found the remains of sculptured walls, forming part of the edifice previously discovered there. The lower half of several colossal figures, amongst them winged men struggling with lions and mythic animals, had been preserved.

Some small objects of interest were discovered in different parts of the ruins, and some additional rooms were explored in the north-west and south-east palaces. In none of them, however, were there sculptures or even inscriptions, except such as were impressed on bricks; nor was there anything new in their construction to require particular description or additional plans. The south-east edifice appears to have been a building of considerable extent. Several rooms were opened to the north of those previously examined. The bricks found of the palace prove that it was partly built by the grandson of Esar-haddon, one of the last of the Assyrian kings. Excavations were subsequently carried on amongst its ruins by Mr. Hormuzd Rassam and Mr. Loftus. The remains of more than one building were discovered beneath its foundations; and it would appear that several kings, amongst whom was Pul, had erected palaces on this site. Several very interesting monuments, amongst them two figures carved in limestone, with an inscription containing a name which Sir Henry Rawlinson interprets as that of Queen Semiramis, were found there.

Cylinder in green Jasper.

Amongst the smaller relics discovered in Assyrian and Babylonian ruins, the most interesting are probably the engraved cylinders or gems, of which a large collection was brought by me to England. They vary in length from a quarter of an inch to about two inches, and are either quite circular, or barrel-shaped, or

---

* Sir Henry Rawlinson and Mr. Hormuzd Rassam afterwards carried on some excavations in the mound of Shereef Khan; but no discoveries

slightly curved inwards like that represented in the accompanying woodcut. They are usually of lapis-lazuli, rock crystal, cornelian, amethyst, chalcedony, agate, onyx, jasper, quartz, serpentine, sienite, oriental alabaster, green felspar, and hæmatite. The workmanship varies in different specimens, that of some being distinguished by considerable sharpness and delicacy, and that of others being so coarse as scarcely to enable us to recognise the objects engraved upon them. The subjects are generally either religious or historical, usually the former, and on many are short inscriptions in the cuneiform character, sometimes containing a royal name, or that of a private individual. These cylinders belong to several distinct periods. The most ancient with which I am acquainted are those of the time of the kings who built the oldest edifices hitherto discovered at Nineveh. From the similarity of the subjects, and of the style of art

Ancient Assyrian Cylinder, in Serpentine.

between them and the sculptures in the north-west palace at Nimroud, I have ventured to assign others collected by me to the same period. Nearly all the cylinders of this class are

of any great importance, except fragments of inscriptions, and an interesting signet cylinder, were made in it. The ruins appear to be those of a temple dedicated to the god Nergal, and the Assyrian name of the place seems to read Tarbisi.

cut in serpentine, and the designs upon them are generally rude and coarsely engraved. The subjects are usually the king in his chariot discharging his arrows against a lion or wild bull, warriors in battle, the monarch or priests in adoration before the emblem of the deity, the eagle-headed god, winged bulls and lions, and other mythic animals, accompanied by the common Assyrian symbols, the sun, the moon, the seven stars, the winged globe, the sacred tree, and the wedge or cuneatic element. An unique specimen, apparently of this period, represents a man armed with a spear, standing

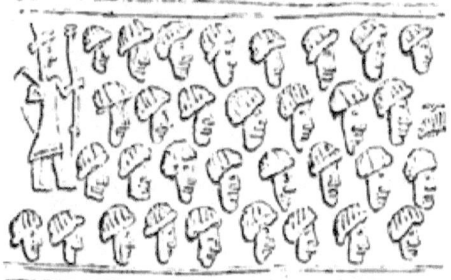 

Assyrian Cylinders, in Serpentine.

in the midst of thirty-two human heads, probably the seal of a successful warrior. Upon another are a turtle, a bird, and a human figure.

The next in order of date are those of the time of Sargon and his successors. To this period belong the cylinder with the fish-god, and that which I believe to be the signet of Sennacherib himself, described in a previous part of this work.* A very fine specimen, cut in agate, represents an Assyrian goddess, perhaps Astarte, or the Moon, with ten stars, and with a dog seated before her. In front of her is the moon's crescent, and a priest in an attitude of adoration. A tree and a rampant goat, both common Assyrian symbols, complete the group. On other cylinders of the same age we find the gods represented under various forms, the king and priests worshipping before them, altars and

* Ante, p. 174. One cylinder bears his name.

the usual mythic emblems. On a small cylinder in white porcelain or quartz is engraved a cow of the Indian breed suckling a calf, an Assyrian emblem, which occurs amongst the ivory carvings discovered at Nimroud.*

Assyrian Cylinder, in Agate.   Assyrian Cylinder, in Porcelain or Quartz.

The pure Babylonian cylinders are more commonly found in European collections than the Assyrian. They are usually engraved with sacred figures, accompanied by a short inscription in the Babylonian cuneiform character, containing the names of the owner of the seal and of the divinity, under whose particular protection he had probably placed

In Iron Hæmatite.   In Jasper.
Babylonian Cylinders.

himself. They are usually cut in a red iron ore or hæmatite, which appears to have been a favourite material for such objects. Many specimens, however, are in agate, jasper, and other hard substances. Amongst the most interesting cylinders of this kind obtained by me is one in spotted sien-

* A similar group is seen in a bas-relief at Khorsabad. Botta, pl. 141.

ite, and one in green jasper, remarkable for the depth of the intaglio and spirit of the design, representing the Assyrian Hercules contending with a buffalo, and a horned human

Babylonian Cylinder, in green Jasper.

figure, with the extremities of a bull, fighting with a lion. Between the two groups is an antelope with long spiral horns, an animal not found at this day in Mesopotamia.

A class of cylinders of very rude workmanship, and generally in hæmatite, are probably of the latest Babylonian period. Upon them are usually found the figures of various deities, and especially of Venus, sometimes represented with the waters of life flowing from her breasts. Amongst the most curious is one in jasper, engraved with a man seated in a car of peculiar construction drawn by four horses: in front of him are seven human heads and two birds.

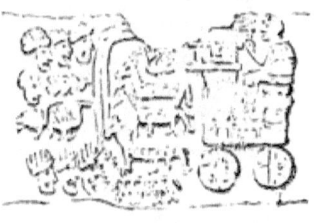

Babylonian Cylinder, in Jasper.

A few cylinders and gems, Assyrian in character, are inscribed with Semetic letters, resembling the Phœnician and cursive Babylonian. They are rare, and have chiefly been found, I believe, in ruins on the banks of the Euphrates to the north of Babylon, near Hit and Ana. I would attribute them, therefore, to the Semetic population which inhabited the districts on the eastern borders of the Syrian desert. They appear to belong to various periods, from the time of the lower Assyrian dynasty to that of the Persian occupation

Cylinders, with Semetic Characters.

of Babylonia. To the first period I assign a cylinder in the British Museum, representing two figures, half man half bull, raising the winged emblem of the deity over the sacred tree. On one side of them is a priest carrying a goat, such as is seen in the Khorsabad sculptures, and on the other a man in the act of worship. Of the Persian epoch an interesting example exists in the same collection. On it is engraved the king contending with a winged human-headed bull and a griffin beneath the image of the god Ormuzd. The first word of the inscription is pure Hebrew, חתם, Katham, 'the seal,' and then follow the names of a man and of his father.

Persian cylinders frequently bear an inscription in the cuneiform character peculiar to the monuments of the Achæmenian dynasty. The most interesting specimen of this class is a well-known gem of green chalcedony in the British Museum, on which is engraved king Darius in his chariot, with his name and that of his father. This was probably a royal signet. Another, in the same collection, bears the name of one Arsaces, who appears to have been a chamberlain, or to have held some other office in the Persian court. The device represents the god Typhon (?)* full-faced, holding a lotus flower in each hand beneath the sym-

* Represented as on Egyptian monuments.

bol of the supreme deity supported by two priests. A very fine cylinder in rock crystal, brought by me to this country, and now also in the British Museum, has the god Ormuzd represented as at Persepolis, raised by two winged bulls with

In red Cornelian.   In Chalcedony.

In Rock Crystal.   In Onyx.

Persian Cylinders.

human heads, above an oval, containing the image of a king. The engraving on this gem is remarkable for its delicacy and minuteness.

Persian cylinders are recognised at once by the draperies of the figures, gathered up into folds, as in the sculptures of the Achæmenian dynasty, a peculiarity never found on pure Assyrian or Babylonian monuments; by the crown of the king; by the form of the supreme deity, or Ormuzd, and by the monstrous animals, resembling the sculptures on the walls of Persepolis. Although gems and precious stones of the Arsacian and Sassanian dynasties of Persia, engraved with subjects and mythical figures precisely similar to those on Assyrian and Babylonian relics, are by no means uncommon; yet no cylinders, as far as I am aware, have hitherto been found of those periods. Seals in this form do not appear to have been used after the fall of the Achæmenian power.

It is evident from the specimens above described, that these cylinders were seals or signets to be impressed on clay and other materials on which public and private documents were written. Herodotus states that the Babylonians were accustomed to have their signets constantly with them, as a modern Eastern always carries his seal.* The manner in which they were used is shown in the engraving of an inscribed terracotta tablet from Kouyunjik.† The seal was rolled on the moist clay, at the same time as the letters were impressed.‡ The tablet was then placed in the furnace and baked. All these cylinders have been pierced, and one specimen, found by my workmen in a mound in the desert near the Sinjar, still retained its copper setting. They revolved upon a metal axis like a garden rolling-stone.

Such then were the objects of sculpture and the smaller relics found at Nimroud and Kouyunjik. I will now endeavour to convey to the reader, in conclusion, a general idea of the results of the excavations, as far as they may tend to increase our acquaintance with the history of Assyria, and to illustrate the religion, the arts, and the manners of her inhabitants.

* Lib. i. c. 195. As a written signature is of no value, except in particular cases, in the East, and as all documents to be valid must be sealed with seals bearing the names of the parties to them, the engraved signet is of great importance, and the trade of an engraver one of considerable responsibility. The punishment for forging seals is very severe, and there are many regulations enforced for securing their authenticity.
† Ante, p. 170, 171.
‡ Compare Job, xxxviii. 14. 'It is turned as clay to the seal.'

CHAPTER XIV.

Results of the discoveries to chronology and history—Names of earliest Assyrian kings—Annals of Tiglath Pileser I.—The period of his reign—The dynasty of the Nimroud kings—Sardanapalus I.—His successor—Mention of Jehu, king of Israel—Annals of Tiglath Pileser II.—Mention of Menahem—Annals of Sargon—of Sennacherib—of Esarhaddon—of his son and grandson—Nature of Assyrian records—Political condition of Assyria—Religion—Extent of Nineveh—Assyrian architecture—Sennacherib's palace at Kouyunjik—The palaces at Nimroud—Fortifications of Nimroud, Khorsabad, and Kouyunjik—Conclusion.

SINCE the first discovery of the ruins on the site of the great city of Nineveh, a mass of information, scarcely to be overrated for its importance and interest, has been added to our previous knowledge of the early civilisation, history, and comparative geography of the countries watered by the Tigris and Euphrates, and of those which were once included within the Assyrian and Babylonian empires. When in 1849 I published the narrative of my first expedition to Assyria, the inscriptions recovered from the remains of the buried palaces were still a sealed book; for although attempts had been made to interpret some of them, those attempts were rather founded upon ingenious conjectures than upon any well-established philological basis. Since that time great progress has been made in the decipherment of the cuneiform character, and the general contents of the Assyrian and Babylonian inscriptions can now be ascertained with some certainty, although we may not be able to give the exact meaning of a large number of words and passages, or to render the true sound of each sign or letter. This remarkable result we owe to the labours of four English scholars, the late Dr. Hincks, Sir Henry Rawlinson, Mr. Fox Talbot, and Mr. Norris, and of the French orientalists, M. Oppert and M. Ménant.* This work would not be complete were I not to give a general sketch of the results of their investigations as well as of my own researches, confining myself, however, to the history of Assyria.†

The earliest kings of which any mention has yet been discovered in the cuneiform inscriptions are supposed to have reigned in Assyria from about 1650 to 1550 B.C. Their names, the reading of which is extremely doubtful,‡ are found together on the fragment of a clay tablet, now in the British Museum, containing, it is believed, portions of a synchronous history of Assyria and Babylonia, but admitted to belong to a period nearly one thousand years later than the date assigned to those kings themselves. They appear to have had family alliances with the kings of Babylon, and to have also been at war with them. But the theories as to the time of their reign, and as to the part they are supposed to have played in Assyrian history, appear to me to rest upon the most slender foundations. No monuments, remains, or inscriptions have yet been discovered in Assyria, which can be assigned to them, or to the time in which they are believed to have lived; and the earliest mention of a royal name which corresponds with one of the three borne by these primitive kings is found in a tablet belonging, it is conjectured, to the 11th century B.C.

One other name, which has been conjecturally assigned to this early period, exists on a fragment of a tablet containing a genealogical list.§ We then come to the names of six kings, who appear to have followed in direct succession from father to son, and who are supposed to have reigned be-

---

* A short account of the history of cuneiform decipherment will be found in the introduction to this volume.

† For a complete resumé of the results of the labours of the Assyrian decipherers, see the Rev. G. Rawlinson's 'Ancient Monarchies,' chap. ix. vol. ii., which contains, it is presumed, the last views of his brother, Sir H. Rawlinson, on the subject of Assyrian history and chronology, as derived from the inscriptions.

‡ Sir H. Rawlinson calls them Asshur-bel-nisr, Nuzur-Asshur, and Asshur-Vatila.

§ Sir H. Rawlinson reads the name 'Bel-sumili-Kapi: M. Oppert, Bel-kat-irassu.

tween 1350 and 1230 B.C. These names are found on inscribed bricks from Kalah Sherghat, on tablets containing genealogical lists, and in inscriptions belonging to kings of a much later date. To the fourth king of this dynasty, whose name is believed to correspond with the biblical Shalmaneser, although he reigned some centuries before that monarch, Sir H. Rawlinson attributes the foundation of Calah, which is supposed to be the name of the city marked by the ruins of Nimroud. He appears to have been a warlike ruler, to have conquered distant provinces, and to have built new cities. His son, whose name is read by Sir H. Rawlinson, Tiglathi-Nisr, or Tiglath-Ussur, and, by M. Oppert, Tuklat-pal-assar, corresponding with that of the biblical Tiklath Pileser, calls himself 'Conqueror of Babylon.' Of these six kings no monument has been discovered in Assyria.

After an interval, to which no royal name yet discovered can be assigned, we find another list of six kings in direct succession. They are believed to belong to a new dynasty which established itself on the Assyrian throne. Their names are found on clay tablets and cylinders, and one of them, Tiglath Pileser II., has left a sculptured monument, consisting of his effigy and an inscription, in a cavern, from which issues one of the sources of the eastern branch of the Tigris.* The date of this king's reign, if the cuneiform inscriptions are rightly interpreted, may be approximately if not accurately fixed, and enables us for the first time to tread with some certainty the treacherous ground of Assyrian chronology. Sennacherib, in one of the inscriptions discovered at Bavian,† declares that he recovered from Babylon certain images of the gods, which had been captured 418 years previously by a king of that city from Tiglath Pileser. As the Bavian tablets are supposed to have been carved by Sennacherib in the 10th year of his reign, or about B.C. 694, if a correct computation of time were kept

---

* This tablet was discovered by Mr. John Taylor, H. M. consul at Diarbekr. His attention had been directed to it by Sir H. Rawlinson, who had found mention of it in an inscription of Sardanapalus, the founder of the north-west palace at Nimroud; an important proof of the general accuracy of the interpretation of the cuneiform character.

† See ante, p. 71.

by the Assyrians, and there is every reason to believe, from the various chronological tables that have been preserved to us, that such was the case. Tiglath Pileser must have been on the throne about the year 1112 B.C.

This king is also the first of whose reign we have any detailed annals. They are preserved on three clay cylinders discovered at Kalah Sherghat, and on some fragments of tablets, and are those mentioned in the introduction to this volume, as having been submitted to the independent decipherment of the four principal interpreters of the cuneiform character. He appears, from these records, to have carried his arms into the mountainous countries to the north and west of Assyria, to have conquered and rendered tributary to Assyria several nations between the river Euphrates and the Mediterranean Sea, and to have successfully invaded Babylonia. • In his annals he also celebrates his prowess as a hunter, and describes the number of lions, wild bulls, and other savage animals which he slew; and records the building and repair of various temples to the gods,* giving details as to their mode of construction and of the materials used, which can only be translated conjecturally.

Of the son of Tiglath Pileser† we have no records, and there is apparently the lapse of more than a century and a half during which, with the exception of the names of two kings, supposed to have lived about this time,‡ we have no materials whatever for Assyrian history. About 930 B.C. a king ascended the throne, who transmitted it in direct descent through six generations. Amongst his descendants and successors were the two great Assyrian conquerors, who built the north-west and centre palaces at Nimroud. The names of the kings of this dynasty and the proof of their descent are found in an important canon, inscribed on a clay tablet, and in the inscriptions on slabs of alabaster and stone, and on bricks discovered in various ruins in Assyria. Of the first

* One of these temples is said, in an inscription, to have been founded 641 years before by a king of Assyria, or highpriest of Asshur, who would consequently have reigned between 1800 and 1700 B.C.
† His name is read Asshur-bel-kala.
‡ The names are read Asshur-mazur and Asshur-iddin-akhi (Rawlinson).

three we have no monuments nor records;* of the fourth we have the fullest annals. His name has been read variously as Asshur-idanni-pal and Asshur-izzar-pal by Sir H. Rawlinson, Asshur-yuzhur-bal by Dr. Hincks, Asshur-akh-bal by Mr. Fox Talbot, and Assur-idanna-palla by M. Oppert; and it has been identified, as I have before stated, with that of Sardanapalus, which is evidently a Greek corruption or form of an Assyrian word. He is believed to have reigned twenty-five years, and, by some, to have been one of the kings of this name mentioned in classic history.

In the course of this work the great palaces and temples which he built, and the elaborate inscriptions which he set up to commemorate his wars and the extent of his empire, have been fully described. It is difficult to say how far his conquests were carried to the north and east of Assyria, as we cannot identify, with any certainty, the names of the numerous countries, districts, and cities which occur in the inscriptions; but it is probable that he penetrated far into Media, Armenia, and Asia Minor. He seems to have reduced the whole of northern Mesopotamia under his sway, and to have crossed the Euphrates into Syria, receiving tribute from, if not actually capturing, the cities of the Phoenician coast of the Mediterranean. He was no less great in the chase than in war; and he has recorded in his inscriptions, and has celebrated on the sculptured walls of his palace, his contests with lions, wild bulls, and other animals.† It would further appear from the inscriptions, that he constructed parks or preserves at Nineveh, in which wild beasts were kept,

---

* Their names, according to Sir H. Rawlinson, were Asshur-danan-il, Iva-lash (or Vul-lush or Yama-zala-khush), and Tiglathi-Nin (or Tiglathi-Ninip, or Tiglath-Ussur); according to M. Oppert, Assur-idil-il, Hulikh-Khus, and Tuklat-pal-asar. Dr. Hincks reads the third name 'Shimish-bar.' The last two names occur with that of Asshur-idanni-pal (Sardanapalus) on the bricks and slabs from the north-west palace at Nimroud.

† According to Sir Henry Rawlinson, amongst these animals were wild sheep, red deer, fallow deer, wild goats or ibexes, leopards, bears, wolves, jackals, wild boars, foxes, hyænas, wild asses, ostriches, &c. The list of them is found on the obelisk of white limestone discovered by Mr. H. Rassam, and now in the British Museum.

probably for the chase; amongst them the elephant is supposed to be mentioned.

Sardanapalus I. was succeeded by his son, whose name is read Shalmaneser by Sir H. Rawlinson, and Divanu-Bara by Dr. Hincks. Of this king we have the fullest records, inscribed on the black obelisk, on the winged bulls discovered in the centre palace at Nimroud, and on various monuments and tablets from different Assyrian ruins. He seems to have reigned for thirty-five years, and to have commanded in person no less than twenty-three military expeditions. The countries which he reduced, and from which he enforced the payment of tribute, appear to have included the whole of Chaldæa and Babylonia down to the Persian Gulf, Syria, Phœnicia, northern Mesopotamia, parts of Asia Minor and Armenia, of Media, and even, it is believed, of Persia. The nature of the objects brought to him by his tributaries show the extent of his dominions.* Two of his campaigns were directed against Khazail (Hazael), king of Damascus,† and amongst his tributaries is mentioned 'Jehu, the son of Khumri' (Omri). This monarch was not, as we know, the son, although one of the successors of Omri; but the term 'son of' was no doubt used in those days, as it still is in the East, to denote close connection between two persons, either by descent or succession. Thus we find in Scripture the same person called 'the son of Nimshi' and 'the son of Jehoshaphat, the son of Nimshi.'‡ The capital city of Jehu is called Samaria, and this name appears to be interchangeable in the inscriptions with Beth-Omri, or the house of Omri, so called, according to a common Eastern custom, after its founder.§ This fact, the discovery of which we owe to the late Dr. Hincks, furnishes a striking proof of the correctness of the interpretation of the cuneiform character. Mr. George Smith, whilst calendaring the Assyrian tablets

---

* See 'Nineveh and its Remains,' p. 245. They include the elephant and rhinoceros.
† 1 Kings, xix. 15
‡ Compare 1 Kings, xx. 16 and 2 Kings, ix. 2.
§ Omri 'bought the hill Samaria of Shamar, for two talents of silver, and built on the hill, and called the name of the city which he built after Shamar, owner of the hill, Samaria.' (1 Kings, xvi. 24.)

in the British Museum, has recently found a short inscription, in which it is stated that Shalmaneser received Jehu's tribute in the eighteenth year of his reign, which enables us to fix the date of this event at about 840 B.C.*

Shalmaneser's son, whose name has been read by Sir H. Rawlinson as Shamash-Vul, Shamsi-Yama, and Shamas-Iva, by Dr. Hincks as Shamsi-Yav, and by M. Oppert as Samsi-Hu, is supposed to have reigned fourteen years. He raised a stele, or arched tablet, similar to that of Sardanapalus, at Nimroud. It bears his image and an inscription, in a somewhat complicated form of cuneiform writing, containing the annals of the first four years of his reign.† He warred with the country to the north and west of Assyria and with Babylonia, whose king he totally defeated, apparently reducing his country to the position of a dependency on the Assyrian empire.

Of the son and successor of this king‡ we have one or two detached slabs§ and two statues with dedicatory inscriptions to Nebo, found at Nimroud; and his name occurs on a brick from the mound of Nebbi Yunus. He appears to have captured the city of Damascus, to have exacted the usual tribute from Tyre, Sidon, and the cities on the Phœnician coast, and from Khumri (Samaria), Palestine, and Edom (written 'Hudum' in the cuneiform character). The Medes and Persians were also subject to him, and he may have reigned over Babylon.‖ His wife seems to have borne a name which corresponds with that of the classical Semiramis,¶ with whom, according to some, she is to be iden-

---

* Athenæum for Sept. 29, 1866. The passage runs thus:—'In my eighteenth year, the sixteenth time, the river Euphrates I crossed. Hazael of Syria put confidence in his army to oppose me: his numerous soldiers he gathered together; Sanirusitsi (?) in the mountains of Lebanon he made his stronghold. With him I fought, and defeated him. 16,000 of his warriors were slain. I took his spoil, 1131 chariots, 470 horsemen, and his camp, which he abandoned, and fled away. At that time, the tribute of Yahua (Jehu), the son of Khumri, I received.'

† This stele is now in the British Museum.
‡ Iva-lush, or Ku-likh-khus, IV.
§ Nineveh and its Remains, p. 273.
‖ Mr. Fox Talbot (Journal of the Asiatic Society, vol. xix. p. 182).
¶ 'Sammuramit,' see Introduction.

tified. He was the builder of the upper chambers at Nimroud, described in the narrative of my first expedition.* From a brick bearing his name, found in the mound of Nebbi Yunus, he appears to have raised a palace or temple there, but no remains of that building have as yet been discovered.

Three kings are mentioned in the fragments of the canon discovered at Kouyunjik as reigning after Iva-lush IV., of whom no annals nor monuments have been preserved.† The next monarch of whom we have any sculptured records and buildings was Tiglath-Pileser, the third king of that name, who is known to us as having carried into captivity a part of the Jewish tribes.‡ He reigned, according to the Assyrian canon, eighteen years. He added to Shalmaneser's palace in the centre of the mound, and built a new palace for himself at its north-eastern corner. Both buildings appear to have been destroyed by Esar-haddon, who used the materials for the construction of his own dwelling-place, of which the remains were discovered in the south-west corner of the Nimroud Mound. Above the ruins of Tiglath Pileser's palace in the south-east corner, which appears to have been an edifice of some magnificence, one of his successors, a hundred years afterwards, erected a new royal residence. A large number of bas-reliefs, taken from their original places, some heaped up ready for removal, others built into the walls of the south-west palace, were discovered at Nimroud.§ On one of them, representing war-chariots following the king, is an inscription in which Dr. Hincks detected the name of Menahem, king of Israel, who is mentioned amongst other princes paying tribute to Tiglath Pileser in the eighth year of his reign.‖

* Nineveh and its Remains, p. 272.
† Their names, according to Sir H. Rawlinson, were Shalman-ussur (the 3rd), Asshur-danin-il (the 2nd), and Asshur-zala-Khus.
‡ 1 Chron. v. 26, 2 Kings, xv. 29. Of the name of Pul, king of Assyria, who is mentioned in Chronicles and in 2 Kings (xv. 19, 29), as having carried away the Jews, no trace has hitherto been found in the cuneiform inscriptions. This fact has led to the conjecture that he was identical with Tiglath Pileser. The arguments for and against this identification are stated in Rawlinson's 'Ancient Monarchies,' vol. ii. 386-389.
§ See 'Nineveh and its Remains,' p. 275.
‖ This very important and interesting discovery was first announced by Dr. Hincks in the 'Athenæum' for January 3, 1852.

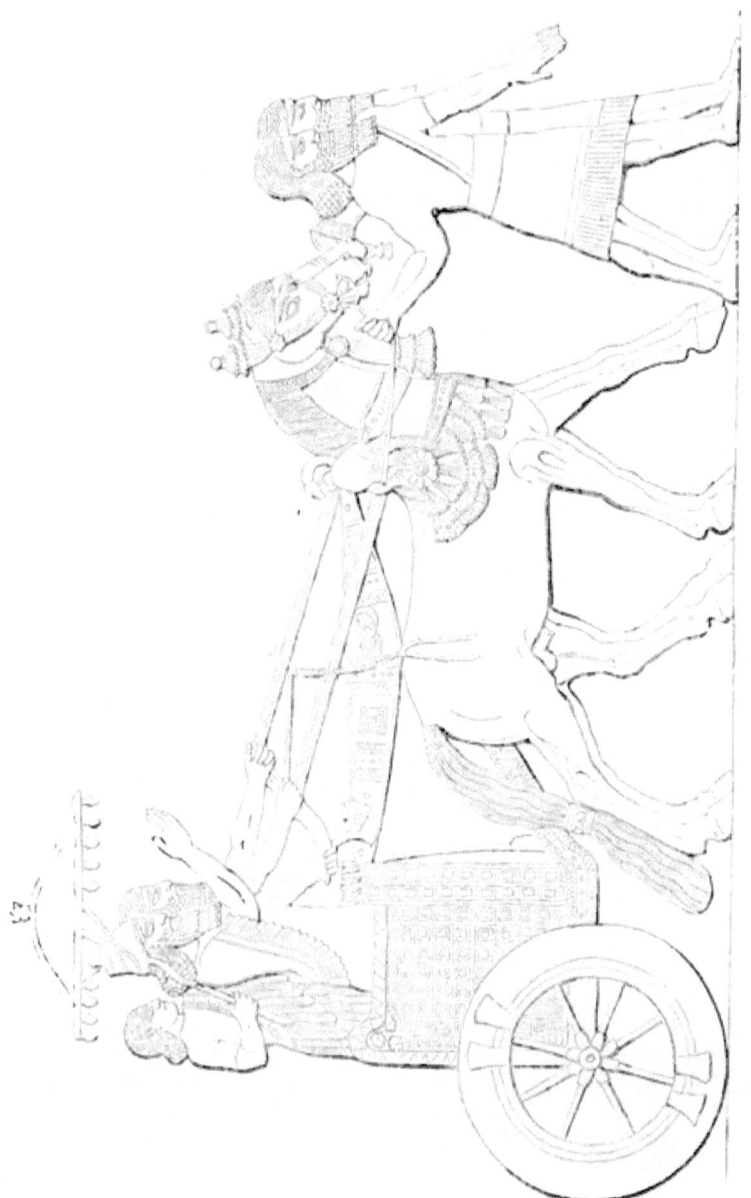

Bas-relief, representing Pul, or Tig'ath Pileser. Nimroud.

Unfortunately the fragmentary state of the monuments and bas-reliefs of this king prevents the restoration, in a complete shape, of his annals. He appears, in the first year of his reign, to have carried his arms into Babylonia and Chaldæa, where he received the submission of a king bearing the familiar biblical name of Merodach Baladan.* It cannot be ascertained clearly from the inscriptions, in what year of his reign he undertook his expedition into Syria and Palestine. It has been conjectured that it was in the fourth. He subdued Samaria (in which Menahem reigned), Damascus, Tyre (whose king bore the name of Hiram), and, apparently, some of the Arab tribes inhabiting Arabia Petræa and the Sinaitic peninsula, who were ruled by a queen. His campaign against Pekah, king of Israel, described in the Second Book of Kings,† during which he captured several Jewish cities, and carried their inhabitants into captivity, probably took place some years later, but no distinct mention of it has yet been found in the inscriptions.

From the various fragments found at Nimroud, some scattered notices of the further campaigns of this king in Syria and Palestine may be recovered,‡ but they cannot as yet be placed in chronological order. Several names of places and persons, familiar to us from their mention in Scripture, may be detected in them, such as Rezin (?), Pekah (?), Magidu (Megiddo), Duru (Dor), and Yahu-Khazi (?), king of Judah, believed to be Ahaz. He also warred against the countries to the north of Assyria.

The mention in the inscriptions of the wars of Tiglath Pileser with the Jews enables us to fix the date of his reign at about 744 to 726 B.C.

Tiglath Pileser is supposed to have been succeeded by Shalmaneser, who warred against Hosea, king of Israel, and captured Samaria,§ but no mention of him has yet been

---

* 2 Kings, xx. 12 (where he is called *Berodach*-Baladan), 1 Isaiah, xxxix. 1.

† Ch. xv. 29.

‡ In the 'Athenæum' of August 22, 1863 (No. 1869, p. 245), will be found some valuable notices of the reign of this king, of Sargon, and of other Assyrian monarchs, by Sir H. Rawlinson.

§ 2 Kings, xvii.

found in the Assyrian inscriptions. It has consequently been suggested, either that he was an usurper, of whom the traces have been destroyed, or that he was identical with Sargon.*

The next king of whom we have monuments and contemporary annals was Sar-kin, or Sargin, the Sargon of Scripture, the builder of the palace at Khorsabad, discovered by M. Botta, and the sculptures from which form the principal part of the Assyrian collection now in the Louvre. This king is believed to have been an usurper, and to have founded a new dynasty, as no mention is made in the inscriptions, according to the usual custom of the Assyrians, of his father. The Khorsabad monuments, and the various tablets on gold, silver, and other materials, and the clay cylinders discovered in the ruins, furnish us with fifteen or sixteen years of the annals of his reign. His first campaign was against the Susianians, or Elamites. He then turned his arms against Samaria, subdued the city, over which he placed an Assyrian governor, and carried away 27,280 (or 24,000) of the inhabitants as captives into Assyria. He next overthrew and put to death a king of Hamath, named Yahu-bid, or Ilu-bid (?). Having conquered Syria and Palestine, he appears to have marched to the borders of Egypt, where he encountered the united armies of the Philistines and of an Egyptian prince, whose name is read 'Shebek' (Sabaco?), and whose title appears to be 'Sultan' of Egypt. He defeated them, capturing the king of Gaza. His next great campaign was against the tribes of Arabia, during which he penetrated into a part of that country which had not before been subdued by the Assyrian kings, and carried away some of its inhabitants to Nineveh. The result of this successful expedition appears to have been the submission of a Pharaoh (king of Egypt), of Ithamar (?) king of the Sabæans, and of Tsamsi (?) queen of the Arabs, who sent tribute and presents to Sargon, amongst which were gold, horses, and camels.

Parts of Syria must have revolted a second time against his rule, for we find Sargon, three years after his successful

* The Rev. G. Rawlinson, 'Ancient Monarchies,' vol. ii. p. 401.

campaign against Arabia, besieging and capturing Ashdod.*
He thence marched against Egypt, whose king, Shebek, appears to have aided the king of Ashdod. If the inscriptions are rightly interpreted, not only did this monarch send an embassy to Assyria, but even the king of Meroe, or Ethiopia, who had never before submitted to an Assyrian ruler, humbled himself before Sargon.

Successful wars against Susiana and Babylonia followed. Merodach Baladan, the king of the latter country, was defeated, and carried captive to Nineveh, and his palace plundered and capital burnt. At Babylon, Sargon received embassies from a country 'in the middle of the sea of the rising sun,' supposed to be some island in the Persian Gulf, of whom the kings of Assyria had never before even heard the name; and, on his return to Nineveh, from seven kings of the island of Cyprus, which is described as being 'at the distance of seven days from the coast in the sea of the setting sun.' Striking evidence of the correctness of the interpretation of the cuneiform inscriptions is furnished by the actual discovery of a stele with the effigy of Sargon, and an inscription containing his name and titles, on the site of the ancient Idalium in Cyprus.† Whether Sargon himself ever visited the island, or whether its inhabitants consented to erect this stele as a proof of their submission to the king of Assyria, does not appear from the inscriptions.

Sargon did not confine his expeditions to the countries to the south and west of Assyria: he also subdued many nations and tribes to the north and east, in the mountainous countries of Asia Minor, Armenia, Media, and Persia. Full details of his wars in those regions, and of the various kingdoms, provinces, and cities which were included in his vast dominions, are contained in the inscriptions, but with one or two exceptions the identification of the geographical names is more than doubtful.

---

* This was probably the campaign alluded to in Isaiah (xx. 1), where alone, in the Old Testament, Sargon is mentioned by name.
† This highly interesting and important monument is now in the museum at Berlin. It is similar in shape to the stele of Sardanapalus, discovered at Nimroud. See ante, p. 178.

The principal edifice erected by Sargon was his palace at Khorsabad, the ruins of which bore his name even long after the Arab occupation of Assyria.* He rebuilt, according to the inscriptions, the walls of Nineveh, and erected in the city a temple to Nebo; and we learn from an inscription carved on the walls of a chamber in Sardanapalus's palace at Nimroud,† that he added to and repaired that building.‡ He also declares that he restored the great sanctuaries of Sippara, Nipours, Babylon, and Borsippa.

Sargon was succeeded by his son Sennacherib, whose name in the Assyrian inscriptions is to be read, according to Sir H. Rawlinson, Sin-akhi-erba; according to Dr. Hincks, Tsin-a skhirib; and, according to M. Oppert, Sin-akh-arib. I have described, in the preceding pages, the magnificent monuments which he raised, and have given a short account of the principal events of his reign, as contained in his annals.§ He built from its foundations the splendid palace at Kouyunjik, and the walls and gates of the great inclosure in which that edifice stood. According to the inscriptions he restored the ancient dwelling-place of the Assyrian kings at Nineveh, supposed to have stood on the mound of Nebbi Yunus. He erected a temple, dedicated to Nergal, at Tarbisi (Shereef Khan), of which the ruins have been discovered;|| constructed canals, aqueducts, embankments, and other great public works; and, according to the Bavian tablets, brought supplies of drinking water in pipes to Nineveh. His records contain a full account of the mode of construction of his palaces, the materials employed, from whence they were brought, and the various nations, captives taken during his wars, employed in the work. We have abundant materials for the history of Sennacherib in the

---

* Yakuti, the Arab geographer, calls the place Saroun, or Saraghoun. See 'Nineveh and its Remains,' p. 113.

† See 'Nineveh and its Remains,' p. 271. This inscription contains the name of Judæa (Iahouda).

‡ The annals of Sargon have been translated at full length by M. Oppert: 'Les Inscriptions Assyriennes des Sargonides et les Fastes de Ninive,' first published in 'Annals de Philosophie Chrétienne,' vol. vi. 5th series.

§ Chap. ii. || See ante, p. 342.

inscriptions on the walls of his palace, on detached slabs, on cylinders and tablets of clay, and on the monuments carved by him on the rocks at Bavian, at the mouth of the Nahr el Kelb in Syria, and in other parts of his vast dominions. He appears to have reigned about 24 years (from 704 to 680 B.C.), and was succeeded by his son Esar-haddon.

The name of this king is written in the cuneiform character, Asshur-akh-iddina, or Asshur-akh-idin. The principal materials for the history of his reign are found on two clay cylinders, now in the British Museum, the inscriptions on which contain the description of nine of his campaigns. His first war appears to have been against the cities of Phœnicia, and he crossed the sea to Cyprus, where he captured the king of Sidon who had fled thither. He destroyed the cities of the coast, and brought their inhabitants captives to Assyria. Like his predecessors, he carried his arms into Cilicia, and the mountainous country to the north and north-west of Assyria; and it is believed that the name of a tribe which he conquered can be identified with the Cimmerians, who would thus appear for the first time in history. Successful expeditions into Chaldæa, Babylonia, and Edom occupied a considerable part of his reign; and he appears to have even crossed the desert, and to have led an army in person into the almost inaccessible regions of Arabia.

Esar-haddon, in the annals of his son, is described as the conqueror of Egypt and Ethiopia, where Tirhakah then reigned, and he adds the title of 'King of the kings of Egypt, and conqueror of Ethiopia,' to those usually borne by the Assyrian monarchs; but of his campaigns in those countries, and of his wars against Manasseh, king of Judah, whom he captured and carried in chains to Babylon,[*] no mention has yet been found in any inscription. Esar-haddon's annals appear to give a full account of the various palaces and temples which he built, and of the materials, including precious metals and woods, which he employed in their construction; but we are not yet sufficiently acquainted with the reading and meaning of the architectural and other

---

[*] 2 Chron. xxxiii.

technical terms used in the Assyrian inscriptions to be able to translate these descriptions satisfactorily. We know that the south-west palace at Nimroud was built by him out of materials taken from edifices raised by former kings; and that the ruins of one of his palaces exist in the mound of Nebbi Yunus and at Shereef Khan. He also appears to have erected a royal residence at Babylon, of which no traces have hitherto been found.

Esar-haddon was succeeded, apparently after a reign of about thirteen years, by his son, Asshur-bani-pal, whose conquests appear to identify him with that Sardanapalus, the son of Anacyndaraxes, whose tomb at Tarsus and its inscription have been so frequently described and commented upon by ancient classic writers.* Of the principal events of his reign we have abundant illustrations in the sculptures and inscriptions from the palace which he built at Kouyunjik, and the ruins of which were discovered after my departure from Mosul by Mr. Hormuzd Rassam. He appears to have reduced to the condition of Assyrian provinces almost the whole of Egypt and Ethiopia, and to have carried off from those countries a vast treasure by way of booty. The name of Gyges, king of Lydia, is believed to have been found in his inscriptions, as also an account of his wars with the Cimmerians, who, according to Herodotus, invaded Lydia about this time. His campaigns in Susiana, or Elam, are recorded in the sculptures which he placed in the Palace of Sennacherib at Kouyunjik, and which have been described in a former part of this volume.† Like the early Nimroud king, who bore a name very similar, he was a great hunter, and his

---

* Several versions have been given of this celebrated inscription. The one generally received is the following:—'Sardanapalus, son of Anacyndaraxes, built Tarsus and Anchiale in one day. Do thou, O stranger, eat and drink, and amuse thyself; for all the rest of human life is not worth so much as *this*'—the king being represented in the act of snapping his fingers. Mr. Rawlinson ('Ancient Monarchies,' vol. ii. p. 501) has conjectured, and I am inclined to agree with him, that the tomb was really a stele, containing the usual effigy of the king in an arched frame, similar to that found at Nimroud (see p. 178); and that the raised hand suggested the idea that he was represented as snapping his fingers.

† See chap. x.

exploits in the chase, especially against the lion, were celebrated in elaborate and spirited bas-reliefs on the walls of his palace. Of his reign we have a vast collection of clay tablets, containing inscriptions of great interest, importance, and variety, discovered in the chamber of records and elsewhere at Kouyunjik."*

The son and successor of Asshur-bani-pal is the last Assyrian king of whom we find any mention amongst the remains discovered at Nineveh; and there is every reason to believe that with him ended the Assyrian empire, and the very existence of its great capital. We have no sculptures nor records that can be attributed to his reign, and his name only occurs on bricks discovered in the ruins of the south-east palace, which he appears to have rebuilt. It is believed to read Asshur-emid-ilin, or Asshur-kinat-ill-kain, according to Sir H. Rawlinson; or Asshur-idil-il, according to M. Oppert; and he had two predecessors of the same name.† He may perhaps be identified with the Saracus of the Greeks, or with that Sardanapalus whose inglorious reign terminated (B.C. 606) with the capture and destruction of Nineveh by the Medes, and his own self-immolation amidst the flames of his burning palace.‡

As I have thus given a general sketch of the contents of the inscriptions discovered in the Assyrian ruins, it may not be out of place to make a few observations upon the nature of the Assyrian records, and their importance to the study of Scripture and profane history. In the first place, the care with which the events of each king's reign were chronicled is worthy of remark. They were usually written, as we have seen, in the form of regular annals; and in some cases, as on the great monoliths at Nimroud, the royal progress during a campaign appears to be described almost

---

* See chap. vii.

† According to M. Oppert, there were seven Assyrian kings who bore names corresponding with the Greek Sardanapalus. The last of the name reigned from B.C. 625 to 606.

‡ In one of the inscriptions of Sargon he is supposed to declare that 'about 350 kings reigned before him in Assyria.' (Oppert, 'Inscriptions des Sargonides,' p. 37.) As it has been seen, the names of only 29 have been found in the inscriptions.

day by day. They are, in some respects, not unlike the historical books of the Jews. There is, however, this marked difference between them, that whilst the Assyrian records are nothing but a dry narrative, or rather register, of military campaigns, spoliations, and cruelties, events of little importance but to those immediately concerned in them, the historical books of the Old Testament, apart from the deeds of war and blood which they chronicle, contain the most interesting of private episodes, and the most sublime of moral lessons. It may, however, be objected, that these Assyrian inscriptions being merely records of national events, such as at this day might be placed upon public monuments, did not admit of any irrelevant reflections, or of the details and incidents of private life; but that the Hebrew books being more strictly a connected and written history, the author could draw his own inferences, and point out to his readers the moral of his story. The Assyrians, it may be added, might have had similar volumes, which have long since perished. This conjecture is partly confirmed by the discovery of more private documents, such as the clay cylinders and tablets described in the preceding pages.

The monuments of Nineveh, as well as the testimony of history, tend to prove that the Assyrian monarch was a thorough Eastern despot, unchecked by popular opinion, and having complete power over the lives and property of his subjects—rather adored as a god than feared as a man, and yet himself claiming his authority and the absolute obedience of his people in virtue of his reverence for the national deities and the national religion. It was only when the gods themselves seemed to interpose that any check was placed upon the royal pride and lust; and it is probable that when Jonah entered Nineveh crying to the people to repent, the king, believing him to be a special minister from the supreme deity of the nation, 'arose from his throne, and laid his robe from him, and covered him with sackcloth, and sat in ashes.'*

* It was not necessary to the effect of his preaching that Jonah should be of the religion of the people of Nineveh. I have known a Christian priest frighten a whole Mussulman town to tents and repentance by publicly proclaiming that he had received a divine mission to announce a coming earthquake or plague.

The Hebrew state, on the contrary, was, to a certain extent, a limited monarchy. The Jewish kings were amenable to, and even guided by, the opinion of their subjects. The prophets boldly upbraided and threatened them; their warnings and menaces were usually received with respect and fear. 'Good is the word of the Lord which thou hast spoken,' exclaimed Hezekiah to Isaiah, when the prophet reproved him for his pride, and foretold the captivity of his sons and the destruction of his kingdom;* a prophecy which none would have dared utter in the presence of the Assyrian king, except, as it would appear by the story of Jonah, he were a stranger. It can scarcely, therefore, be expected that any history other than bare chronicles of the victories and triumphs of the kings, omitting all allusion to their reverses and defeats, could be found on the public monuments of Assyria.

It is remarkable that the Assyrian records should, on the whole, be so free from the exaggerated forms of expression, and the magniloquent royal titles, which are found in Egyptian documents of the same nature, and even in those of modern Eastern sovereigns. Internal evidence proves their truthfulness so far as they go. We are further led to place confidence in them by the very minuteness with which they even give the amount of the spoil; the registrars, 'the scribes of the host,' as they are called in the Bible :† being constantly seen in the bas-reliefs, writing down the various objects brought to them by the victorious warriors,—the heads of the slain, the prisoners, the cattle, the sheep,‡ the furniture, and the vessels of metal.

The next reflection arising from an examination of the Assyrian records relates to the political condition and constitution of the empire, which appear to have been of a very peculiar nature. The king, we may infer, exercised but little

---

* 2 Kings, xx. 19. † 2 Kings, xxv. 19.

‡ Driving away the cattle and sheep of a conquered people, and accounting them amongst the principal spoil, has ever been the custom of Eastern nations who have not altogether renounced a nomadic life, and whose chief wealth consequently consists in these animals. When Asa defeated the Ethiopians, 'he carried away sheep and camels in abundance, and returned to Jerusalem.' (2 Chron. xiv. 15.)

direct authority beyond the districts in the immediate neighbourhood of Nineveh, although he was constantly carrying his arms into the surrounding countries. The Assyrian dominions, as far as we can yet learn from the inscriptions, did not at any time extend much further than the central provinces of Asia Minor and Armenia to the north, not reaching to the Black Sea, though probably to the Caspian. To the east they occasionally included Media and the western provinces of Persia; to the south, Susiana, Babylonia, and the northern part of Arabia. To the west the Assyrians may have penetrated into Lycia, and perhaps Lydia; and Syria and Palestine were considered within the territories of the great king; Egypt and Meroe (Æthiopia) were the farthest limits reached by the Assyrian armies. According to Greek authors, however, a much greater extent must be assigned to Assyrian influence, if not to the Assyrian empire; and we may hereafter find that such was in fact the case. I am here merely referring to the evidence afforded by actual records as far as they may be assumed to have been deciphered.

The empire appears to have consisted of a number of tributary states, whose kings were so far independent that they were only bound to furnish troops to their supreme lord in time of war, and to pay him yearly a certain tribute. Hence we find successive Assyrian kings fighting with exactly the same nations and tribes, some of which were scarcely more than four or five days' march from the gates of Nineveh. On the occasion of every change at the capital, these tributary states seem to have striven to throw off the Assyrian yoke, and to have begun by refusing to pay their customary tribute. A new campaign was consequently necessary to bring them to obedience. We learn from the inscriptions, that when a city or kingdom was thus subdued, however near it might have been to Nineveh, when not actually forming a part of the imperial district, a new ruler was appointed to it with the title of 'King,' written in the same cuneiform characters on the monuments as when applied to the head of the empire.* Hence, too, the Assyrian armies, like those of Xerxes described by Herodotus,† were made up of various nations, retaining their own costumes, arms, and modes of warfare.

The Jewish tribes, as it had long been suspected by biblical scholars, can now be proved to have been tributaries to the Assyrian king, from a very early period, indeed long before the time inferred by any passage in Scripture. Whenever an expedition against the kings of Judah or Israel is mentioned in the Assyrian records, it is stated to have been undertaken on the ground that they had not paid their customary tribute.‡

The political state of the Jewish kingdom under Solomon appears to have been very nearly the same as that of the Assyrian empire. The scriptural account of the power of the Hebrew king resembles, almost word for word, some of the paragraphs in the great inscriptions at Nimroud. 'Solomon reigned over the kingdoms from the river unto the land of the Philistines, and unto the border of Egypt: they brought presents and served Solomon all the days of his life. . . . . He had dominion over all the region on this side the river, from Tipsah even unto the Azzah, *over all the kings* on this side the river.'§

The political condition of Assyria can only be compared in modern times with that of India, when the peninsula was divided into numerous distinct sovereignties under a nominal dependence on the emperor of Delhi as the head of the

---

* This fact illustrates the passage in Isaiah (x. 8, 9), 'For he saith, *Are not my princes altogether kings?* Is not Calno as Carchemish? Is not Hamath as Arpad? Is not Samaria as Damascus?'

† Lib. vii.

‡ The same thing may, indeed, be inferred from several passages in Chronicles and Kings. See particularly 2 Kings, xvi. 7, xvii. 4. In the cuneiform inscriptions, Judæa is called 'Iahouda,' and Israel 'Beth Khumri,' or House of Omri, a name also given to Samaria, the capital.

§ 1 Kings, iv. 21 and 24. '*He reigned over all the kings* from the river even unto the land of the Philistines and to the border of Egypt;' and the kings 'brought him every man his present, vessels of silver, and vessels of gold, and raiment, harness, and spices, horses and mules, a rate year by year.' (2 Chron. ix. 24, 26.) Such were probably the very articles brought yearly to the Assyrian kings, and enumerated in their records.

Mogul dynasty; or to that of Turkey in the last century, when the empire was made up of a number of semi-independent pashalics, governed by hereditary rulers, from whom the Sultan demanded little more than yearly tribute, and a contribution of troops in war, though invested with an absolute power over them of life and death, arising from his mixed political and religious character, sometimes exercised and submitted to in a manner inexplicable to those unacquainted with the Eastern character.

The custom of the Assyrians, so frequently alluded to in the inscriptions, of removing the inhabitants of conquered cities and districts to distant parts of the empire, and of replacing them by colonists from Nineveh, or from other subdued countries, is recorded in the books of the Old Testament. It has been generally inferred that there was but one carrying away, or at the most two, of the people of Samaria, although three, at least, appear to be distinctly alluded to in the Bible; the first, by Pul; the second, by Tiglath-Pileser; the third, by Shalmaneser.* It was not until the time of this last king that Samaria was destroyed as an independent kingdom. On former occasions only the inhabitants of the surrounding towns and villages seem to have been taken as captives. Such we find to have been the case with many other nations, who were subdued or punished for rebellion by the Assyrians. The conquerors, as we also learn from the inscriptions, established the worship of their own gods in the conquered cities, raising altars and temples, and appointing priests for their service. So after the fall of Samaria, the strangers who were placed in its cities, 'made gods of their own and put them in the houses of the high places which the Samaritans had made.'†

The vast number of families thus sent to dwell in distant countries, must have wrought great changes in the physical condition, language, and religion of the people with which they were intermixed. When the Assyrian records are with more certainty interpreted, we may, perhaps, be able to ex-

---
* 1 Chron. v. 6, 26; 2 Kings, xvii. 6, xviii. 11.
† 2 Kings, xvii. 29.

plain many of the anomalies of ancient Eastern philology and comparative geography.

We further gather from the records of the campaigns of the Assyrian kings, that the country, both in Mesopotamia and to the west of the Euphrates, now included in the general term of 'the Desert,' was at that remote period teeming with a dense population both sedentary and nomade; that cities, towns, and villages arose on all sides; and that, consequently, the soil brought forth produce for the support of this great congregation of human beings. It will have been seen from many parts of the foregoing narrative, that there are still traces in these now desolate regions, of their ancient wealth and prosperity. Mounds of earth, covering the ruins of buildings, or the sites of fenced stations and forts, are scattered far and wide over the plains. When the winter rains furrow the face of the land, inscribed stones and gems, broken pottery, and masses of brickwork, the certain signs of former habitations, are everywhere found by the wandering Arab. All those settlements depended almost exclusively upon artificial irrigation. Hence the dry beds of enormous canals and countless watercourses, which are spread like a network over the face of the country. Even the traveller, accustomed to the triumphs of modern science and civilisation, gazes with wonder upon these gigantic works, and reflects with admiration upon the industry, the skill, and the power of those who made them. And may not the waters be again turned into the empty channels, and may not life be again spread over those parched and arid wastes? Upon them no other curse has alighted than that of a false religion and a listless race.

Of the information as to the religious system of the Assyrians which may be derived from the inscriptions, I am still unwilling to treat in the present state of our knowledge of their contents.* It is highly probable that the large collection of clay tablets now in the British Museum may hereafter furnish us with important matter connected with the sub-

---

* All that can be said upon the subject, and the greater part of this is mere guesswork and speculation, may be found in the Rev. G. Rawlinson's 'Ancient Monarchies,' vol. ii. chap. viii.

ject; but a far more intimate acquaintance with the writing and language than we yet possess is required before the translation of such documents can be fully relied on. All we can now venture to infer is, that the Assyrians worshipped one supreme god, as the great national deity under whose immediate and special protection they lived, and their empire existed. The name of this god appears to have been Asshur, who is called the 'father of the gods' in the inscriptions. It was identified with that of the empire itself, always called 'the country of Asshur;' it entered into the names of many kings and private persons, and was also applied to particular cities. This god is typified by the winged figure in the circle. With Asshur, but apparently far inferior to him in the celestial hierarchy, although called the great gods, were associated twelve other deities. Some of them may possibly be identified with the divinities of the Greek Pantheon. They may have presided over the twelve months of the year, and the vast number of still inferior gods, in one inscription, I believe, stated to be no less than 4000, over the days of the year, various phenomena and productions of nature, and the celestial bodies. It is difficult to understand such a system of polytheism, unless we suppose that whilst there was but one supreme god, represented sometimes under a triune form, all the so-called inferior gods were originally mere names for events and outward things, or symbols and myths. Although at one time generally accepted as such even by the common people, their true meaning was only known in a corrupted age to the priests, by whom they were turned into a mystery and a trade. It may, indeed, be inferred from many passages in the Scriptures, that a system of theology not very different from the Assyrian prevailed at times amongst the Jews themselves.

The question as to the space occupied by the city of Nineveh at the time of its greatest prosperity is still far from being set at rest. Some believe the inclosures of Nimroud, Kouyunjik, and Khorsabad, and the small mounds of Shereef-Khan, scarcely three miles from Kouyunjik, as well as others in the immediate neighbourhood, to be the remains of distinct cities. But the supposition that any one of these groups of mounds represents the city of Nineveh can in no way be reconciled with the accounts in Scripture, and in the Greek authors, which so remarkably coincide as to its extent; a difficulty which leads Sir H. Rawlinson to say, that all these ruins 'formed one of that group of cities which, in the time of the prophet Jonah, were known by the common name of Nineveh.'[*] It is indeed true, that, on bricks from different mounds, distinct names appear to be given to each locality, and that those from Kouyunjik are inscribed with the name of Nineveh, whilst those from Nimroud and Khorsabad bear other names which have not yet been satisfactorily deciphered.[†] These names are preceded by a determinative monogram assumed to signify a city, but which undoubtedly also applies to a fort or fortified palace.[‡] Nahum describes Nineveh as a city of many strongholds and gates,[§] and such I believe it to have been, each fort or stronghold having a different name. The most important, as it was the best defended, may at one time have been the palace at Kouyunjik, which being especially called Nineveh, gave its name to the whole city. By no other supposition can we reconcile the united testimony of ancient writers as to the great size of Nineveh with the present remains.

It is very doubtful whether these fortified inclosures contained many buildings besides the royal palaces, and such temples and public edifices as were attached to them. At Nimroud excavations were made in various parts of the inclosed space, and it was carefully examined with a view to ascertain whether any foundations or remains of houses still existed. None were discovered except at the south-eastern

---

[*] On the Inscriptions of Babylonia and Assyria, p. 417.

[†] Col. Rawlinson reads the name of Levkeh or Calah on the bricks from Nimroud, and consequently identifies the ruins with the Calah of Genesis, one of the primitive cities of Assyria; but I cannot believe that the four cities mentioned in the Bible could have stood within so short a distance of each other, particularly as we are told that Resen, 'a great city, was *between* Nineveh and Calah.' (Genesis, x. 12.)

[‡] In like manner one common determinative sign signifies a country, a hill, and a mine. (Dr. Hincks' 'Mem. on the Assyro-Babylonian Phonetic Characters,' note, p. 301; Transactions of the Royal Irish Academy, vol. xxii.) It appears to be also used on some bricks in the same way as the determinative sign described in the text.

[§] Chap. iii. 12-14.

corner, where, as already described,* the height of a mound above the natural level of the soil at once showed the existence of ruins. In some parts of the inclosure the conglomerate rock is almost denuded of earth.

Such is also the case opposite Mosul. The remains of one or two buildings appear to exist within the inclosure containing the mounds of Kouyunjik and Nebbi Yunus; but with these exceptions there are no indications whatever of ancient edifices, and the conglomerate rock is, as at Nimroud, on a level with the surrounding soil.

At Khorsabad, the greater part of the inclosed space is so much *below* the surrounding country, that it is covered with a marsh formed by the small river Khauser, which flows near the ruins. Within the walls, which are scarcely more than a mile square, can only be traced the remains of one or two buildings, and of a propylæum, standing below the platform, and about two hundred yards from the ascent to the palace,† but they are at once perceived by well-defined inequalities in the soil.

After repeated careful examinations of the ruins and of the spaces inclosed by the ramparts of earth, I am still inclined to the opinion that they were royal dwellings with their dependent buildings, and parks or paradises, fortified like the palace-temples of Egypt, capable of standing a prolonged siege, and places of refuge for the inhabitants in case of invasion. They may have been called by different names, but they were all included within the area of that great city known to the Jews and to the Greeks as Nineveh. I will not venture to say that the whole of this vast space was thickly inhabited or built upon. We must not judge of Eastern cities by those of Europe. In Asia, gardens and orchards, containing suburbs and even distinct villages collected round a walled city, are all included by the natives under one general name. Such is the case with Isfahan and Damascus, and such I believe it to have been with ancient Nineveh. It appears to me quite inconsistent with Eastern customs,

---

* P. 54.
† From this propylæum came the two colossal bulls in the British Museum; it was part of the royal palace.

as well as with historic testimony, to place within so short a distance of each other several great and distinct cities. Recent researches have in no way shaken the opinion that I ventured to express in my former work, partly founded upon arguments derived from the fact of each of these separate fortified palaces having been built by different kings.

A few remarks are necessary on the architecture and architectural decorations, external and internal, of the Assyrian palaces. The inscriptions on their walls, especially on those of Kouyunjik and Khorsabad, appear to contain important and even minute details, not only as to their general plan and mode of construction, but even as to the materials employed for their different parts, and for the objects of sculpture and ornaments placed in them.* This fact furnishes another remarkable analogy between the records of the Jewish and the Assyrian kings. To the history of their monarchs and of their nation, the Hebrew chroniclers have added a full account of the building and ornaments of the temple and palaces of Solomon. In both cases, from the use of technical words, we can scarcely hope to understand, with any degree of certainty, all the details. It is impossible to comprehend, by the help of the descriptions alone, the plan or appearance of the temple of Solomon. This arises not only from our being unacquainted with the exact meaning of various Hebrew architectural terms, but also from the difficulty experienced even in ordinary cases, of restoring from mere description an edifice of any kind. In the Assyrian inscriptions we labour, of course, under still greater disadvantages. The language in which they are written is as yet but very imperfectly known, and although we may be able to explain with some confidence the general meaning of the historical paragraphs, yet when we come to technical words relating to architecture, even with a very intimate acquaintance with the Assyrian tongue, we could scarcely hope to ascertain their precise signification. On the other hand, the

* Capt. Jones ('Journal of the Asiatic Society,' vol. xv. p. 326) has calculated that the mound of Kouyunjik contains 14,500,000 tons of earth, and that its construction would have taken 10,000 men for twelve years.

materials, and the general plan of the Assyrian palaces are still preserved, whilst of the great edifices of the Jews, not a fragment of masonry, nor the smallest traces, are probably left to guide us. But, as Mr. Fergusson * has shown, the architecture of the one people may be illustrated by that of the other. With the help of the sacred books, and of the ruins of the palaces of Nineveh, together with those of cotemporary and later remains, as well as from customs still existing in the East, we may, to a certain extent, ascertain the principal architectural features of the buildings of both nations.

Before suggesting a general restoration of the royal edifices of Nineveh, I shall endeavour to point out the analogies which appear to exist between their actual remains and what is recorded of the temple and palaces of Solomon. In the first place, as Sennacherib in his inscriptions declares himself to have done, the Jewish king sent the bearers of burdens and the hewers into the mountains to bring great stones, costly stones, and hewed stones,† to lay the foundations, which were probably artificial platforms, resembling the Assyrian mounds, though constructed of more solid materials. We have the remains of such a terrace or stage of stone masonry, perhaps built by king Solomon himself, at Baalbec. The enormous size of some of the hewn stones in that structure, and of those still remaining in the quarries, some of which are more than sixty feet long, has excited the wonder of modern travellers. The dimensions of the temple of Jerusalem, threescore cubits long,‡ twenty broad, and thirty high, were much smaller than those of the great edifices explored in Assyria. Solomon's own palace, however, appears to have been considerably larger, and to have more nearly approached in its proportions those of the kings of Nineveh, for it was one hundred cubits long, fifty broad, and thirty high. "The

---

* See his highly interesting work, entitled 'The Palaces of Nineveh and Persepolis restored,' to which I have had frequent occasion to refer in the remarks in the text, and to which I take this opportunity of acknowledging my obligations.
† 1 Kings, v. 15.
‡ The Jewish cubit appears to have been about eighteen inches.

porch before the temple,' twenty cubits by ten,* may have been a propylæum, such as was discovered at Khorsabad in front of the palace. The chambers, with the exception of the oracle, were exceedingly small, the largest being only seven cubits broad, 'for without, *in the wall* of the house, he made numerous rests round about, that *the beams* should not be fastened in the walls of the house.' The words in italics are inserted in our version to make good the sense, and may consequently not convey the exact meaning, which may be, that these apartments were thus narrow in order that the beams might be supported without the use of pillars, a reason already suggested for the narrowness of the greater number of chambers in the Assyrian palaces. These smaller rooms appear to have been built round a large central hall called the oracle, the whole arrangement thus corresponding with the courts, halls, and surrounding rooms at Nimroud, Khorsabad, and Kouyunjik. The oracle was twenty cubits square, smaller far in dimensions than the Nineveh halls; but it was twenty cubits *high*—an important fact, illustrative of Assyrian architecture, for as the building itself was thirty cubits in height, the oracle must not only have been much loftier than the adjoining chambers, but must have had an upper structure of ten cubits.† Within it were the two cherubim of olive wood ten cubits high, with wings each five cubits long, 'and he carved all the house around with carved figures of cherubim and palm trees, and open flowers, within and without.' The cherubim have been described by Biblical commentators as mythic figures, uniting the human head with the body of a lion, or an ox, and the wings of an eagle.‡ If for the palm trees we substitute the sacred tree of the Nineveh sculptures, and for the open flowers the Assyrian tulip-shaped ornament—objects most probably very nearly resembling each other—we find that the oracle of the temple was almost

---

* The height, according to 2 Chron. iii. 4, was 120 cubits, which would appear to be an error in the text, although Josephus gives the same dimensions, adding an upper story or structure.

† Mr. Fergusson has pointed out, from the account of Josephus, the probability of the temple having had two stories. (The Palaces of Nineveh restored, p. 222.)

‡ See Calmet's 'Dictionary of the Bible.'

identical, in general form and in its ornaments, with some of the chambers of Nimroud and Khorsabad. In the Assyrian halls, too, the winged human-headed bulls were on the side of the wall, and their wings, like those of the cherubim, 'touched one another in the midst of the house.'* The dimensions of these figures were in some cases nearly the same in the Jewish and Assyrian temples, namely, fifteen feet square. The doors were also carved with cherubim and palm trees, and open flowers; and thus, with the other parts of the building, corresponded with those of the Assyrian palaces. On the walls at Nineveh the only addition appears to have been the introduction of the human form and the image of the king, which were an abomination to the Jews. The pomegranates and lilies of Solomon's temple must have been nearly identical with the usual Assyrian ornament, in which, and particularly at Khorsabad, the pomegranate frequently takes the place of the tulip and the cone.

But the description given by Josephus of the interior of one of Solomon's houses, still more completely corresponds with and illustrates the chambers in the palaces of Nineveh. 'Solomon built some of these (houses) with stones of ten cubits, and wainscoted the walls with other stones that were sawed, and were of great value, such as were dug out of the bowels of the earth, for ornaments of temples, &c. The arrangement of the curious workmanship of these stones was in three rows; but the fourth was pre-eminent for the beauty of its sculpture, for on it were represented trees, and all sorts of plants, with the shadows caused by their branches and the leaves that hung down from them. These trees and plants covered the stone that was beneath them, and their leaves were wrought so wonderfully thin and subtile, that they appeared almost in motion; but the rest of the wall, up to the roof, was plastered over, and, as it were, wrought over with various colours and pictures.'†

To complete the analogy between the two edifices, it would appear that Solomon was seven years building his temple,

---

* See woodcut in the following page.
† Josephus, b. viii. c. 2. Fergusson's 'Palaces of Nineveh,' p. 229.

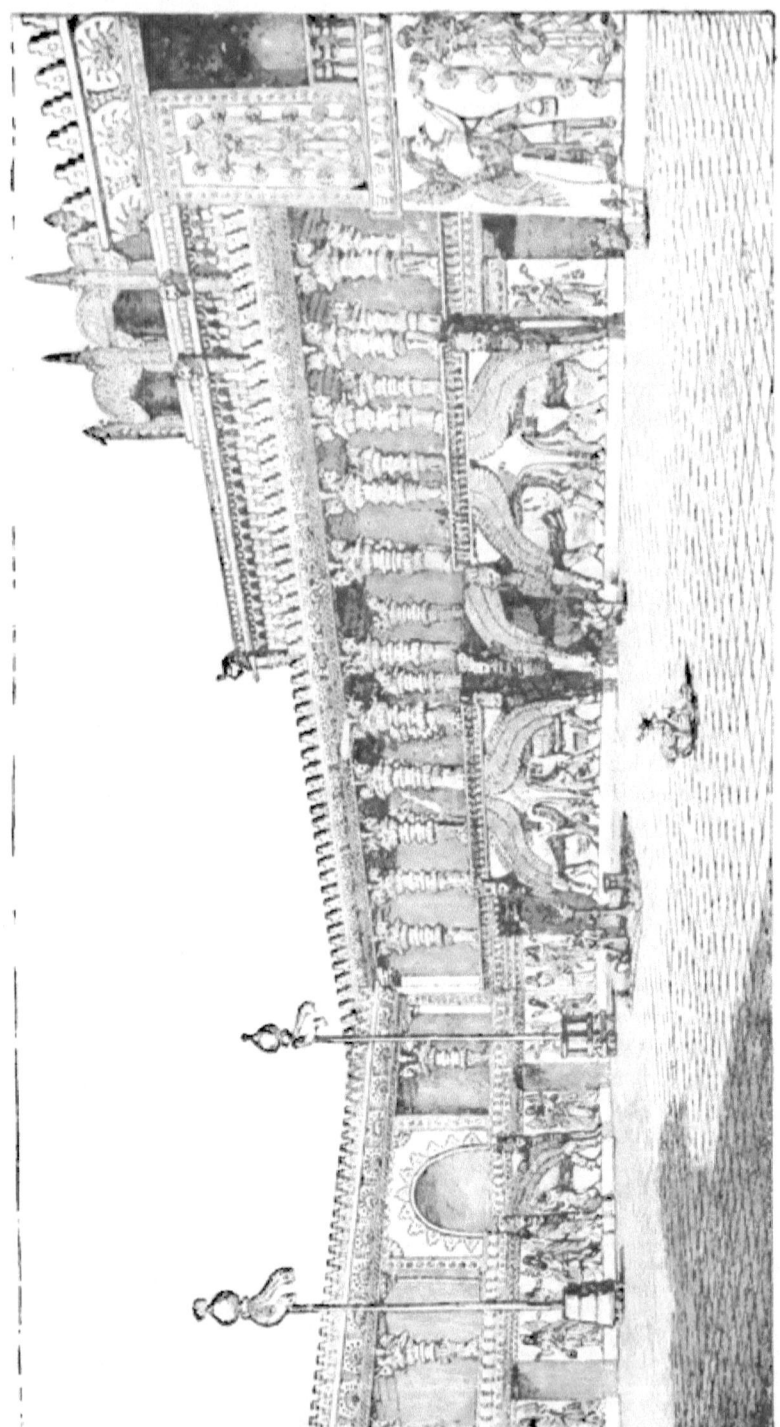
Court of Sargon's Palace at Khorsabad, restored after Fergusson.

and Sennacherib about the same time in erecting his great palace at Kouyunjik.*

The ceiling, roof, and beams of the Jewish temple were of cedar wood. The discoveries in the ruins at Nimroud show that the same precious wood was used in the Assyrian edifices; and the king of Nineveh, as we learn from the inscriptions, sent men, precisely as Solomon had done, to cut it in Mount Lebanon. Fir was also employed in the Jewish buildings, and probably in those of Assyria.†

In order to understand the proposed restoration of the palace at Kouyunjik from the existing remains, the reader must refer to the plan of the excavated ruins.‡ It will be perceived that the building does not face the cardinal points of the compass. I will however assume, for convenience sake, that it stands due north and south. To the west, therefore, it immediately overlooked the Tigris; and on that side rose one of its principal façades. The edifice must have stood on the very edge of the platform, the foot of which was at that time washed by the river. If, therefore, there were any access to the palace on the river front, it must necessarily have been by a flight of steps, or an inclined way leading down to the water's edge, and there might have been great stairs parallel to the basement wall as at Persepolis. Although from the fact of there having been a grand entrance to the palace on this side, it is highly probable that some such approach once existed, no remains whatever of it have been discovered. The western façade, like the eastern, was formed by five pairs of human-headed bulls, and numerous colossal figures, forming three distinct gateways.

The principal approach to the palace appears, however, to have been on the eastern side, where the great bulls bearing the annals of Sennacherib were discovered. In the frontispiece to this volume I have been able, by the assistance of Mr. Fergusson, to give a restoration of this magnificent façade and entrance. Inclined ways, or broad flights of

---

* It will be remembered that the annals on the bulls of Kouyunjik include six years of his reign, and were, therefore, probably inscribed on them in the seventh year.
† 1 Kings, v. 8.   ‡ See Plan I. p. 4.

steps, appear to have led up to it from the foot of the platform; and the remains of them, consisting of huge squared stones, are still seen in the ravines, which are but ancient ascents, deepened by the winter rains of centuries.* From this grand entrance direct access could be had to all the principal halls and chambers in the palace; that on the western face, as appears from the ruins, only opened into a set of eight rooms.

The chambers hitherto explored appear to have been grouped round three great courts or halls marked Nos. VI., XIX., and LXIV. on the Plan. It must be borne in mind, however, that the palace extended considerably to the northeast of the grand entrance, and that there may have been another hall, and similar dependent chambers in that part of the edifice. To the east of hall LXIV., and to the north of No. VI., there were also remains of buildings. Only a part of the palace has been hitherto excavated, and we are not consequently in possession of a perfect ground-plan of it.

The general arrangement of the chambers at Kouyunjik is similar to that at Khorsabad, though the extent of the building is very much greater. The Khorsabad mound falls gradually to the level of the plain, and there are the remains of a succession of broad terraces or stages. Parts of the palace, such as the propylæa, were actually beneath the platform, and stood at some distance from it in the midst of the walled inclosure. At Kouyunjik, however, the whole of the royal edifice, with its dependent buildings, appears to have stood on the summit of the artificial mound,† whose lofty perpendicular sides could only have been accessible by steps, or inclined ways. No propylæa, or other edifices connected with the palace, have as yet been discovered below the platform.

The inscriptions, it is said, refer to four distinct parts of the palace, three of which, inhabited by the women, seem subsequently to have been reduced to one. It is not clear whether they were all on the ground-floor, or whether they

* Remains of such a flight of steps, and of grand propylæa formed by winged bulls, were subsequently discovered by M. Place at Khorsabad.
† Such also appears to have been the case at Nimroud.

The Great Hall of Sardanapalus' Palace, restored.

To face page 383

formed different stories. Mr. Fergusson, in his ingenious work on the restoration of the palaces of Nineveh, in which he has, with great learning and research, fully examined the subject of the architecture of the Assyrians and ancient Persians, endeavours to divide the Khorsabad palace, after the manner of modern Mussulman houses, into the Salamlik or apartments of the men, and the Harem or those of the women. The division he suggests must, of course, depend upon analogy and conjecture; but it may, I think, be accepted as highly probable, until fuller and more accurate translations of the inscriptions than can yet be made may furnish us with some positive data on the subject. In the ruins of Kouyunjik there is nothing, as far as I am aware, to mark the distinction between the male and female apartments. Supposing Mr. Fergusson's theory to be correct, and following the analogy between the two buildings, the court marked XIX. on the Plan would best correspond with the harem court of Khorsabad. Of a temple no remains have as yet been found at Kouyunjik, nor is there any high conical mound as at Nimroud and Khorsabad.

In all the Assyrian edifices hitherto explored we find the same general plan. On the four sides of the great courts or halls are two or three narrow parallel chambers opening one into the other. Most of them have doorways at each end leading into smaller rooms, which have no other outlet. It seems highly probable that this uniform plan was adopted with reference to the peculiar architectural arrangements required by the building, and I agree with Mr. Fergusson in attributing it to the mode resorted to for lighting the apartments.

In my former work I expressed a belief that the chambers received light from the top. Although this may have been the case in some instances, yet recent discoveries now prove that the Assyrian palaces had more than one story. Such being the case, it is evident that other means must have been adopted to admit light to the inner rooms on the ground-floor. Mr. Fergusson's suggestion, that the upper part of the halls and principal chambers was formed by a row of pillars supporting the ceiling and admitting a free circulation of light and air, appears to me to meet, to a certain extent, the difficulty. It has, moreover, been borne out by subsequent discoveries, and by the representation of a large building, apparently a palace, on one of the bas-reliefs from Kouyunjik.* In the accompanying woodcut an edifice is seen with openings at equal distances

Exterior of a Building (From a Bas-relief at Kouyunjik.)

immediately beneath the roof, each opening being formed by two low columns with capitals resembling the Ionic. In the restoration of the exterior of the Kouyunjik palace forming the frontispiece to this volume, pillars with similar capitals have been adopted in preference to those taken by Mr. Fergusson from Persepolis, which, although undoubtedly,

* See also 2nd series of 'Monuments of Nineveh,' Plate 40.

like the other architectural details of those celebrated ruins, Assyrian in character, are not authorised by any known Assyrian remains.*

Although the larger halls may have been lighted in this manner, yet the inner chambers must have remained in almost entire darkness. And it is not improbable that such was the case, to judge from modern Eastern houses, in which the rooms are purposely kept dark to mitigate the great heat. The sculptures and decorations in them could then only be properly seen by torchlight. The great courts were probably entirely open to the sky, like the courts of the modern houses of Mosul, whose walls are also adorned with sculptured alabaster. The roofs of the large halls must have been supported by pillars of wood or brickwork. It may be conjectured that there were two or three stories of chambers opening into them, either by columns or by windows. Such appears to have been the case in Solomon's temple; for Josephus tells us that the great inner sanctuary was surrounded by small rooms, 'over these rooms were other rooms, and others above them, equal both in their measure and numbers, and these reached to a height equal to the *lower part* of the house, for the upper had no buildings about it.' We have also a similar arrangement of chambers in the modern houses of Persia,† in which a lofty central hall, called the Iwan, of the entire height of the building, has small rooms in two or three separate stories opening by windows into it, whilst the inner chambers have no windows at all, and only receive light through the door. Sometimes these side chambers open into a centre court, as I have suggested may have been the case in the Nineveh palaces, and then a projecting roof of woodwork protects the carved and painted walls from injury by the weather. Curtains and awnings were no doubt suspended above the

---

* See frontispiece to Mr. Fergusson's 'Palaces of Nineveh restored.' The pure Ionic volute occurs amongst the bronze ornaments from the throne in the British Museum. There is, however, amongst the small objects brought by me to this country, what appears to be part of a double bull precisely similar to the capitals of Persepolis. Between the figures is a groove for the beam. It may have belonged to some model of a building or of a column.

† Especially of Isfahan, Hamadan, and Kermansh h.

windows and entrances in the Assyrian palaces, to ward off the rays of the sun.

Although no remains of pillars have hitherto been discovered in the Assyrian ruins, I now think it highly probable, as suggested by Mr. Fergusson, that they were used to support the roof. The sketch of a modern Yezidi house in the Sinjar, given in a previous part of this volume,† is a good illustration not only of this mode of supporting the ceiling, but of the manner in which light may have been admitted into the side chambers. It is curious, however, that no stone pedestals, upon which wooden columns may have rested, have been found in the ruins; nor have I found marks of them on the pavement. I can scarcely account for the entire absence of all such traces. However, unless some support of this kind were resorted to, it is impossible that the larger halls at Kouyunjik could have been covered in. The great hall, or house as it is rendered in the Bible,‡ of the forest of Lebanon was thirty cubits high, upon four rows of cedar pillars with cedar beams upon the pillars. The Assyrian kings, as we have seen, cut wood in the same forests as King Solomon: and probably used it for the same purposes, namely, for pillars, beams, and ceilings. The dimensions of this hall, 100 cubits (about 150 feet) by 50 cubits (75 feet), very much resemble those of the centre halls of the palaces of Nineveh. 'The porch of pillars' was fifty cubits in length; equal, therefore, to the breadth of the hall, of which, I presume, it was a kind of inclosed space at the upper end, whilst 'the porch for the throne where he might judge, even the porch of judgment .... covered with cedar wood from one side of the floor to the other,' was probably a raised place within it, corresponding with a similar platform where the host and guests of honour are seated in a modern Eastern house. Supposing the three parts of the building to have been arranged as I have suggested, we should have an exact

---

* See woodcut, p. 327. † P. 96.
‡ 1 Kings, vii. 2. It is only by supposing it to have been one great hall that we can understand the proportions and form of the building as subsequently given. The Hebrew word, as its Arabic equivalent still does, will bear both meanings. Pharaoh's daughter's house, which was '*like unto the porch*,' was probably the harem or private apartment.

counterpart of them in the hall of audience of the Persian palaces. The upper part of the magnificent hall in which I have frequently seen the governor of Isfahan, was divided from the lower part by columns, and his throne was a raised place of carved woodwork adorned with rich stuffs, ivory, and other precious materials. Suppliants and attendants stood outside the line of pillars, and the officers of the court within. Such also may have been the interior arrangement of the great halls in the Assyrian edifices.

That the Nineveh palaces had more than one story, at least in some parts if not in all, can now no longer be doubted. The inscriptions appear to describe distinctly the upper rooms; and at Kouyunjik, as it has been seen, an inclined way was discovered leading to them.[*] If there had not been an upper structure, it would be impossible to account for the enormous accumulation of rubbish, consisting chiefly of remains of building, over the ruins of Kouyunjik and Khorsabad. These upper rooms were probably built of sundried bricks and wood, but principally of the latter material, and may have been connected with the lower by winding staircases, as in the temple of Solomon, and by inclined ways. The roofs were flat, like the roofs of modern Eastern houses.

I have already described the interior decorations of the Assyrian palaces,[†] and have little more to add upon the subject. The walls of Kouyunjik were more elaborately decorated than those of Nimroud and Khorsabad. Almost every chamber I explored there, and they amounted to above seventy, was panelled with alabaster slabs carved with numerous figures and with the minutest details. Each room appears to have been dedicated to some particular event, and in each, apparently, was the image of the king himself. In fact, the walls recorded in sculpture what the inscriptions did in writing,—the great deeds of Sennacherib in peace as well as in war. It will be remarked that, whilst in other Assyrian edifices the king is frequently represented taking an

---

[*] No. LXI. Plan I. p. 4.
[†] Nineveh and its Remains, chap. xiii.

active part in war, slaying his enemies, and fighting beneath a besieged city, Sennacherib is never represented at Kouyunjik otherwise than in an attitude of triumph, in his chariot or on his throne, receiving the captives and the spoil. Nor is he ever seen torturing his prisoners, or putting them to death with his own hand.

There were chambers, however, in the palace of Sennacherib, as well as in those at Nimroud and Khorsabad, whose walls were simply coated with plaster, like the walls of Belshazzar's palace at Babylon.* Some were probably richly ornamented in colour with figures of men and animals, as well as with elegant designs; or others may have been panelled with cedar wainscoting, as the chambers in the temple and palaces of Solomon, and in the royal edifices of Babylon. Gilding, too, appears to have been extensively used in decoration, and some of the great sphinxes may have been overlaid with gold, like the cherubim in Solomon's temple.†

At Kouyunjik, the pavement slabs were not inscribed as at Nimroud; but those between the winged bulls, at some of the entrances, were carved with an elaborate and very elegant pattern.‡ The doors were probably of wood, gilt and adorned with precious materials, like the gates of the temple of Jerusalem, and their hinges appear to have turned in stone sockets, some of which were found in the ruins. To ward off the glare of an Eastern sun, hangings or curtains, of gay colours and of rich materials, were probably suspended to the pillars supporting the ceiling, or to wooden poles raised for the purpose, as in the palaces of Babylon and Shushan.

The excavations carried on at Nimroud have enabled me to restore, to a certain extent, the various buildings on the platform, and to obtain some idea of their original appearance. I have endeavoured, with the able assistance of Mr

---

* Daniel, v. 5.
† 1 Kings, vi. 28. I cannot, however, but express my conviction that much of the metal called gold, both in the sacred writings and in the profane authors of antiquity, was really copper, alloyed with other metals, the aurichalcum, or orichalcum, of the Greeks, such as was used in the bowls and plates discovered at Nimroud.
‡ 2nd series of the 'Monuments of Nineveh,' plate 56.

Fergusson, to convey in the frontispiece to this volume, and in that to the second series of my larger work on the 'Monuments of Nineveh,' the general effect of these mag-

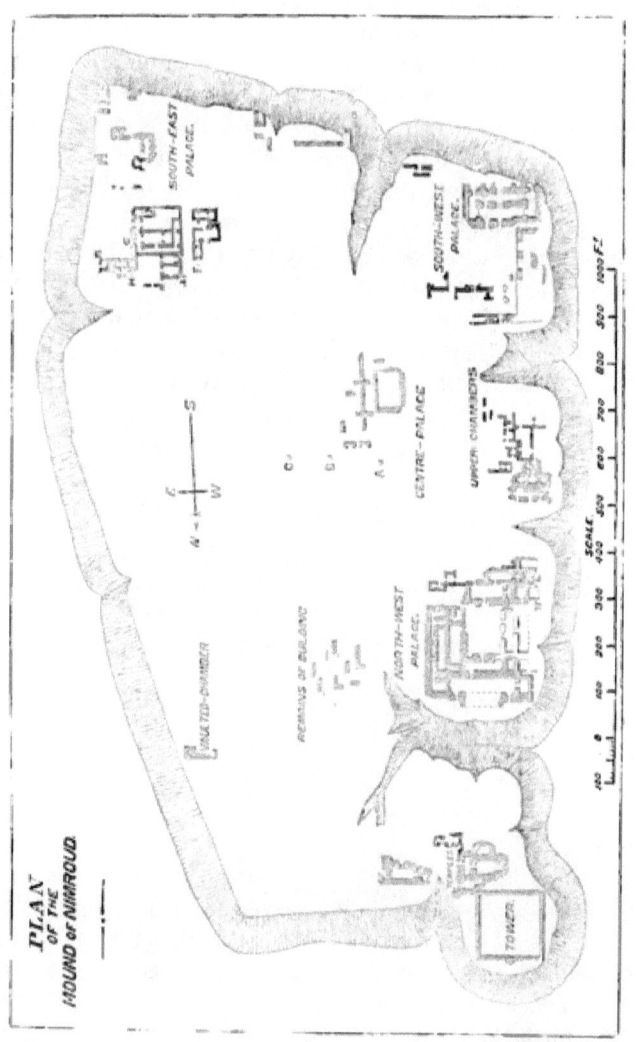

nificent edifices when they still rose on their massy basement, and were reflected in the broad stream of the Tigris.

I must refer the reader, who desires to follow me in the following description, to the accompanying general plan of the platform and palaces at Nimroud.

On the artificial platform, built of regular layers of sun-dried bricks in some parts, and of rubbish in others, but cased on all sides with solid stone masonry, stood at one time several buildings. The intervals between them were paved with stone, or with large kiln-burnt bricks, from one and a half to two feet square. At the north-western corner rose the great tower, the tomb of Sardanapalus, the founder of the principal palace, already described.* The upper part, built of brick, was most probably painted, like the palaces of Babylon, with figures and mythic emblems. Its summit, I conjecture, to have consisted of several gradines or stages, like the top of the black obelisk, and I have ventured to crown it with an altar on which may have burned the eternal fire. Adjoining this tower were, as we have seen, two small temples, dedicated to two of the principal gods.

Mound of Nimroud.

Between the small temples and the north-west palace were two great flights of steps, or inclined ways, leading up from the margin of the river. Their sites are still marked by deep ravines. They ended in a broad paved terrace. The principal façade and entrance of the north-west palace was to the north, facing the tower, and nearly resembled those of the palaces of Kouyunjik and Khorsabad. The two

* Chap. i.

gateways formed by sphinxes with the human form to the waist,* were united by colossal human-headed bulls and lions and winged figures. The remains of no other great entrance to this palace have yet been discovered, but I have little doubt, from several indications in the ruins, that there was a similar façade on the river side, and that a terrace, reached by broad flights of steps, overlooked the Tigris.

To the south of the north-west palace was a third ascent to the summit of the platform, also marked by a ravine in the side of the mound. Beyond it were the upper chambers, built by the fourth king in succession from Sardanapalus, probably over the remains of an earlier edifice. Excavations made in different parts of the small mound covering their ruins, show that they consisted of three distinct groups, built round a tower or solid central mass of sundried bricks.

The upper chambers were separated from the palace of Esar-haddon, the most southern on this side of the platform, by a fourth grand approach to the terraces. Remains of great blocks of stone, of winged bulls, and of colossal figures in yellow limestone, were found in the ravine.

Esar-haddon's palace was raised some feet above the north-west and centre edifices. It had been so entirely destroyed by fire, and by the removal of the slabs from its walls, that a complete ground-plan of it could not be restored. In the arrangement of its chambers, as far as I was able to judge from the ruins, it differed from other Assyrian buildings with which we are acquainted. The centre court, above 220 feet long and 100 broad, opening at the northern end by a gateway of winged bulls on a terrace, which overlooked the grand approach and the principal palaces, and at the opposite end having a triple portal guarded by three pairs of colossal sphinxes, which commanded the open country and the Tigris winding through the plain, must have been a truly magnificent feature in this building. It occupied the corner of the platform, and an approach, of which considerable remains still exist, led up to it from the plain on the southern side. Around the grand court appear to have been built a number of small chambers; and

---

* See woodcut, p. 52, 'Nineveh and its Remains.'

this Assyrian edifice probably answers in its general plan, more than any other yet discovered, to the descriptions in the Bible of the palace of Solomon, especially if we assume that the ante-chamber, divided into two parts, corresponds with the portico of the Jewish structures.

The palace of Esar-haddon was considerably below the level of that of his grandson, and was separated from it by what appears, from a very deep and wide ravine, to have been the principal approach to the platform. The south-east edifice was very inferior, both in the size of its apartments and in the materials employed in its construction, to the other royal buildings. It was built when the empire was fast falling to decay, and, as is usual in such cases, the arts seem to have declined with the power of the people. In this palace there was no great hall, nor even any sculptured slabs. It consisted of a number of rooms of small proportions, panelled below by limestone slabs, roughly hewn and not much above three feet and a half high. The upper part of the walls was simply plastered. I could not find any traces of a grand entrance, façade, or exterior architecture, and recent excavations have only led to the discovery of a few new chambers containing no objects of interest. There are, however, the remains of an earlier building beneath it. The terraces to the west, overlooking the approach from the plain, were floored with thick lime-plaster or cement, which still remains.

Returning northwards, we come to the only traces of an approach on the eastern side of the platform, and consequently from the interior of the walled inclosure. On this part of the platform no ruins have hitherto been discovered, although there are undoubtedly traces of buildings in several places, and I think it not improbable that a temple, or some similar edifice, stood there.

It only remains for me to mention the palace in the centre of the platform. Excavations carried on during the second expedition, brought to light the walls of a few additional chambers and numerous fragments of interesting sculptures.*

* Amongst them were winged figures struggling with mythic animals, and various other groups, such as are seen on cylinders and on the robes

But the edifice was so utterly destroyed by Esar-haddon, who used the materials in the construction of his own dwelling-place, that it is impossible to ascertain its general plan, or even the arrangement of any of its rooms.

Around this edifice was a pavement of large square bricks, extending on one side to the north-west palace and the small

Plan of Mound and Inclosure of Nimroud.

temples, and on the other to the upper chambers, Esar-haddon's palace, and that of his grandson.

In the ramparts of earth, marking the inclosure wall of Nimroud to the north, fifty-eight towers can still be distinctly traced. To the east there were about fifty, but all traces of some of them are entirely gone. To the south the wall has almost disappeared, so that it could not have been of great

of the king in the north-west palace. They appear to have been sculptured in colossal proportions on the walls of this palace.

size or thickness on that side. The level of the inclosure is here, however, considerably above the plain; and it is not improbable that the Tigris actually flowed beneath part of it, and that the remainder was defended by a wide and deep ditch, either supplied by the small stream still running near the ruins, or by the river.

At the south-eastern corner of the inclosure, as I have already mentioned,* is a mound of considerable height, and the remains of a square edifice which may have been a fort or tower. I searched in vain for traces of gates in the walls on the northern side. A high double mound, which probably marks the ruins of an entrance, was excavated; but no stone masonry or sculptured figures were discovered. I conclude, therefore, that the gateways of the quarter of Nineveh represented by Nimroud were not, like those of the more northern divisions of the city, adorned with sculptures, but were built of the same materials as the walls.

It is evident that the inclosure of Nimroud was regularly fortified, and defended by walls built for the purpose of resisting an enemy, and sustaining a siege. That of Khorsabad was precisely similar. There also the platform, on which the great palace stood, formed part of the walls,—a fact for which I can scarcely offer any satisfactory explanation. It would seem more consistent with security that the dwelling of the king, the temples of the gods, and the edifices containing the archives and treasures of the kingdom, should have been in the centre of the fortifications, equally protected on all sides. The palaces of Nimroud and Kouyunjik, built on a platform, which was washed on one side by a deep and broad river, were, to a certain extent, guarded from the approach of an enemy. But at Khorsabad such was not the case. The royal residence overlooked the plain country, and was accessible from it, unless the summit of the platform were strongly fortified on the western side, of which there is no trace.

Of the fortified inclosures still existing, that defending Kouyunjik is the most remarkable, and was best calculated to withstand the attack of a powerful and numerous army.

* See p. 54.

FORTIFICATIONS OF KOUYUNJIK.

Its form, it will be perceived, was irregular. The wall facing the river (*a*), including the mounds of Kouyunjik and Nebbi Yunus, and the northern (or north-western) wall (*b*), are at right angles to each other, and are nearly straight.*

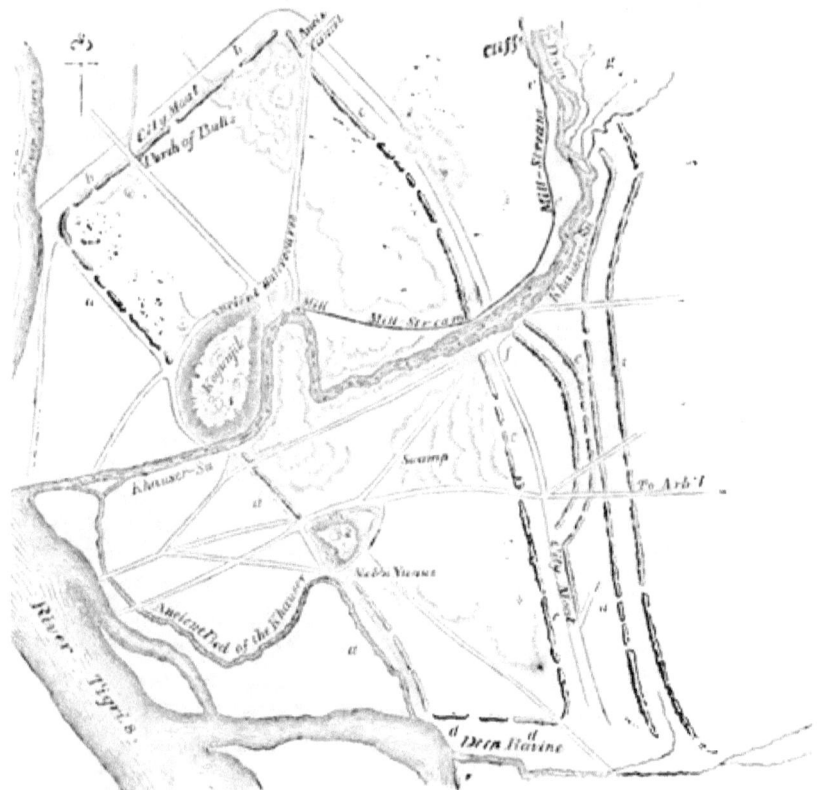

Plan of Mound and Inclosure of Kouyunjik.

From the eastern corner of the northern face, the inner wall (*c*), which is about 16,000 feet, or three miles in length, curves towards the southern end of the western, the two being about 1,000 yards apart at their extremities (*d*). The whole extent

---

* Plate 70, in the 2nd series of the 'Monuments of Nineveh' will convey an idea of the nature of the earthen ramparts forming the inclosure round Kouyunjik. The upper lithograph represents the northern line of wall.

of the walls is thus about eight miles. On the four sides are the remains of towers and curtains, and the walls appear to have consisted of a basement of stone and an upper structure of sundried bricks. The top of the stone masonry was ornamented with gradines as at Nimroud.* There were probably numerous gateways, and their sites are still marked by mounds exceeding those around in height and size; but the only two which have hitherto been explored are in the northern and eastern walls, and have been described in a previous chapter.†

Ornament on Top of Walls. (Kouyunjik.)

The western wall (*a*), 13,000 feet in length, was washed by the river, and needed no other defence.‡ A deep moat, of which traces still exist, was excavated beneath the northern wall. (*b*) That to the south (*d*) was protected by a ditch and by the Tigris. The side most accessible to an enemy was that to the east (*c*), and it was accordingly fortified with extraordinary care and strength. The small river Khauser flows nearly in a direct line from the hills towards the northeastern corner of the inclosure, but makes a sweep to the south (*e*) before reaching it, and after running for some distance beneath a perpendicular bank formed by conglomerate hills (*g*) parallel to it, but, about three-quarters of a mile from it, again turns to the westward (at *f*), and enters the eastern wall almost in its centre. It then traverses the entire inclosure, winds round the base of Kouyunjik, and falls into the Tigris. Nearly one-half of the eastern wall was, consequently, provided with natural defences. The Khauser served as a moat; and the conglomerate ridge, increased

---

* Several blocks of limestone cut into this form, and evidently fallen from the tops of the walls, are scattered about the ruins. It is possible that the upper structure of sundried bricks may have been similarly ornamented.

† Chap. i.

‡ It will be borne in mind that the Tigris has now changed its course.

by artificial means, as a strong line of fortification. The remains of one or more ramparts of earth are still to be traced between the stream and the inner wall, but they could not have been of very considerable size. The north-eastern extremity of these outer defences appears to have joined the ditch which was carried along the northern face of the inclosure, thus completing the fortifications on this side.

Below, or to the south of the Khauser, the inner wall was defended by a complete system of outworks. In the first place a deep moat, about one hundred and fifty feet wide, was dug immediately beneath it, and was divided for half its length into two parts by a high rampart. A parallel wall (*h*) was then carried from the banks of the Khauser to the dyke on the southern side of the inclosure, as well as a second moat, about one hundred and eight feet wide, and of considerable depth, probably supplied by the Khauser. A third wall (*i*), the remains of which are above one hundred feet high on the inner face, abutted to the north on the ridge of conglomerate hills (*g*), and completed the outer defences. A few mounds rising in the level country beyond, the principal of which, near the southern extremity of the lines, is called Tel-ez-zembil (the Mound of the Basket), appear to have been fortified outposts; probably detached towers, such as are represented in the bas-reliefs of Kouyunjik.*

An enemy coming from the east, the side on which the inclosure was most open to attack, had consequently first to force a stupendous wall strengthened by detached forts. Two deep ditches and two more walls, the inner being scarcely inferior in size to the outer, had then to be passed before this part of the city could be taken.† The remains still existing of these fortifications almost confirm the statement of Diodorus Siculus, that the walls were a hundred feet high, and that three chariots could drive upon them abreast; and lead

---

* See 2nd series of 'Monuments of Nineveh,' Plate 43.
† The distance from the inside of the inner wall to the inside of the outer is about 2007 feet. Allowing 200 feet for the outer, the breadth of the whole fortifications would be about 2200 feet, or not far from half a mile.

to the conclusion that, in describing the ramparts forming the circuit round the whole city, ancient historians were confounding them with those which inclosed only a separate quarter, or a royal residence, as they have also done in speaking of those of Babylon. Whilst the inner walls were constructed of stone and brick masonry, the outer appear to have consisted of little else than of the earth, loose pebbles, and rubble dug out from the moats, which were cut with enormous labour into the solid conglomerate rock.*

The walls and moats around Kouyunjik were a favourite ride during my residence among the ruins. The summit of the outer ramparts commands an extensive and beautiful prospect over the great mounds, the plains bounded by the several mountain ranges of Kurdistan, the windings of the river, and the town of Mosul. 'Niniue (that which God himself calleth that Great Citie) hath not one stone standing, which may giue memorie of the being of a towne : one English mile from it is a place called Mosul, a small thing, rather to be a witnesse of the other's mightenesse, and God's iudgement, than of any fashion of magnificence in itselfe.'† Such are the simple though impressive words of an old English traveller, who probably looked down upon the site of Nineveh from the same spot two centuries and a half ago.

Beaten tracks from the neighbouring villages have for ages led, and still lead, through the ruins. Along them Arabs and Kurds with their camels and laden beasts may be seen slowly wending their way to the town. But the space between the walls is deserted except by the timid gazelle and the jackals and hyenas which make their dens in the holes and caves in the sides of the mounds and in the rocky banks of the ancient ditches.

The spring rising in the inner circuit of the eastern walls, called by the Arabs Damlamajeh, and described by Mr. Rich,‡ is a small pool of cool and refreshing water in a

---

* If the city, or this part of it, were ever taken by the river having been turned upon the walls, as some ancient authors have declared, the breach must have been made at the north-western corner. There are no traces of it.

† Sir Anthony Shirley's Travels in Persia. Purchas, vol. ii. p. 1387.

‡ Narrative of a Residence in Kurdistan, vol. i. pp. 40, 51.

natural cavern, the entrance to which is adorned with an arch, cornice, and stonework, evidently of Roman construction. Upon the masonry are still to be traced the names of Mrs. Rich, and of the companions of the distinguished traveller.

CONCLUSION.

The time was drawing near for my departure. Once more I was about to leave the ruins amidst which I had spent so many happy hours, and to which I was bound by so many pleasant and solemn ties; and probably to return no more.

I only waited the arrival of Abde, the late Pasha of Baghdad, who was now on his way to his new government of Diarbekr. He was travelling with a large company of attendants, and without a strong escort it was scarcely prudent to venture on my journey. It was doubly necessary for me to have proper protection, as I took with me the valuable collection of bronzes and other small objects discovered in the ruins. I gladly, therefore, availed myself of this opportunity of joining so numerous and strong a caravan.

At length, after the usual Eastern delays, the Pasha arrived at Mosul. He remained encamped outside the town for two or three days, and during that time visited the excavations, his curiosity having been excited by the description he had received of the wondrous idols dug out of the ruins. He marvelled at what he saw, as a Turk marvels at strange things which he can neither understand nor explain. It would be in vain to speak to him of the true objects of such researches, the knowledge they impart, the lessons they teach, or the thoughts they beget.

CONCLUSION.

In these pages I have occasionally indulged in reflections suggested by the scenes I have had to describe, and have ventured to point out the moral of the strange tale I have had to relate. I cannot better conclude than by showing the spirit in which Eastern philosophy and Mussulman resignation contemplate the evidences of ancient greatness and civilisation, suddenly rising up in the midst of modern ignorance and decay. A letter in my possession contains so true and characteristic a picture of the feelings that such an event excites in the mind of a good Mohammedan, that I here give a literal translation of its contents. It was written to a friend of mine by a Turkish Cadi, in reply to some inquiries as to the commerce, population, and remains of antiquity of an ancient city, in which dwelt the head of the law. These are its words:—

'My illustrious Friend, and Joy of my Liver!

'The thing you ask of me is both difficult and useless. Although I have passed all my days in this place, I have neither counted the houses, nor have I inquired into the number of the inhabitants; and as to what one person loads on his mules and the other stows away in the bottom of his ship, that is no business of mine. But, above all, as to the previous history of this city, God only knows the amount of dirt and confusion that the infidels may have eaten before the coming of the sword of Islam. It were unprofitable for us to inquire into it.

'Oh, my soul! oh, my lamb! seek not after the things which concern thee not. Thou camest unto us, and we welcomed thee: go in peace.

'Of a truth, thou hast spoken many words; and there is no harm done, for the speaker is one and the listener is another. After the fashion of thy people thou hast wandered from one place to another until thou art happy and content in none. We (praise be to God!) were born here, and never desire to quit it. Is it possible then that the idea of a general intercourse between mankind should make any impression on our understandings? God forbid!

'Listen, oh my son! There is no wisdom equal unto the belief in God! He created the world, and shall we liken ourselves unto him in seeking to penetrate into the mysteries of his creation? Shall we say, behold this star spinneth round that star, and this other star with a tail goeth and cometh in so many years! Let it go! He from whose hand it came will guide and direct it.

'But thou wilt say unto me, Stand aside, oh man, for I am more learned than thou art, and have seen more things. If thou thinkest that thou art in this respect better than I am, thou art welcome. I praise God that I seek not that which I require not. Thou art learned in the things I care not for; and as for that which thou hast seen, I defile it. Will much knowledge create thee a double belly, or wilt thou seek Paradise with thine eyes?

'Oh, my friend! If thou wilt be happy, say, There is no God but God! Do no evil, and thus wilt thou fear neither man nor death; for surely thine hour will come!

'The meek in spirit (El Fakir),

'IMAUM ALI ZADÈ.'

On the 28th of April I bid a last farewell to my faithful Arab friends, and with a heavy heart turned from the ruins of ancient Nineveh.

Last View of Mosul.

INDEX.

ABD

ABDAL BEY, Chief of Mukus, 221
Abd'rubbou, Sheikh, 120. News of the death of his sister, 120
Abd-ul-Azeez, Sheikh of the Jebours, 93
Abd-ul-Azeez hills, 117
Abd-ur-Rahman, Sheikh, 15, 67
Abd-ur-Rahman Agha, Chief of the Hartushi Kurds, 225, 226
Abou-Khaima, mound of, 104
Abou Khameera, ruins of, 88
Abou Maria, village of, 88. Discoveries at, 162
Abou-Salman Arabs, 14
Abra, El, river, 92
Adel Bey, Mudir of Dizza, 197
Adla, Sheikh Suttum's first wife, 134
Afaij Arabs, 308. Visit to the, 313. Souk-el-Afaij, 316. Their manners and customs, 324
Agab, chief of the Afaij Arabs, 308. Visit to, 316
Ague, attacks of, 185
Ain-es-Sufra, Gebel, 186
Akhtamar, Patriarch of, 216. The convent of, 217
Akra, Kurdish town of, 187
Akker-Kuf, mound of, 267
Aldina, village of, 100, 160
Ali Kahal, Sheikh of the mound, 11
Allak, village of, 309
Alouvi hills, 109
Alphabet, cuneiform, Introd. xliv.
American missionaries, their work in the East, 213
Amikh, Armenian rock-inscriptions at, 214
Amran ben Ali, excavations in the mound of, 290

ARM

Anana, mound of, 307
Animals, wild, near Babylon, 323
Antiss, village of, 199
Arabs, attack of, on Nimroud, 55. The rediff of the Bedouins, 81. Arab exhilaration, 93. An encampment, 105. Hospitality, 105, 106, 127. Arab ladies, 107. Their dress, 107. Peace concluded between the Yezidis and Bedouins, 97, 100, 111. News of a death, 120. Arab food, 128. Domestic life of the Bedouins, 131. Their diseases, 132. Polygamy amongst them, 135. Cadis or judges of the Shammar, 140. The Thar, or blood-revenge, 141. Arab lovemaking, 150. The Dakheel, 151. An Arab poet, 153. Arab sagacity, 155. Their expeditions, 162. Savage Arabs, 310, 311. Manners and customs of the Afaij, 324
Ararat, Mount, view of, 226
Arban, arrival at, 114. Discoveries at, 120. Departure from, 139
Arch, the, known to the Assyrians, 38. Examples of the, 38, 53, 77, 79
Architecture, Armenian, 218. Assyrian, 376
Ardzrouni, Armenian royal family of, 217
Armenia, visit to, 198
Armenian ploughmen, 199
Armenian bishop, a, 208
Armenian schools at Wan, 213
Armour, Assyrian, 63, 64
Arms, remains of, found, 63, 64
Army, composition of the Assyrian, 370

ART — BOW

Artamit, or Adremit, Armenian village of, 216
Arts of the Babylonians, 304
Ashayansk, Armenian village of, 219
Ashkaun, Armenian village of, 223
Ashur, the Assyrian god, three-headed emblem of, 174. The supreme god of Assyria, 373
Asses, wild, 115. White, of Baghdad, 265. Chase of the, on bas-reliefs, Introd. xxvii.
Asshur, the ancient capital of Assyria, Sir H. Rawlinson's theory of, Introd. liv.
Assyria, annals of the kings of, 352. Its political condition, 368. Extent of the empire, 360. Its religion, 373. Its architecture, 376. Its civilization, Introd. lv.
Athelé, the tree, at Babylon, 288
Aththenir river, 161
Aurenj, Armenian village of, 221
Author, his illness, 325
Awai, or great dam of the Tigris, 260
Awaythe, the Sheikh, 261
Azeez Agha, of Hillah, 273

BABEL, mound of, 269. Mounds near, 275. The Tower of Babel of early travellers, 278. Excavations in the mound of, 283
Babylon, conquest of, by Sennacherib, 44. Departure for, 260. Ruins of, 274, 275. The walls of the city, 275. Plan of the city, 276. Excavations in the great mound of Babel, 283. The Mujelibé, or Kasr, and excavations in it, 286. Remains of the Jews of the Captivity at, 290, 291. State of the ruins of, 294. Cause of the disappearance of the buildings, 294. History of the city, 297. Its commerce, 297, 299. Its canals and rivers, 300. Its Indian dogs, 303. Its textile fabrics, 303. Its arts, 304. Causes of its fall, 305, 306

Baggage mules, accident to, 229
Baghdad, approach to, 265. City of, 266. Remains of the Babylonian period at, 267
Baghdad, Eski, ruins of, 263
Bairam, festival of, at Wan, 211, 212
Ballads, influence of, on the Bedouins, 154
Bani, Kurdish village of, 191
Baraoost, Kurdish district of, 191
Barber-surgeons, 132, 133
Bardaresh, Kurdish village of, 186
Bas-reliefs discovered at Arban, 121-124
Bash-Kalah, castle of, 199
Bashayi, village of, 326
Battle in a marsh in Southern Mesopotamia, 336
Bavian, visit to the rock-sculptures of, 71-73
Beavers on the Khabour, 136
Beder Khan Bey, his ravages, 236
Behistun, rock-inscription of, Introd. xliii.
Bell, Mr., drowned in the Gomel, 72
Bells, bronze, discovered, 58. The metal used in them, 62
Beltis, Assyrian temple dedicated to the goddess, 180
Bersiyah, Kurdish village of, 191
Beygishni, Kurdish stronghold of, 192
Bir Hillan, village of, 186
Birikapra, Kurdish village of, 189
Birs Nimroud, visit to, 277. Proposed restoration of, 280.
Bishop, a Nestorian, 235
Bitumen-pits at Nimroud, 68
Blood-revenge of the Arabs, 141
Boats in bas-reliefs, 76. Of the Afaij Arabs, 314
Boraij Arabs, 103. Their encampment, 105. Their women, 107
Bouran, deserted villages of, 100
Bowen, Rev. Mr., 204
Bowls, bronze, discovery of, 95.

INDEX.   405

BRA

Glass, 65. Inscribed earthen, 291
Bracelets, Arab, 107
Bread of the Arabs, 128
Bricks, painted, 55. Babylonian, 287, 295. Enamelled Babylonian, 288, 295
Bronzes, discovery of, 57. Bells, 58
Buffaloes of the Afaij Arabs, 315
Bukra, village of, 95. Interior of a house at, 96
Bulls, winged human-headed, found at Kouyunjik, 8, 17, 40, 46. Bas-reliefs representing the moving of the, 18. The bulls at the gateway of Kouyunjik, 30. At the entrance to the palace of Sennacherib, 41. Those found at Arban, 121
Burning-glass, a, 67
Bustard of the desert, 110
Butter of the Arabs, 131

CAMELS, Arab, 159. In bas-reliefs, 75, 333
Canals, network of ancient Babylonian, 268, 269, 300, 330
Camp, fortified, in bas-reliefs, 76
Campaign, an Assyrian, 166
Captives, 48, 51, 76, 77, 254, 333. Put to the torture, and flayed alive, 254, 256
Castle, or fortified camp, ground-plan of a, 50
Catholic Chaldæans amongst the Kurds, 189
Cauldrons, copper, discovered, 58, 59
Causeway, Assyrian, from Bavian to Nineveh, 74
Cavern, natural, near Koukab, 142. At Gunduk, 188. Near Wan, 209, 211
Cedar beams in the temple at Nimroud, 180
Chaal, Nestorian district of, 237
Chaldæans, their superstitions, 291
Charderrah, sulphur springs of, 198

DES

Charms, Eastern, 292
Chappata, visit to the Kurdish valley of, 192
Chichi Kurds, 146
Chilgiri, Nestorian village of, 224
Chronology, Assyrian, 71. Restoration of, Introd. liii.
Church, an ancient Nestorian, 234
City, capture of a, 9, 29. A double-walled, 77
Coffins discovered at Babylon, 284. And at Niffer, 320. Vast numbers of them at Wurka, 322
Colours used by the Assyrians, 55
Conduits, Assyrian, at Bavian, 73
Conquest of a district, bas-relief of, 42
Cooper, Mr., returns to Europe, 216
Corn-mills, hand, Arab, 128
Ctesiphon, palace of, 327
Cubes inlaid with gold, 64
Cuneiform character, investigations of the, Introd. xxxviii. Trilingual inscriptions of Persia, xxxix. Testimony of a committee of gentlemen as to the correctness of various renderings, xlviii.
Cups, bronze, found, 59, 61
Cursive characters of the Assyrians, 171
Cuth and the Cuthites, 305 *note*
Cylinders, Assyrian, 169, 343. Babylonian, 304, 346. Persian, 349

DAGON, the fish-god, 168, 177. Found on an Assyrian cylinder, 168. Extent of the worship of, 168
Dakheel, or protection, of the Arabs, 151
Damalamajeh, spring of, at Kouyunjik, 399
Deity, the fish, 168. The three-headed, 174
Deloul, or dromedary, 133. Its speed and endurance, 134. Heads of Arab delouls, 312
Desert and its delights, 137

Dishes, bronze, found, 59-61
Diz, valley of, 220. Villages of, 229
Dizza, village of, 197. Armenian Christians of, 198
Dogs of the Babylonians, 303
Drain, vaulted, beneath south-east and north-west palaces, 53, 54
Dujail canal, 330
Dura, plain of, 262

EAGLE-HEADED monsters, 8
Eclipses, how regarded by ignorant Mohammedans, 315
'Effendi, the,' of the Mendka tribe, 93
Egyptian scarabæi found at Arban, 125. Royal Seal of Sabaco II. found at Kouyunjik, 173
Elam invaded by Sennacherib, 46
Embossed vessels, 62
Emin, Mohammed, Sheikh of the Jebour, 81, 114. Description of, 119. His family, 119, 120. His hospitality, 127. His visit to Suleiman Agha, 139-147
Encampment in the Desert, 87
Esar-haddon, annals of the reign of, 364. Palace of, 391
Esau, chief of Mirkan, 95
Eulukæus of the Greeks, king of Phœnicia, 44
Eunuchs in the sculptures at Kouyunjik, 250
Evil spirit, bas-relief of the, 177
Excavations, renewal of, 1
Ex-voto offerings in the East, 187
Ezekiel, tomb of, 281, 282
Ezra, tomb of, 282 *note*

FALCON, a trained, 115
Ferhan, chief of the Shammar Arabs, 159
Fezullah Bey, Mir of Baradost, 192
Fish-god of the Philistines and Phœnicians, 168. Bas-relief of the, 177

Flowers of Mesopotamia, 114, 137, 160. Of the mountains in Armenia, 226
Footstool, the royal, discovered, 66
Fortifications of Nimroud, 395. Of Kouyunjik, 397
Fountain, Assyrian, at Bavian, 73
Fuel of the Arabs, 129
Fukka ponds, 101

GABARA, village of, 102
Gardens, Assyrian, 78, 79. Hanging, 79
Gateway, discovery of a, at Kouyunjik, 30
Gazelle, hunting the, Introd. xxix.
Gems, engraved, of the Babylonians, 304. Of the Assyrians, 343
Ghaonr, or Ghiaver, Kurdish district of, 196, 197
Gherdi, visit to, 193
Glass bowls discovered, 65. Decomposition of, 65. Glass ornaments discovered at Babylon, 290
Gods, images of the, carried away from the conquered nations, 75. The deities of the Babylonians, 289
Gomel River, 71, 72, 74
Grotefend, his investigations of the arrow-headed character, Introd. xxxviii.
Gundi-Gayli, village of, 100
Gunduk, rock-tablets of, 188. Cave of St. John at, 188
Gunduktha, village of, 236

HAKKIARI, visit to the province of, 197
Hamoud Arabs, 113
Hamza, village of, 309
Hare-hunt, a, 56
Harouna, valley of, 196
Harouni, Kurdish village of, 191
Hartushi Kurds, visit to the, 225
Hashtgah, Kurdish village of, 188

HAT

Hathail, wound of, 92
Haweeza hills, 113
Hawking in the Desert, 110, 112. A trained falcon, 115
Head-dress of captives, 19
Heads of the slain, brought to the registrars, 9
Hebrew inscriptions on earthenware bowls, 290
Helmets of Jewish warriors, 48
Hercules, the Assyrian, 40, 72. Temple dedicated to, 175
Heren, Kurdish village of, 189
Herki, their periodical migrations into Kurdistan, 196
Hezekiah, king of Judah, annals of his war with Sennacherib, 45
Hillah, town of, 270. Departure from, 308
Hindostan, Armenian village of, 203
Hincks, Dr., his decipherment of the cuneiform inscriptions, Introd. xlvi. His death, and ill requital of his labours, xlvi. *note*
Hinge-sockets of the palace-gate at Nimroud, 52
Hittites, expedition of Sennacherib against the, 44
Hol, the, 156
Horses, Assyrian, 165. Ornaments of, 59, 165, 250. Arab, 102, 104, 158, 159
Houses of the Yezidis, 97
Howar of the Tai Arabs, 56. Visit to the, 58
Hunting scenes on Assyrian basreliefs, Introd. xxiii.
Hussein, Cawal, tomb of, 100
Hymer, El, mound of, 306

I AHYA Bey, Mir of Rua, 193
Iron instruments found, 63, 64
Irrigation, mode of, 24
Ismail Agha of Tepelin, 198
Iva-lush, King, annals of, 357
Ivory ornaments discovered, 52
Izzet Pasha, visit to, 200

KHA

J ARS, discovery of, 58, 59
Jasim, Seyyid, 308
Jedaila, village of, 102
Jehu, King of Israel, mention of, 356
Jelu mountain, 230, 231
Jelu pass, 231
Jelu, valley of, 232. The Nestorians of, 233
Jeraiba hills, 111
Jerujer river, 144, 145
Jews, dress of the captive, of Lachish, 48, 51. Descendants of, on the Khabour, 126. Jewish families residing among the Kurds, 194. And among the Armenians, 200. Remains of the Jews of the Captivity at Babylon, 290. The 'Lord Prince of the Captivity,' 293
Jezirch, villages in the, 309
Jonah, excavations in the tomb of, 341
Jones, Captain, his recovery of the lost lion, 70
Journey, preparations for a, in the East, 83
Judah, war of Sennacherib against, 45
Julamerik, 227, 228
Jumjumah, excavations in the mound of, 290

K ALAH SHERGHAT, excavations at, 332. The site of the primitive Assyrian capital, Introd. xxxv. liv.
Kadesia, 264. Battle of, 264
Kaimawa, Kurdish village of, 186
Karboul, Sheikh, 311
Karnessa-ou-Daoleh, peak of, 226
Kemball, Captain, at Baghdad, 266
Khabour, visit to the banks of the, 80. Its beauty, 80, 114. Encampment on the, 115, 116, 118. Artificial mounds on the, 117. The Chebar of the Captivity, 126. Turtle in the, 136 Lions

KHA

on the, 136. Banks of the river, 139. Game on the, 140.
Khan-i-resh, Kurdish village of, 192
Kharala river, 92
Khatouniyah, town and lake of, 157
Khawassan, valley of, 203
Khersa, village of, 100
Khoraif, Sheikh Suttum's rediff, 81
Khorous Klissia, in Kurdistan, 220
Kerraniyah, village of, 103
King, the, on his throne, 49. Bas-relief of the King, 178. The King attired as high-priest, 182, 183. Names of the earliest kings, 350. Power of the kings of Assyria, 367.
Kirikor, the Armenian monk, 217
Kochannes, visit to, 227
Kochers, Kurdish tribe of, 191
Kormawor, Armenian church of, 215
Kosh-Ab, castle of, 201, 202
Koukab, volcanic cone of, 142, 143, 155. The name, 144. View from the, 144
Kouyunjik, return to, 3. Discoveries there, 4. Character of the sculptures at, 11. Description of the chambers at, 17. Discovery of a gateway, 30. Of the entrance to Sennacherib's palace, 40. Bas-reliefs discovered at, 163. Discoveries at, during the summer, 238. And during the author's visit to Babylon, 333. Contents of the mound of Kouyunjik, 376. Sennacherib's palace at, 381. Plan of the mound and enclosure of, 395. Fortifications of, 395–397. Subsequent excavations in the mound of, Introd. xix.
Kowee, or strength money, 111
Kurds, their tents and encampments, 145–147. Visit to their villages, 186, 197. Their hospitality, 189. Their dress, 190. Nomade tribes, 191. Lan-

MEC

guages used by the tribes, 192. Kurds of Wan, 212. Of Hartushi, 225
Kurdistan, villages of, 186, 197. Scenery of Upper, 201
Kushna, village of, 100

LACHISH, sculptures representing the siege of, 45, 47
Larissa, wall of, 37
Latiff Agha, 15
Lens, rock-crystal, discovered, 65
Lewen, Nestorian district of, 226
Lion discovered at Arban, 123, 124. Existing on the banks of the Khabour, 136. Present of two, at Hillah, 271. Babylonian, 271. In the jungles about Niffer, 323
Lions, human-headed, at Nimroud, 52. Visit to the, by night, 67. Removal of, to the river, 68. Loss and recovery of one of them, 70. Colossal lions at the temple of Beltis, 180. Hunting lions, Introd. xxiv.
Locusts eaten as food, 165
Love-making of the Arabs, 150
Luliya, king of Phœnicia, 44

MAALAGA springs, 112
Madis, visit to, 228
Magnifying-glass, a, 67
Mahmoud, Khan, Armenian rebel chief, 219
Mahmoudiyah, valley of, 201
Makloub, Gebel, 70. Beauty and coolness of, 74. The valley between the southern and northern ridges, 186
Mar Hananisho, 195. Convent of, 195
Mar Isho, Bishop of Shemisden, 194, 195
Mar Shamoun, Patriarch of the Nestorians, 227
Mardin, view from, 97 *note*
Martha Akhtayiah, village of, 235
Mechanical powers of the Assyrians, 26

Median wall, the, 331
Mehemet Pasha, of Wan, 205
Meher Kapousi, Armenian tradition respecting the, 210
Mehlaibiyah, mound of, 140
Menahem, King of Israel, mention of, on the sculptures, 358
Mendka, Sinjar tribe of, 93
Merodach-Baladan, King of Babylon, defeated by Sennacherib, 44, 362. Records of the expedition, 71, 362
Merwanen, Nestorian village of, 224
Metallurgy, Assyrian knowledge of, 62
Mijwell, the Boraij Arab, 140. His envy of the Kurds, 150. His domestic affairs, 150
Milli Kurds, visit to the, 147
Mirage seen from Baghdad, 328
Miran Bey, of Shirwan, visit to, 191
Mirkan, village of, 94
Moghamis, Arab warrior, 114, 115, 137
Mohammed Seyyid Pasha, of Akra, 188
Monolith, inscriptions on a, 179
Monster, discovery of the bas-relief of a, at Nimroud, 177
Mosul, return to, 2. Improvement in the government of, 13. Departure from, for the Khabour, 83. The summer in, 185. Departure from, for the mountains, 185
Mosul, Eski, 162
Mounds of Mesopotamia, 306, 307, 311
Mousa Agha, chief of the Milli Kurds, visit to the, 147. His mother, 148
Mousa Bey, chief of Shemdeena, 193
Mukus, Armenian valley and district of, 219-221. River of, 220. Village of, 220
Mules of Susiana, 248 *note*
Munaif, salt lake of, 101
Murad, chief of Aldina, 160

Murad, tomb of, 95
Musicians and musical instruments of the Assyrians, 252, 253
Musk-bag of the beaver, 136
Mustafa Agha, chief the Zibari tribes, 189

NAHAB, encampment at, 140
Naharwan, canal of, 263
Namet Agha, chief of the Zibari tribes, 189
Nara, Nestorian village of, 235
Narek, Armenian festival at, 216. Church at, 216, 219
Nebbi Yunus, excavations in the mound of, Introd. xx.
Nebo, statue of the god, Introd. xxxii.
Nebuchadnezzar, name of, at Baghdad, 267
Nera, Kurdish village of, 193
Nerin, castle of, 202, 203
Nestorians, the, in Shemisden, 195. Persecuted by their enemies, the Herki, 196. Their villages in Armenia, 224. A Nestorian family, 224. Their zomas, or summer encampments, 225. Their dress, 225. Oppressed by the Turks, 228, 232. A Nestorian bishop, 234, 235, 236
Niello, Assyrian specimens of, 64
Niffer, visit to the mound of, 312, 313. Excavations at, 319
Night, an Eastern, 185
Nikoos, the Armenian architect, 210
Nimroud revisited, 12. Sir H. Rawlinson at, 15. Discoveries in the high conical mound at, 33. Palace of Tiglath Pileser at, 52. Vaulted drain at, 53. Attacked by Arabs, 55. Bitumen springs at, 68. Flood at, 175. Palaces at, 388. Mound of, 390. Enclosure of, 393
Nimroud, Birs, visit to the, 277. Proposed restoration of, 280. View from the, 281
Nimroud Dagh, in Armenia, 203

NIN

Nineveh, discovery of the city-gate of, 31–33. Extent of the city, 373
Nose-rings of the Arab women, 107
Nourdooz, Armenian district of, 222
Nourtchouk, visit to, 203
Numerals, Assyrian, determined by Dr. Hincks, Introd. xlvii
Nur-Ullah Bey, residence of, 200. His banishment, 200

OBELISK discovered at Kouyunjik, Introd. xxii.
Omar Agha, Kurd chieftain, 222
Om-el-Dhiban, 110
Ophthalmia among the Arabs, 132
Opis, Chaldæan city of, 264
Ossofa, village of, 99
Owl of the Desert, 110
Ozair Agha, 91

PADIYA, or Padi, King of Ekron, restored by Sennacherib, 44
Pagwantz, castle of, in Armenia, 219
Painted bricks, 55
Palaces, Assyrian, 377
Parks, or paradises, of Sardanapalus I., at Nineveh, 355. Of the Assyrians, 375
Partridges, gigantic, in Upper Kurdistan, 201
Pay-day with the Arabs, 16
Pedestals, Assyrian, 339, 340
Perauniss, Kurdish village of, 198
Phœnicia conquered by Sennacherib, 44
Pillars, bases of, at Kouyunjik, 339
Piran mountain, 191
Place, M., his excavations, Introd. xx., xxxiv.
Poet, an Arab, 152
Polygamy among the Arabs, 135
Pul, King, of the Scriptures, 358 *note*
Pulo, chief of Ossofa, 99

SAH

QUARRIES, Assyrian, 28

RABBAN AUDISHO, village of, 229
Rabshakeh, or chief cup-bearer, 48, 75
Rassam, Mr. C., his excavations at Kouyunjik, Introd. xix.
Rassam, Mr. H., 16, 93. His illness at Umjerjeh, 147. Attacked by ague, 185. His explorations, Introd. xxi.
Rassam, Mrs., among the Bedouins, 137
Rathaiyah, wife of Sheikh Suttum, 108, 112, 118, 135
Rawlinson, Sir H., at Nimroud, 15. His translation of the rock-inscription at Behistun, Introd. xliv.
Records and public documents of the Assyrians, mode of keeping the, 168, 169. Chambers of, 169. Their importance to the study of sacred and profane history, 366
Rediff of the Bedouins, the, 81
Religion of the Assyrians, 373
Rhawandiz mountains, 191
Rheumatism, Arab cures for, 132
Rhoua hills, 113
Rishwan, chief of the Boraij Arabs, 103, 106. Tents of his tribe, 105. Visit to him, 105
Rizan, Kurdish village of, 190
Rock-sculptures at Bavian, 71–73. At Gunduk, 188. At Wan, 208, 209
Roofs, conical, 26
Rua, Kurdish village of, 193
Ruffo, chief of Gabara, 102

SABACO II., King of Egypt, discovery of his seal at Kouyunjik, 173
Sacrifices of the Assyrians, 75
Sahaghi castle, 86
Sahiman, the Boraij Arab, 104. His wife, 106. His recovery of the stolen horses, 332.

SAK

Saklawiyah canal, 268
Saladin, 94. Birthplace of, 262
Saleh, brother of the Sheikh of the Tai, 56
Samaria, destruction of the city of, 371
Samarrah, city of, 263. Tombs at, 263
Sandhills, moving, 309
Sandwith, Dr., 1. Returns to Europe, 216
Saoud, the Bedouin poet, 153
Sarcophagi found at Arban, 125
Sardanapalus, tomb of, 37. Discovery of a small temple of, 175. Bas-relief of the King, 178. Record of his campaigns and victories, 179. Annals of his reign, 355. His palaces and temples, 355. Records of him and of his father, 366. Discovery of his palace, Introd. xxii. At banquet, xxxi.
Sargon, annals of the reign of, 361
Sayhel river, 158
Schulz, scene of the murder of, 199
Seals, discovery and impressions of royal, 172. Importance of seals in the East, 350
Sekkiniyah, village of, 103
Semiramis, Queen, her foundation of Wan, 206. Wife of Iva-lush, 357, and Introd. xxxiii.
Semitic characters on cylinders, 348
Sennacherib, discoveries in the palace of, at Kouyunjik, 4. The King going to, and returning from, battle, 7, 10. Superintending the placing of a human-headed bull, 25, 28. Receiving captives, 30. Murdered, 31. Grand entrance to his palace discovered, 40. Inscriptions containing the annals of his reign, 44. Account of his war with Hezekiah, 44, 45. His other conquests, 46. On his throne before Lachish, 49. His throne and footstool in the British Museum, 66. Representations

SUL

of him at Bavian, 71. His expedition against Babylon, 44, 71. Discovery of his signet cylinder, 174. Figure of him in a bas-relief, 240. Annals of the reign of, 363. His palace at Kouyunjik, 381
Seramus, village of, 229
Ser-i-resh mountain crossed, 192, 193
Shabaneh Arabs, 311
Shabib Agha, governor of Hillah, 272
Shahir, Saleh, 13
Shalmaneser, annals of, 356
Shammar Arabs, cadis or judges of the, 140
Shattak, Armenian district of, 222. Town of, 222
Shemdeena, Kurdish district of, 193, 194
Sheneena, or sour milk, of the Arabs, 131
Shereef-Khan, discoveries at, 344
Shields, bronze, 63. 'Bosses of the bucklers,' 64
Shirwan, visit to the district of, 191
Siokh, Armenian town of, 223
Shomal, visit to the villages of the, 94
Shushan, city of, in the sculptures, 251
Sieges, on bas-reliefs, 8, 9, 29, 47, 239, 240, 338
Singers meeting the returning conquerors, 252
Sinjar, Belled, visited, 93, 160. Ruins of the town of, 94. Villages of the, 94, 95. View from the Sinjar hill, 95
Small-pox among the Arabs, 132
Snake-charmer, a Yezidi, 101
Soulak, the dried-up spring, 102
Sourasor, Nestorian village of, 196
Sow, wild, in bas-relief, 23
Stag, in bas-relief, 23
Storms in Mesopotamia, 88, 135
Subhan Dagh, 203
Suffeyra river, 158
Suleiman Agha, visit to, 139, 145

SUL

Sulphur springs near Charderrah, 108
Summaichah, village of, 330
Summer in Mesopotamia, 185
Susiana, conquest of the people of, 238
Suttum, Sheikh of the Boraij Arabs, 81, 84. His rediff, 84. His deloul, 84. Messenger from his father, 92. His white mare, 102. His wife, 108, 112, 118. His tact and intelligence, 118. His wives, 134, 135. His delight in the desert, 137. His complaints, 161
Syria, expedition of Sennacherib against, 44
Syriac inscriptions on earthenware bowls, 290

TABLETS, inscribed clay, 170–173
Tahar, the Kurdish Sheikh, 194
Tahlel of the Arab women, 70
Tai Arabs, their attack on Nimroud, 56. Visit to the Howar of the, 57
Tanzimat, the, 13
Tartan, or general of the Assyrian forces, 48, 251
Tekrit, town of, 262, 331
Tel Abib, 126
Tel Athur, 55
Tel Ermah, 89
Tel Jemal, 92
Tel Kef, village of, 2
Tel Umjerjeh, 146
Tellana, Nestorian village of, 196
Temminah, the, of the Turks, 147
Temple, discovery of a small, at Nimroud, 175, 176. And of a second there, 180
Terraces, cultivated, of the Sinjar, 95
Thar, or Arab law of blood-revenge, 141
Throne, the, of Sennacherib, 49. Discovery of the royal throne, 65
Tiglath Pileser I., building of, at Nimroud, 52. Annals of, 353

WUR

Tiglath Pileser II., annals of, 358
Tigris, some of the principal sources of the Eastern branches of the, 220, 222. Descent of the river, 261. The river near Baghdad, 264
Tin used by the Assyrians, 62
Tkhoma, ravages of the Kurds and Turks in, 236
Tkhoma Gowaia, visit to, 237
Tombs in the rock at Wan, 209. Absence of Assyrian tombs, 340
Tower, discovery of, at Nimroud, 35. On a bas-relief, 39. A tower like the pictures of the Tower of Babel, 263
Truffles in the desert, 130
Turks, their oppression of the Christian communities of Asia, 232, 236
Turtle, a, caught, 136

USGAH, mound of, 92

VASTAN, Armenian town of, 217
Vineyards of Bouran, 100
Volcano of Koukab, 143

WAN, visit to the lake and city of, 203. Jewish families residing near, 200. Description of the city of, 205. Ancient inscriptions at, 208. Tombs in the rock at, 209. Armenian schools at, 213
Warriors, Assyrian, 239
Warriors, Jewish, dress of, 48
Wine-strainer found, 59, 61
Women, Yezidi, 98. Boraij, 107. Arab, grinding corn, 128. Domestic life of the Arab women, 133. Women of the Milli Kurds, 148–150. Of the Zibari Kurds, 189. And of Armenia, 216
Wurka, vast numbers of coffins at, 322

X

XERXES, inscription of, at Wan, 208

Y

YAKOUB, rais of Asheetha, 12
Yavan, 47
Vedi Klissia, Armenian convent of, 203. Visit to, 215
Yezidis, their industry, 95. And cleanliness, 97. Their houses, 97. Women of the, 98. Dress of the people, 98. Group of, 99. A snake-charmer, 101. Peace concluded between the Yezidis and Bedouins, 97, 100, 111
Yohanna, Guppa d'Mar, 188
Yusuf Beg hills, 109

Z

ZAB river, 188, 189, 190. Valley of the, 199
Zachariah, patriarch of Armenia, tomb of, 218
Zerga, plain of, 86, 87
Zerin, Nestorian village of, 232
Ziarehs of the Yezidis, 99, 100
Zibari, district of, 189
Zibbliyah, mound of, 322
Zimzim, cavern of, near Wan, 211
Zobeide, tomb of, 265. Her tribe, 270

www.ingramcontent.com/pod-product-compliance
Lightning Source LLC
Chambersburg PA
CBHW022111300426
44117CB00007B/672